Short Stories by Jesus

THE ENIGMATIC PARABLES OF A CONTROVERSIAL RABBI

AMY-JILL LEVINE

HarperOne
An Imprint of HarperCollinsPublishers

HarperOne

SHORT STORIES BY JESUS: *The Enigmatic Parables of a Controversial
Rabbi*. Copyright © 2014 by Amy-Jill Levine. All rights reserved.
Printed in the United States of America. No part of this book may
be used or reproduced in any manner whatsoever without written
permission except in the case of brief quotations embodied in
critical articles and reviews. For information address HarperCollins
Publishers, 195 Broadway, New York, NY 10007.

HarperCollins books may be purchased for educational, business,
or sales promotional use. For information please e-mail the Special
Markets Department at SPsales@harpercollins.com.

HarperCollins website: http://www.harpercollins.com

HarperCollins®, 📖®, and HarperOne™ are trademarks of
HarperCollins Publishers.

FIRST EDITION

Designed by Ralph Fowler

Library of Congress Cataloging-in-Publication Data

Levine, Amy-Jill.
Short stories by Jesus : the enigmatic parables of a controversial rabbi
/ Amy-Jill Levine.
    pages cm
ISBN 978–0–06–156101–6
1. Jesus Christ—Parables. I. Title.
BT375.3.L48 2014
226.8'06—dc23   2014012012

14 15 16 17 18 RRD(H) 10 9 8 7 6 5 4 3 2 1

For Jay, Sarah Elizabeth, and Alexander David

Contents

How We Domesticate Jesus's Provocative Stories

Parables, stories some only a sentence or two long, are often seen as the hallmark of Jesus's teaching. As Mark 4.33–34 puts it: "With many such parables he spoke the word to them, as they were able to hear it; he did not speak to them except in parables, but he explained everything in private to his disciples." Few of these private explanations have been preserved. The crowds then needed to find their own understandings, and we too must find ours.

It is a very good thing that the interpretations, if indeed Jesus did provide them, have not come down to us. The Gospel writers, in their wisdom, left most of the parables as open narratives in order to invite us into engagement with them. Each reader will hear a distinct message and may find that the same parable leaves multiple impressions over time. Different audiences inevitably hear different messages, just as today a listener who is poor or in ill health may form a different interpretation of the Rich Man and Lazarus than a person with a seat on the stock exchange or extended credit from Neiman Marcus. The parable of the Lost Son will convey different nuances to parents than to children, to the irresponsible and indulged (if such children pay attention at all) than to the faithful and overlooked. Reducing parables to a single meaning destroys their aesthetic as well as ethical potential. This surplus of meaning is how poetry and storytelling work, and it is all to the good.

It may also be a good thing that we do not have the explanations that Mark's disciples heard and remembered. The Twelve, despite their commission by Jesus, consistently misunderstand him. They do not understand the parable of the Sower, and Jesus despairs of their understanding any of the other parables: "And he said to them, 'Do you not understand this parable? Then how will you understand all the parables?'" (Mark 4.13). Their lack of understanding shows when Jesus tells them to feed the crowds and they sarcastically respond, "Are we to go and buy two hundred denarii worth of bread, and give it to them to eat?" (6.37). Following the feeding miracles, Jesus cautions them, "Beware of the yeast of the Pharisees and the yeast of Herod" (8.15). The disciples then say to one another, "It is because we have no bread." Not only have they forgotten that Jesus can cater; they have also missed the implications of Jesus's metaphorical message. No doubt when they heard the parable of the yeast they worried about whether the dough was gluten-free.

Although Peter, Andrew, James, and John are seasoned fishermen, they are afraid of being shipwrecked in a storm, and Jesus—who had been asleep in the boat—has to rebuke them for their lack of faith (Mark 4.40). They doubt his awareness of his healing powers (5.31); they don't understand his argument that "there is nothing outside a person that by going in can defile, but the things that come out are what defile" (7.15); Peter questions his mission, and Jesus responds by calling him "Satan," which is not a compliment (8.33); they seek to prevent parents and caregivers from bringing their children to Jesus (10.13–16) despite his telling them to welcome children (9.37); Judas betrays him (14.45); Peter, James, and John fall asleep when he is in agony in Gethsemane (14.37); Peter then denies him (14.68); and they all flee from the cross.

Nor, alas, are the named women followers much better when it comes to understanding him. Mary Magdalene, Mary the mother of James, and Salome go to the tomb on Sunday morning to "anoint" the body (Mark 16.1). Not only do they ask, too late to suggest any advance planning, "Who will roll away the stone for us from the entrance to the tomb?" (16.3); they are too late with their ointments: at the first supper of Jesus's final week, an unnamed woman had already anointed him (14.8).

Mark's disciples are not the best candidates for accurately preserving explanations of parables. Whether they were as clueless as Mark portrays them, or whether the evangelist has deliberately portrayed them as in need of re-medial instruction, the literary effect of their descriptions is the same. Mark is telling readers, "Go beyond the disciples, be open to the mystery and the challenge, interpret for yourselves." And we readers should be reassured that if Peter, James, and John, even after failing, can find rehabilitation and stay with the program, there's hope for the rest of us.

Granted, we should not be too hard on the disciples. They were looking for something within their comfort zone and, like many, resisted what the parables might convey. Moreover, Jesus was requiring that they do more than listen; he was asking them to think as well. He tells the Twelve, "To you has been given the mystery of the kingdom of God, but for those out-side, everything comes in parables; in order that 'they may indeed look, but not perceive, and may indeed listen, but not understand'" (Mark 4.11–12; see also Matt. 13.11–13). "Mystery" is here not indicative of something ar-cane or in need of a special key to unlock a singular meaning. What makes the parables mysterious, or difficult, is that they challenge us to look into the hidden aspects of our own values, our own lives. They bring to the surface unasked questions, and they reveal the answers we have always known, but refuse to acknowledge. Our reaction to them should be one of resistance rather than acceptance. For our own comfort, we may want to foreclose the meaning rather than allow the parable to open into multiple interpretations. We are probably more comfortable proclaiming a creed than prompting a conversation or pursuing a call.

Religion has been defined as designed to comfort the afflicted and to af-flict the comfortable. We do well to think of the parables of Jesus as doing the afflicting. Therefore, if we hear a parable and think, "I really like that" or, worse, fail to take any challenge, we are not listening well enough.

Such listening is not only a challenge; it is also an art, and this art has become lost. Down through the centuries, starting with the Gospel writers themselves, the parables have been allegorized, moralized, christologized, and otherwise tamed into either platitudes such as "God loves us" or "Be nice" or, worse, assurances that all is right with the world as long as we be-lieve in Jesus. Too often we settle for easy interpretations: we should be nice like the good Samaritan; we will be forgiven, as was the prodigal son; we should pray and not lose heart like the importuning widow. When we seek universal morals from a genre that is designed to surprise, challenge, shake up, or indict and look for a single meaning in a form that opens to multiple interpretations, we are necessarily limiting the parables and, so, ourselves.

If we stop with the easy lessons, good though they may be, we lose the way Jesus's first followers would have heard the parables, and we lose the genius of Jesus's teaching. Those followers, like Jesus himself, were Jews, and Jews knew that parables were more than children's stories or restatements of common knowledge. They knew that parables and the tellers of parables were there to prompt them to see the world in a different way, to challenge, and at times to indict.

We might be better off thinking less about what they "mean" and more about what they can "do": remind, provoke, refine, confront, disturb . . . .

The Parables in Israel's Scriptures

The origins of this provocative genre, with its personal, social, and moral barbs, appear in the scriptures of Israel, the books that comprise what the church traditionally calls the Old Testament and the synagogue calls the Tanakh (an acronym for *Torah,* or Pentateuch; *Nevi'im,* or Prophets; and *Ketuvim,* or Writings). The book of Judges records how a fellow named Abimelech slaughters all but one of his brothers in his attempt to secure rule over the city of Shechem. The youngest brother, Jotham, hides and survives. Following Abimelech's royal investiture, the surviving brother stands on Mt. Gerizim (the site of what will be the Samaritan temple, where the woman at the well in John 4 will worship) and tells the following parable to the leading men of the city:

> The trees once went out to anoint [Heb. *limshoach,* Gk. *chrisai,* the same root from which "Messiah" and "Christ" derive] a king over themselves. So they said to the olive tree, "Reign over us." The olive tree answered them, "Shall I stop producing my rich oil by which gods and mortals are honored, and go to sway over the trees?" Then the trees said to the fig tree, "You come and reign over us." But the fig tree answered them, "Shall I stop producing my sweetness and my delicious fruit, and go to sway over the trees?" Then the trees said to the vine, "You come and reign over us." But the vine said

to them, "Shall I stop producing my wine that cheers gods and mortals, and go to sway over the trees?" So all the trees said to the bramble, "You come and reign over us." And the bramble said to the trees, "If in good faith you are anointing me king over you, then come and take refuge in my shade; but if not, let fire come out of the bramble and devour the cedars of Lebanon." (9.8–15)

In this parable, members of society with something of value to contribute neither seek nor want political office; only the bramble, which has nothing to offer, accepts the job, and he does so with the threat that he will destroy those who oppose him. The point, hardly subtle, is a challenge to any who might seek to rule and to any who are in positions of authority. Candidates for office—especially those who have not proven themselves in any way save for good family connections (Abimelech's name means, in Hebrew, "My father is king"; his dad, Gideon the judge, was not known for his refinement) and generous coffers (Abimelech has access to the treasury at the temple of Baal Berith)—may still hear a warning today, even as their opponents might both chuckle and, if they are wise, take the same warning.

The setting of the parable, Shechem, later called Samaria, and the notice of Mt. Gerizim should not go unremarked in a study of the parables of Jesus. Judges 9, as we will see, provides one of the subtexts for the famous parable of the Good Samaritan.

Second Samuel 12.1–7 records the prophet Nathan's famous parable of the Ewe Lamb. Nathan was King David's court prophet (think of Billy Graham to Richard Nixon, or perhaps Joel Hunter to Barak Obama), the figure who spoke to the conscience of the king. Following David's adultery with Bathsheba and then his arranging the murder of Bathsheba's husband, Uriah (imagine, a politician who has an affair and then attempts to cover it up!), Nathan tells the king about "two men in a certain city, one rich and the other poor." The rich man had large flocks, but the poor man had only one little ewe lamb—let's call her Fluffy—who was "like a daughter to him." When a visitor came to the rich man and it was time for dinner, the rich man took little Fluffy, butchered her, and served her for dinner.

That's the parable, and David, who takes it as an actual story, is incensed: "Then David's anger was greatly kindled against the man. He said to Nathan, 'As the LORD lives, the man who has done this deserves to die'" (2 Sam.

12.5). It gives most readers no small degree of satisfaction when Nathan then proclaims, "You are the man!" David hears the parable and indicts himself.

This parable too should echo in the ears of anyone hearing Jesus's parables that begin, "There was a rich man who . . . ." His first-century audience was already primed to hear that the rich man did something oppressive to the poor man. The shock of Nathan's parable is that the one condemned is the parable's intended target, David himself; he was able to recognize, finally, the gravity of his sin.

Abimelech and his supporters recognized Jotham's challenge; David recognized Nathan's critique. They were able to listen; they heard their indictment. Words can wound, and stories can condemn, challenge, or provoke. We readers can hear those challenges from Judges and 2 Samuel, because we have the broader narrative context in which the parables were told.

The scriptures of Israel offer a number of such parables, and in each case we readers, like the people to whom the tales were originally addressed, are forced to make a choice. What would *we* do? Second Samuel 14.5–8 offers a parable that raises the question of capital punishment in the case in which one brother kills another. Should the execution be carried out and so leave a mother childless and a widow's "husband neither name nor remnant on the face of the earth"? The idea of losing both children is not a new story. It reminds us of the first fratricide, of Cain's killing his brother, Abel, and it anticipates additional stories of lost sons, including the famous parable of the Prodigal Son.

Parables are not restricted to those found in what the church calls the Old Testament and the synagogue the Tanakh. They would have been told at home in the evening after dinner or in the workshops and the fields and the synagogues. Stories are part of culture, and parables are a major part of Jewish culture.

Rabbinic texts—Jewish texts compiled after Jesus's time but containing materials that may well date from years before his birth—record numerous parables. The rabbinic parables frequently take the form, "I will tell (*emshal*) you a parable (*mashal*). To what can the thing be compared?" Likewise, Jesus frequently introduces parables with the expression, "The kingdom of heaven is like . . . ." To grasp the implications of the comparison—the term "parable" comes from the Greek *para*, "along side, together with," as in "parallel" or "paradox," and *balo*, "to cast," "to throw"—we need to understand the nuances of each side of the equation. We immediately realize that, with such comparisons, no single meaning can ever be determined, just as no single metaphor or simile can be restricted.

Robert Burns's famous poem, "O my Luve's like a red, red rose, / That's newly sprung in June," offers a good test case. The simile comparing love to a rose blossoms into multiple interpretations, but some are better than others. Perhaps his love is better by the dozen, or fresher if kept in water, or prickly with thorns. Or perhaps his love will fade as quickly as the flower wilts in the summer heat. Like a poem (another simile), a parable will evoke numerous interpretations; it is our job to sort through them.

The "kingdom of heaven" will convey different specific ideas to different people. For some it is a time when all pain will cease, and Jesus "will wipe every tear from their eyes" (Rev. 21.4). For others, it's a place with pearly gates and golden slippers. The Gospels give some hints, aside from parables, as to what this heavenly realm looks like. Ironically, it may not be what many of us would want. I do wonder, do all those who pray, "Your kingdom come, your will be done," really want a change in the status quo, or are they pretty satisfied with the "kingdom" we have in the here and now? Do they really want the time when, as Jesus promises, the first will be last and the last first (Matt. 19.30), when a final judgment occurs, or when we are assessed not by whether we said, "Lord, Lord" (Matt. 7.21–22; 25.11; Luke 6.46), but whether we loved our enemy and fed the hungry? The challenge has already begun, and we're barely through with the Introduction.

The importance of parables in Jewish thought is indicated by a comment found in an early commentary on the Song of Songs. By the way, study of Song of Songs, also known as Canticles or Song of Solomon, provides a very good example of how to distinguish parable from allegory. A parable requires no external key to explain what its elements mean; an allegory does. Song of Songs is generally understood, by the communities that hold it sacred, to be an allegory, not a parable. For Jews, the poem is traditionally understood as the love song between God and Israel. Catholic teaching traditionally sees the text as the love song between Christ and the church. For many Protestants, it is the love song between God and the individual soul. Then again, for biblical scholars it is (also) a love song between a man and a woman who have the hots for each other, and so it is in its original context neither allegory nor parable.

Here's what a Jewish text called *Song of Songs Rabbah,* a commentary on the Song of Songs, says about the parable: "Do not let the parable (*mashal*) appear of little worth to you. Through a parable, a person can fathom words of Torah." Then the text offers a parable: "Consider the king who has lost a gold coin or a precious pearl in his house. May he not find it by the light of a wick worth no more than an *issar* [a penny]?" The commentary then reinforces the point: "Likewise, do not let the parable appear of little worth to you. By its light, a person may fathom words of Torah" (I, 1, 8). Just as the rabbinic text notes that parables are a means for understanding Torah—not just the Pentateuch, but all Jewish teachings and the traditions—so Jesus the Jew uses parables to help his followers understand the kingdom of heaven.

The commentary hints at an additional aspect of parables, that is, their humor. In Jesus's parable of the Lost Coin, a woman lights her lamps and sweeps her house to find her missing money. A king would not do this; he has staff for such annoyances. To picture the king on his hands and knees, searching for one coin or one pearl out of an entire treasury box, is to picture something foolish, something humorous. It is also to picture something potentially desirable, or challenging: a ruler who gets off his throne and down into the dirt, like the rest of us, to find what he needs. There is a touch of the absurd in the rabbinic parable, as there is in many of the parables Jesus told.

Context Matters

There's an old saying in biblical studies (I first heard it from Ben Witherington III) that a text without a context is just a pretext for making it say anything one wants. But the more we know about the original contexts, the richer our understanding becomes, and the greater our appreciation for the artists and composers who created the works initially.

In order better to hear the parables in their original contexts and so to determine what is normal and what is absurd, what is conventional and what is unexpected, we need to do the history. We need to determine how Samaritans and Jews related to each other; what the cultural expectations of fathers and sons were; how day laborers and vineyard owners established their contractual obligations; what social roles were open to women; and who went to the Temple to pray and why. If we get the context wrong, we'll get Jesus wrong as well. The parables are open-ended in that interpretation will take place in every act of reading, but they are also historically specific. When the historical context goes missing or we get it wrong, the parables become open to problematic and sometimes abusive readings.

The best modern example I have for explaining the importance of the context for understanding stories is *The Rocky and Bullwinkle Show,* which aired on U.S. television from 1959 to 1964. Dudley Do-Right gave me my initial fascination with all things Canadian; the WABAC (i.e., "way back") machine belonging to Peabody the dog and his "pet boy" Sherman prompted my interest in history; and both "Fractured Fairy Tales" and "Aesop and Son" taught me to question all stories with morals as well as to appreciate the pun. Then there was Rocket J. Squirrel, who, together with his companion, Bullwinkle J. Moose, saved the world, often. For children, the show was funny—what's not to like about moose and squirrel?

What we children missed was the social satire. I had no clue why the bad guys had the Russian-sounding names of Boris Badenov and Natasha Fatale. Then again, I thought Wossamotta U was an institute of higher education in Frostbite Falls, Minnesota (part of my early interest in academics). I had not heard of Boris Godunov the czar, let alone Pushkin's play or Mussorgsky's opera. I didn't know what a "femme fatale" was, so Natasha's last name simply sounded exotic. What I also missed, and why cultural context is so important, were the references to the Cold War. Along with the puns on names (regarding which I would be remiss not to mention J. Robert Oppendowner, Bermuda Schwartz, and the Ruby Yacht of Omar Khayyam), the cartoon was engaging in social commentary. I could appreciate Moose and Squirrel, but I could not appreciate them fully, because I missed the context.

In listening to parables and appreciating them within their initial context, we also do well to listen for echoes of Israel's scriptures, since the parables evoke earlier stories and then comment on them. "There was a man who had two sons . . ." (Luke 15.11) is the beginning of what is traditionally called the parable of the Prodigal Son. Jesus's Jewish audience would be reminded of other men and their two sons: Cain and Abel, the sons of Adam; Ishmael and Isaac, the sons of Abraham; Jacob and Esau, the sons of Isaac; and so on. Reading the parable in light of the antecedent narratives creates surprise and challenge; in turn, reading the antecedent narrative in light of the parable opens a host of new insights.

Another maxim that frequently holds for biblical studies is that the world of the people who wrote and first heard the texts is different from our world. We cannot map onto their cultures and contexts our own values or expectations. What seems odd to us might be perfectly normal to them: fathers did divide their property via bequests prior to their death; judges were not always expected to act according to strict standards of justice; vineyard owners did their own hiring; kings destroyed enemy countries rather than determining how best to exploit the resources of the conquered areas.

On the other hand, these distinctions can be taken to extremes. Sometimes what seems odd to us really *is* odd. A woman does not "hide" yeast in dough, yet this is the verb that both Matthew and Luke use to describe the activity. Here we are already misled by most English translations, which render the Greek verb for "hide" as "mix" and so obscure the subversive nature of the parable. Mustard seeds do not yield giant trees; vineyard owners do not typically provoke their workers by setting up false expectations. The trick is to determine what is surprising in the parable, and what is not. And there is much in Jesus's parables that surprises.

The Parables of Jesus

When we turn to Jesus's parables, we do well to hear them as the people who first heard them, Jews in the Galilee and Judea, did and thus to recover as best as we can the original provocation. To do so requires several leaps of faith.

The first leap concerns what Jesus himself said, for we do not know with certainty if Jesus actually told the parables recorded in the Gospels. Second, even if he did tell them, we know with certainty neither the composition of the audience nor their reaction. Third, it is unlikely, were he to have composed these parables, that he only used them on one occasion or told them exactly the same way each time.

The concern for the "authenticity" of the parables relates to the broader issue of what is known as "historical Jesus studies." We do not have access to Jesus directly; he leaves us no writing, no autobiography, no sanctioned biography. To be blunt, he leaves us neither a physical body nor a body of writing. If the only Gospel we had were that traditionally attributed to

John, we would have no parables; nor would we have accounts of Jesus's baptism by John, his exorcisms, or his famous saying, "Give therefore to the emperor the things that are the emperor's, and to God the things that are God's" (Matt. 22.21; Mark 12.17; Luke 20.25). The parables appear only in the synoptic Gospels (Matthew, Mark, and Luke), although a few are repeated and a few distinct ones are presented in the noncanonical Coptic *Gospel of Thomas*.

Instead of having an unmediated Jesus, all we have are the memories preserved and filtered through the concerns and confessions of those who proclaimed him Lord or Savior. Moreover, those filters included linguistic ones. Jesus, raised in lower Galilee, would have spoken Aramaic and probably some Hebrew; if he knew Greek, it would have been the Greek needed by an artisan who might take a contract from a Greek speaker in the larger Galilean cities of Sepphoris and Tiberias. Thus when we attempt to interpret his parables, we are interpreting them in their Greek version. As with any translation, something is always lost and something is always added. We do the best we can with what we have.

I do think Jesus spoke in parables despite their absence from John; he would have been at home in the genre. There are several other reasons for thinking he told many, if not most or even all, of the parables recorded in the Gospels.

For example, the parables often express concerns that appear elsewhere in the Jesus tradition; they echo themes heard in his teachings and debates. Jesus is concerned about economics: about giving to those who beg, about the blessings that will come to the poor, about mutual dependence rather than top-down brokerage, about what can be summarized as "kingdom economics," in which the prayer "Forgive us our debts" meant more than sins and included monetary loans. His focus is on laying up treasure in heaven, not on accumulating bank accounts on earth. The parables, with their attention to wealth management, debts, daily wages, land ownership, and lost coins, speak to the same concerns. Luke retains several parables that begin "There was a rich man who . . ."; none is likely to be well loved by owners of Fortune 500 companies. One could claim that Luke invented all these parables, but this would be an overstatement. Rather, the parables sit uneasily in his Gospel. The Rich Man and Lazarus presumes a judgment of heaven and hell already in place prior to Jesus's death and so complicates the role of the cross in salvation; the lines following the parable of the Dishonest Manager show Luke attempting to bring order to a story with no clear morality.

Jesus is also concerned about relationships: between parents and children, siblings, neighbors, and leaders and followers; he emphasizes caring for the other, mutual reciprocity, servant leadership, and humility. The parables sound all these themes. The Sheep and the Goats (Matt. 25.31–46) insists that it is not religious confession, but caring for others—feeding the hungry, visiting people in prison, clothing the naked—that will bring entrance into the heavenly kingdom (if you are unfamiliar with the parable and you find yourself at the pearly gates, where there are lines marked "Sheep" and "Goats," get into the sheep line). Again, the parable runs contrary to church's (later) focus that it is belief in Jesus, Jesus's own fidelity, or the cross and resurrection that conveys eschatological blessing, so despite the parable's presence only in Matthew's Gospel, it most likely comes from Jesus himself.

Next, Jesus is concerned about prioritizing. Expecting the kingdom of heaven to break in, indeed, seeing it already as present in his actions, he demands a reaction: choose life, choose to live the way God wants us to live. His message echoes the warning of his former teacher, John the Baptist: "The time is fulfilled, and the kingdom of God has come near; repent, and believe in the good news" (Mark 1.15; cf. Matt. 4.17). Given this urgency, new forms of living are required: we need to determine what is necessary and what is not (so the Pearl of Great Price); we need to determine when practicality should give way to generosity (so the Laborers in the Vineyard); and we need to be assured that the kingdom is coming, both with our help (the Yeast) and without it (the Mustard Seed).

With regard to Jesus's own presentation, the parables fit his comments about himself and the kingdom he proclaims. In his teachings and his actions, Jesus displays such respect for the people he encounters that he does not spoon-feed them what can only be understood in the heart, not the head. Yes, he makes direct statements—"You shall not murder," "Love your enemies"—but he also teaches through challenge.

For example, he refers to himself as the "son of man," and in so doing he forces his listeners to make a decision. Is he speaking of himself as one human being among others, one who does not know the mysteries of heaven, as in, for example, God's address to Ezekiel, "Son of man, can these bones live?" (37.3, KJV)? Is he recalling humanity's almost divine nature and so almost limitless potential, as in Psalm 8.4–5: "What is man, that thou art mindful of him? and the son of man, that thou visitest him? For thou hast made him a little lower than the angels, and hast crowned him with glory and honour" (KJV; cf. Heb. 2.7, 9). Or is he alluding to the "Son of man" in Daniel 7.13–14, to whom was given "dominion, and glory, and a kingdom, that all people, nations, and languages, should serve him: his dominion is an everlasting dominion, which shall not pass away, and his kingdom that which shall not be destroyed" (KJV)? Or again, is he simply using the Galilean Aramaic idiom for "I"? Any hearing him would need to ask: Is he making messianic claims about himself? Is he speaking of another? Is he talking about all of humanity? Who is this man?

Another reason to see Jesus as speaking not only in parables, but in these parables that have come down to us from the Gospels is their frequent motif of celebration. What is infectiously appealing about Jesus is that he likes to celebrate. He is consistently meeting people not at the altar but at table, whether as host, guest, or the body and blood to be consumed (as in John 6 and the synoptic Last Supper accounts). He is indiscriminate in his dining companions, who include Pharisees, tax collectors, sinners, and even an upscale family consisting of two sisters and a formerly dead brother. The Feeding of the Five Thousand is the one miracle story recounted in all four Gospels. To be in his presence is not only to be challenged and comforted; it is to celebrate at table. There is feasting at the end of the parables of the Lost Sheep and the Lost Coin, and a fatted calf awaits the Lost Son.

Such images are not arbitrary. One dominant Jewish view of the *olam ha-ba,* the "world to come," was of a banquet, a great feast at which one "reclined at table with Abraham, Isaac, and Jacob" (see Matt. 8.11). In his dining, Jesus is providing a foretaste of that messianic age. These images add depth to the parable of the Leaven in particular and to the various stories about banquets. Jesus's parables, with their frequent theme of celebration and their warnings to those who fail to share this joy, unsettle, and at the same time the more we chew on them, the greater the smile that will cross our lips, the more food for thought we have, and the more we want to taste.

In addition to the presence of parables in Jesus's own cultural context and their numerous thematic consistencies with the rest of his teaching, there are other very good reasons for thinking that Jesus taught in parables. For example, not only do we today often think of the parables as a genre especially associated with Jesus; so did the majority of his followers. The non-canonical Gospels and Acts stemming from the second century and later tend not to recapitulate parables as a genre. Most of the so-called Gnostic texts move instead into esoteric teaching, teaching that could not be comprehended by bakers, textile workers, or folks in the Galilean fishing industry.

A fourth reason to think that he spoke the parables is that we see the evangelists wrestling with an attempt to control their meaning. We've already noted Luke's concern for domesticating the parables beginning, "There was a rich man who . . ."; Luke's wrestling continues with other un-ruly stories that defy easy moralization. As we'll see when we turn to the Widow and the Judge, Luke attempts to domesticate the parable by turning it into a lesson about constant prayer. That's not the message a first-century Jewish audience would have heard; nor, as I found in my multiple test read-ings with both Jewish groups and Christian groups unfamiliar with the par-able, is it an interpretation today's listeners come up with either. The same domestication occurs with many of the other parables: the Lost Sheep and Lost Coin were not, *pace* Luke, originally heard as stories of repentance and forgiveness. Nor do I think the Prodigal Son is about repenting or forgiving or even, ultimately, about the prodigal.

Asserting that Jesus taught in parables is not the same thing as saying, however, that the parables as we have them today are exactly the words that Jesus originally spoke. We should also consider the role of the storyteller, for good storytellers adapt their tales to the needs and interests of their audi-ences. The idea of Jesus having a set of three-by-five note cards or an iPad (for Jesus, better an "I-am-pad") on which were inscribed the Good Samaritan or the Pearl of Great Price and from which he read the same story, verba-tim, under different circumstances is unlikely; rather, good teacher that Jesus was—that we can be certain of, or stories by him and of him would not continue to be told—he would have adapted his stories for the needs of each new audience. He also likely honed them, as storytellers, social critics, and, yes, even lecturers do, until he knew what words worked best in what contexts.

A good storyteller repeats material, and the parables, as good stories, are certainly worth repeating. At one time, he might have said, "The kingdom of heaven is like yeast that a woman took . . ." (Matt. 13.33; Luke 13.21); an-other time he might have begun the parable, "The kingdom of the father is like a woman who took a little leaven . . ." (*Thomas* 96). I am not here arguing that the *Gospel of Thomas* is fully independent of the Synoptics; the jury is still out on that question. I do think, however, that *Thomas*'s formulations, a few of which we'll see in the chapters to come, may recognize the multiple ways that Jesus himself may have spoken his parables.

New Testament scholars sometimes evoke the discipline known as "form criticism" in order to explain these textual variations. The concept, which comes from studies of folklore, suggests that each story has a structural outline, and the variants can tell us something about the agenda of those who told the tale. A basic modern analogy is "Cinderella" as told in its several forms, first by the Charles Perrault and then the Brothers Grimm (*Aschenputtel*), which are much grimmer than the Disney version and much more serious than the Jerry Lewis variant *Cinderfella* (despite Dame Judith Anderson in the role of the stepmother).

If evocations of form criticism remind readers who have taken New Testament courses of an incomprehensible lecture that seemed to contain more jargon than information, we might make things easier by comparing form criticism to a toy invented about a decade before Rocky and Bullwinkle: the still popular "Mr. Potato Head." The substantive aspect of this toy is the plastic potato; the eyes, ears, nose, and collar are interchangeable, but each choice a child makes for accessorizing the potato opens the possibility of a new image. For the parables, then, we need to locate the potato, because, to continue this already unfortunate metaphor (parable?), that's where the nutrition is. For the parables, despite the variants and the translation from Aramaic to Greek, we can be relatively sanguine that certain elements, like that potato, remain consistent: the pearl remains a pearl, yeast is yeast, and a tenacious widow is exactly that.

Matthew accessorizes his parables with favorite terms, such as the "kingdom of heaven" rather than the "kingdom of God." The phrasing may reflect the Jewish tradition of avoiding using the divine name but since Matthew uses the term "God" often, it is more likely Matthew thought of the "kingdom of heaven" as an actual place. Matthew also has a tendency to increase the violence of the parables, as a quick comparison of his Wedding Banquet (22.2–14) with Luke's Great Dinner (14.16–24) reveals. The Matthean addition, "The king was enraged. He sent his troops, destroyed those murderers, and burned their city" (22.7) is a reflection of the destruction of Jerusalem by the Roman troops in 70 CE; the point is Matthean, for the first Gospel regards the city's destruction as precipitated by the people's failure to accept Jesus as their king (see 27.25, where "the people as a whole," responding to Pilate's question about what to do with Jesus, issue the ironically prophetic and ultimately tragic cry, "His blood be on us and on our children"). But the main dish of the parable—the rejected invitation by the first invited and the feasting by those who never expected the invitation—remains in place.

That the evangelists adapted these short stories by Jesus is also evident from the parables' literary placement. Luke places the Good Samaritan (10.25–37) just before both the story of Martha and Mary (10.38–42) and the instructions concerning the prayer known as the "Our Father" (11.2–4). The two stories speak of the one who chooses the appropriate action: Mary listens to Jesus's teaching rather than helping Martha serve, and the Samaritan helps the injured man rather than passing by. The prayer asks, "Do not bring us to the time of trial" or, more literally from the Greek, "Do not bring us to the test" (*peirasmos*). As the parable of the Good Samaritan opens, a lawyer stands up to "test Jesus" with his question.

Finally, the evangelists are our first known interpreters of the parables. By adapting the language and providing a setting they have already foreclosed some meanings; by providing explications they foreclose others. For example, Luke 18.2–5 is a parable concerning a widow and a judge. Luke tells us that the parable was told to the disciples about "their need to pray always and not to lose heart" (18.1), that the parable is informative about God's providing swift justice to those who remain faithful, and that the judge is a negative allegorical image for God. Luke's opening contextualization and concluding lesson are not necessary, or even necessarily logical, readings of the parable. For Luke's readers in antiquity or for readers today, a tenacious widow who threatens to give a judge a black eye is not an image of fervent prayer; divine justice has not been swift, for we are still waiting for that kingdom come; and the judge is in no way an image for the divine. Luke turns the parable into an allegory, and so platitude replaces provocation.

From these examples, we learn yet another way of understanding the parables in their first-century context: they needed to have made sense within that context. Thus parables are not completely allegorical; there is no one-to-one correspondence between the details of a parable and the details of the outside world. Sometimes a shepherd is just a shepherd, and not a cipher for

God; a king may be just a king, a landowner someone in need of workers; and a lost sheep is not immediately seen as a sinner, repentant or defiant. Jesus's first-century audience would not think, as some of his later Christian interpreters did, that the good Samaritan who rescues the fellow wounded by robbers is Jesus who saves us from death, or that the prodigal son is Jesus who leaves his home to live in a sinful world and then returns to God the Father. The parables in that first-century context need to make sense without any knowledge of how Jesus's followers came to understand him after the Romans crucified him. They need to make sense not only to those who chose to follow him, but to those who found him just a wise teacher, a neighbor in Nazareth, or a fellow Jew.

The Parables Today

For today's Christians, or indeed anyone interested in what ideas the parables convey, interpretation should not be limited to this historical context. If that were the case, we'd all have to be living in first-century Bibleland, and we'd have to conclude that the Gospels offer a one-size-fits-all model that has not yielded any new inspiration over the past two millennia. The texts must speak to each generation and each individual anew, or they cease to be either scripture or literature and become only markings on a page.

For people who claim to follow Jesus today, whether they regard him as the divine Son or as a rabbi with superb things to say, the parables cannot remain historical artifacts. We should ask, as we should with any literature: How do the messages an original audience would have heard translate over the centuries to the person in the pew, the Bible study, or the classroom? We do not restrict the meaning of *Hamlet* to Elizabethan England; we continue to ask new questions of the *Iliad* and of *Huckleberry Finn*. Each generation looks for new meanings, reads with new sensitivity, and projects onto the text new issues. Good literature continues to yield those new meanings, and the parables are no exceptions. Thus this volume asks two main questions: How do we hear the parables through an imagined set of first-century Jewish ears, and then how do we translate them so that they can be heard still speaking?

The former question is based on the study of Jesus, a Galilean Jew interacting with fellow Jews in the late Second Temple period. This is a study of both Jewish history and Christian history; it is a place where today Jews and Christians might find some common bonds, or at least common challenges. In asking this historical question, I am not seeking to replace the readings that Matthew, Mark, and Luke, or Augustine, or John Wesley, or the local homilist proclaims. I am, rather, seeking to add one more layer, a layer that should prove of import, or at least of interest, to anyone concerned about understanding why anyone would have listened to this Galilean teacher in the first place, let alone bothered to remember his stories. More, in hearing the parables without their millennia of domestication—in hearing them in their rawness—we might hear a new message not only of the kingdom of heaven, but of how to find it on earth.

The latter question is primarily, but not entirely a Christian issue. The parables will continue to be preached from church pulpits and studied in confessional settings, and that is all to the good. Christians will, and should, seek new meanings in the ancient texts; otherwise, to use theological language, they will be putting the Holy Spirit out of business. But there are times when the contemporary study goes awry, when Jesus's Jewish context is mischaracterized, and parables intended to provoke instead become parables that teach prejudice. Thus the chapters in this volume also serve as a corrective, or in some cases a prophylactic (perhaps the only time that term will be used in a study of the historical Jesus), not only for preventing the disease of anti-Judaism from infecting the body of his parables, but also for avoiding the other less toxic but equally distressing moves that turn parables into platitudes.

Auditory Atrophy and Aids to Hearing

When it comes to parables and to ancient texts in general, our listening skills are not as developed as they should be. Not only do we frequently miss the original provocation, and not only do we frequently default to simplistic interpretations; we also often import ahistorical and anachronistic readings that deform the good news of the gospel into something Jesus would neither recognize nor condone.

The reasons for this auditory atrophy are easy to locate. Here are six, among the many.

First, in a number of churches, the parables function as children's stories. That is because children can understand those simple messages. We don't need to know who a Samaritan is or what the term connotes in order to know that the traveler in the parable helps someone who is injured and that helping someone is a good thing. Therefore, parables provide excellent "children's sermons" or "events for all ages"—that part of many liberal Protestant or Unitarian services where the children come forward, usually after the first hymn and before the congregant in charge of the next Habitat for Humanity project or the mission trip makes a pitch for donations.

The youth minister, Sunday school teacher, or pastor (for the smaller churches with limited staff) then provides a show-and-tell: the parable of the Leaven means playing with dough and eating fresh-baked bread; the parable of the Mustard Seed means looking at mustard seeds and perhaps tasting them (providing the always delightful opportunity to see children go "yuck"); the parable of the Prodigal Son allows the children to tell stories about how their mommies and daddies love them. Once we come to associate the parables with children's stories, it becomes difficult to see them as anything but. If the parable of the Pharisee and the Tax Collector is then followed by a rousing chorus of, "Don't wanna be a Pharisee . . . cause they're not fair, you see; don't wanna be a Pharisee, I just wanna be a sheep, Baa, baa, baa, baa,"[1] then the message goes from the simplistic to the, well, baaad.

A second reason we settle for easy interpretations is that many clergy do not take the time to develop the challenge of the parable. Many priests and pastors are reluctant to challenge congregations about matters of social policy, family dysfunction, or how to love the enemy. Sunday morning has become in far too many settings the occasion for a pep talk rather than provocation; the service is designed to comfort rather than to challenge, to assure congregants that despite the changes in the culture, the economy, or the law, something—not just the role of the Christ, but the teaching of the church—remains "the same yesterday and today and forever" (Heb. 13.8). If the congregation also expects the folksy joke or humorous anecdote, a point about current issues, or the speaker's statement of personal orthodoxy, there's even less opportunity to develop the challenge.

It's much safer, in many congregations, to assure the faithful how our souls are saved through divine grace rather than to suggest that our societies are saved through personal and corporate aid to the poor. It's much more comforting to hear that God is a loving father who welcomes us home no matter how much we stray than it is to hear an exhortation to reconcile with the brother, sister, or fellow congregant with whom we have not spoken in twenty years. This approach is a deformation of the biblical text; it is not listening to Jesus with ears to hear.

A third reason for auditory atrophy is the expectation of congregations, who have come to believe that the sermon is monologue, not motivation, that it is designed for entertainment. The service becomes less an opportunity for reconciliation, restoration, and renewal and more a Sunday morning version of what Johnny Carson, Jay Leno, and now Jimmy Fallon provide on weekday nights: a monologue to make us laugh, music to amuse or bemuse us (having paid singers in the choir doesn't hurt, nor does an organ that cost more than most of the congregants will make in their lifetimes), something heartwarming (a children's handbell group, good news about the mission trip), and a commercial or two for the upcoming pancake supper, men's club outing, or program on flower arranging. When church becomes a club, parables become pedestrian. At times then, the problem rests with the person in the pulpit; just as often, the problem rests with the person in the pew.

There is yet a fourth reason why the easy answers work, in addition to their familiarity and comfort value, clergy fear, and congregational resistance. This reason is more pernicious, and it is one that I think few clergy have considered. The clergy actually do think that they are presenting a challenging message when in fact they are, unintentionally, repeating anti-Jewish stereotypes. If the interpreter knows nothing about Jesus's Jewish context other than the stereotype of "Jesus came to fix Judaism, so therefore Judaism—whatever it was—must have been bad," then the parables will be interpreted in a deformed way.

One very common way parables are interpreted is by drawing a contrast between what Jesus taught and what "the Jews" generally understood. Thus, the Prodigal Son teaches that God loves sinners, when "the Jews" thought God only loved the righteous and didn't give a damn about sinners. Such a reading should make no sense to anyone who has read in the scriptures of Israel the stories of Adam and Eve, Cain and David, and indeed the nation of Israel. God does not give up on sinners; to the contrary, God is always waiting for us to repent and return. Whereas humanity may violate God's covenant, God remains faithful. Jews knew that God cared about the sinful; were that not the case, there'd be no reason to send prophets to Israel, or Jonah to Ninevah. For other Christian readers ill-informed about early Judaism, the parable of the Yeast and the parable of the Mustard Seed become teachings that reject Jewish purity laws and even Jewish identity, as if Jews somehow eschewed baked bread and spices, and we should therefore thank Jesus for allowing us to have a hot dog, on a bun, with mustard. These parables have nothing to do with purity laws, and to read yeast and mustard as impure is to misunderstand Judaism even as it is to miss out on some excellent food (for thought).

The parable of the Rich Man and Lazarus is understood, again by some misinformed interpreters, as confronting the Jewish view that the rich are necessarily righteous and the poor necessarily sinners—despite the very Jewish view that God is particularly concerned about the poor, widows, orphans, and strangers. The parable of the Lost Coin, with its prominent female protagonist, is seen to challenge Jewish misogyny, as if Jews never told stories with female protagonists (Ruth, Esther, and Judith would be among those surprised at this claim). Such views make Judaism look hardhearted and exclusivist. They make Jewish practice look superstitious and xenophobic, Jewish morality tantamount to the worship of Mammon, and Jewish views of gender indicate the height of misogyny. Such teachings not only get Jesus wrong, and they not only get Judaism wrong; they inculcate and reinforce bigotry.

These stereotypes are not restricted to the lay pastor who was born again at twelve, who received the call to preach at sixteen, and who regards formal theological education as a waste of time, since the Holy Spirit tells him what to say (I do think such preachers would be doing the Spirit a favor by giving it something to work with). Nor are they restricted to the various Internet sites where sermons can be downloaded and biblical passages explained by anyone with a computer. The fault lies in part in the academy as well.

Here is our fifth reason we misread the parables. The study of homiletics, the art of giving sermons, is moving increasingly away from a historical-critical focus on the biblical text and more toward communication theory, toward what is known as "practical theology," or toward readings from one's own subject position or social location, such as a focus on African American hermeneutics or disability studies. My concern is not the opening of new areas of study; in fact, I find of enormous help the move to claim particular voices that address specific issues. My concern is that attention only to these areas, without attention to Jesus's own cultural context, opens the door not just to anachronism, but to stereotype. The more time we take in finding our own context and so our own voice, the less attention gets paid to Jesus's own context and voice.

Finally, the sixth problem: for some on the more liberal side of the theological scale, students of the Bible are also pulled away from history by the allure of newer approaches—including pretty much anything beginning with "post," as in "postmodern," "postcolonial," "postcritical," and so on. These various approaches arose in part as a response to earlier forms of historical work, in which the historian claimed to be doing objective work, when instead he (it usually was a "he") was projecting his own cultural values and theological views on the ancient materials. However, some of today's generation have tossed out all of historical work; they prefer to find meanings from their own perspective. What the text might have meant to Jesus or to his first followers becomes either an impossible or irrelevant question. The more the parables become detached from their own setting, the more the demons of anti-Jewish readings easily enter.

I am not suggesting that preachers who deliver anti-Jewish messages from the pulpit or academics who wind up inculcating them in the classrooms are bigots. Lack of education is not the same thing as hatred; misinformation is not the same thing as slander. In the numerous cases where I've written to people whose depictions of Judaism are incorrect, I've found the responses almost always gracious and thankful.

The message of Jesus and the meaning of the parables need to be heard in their original context, and that context cannot serve as an artificial and negative foil to make Jesus look original or countercultural in cases where he is not. Yes, today we like what is "countercultural" or "radical" or "unique"— but those are our values and are not necessarily what the parables are conveying. Instead, the parables more often tease us into recognizing what we've already always known, and they do so by reframing our vision. The point is less that they reveal something new than that they tap into our memories, our values, and our deepest longings, and so they resurrect what is very old, and very wise, and very precious. And often, very unsettling.

The following studies of a dozen or so of Jesus's parables are thus works of history and imagination, of critical analysis and playful speculation. The more I study the parables, the more challenged I am by them. One need not have to believe in Jesus as Lord and Savior in order to realize that he had some extraordinary things to say. If I can find such genius in his parables, how much more so should those who worship him be able to listen with more finely attuned ears to hear.

Thus, each chapter begins with my fairly literal translation of a short story by Jesus; if the literalness makes the parable seem unfamiliar, good. Once we can defamiliarize ourselves of our tried-and-true readings, we are in a better position to hear the parable anew. The chapter next locates that story in its historical and literary context and sweeps away the interpretations that distort Jesus's own context. It concludes by offering fresh readings of what the parable might have suggested to its earliest and original listeners and then what we might do with that impression today.

I have chosen the parables here on the basis of what I have to say that is original and in recognition that there is a law of diminishing returns. There is no reason to produce a twenty-page discussion of what one can find in numerous other books on parables. As Martin Bresler said while chairing a meeting of a major Jewish organization and despairing of its ever ending: "Everything that needed to be said was said, but not everyone had said it." This book is not a volume at which well-known interpretations are repeated. To repeat what is already known would be a waste of my time, and yours.

This book is an act of listening anew, of imagining what the parables would have sounded like to people who have no idea that Jesus will be proclaimed Son of God by millions, no idea even that he will be crucified by Rome. What would they hear a Jewish storyteller telling them? And why, two thousand years later, are these questions not only relevant, but perhaps more pressing than ever?

CHAPTER 1

Lost Sheep, Lost Coin, Lost Son

Which person among you, having a hundred sheep and losing one out of them, will not leave behind the ninety-nine in the wilderness and go after the lost until he finds it? And finding, he puts it up on his shoulders; rejoicing. And coming into the house he calls together the friends and the neighbors, saying to them, "Rejoice together with me, because I have found my sheep, the lost one." I say to you that likewise there will be more joy in heaven at one sinner repenting than at ninety-nine righteous, those who have no need of repentance.

Luke 15.4–7

Or what woman, having ten drachmas, if she would lose one drachma, does not light a lamp and sweep the house and seek resolutely until she finds? And when she finds, she calls together (female) friends and (female) neighbors, saying, "Rejoice with me, because I have found the drachma, the one I had lost." Likewise, I say to you, there will be rejoicing before the angels of God at one sinner repenting.

Luke 15.8–10

Some man had two sons. And said the younger of them to the father, "Father, give to me the portion of the property that is falling to me." And he divided between them the life.

And after not many days, gathering together all, the younger son took a journey into a far region, and there he scattered the property through excessive living. And having spent all, there was a strong famine in that region, and he himself began to be in need. And going, he became joined to one of the citizens of that region, and he sent him into his fields to feed pigs. And he was desiring to be filled from the pods that the pigs were eating, but no one was giving to him.

And coming to himself, he said, "How many hired laborers of my father are abounding of bread, but I by famine here am lost? Getting up, I shall go to my father and I shall say to him, 'Father, I have sinned against heaven and before you; not still am I worthy to be called your son; make me as one of your hired laborers.'"

And rising up, he went toward his father. And yet when he was far off, his father saw him, and had compassion, and running, fell upon his neck and continually kissed him.

And said the son to him, "Father, I have sinned against heaven and before you; not still am I worthy to be called your son."

And said the father to his slaves, "Quickly carry out a robe, the first, and put it on him, and give the ring to his hand and sandals to the feet. And bring the calf, the grain-fed one, sacrifice and, eating, we may rejoice. Because this, my son, was dead, and he came back to life; he had been lost, and was found." And they began to rejoice.

And his son, the elder, was in the field, and as he, coming, drew near to the house, he heard symphony and chorus. And calling over one of the servants he inquired what these things might be. And he said to him, "Your brother has come, and your father has sacrificed the grain-fed calf, because he received him healthy."

And he became angry, and he did not want to go in. And his father, going out, comforted/urged him.

And answering, he said to his father, "Look, all these years I am slaving for you, and not one commandment of yours have I passed by, and for me not one young goat did you give so that with my friends I might rejoice. But when your

son, this one, the one who ate up your life with whores came,
you sacrificed for him the grain-fed calf.

And he said to him, "Child, you always with me are, and
everything that is mine is yours. But it remains necessary
to cheer and to rejoice, because your brother, this one, was
dead, and lived to life, and being lost, even he was found."

Luke 15.11–32

According to Luke, the narratives traditionally called the parable of the Lost Sheep, the parable of the Lost Coin, and the parable of the Prodigal Son are about sinners repenting and God graciously offering forgiveness and reconciliation. Luke misleads by turning the parables into allegories. It is unlikely a first-century Jewish listener would hear the first two parables and conclude that they have something to do with sheep repenting or coins confessing. Sheep eat, sleep, poop, produce wool, and give milk—but an awareness of sin or a sense of eschatological salvation is not part of ovine nature. Although one could adduce Psalm 119.176—"I have gone astray like a lost sheep; seek out your servant, for I do not forget your commandments"—the parable offers no angora angst or merino *metanoia* (Gk., "repentance"). Neither sheep nor coins have the capability to repent, and I doubt the younger brother does either.

If any blame is to be assigned in the first two parables, then the shepherd and the woman are at fault, for they "lost," respectively, the sheep and the coin. Were the parables called "The Shepherd Who Lost His Sheep" and "The Woman Who Lost Her Coin," we might be closer to an earlier meaning. Regarding the issue of fault in the third parable, were the prodigal son a sinner for demanding his inheritance—which is unlikely to be the case, as we'll see—he had help; his father, instead of disciplining him, abetted his request by complying with it. Thus this parable too might be renamed: "The Father Who Lost His Son(s)."

Not only do many of Luke's readers, as numerous sermons and studies attest, regard the three parables as about sinning and repenting; they also see the parables as correcting an artificially constructed, pernicious Judaism—

and at this point a harmless allegory becomes a dangerous stereotype. Common is the claim that the parables, especially the third, reveal an extravagant, earth-shattering image of a God the Father who forgives, as if Jews had no notion of a divinity who seeks relationship and reconciliation. Common is the view that the older son is an allegorical representation of the Jews, who slavishly serve God the Father in order to earn a reward, while Jesus proclaims salvation by grace. And common is the interpretation that the prodigal, given his connection to pig farming, represents gentile Christians, whereas the older brother, the stereotypical Jew, resents God the Father's outreach beyond the so-called chosen people, with their elitist, nationalistic attitudes.

In these readings and more, the younger son is the repentant Christian, the older son is the Pharisee or the Jewish people, and the father is God. Such interpretations not only yank the parable out of its historical context; they lessen the message of Jesus and bear false witness against Jews and Judaism.

In its original context, the parable of the Prodigal Son would not have been heard as a story of repentance or forgiveness, a story of works-righteousness and grace, or a story of Jewish xenophobia and Christian universalism. Instead, the parable's messages of finding the lost, of reclaiming children, of reassessing the meaning of family offer not only good news, but better news.

Titles Matter

The term "prodigal son" does not appear in the parable most often known by that name. The earliest reference is from the church father Jerome (347–420), who speaks of having written "on the prudent and the prodigal sons."[1] Nevertheless, the label "Prodigal Son" necessarily influences both what messages we take from the parable and what lessons we fail to hear.

On the simplest level, far too many people think the term "prodigal" has a partially positive connotation, such as "adventurous" or "daring" or "ambitious." A few students who did not do well on their SATs hear "prodigal" and think "prodigy." The word "prodigal" indicates wasteful spending, financial recklessness. Aristotle wrote, ". . . [W]e call prodigal those who lack self-restraint and who, in their licentiousness, spend lavishly. Hence the prodigal are held to be very base people, since they have many vices simultaneously."[2] Contrary to today's appropriations of the term, such as *Prodigal Magazine*, a Christian "online publication that is passionate about helping people live and tell good stories,"[3] or Prodigal, a global hedge fund that promotes "innovation in financial services,"[4] or the various claims that speak of God's interest in "reckless," "radical," or "extreme" love, there is nothing complimentary about being prodigal, that is, in wasting resources for personal gratification.

Despite the connotations of prodigality, the traditional interpretation of the parable actually forecloses rather than opens it up to broader meaning. The prodigal disappears from the second half of the narrative; therefore, when readers focus only on the prodigal, it is a prodigal act. It wastes the rest of the story, and it tosses aside the several profound challenges it offers.

Better is "The Prodigal and the Prudent," as Jerome had it. Also plausible is "The Lost Son," which is how the parable is known in Egyptian Christian sources; this title has the added value of opening the question: "Which son is lost?" Lebanese Christians refer to "The Clever (Arabic *shatter*) Son," a title that plays on the similar term *shatr,* meaning "divide" or "separate."[5] Thus the younger son is "the clever and separated." In Germany, *Der verlorene Sohn,* "The Lost Son," is the common title, although ironically the traditional German reading sees the title as applying only to the younger son. At least with this designation, the younger son's ambiguous character is open for discussion.

On my more cynical days, I am inclined to call the story the parable of "The Absent Mother." "The Symphony and Chorus," "The Grain-Fed Calf," and "Dissolute Living" are also possibilities, although not in this volume.

The main reason that the name Prodigal Son caught on was Christian focus on the younger son's character. In the early years of the church, some patristic readers, who never met an allegory they didn't like, saw the younger son as Jesus himself. This Beloved Son left the paradise of his heavenly father, went to dwell in the world of sin, engaged in a gentile mission indicated by his becoming a servant to a pig farmer (by definition, a gentile), and then returned home to be welcomed with ring and robe and feasting. In a number of such appropriations, the elder brother goes missing entirely.[6] This reading, which requires a decoder key (e.g., the Christ hymn in Phil. 2.6–11) to explain the allegorical connections, is not something Jesus's Jewish audience would have heard.

Although the idea that the prodigal is Jesus has become less popular, from antiquity to the present the view that the father is God the Father has prevailed. As early as the second century, the North African church father Tertullian made the connection: "Who is that father to be understood by us? God, surely; no one *is* so truly a Father, no one so rich in paternal love."[7] I do wonder about Tertullian's own parenting, for surely other dads have been generous to a fault (literally) with their younger children.

This allegorical connection is then exploited by more recent commentators who insist that the father's welcoming of the prodigal not only surprises, but transgresses cultural standards of honor. Here is a standard trope that misrepresents Judaism. According to this reading, Jesus creates a new image of the divine to replace the demanding, stern, and punishing God of Judaism. Swiss theologian Eduard Schweizer goes as far as to claim that "those who nailed [Jesus] to the cross because they found blasphemy in his parables—which proclaimed such scandalous conduct on the part of God— understood his parables better than those who saw in them nothing but the obvious message, which should be self-evident to all, of the fatherhood and kindness of God, meant to replace a superstitious belief in a God of wrath."[8] Perhaps he missed such Jewish texts as Psalm 23, which states, "The Lord is my shepherd," not "The Lord is my sadist."

Just as the father is today usually seen as a cipher for God and the prodigal as the Christian who repents of his sin and is welcomed back by the gracious God, so also that older brother, out in the field, remains the Jew or, in a variation on that theme, the "Pharisaic Christian" (in such settings, the label "Pharisee" is never a compliment), who obeys the Father out of a sense of duty rather than of love, who mistakenly thinks that one must earn God's grace, and who refuses to welcome the marginal, outcasts, gentiles, or whatever group Christian readers see themselves as welcoming and the Jews, conversely, as rejecting. Or, as New Testament scholar Klyne Snodgrass puts it, "At least [Luke] ch. 15, if not the whole of 14.1–17.10, is focused on the gospel for the outcasts."[9]

As early as around 383, Jerome claimed that the elder brother represented unrepentant Israel; in the field, he is "far from the grace of the Holy Spirit, banished from his father's counsel."[10] Apparently Jerome did not quite make it to the end of the parable, where the father attempts to reconcile with his older son and states, "Everything I have is yours." Augustine similarly reads the elder brother as "the people of Israel following the flesh . . . toiling with reference to earthly things."[11] Calvin rejects limiting the elder brother to the Jews and extends the reference to "hypocrites with intolerable pride";[12] the move still condemns the older son by attributing to him motives that the parable leaves unmentioned. Yet another variant, albeit out of the mainstream, is the present-day identification of the unforgiving elder brother with Simon Wiesenthal, the Jewish American Nazi hunter.[13] Underlying this unfortunate reading is the view that Nazi hunters should let bygones be bygones. The comparison of the personal spending of one's fortune in dissolute living with genocide strikes me as a tad overstated.

Such positive readings of the father and the prodigal and negative readings of the older brother are prompted substantially by Luke's contextualization, to which we now turn. Luke places the three parables after these words:

> Now all the tax collectors and sinners were coming near to listen to him. And the Pharisees and the scribes were grumbling and saying, "This fellow welcomes sinners and eats with them." (Luke 15.1–2)

We can see Luke's hand at work by comparing Luke 15 with Matthew's version of the first of those three stories.[14] Matthew 18.10–14 offers more or less the same first parable, but with a much different context:

> Take care that you do not despise one of these little ones; for, I tell you, in heaven their angels continually see the face of my Father in heaven. What do you think? If a shepherd has a hundred sheep, and one of them has gone astray, does he not leave the ninety-nine on the mountains and go in search of the one that went astray? And if he finds it, truly I tell you, he rejoices over it more than over the ninety-nine that never went astray. So it is not the will of your Father in heaven that one of these little ones should be lost.

Speaking neither to sinners and tax collectors nor to Pharisees and scribes, but to his own disciples, Matthew offers in the two center sentences of that passage a parable that can legitimately be called the Lost Sheep (vv. 12–13). The NRSV, however, cleans up the language by describing the sheep as having "gone astray," whereas the Greek (*plano*) has the main connotation of "deceive/deception." A better translation would be: "If a person has a hundred sheep and one of them is deceived, does he not leave the ninety-nine upon the mountain and going, seek the deceived? And if he comes to find it—amen, I say to you—that he rejoices over it more than over the ninety-nine who were not deceived." The opening (v. 10) and concluding (v. 14) verses—the context—appear to be from the hand of the evangelist, who favors designations such as "little ones" and "Father in heaven."

For Matthew, the parable is about the church's responsibility to care, doctrinally, for its members, who may be deceived by false claims. The allegory is stronger here: it is the sheep who is "deceived." For Luke, the parable is about repenting and forgiving. Both evangelists had the story, and each recontextualized it to make a point consistent with the rest of the Gospel. Detached from either context, the parable may well have had quite a different message.

For Luke, the three parables are designed to show the different concerns of two groups of people: those with whom the Gospel readers are to identify (sinners and tax collectors) and those whom the readers are to reject (Pharisees and scribes). Luke's Gospel gives us numerous negative portraits of Pharisees and several darling images of tax collectors. In Luke, some of those who come to John the Baptist in repentance are tax collectors (3.12), as is one of Jesus's disciples (5.27). Tax collectors acknowledge divine justice (7.29), and one of them finds reconciliation in the Jerusalem Temple (18.14). And of course there's Zacchaeus (whose name basically means "Mr. Righteous"), the chief tax collector and richest guy in town, who, because he is short, climbs a sycamore tree to see Jesus as he enters Jericho (19.1–10).

The Pharisees and scribes, for Luke's readers, tend to remain coded as Jews, and thus a number of readers go even further than Luke in applying stereotypes. For example, in some commentaries, these "sinners and tax collectors" are understood to be people who "abandoned the law and for all practical purposes had denied God's covenant with Israel."[15] Then, with amazing sleight of hand, these tax collectors and sinners become "outcasts," and the parable is understood to be about "the Pharisaic refusal out of envy and resentment to accept this good news extended to the outcast. . . . They, like the elder son, had stayed within the covenant, . . . they had never broken any of the commandments. But (the story suggests) they regarded themselves not as sons so much as slaves. And they resented others being allowed into the people without cost."[16]

For a first-century Jew, and even for Luke's Gospel, the tax collectors and sinners are not those who have "abandoned the law" or "denied the covenant." That Jesus tells a parable in which a tax collector prays in the Jerusalem Temple does suggest some investment in that covenant. The problem with "tax collectors" is not that they denied the covenant; it is that they work for Rome and so would be seen by many within the Jewish community as traitors to their own people.

Sinners are not "outcasts"; they are not cast out of synagogues or out of the Jerusalem Temple. To the contrary, they are welcome in such places, since such places encourage repentance. The Gospels generally present sinners as wealthy people who have not attended to the poor. That is a dandy definition of the term. Thus, in a first-century context, sinners, like tax collectors, are individuals who have removed themselves from the common welfare, who look to themselves rather than to the community.

The problem is that many of us today hear "sinner" and think only in religious categories. The sinner is the one who "breaks the Law," but the "Law" becomes understood not in terms of "Love your neighbor as yourself" or "Leave the corners of your field for the poor," but in terms of earning one's way into heaven, legalism, or works-righteousness. Many Christian readers, already primed to think of Law as the antithesis of grace and as a "burden," come to identify with the "sinner" who is freed from this dreadful legalism. Again, this is not what first-century (or twenty-first-century) Jews would hear.

Similarly, there are no "outcasts" in any of the three parables in Luke 15. The shepherd did not expel the sheep for bleating a blasphemy or grazing on nonkosher grass. The sheep did not sin. Rather, the shepherd lost the sheep. Similarly, the coin was not cast out; the woman was looking for her money, not divesting from it. Nor was the prodigal cast out; he walked out on his own two feet, or perhaps on a horse he bought with his inheritance. Once the term "outcast" is used in reference to Jesus's Jewish context, dualistic models are in place, negative stereotypes of Judaism are implied, and Christian apologetic is well under way.

We need not have negative views of Pharisees in order to understand the parables. To the contrary, such readings reverse general Jewish views. The Pharisees were the ones respected by the people at large. Paul, the only self-identified Pharisee from whom we have written records, trots out his Pharisaic origins as something worthy of admiration (although heaven forbid he would boast; see Phil. 3.5). As for sinners—that is, those who think about themselves and not of others—Paul provides the standard instruction. In 1 Corinthians 5.11, Paul advises his fledging church, "But now I am writing to you not to associate with anyone who bears the name of brother or sister who is sexually immoral or greedy, or is an idolater, reviler, drunkard, or robber. Do not even eat with such a one." They are the ancient drug pushers, insider traders, arms dealers, and, especially, colonial collaborationists. And yes, Jesus eats with them—that's part of his genius, that he recognizes that they are part of the community and he goes out to get them.

Both Matthew and Luke have provided our parables with a context, and in so doing they have begun the process of interpretation. We do well to see what the parables might have meant prior to their reception as Matthew's "instruction for church leaders" and Luke's "we love tax collectors, but Pharisees not so much."

Lost Sheep

Traditional interpretations see the sheep as the believer who has strayed from the fold; the one in search is Jesus or one of his representatives, who makes every effort to save this lost sheep from destruction; and the friends who join in feasting at the end are the church. This is an encouraging message; it is certainly good news. What has gotten lost, however, is any provocation, any challenge. A second listen is in order.

Which person among you, having a hundred sheep and
losing one out of them . . . **(Luke 15.4a)**

The question would provoke from the majority of people in Jesus's audience
the answer, "Not I." Most peasants do not own a hundred sheep. The parable's opening presupposes a person of some means. So does the story of the
woman who has lost her silver coin and the father who has a sufficiently large
estate to have fatted calves, lots of clothing, and good accessories. Although
"having" might simply mean "having charge over," the image conveyed by
all three parables is that of substance. Perhaps it is those who "have" who are
more likely to fail to notice what is missing.

That audience might have remarked on the owner's recognition that a
sheep was missing. If one has five sheep, noting only four on the hillside
would be easy to do. It is less easy, perhaps impossible, to notice one missing out of one hundred; most people, expecting a hundred coins in a jar or
daisies in a field, could not spot one missing without not only counting, but
also organizing into rows. One out of a hundred is easy to overlook, but as
soon as the owner recognizes his loss, he takes whatever steps are needed
in order to bring the group to wholeness. Even a missing 1 percent must be
noticed. And if he can notice the missing one and diligently seek to find it,
he reminds listeners that perhaps they have lost something, or someone, as
well, but have not noticed it. Before the search can begin, we need to notice
what, or who, is not there.

The initial audience may also have had some concerns about the owner of
those sheep. At fault, if there is blame to be assigned for the missing sheep,
is the one who was to watch over the flock. The story could have gone otherwise. In Matthew's version of this parable, as we have seen, it is the sheep
that has been deceived (Matt. 18.12–14; *Thomas* 107). But in our parable,
with the fellow having lost the sheep, the idea that the owner is Jesus or God
is compromised. The owner is an owner, and he is down one animal. Rather
than the parable of the Lost Sheep, the same short story could be called the
parable of the Initially Oblivious Owner.

... will not leave the ninety-nine in the wilderness and go
after the lost until he finds it? **(Luke 15.4b)**

The seeker who leaves ninety-nine sheep to find one will have, at the end
of the day, only one sheep. Sheep are not among the animal kingdom's
brightest creatures. Sheep stray. When in John 10 Jesus—who here really
is the "Good Shepherd"—describes how the shepherd "calls his own sheep
by name" (10.3), he is being generous; sheep may recognize the voice of the
shepherd, but they do not know their own names. "Here, Fluffy" or "Here,
Lamb Chop" (one does wonder about naming a sheep "Lamb Chop," but
then again neither sheep nor sock puppets would understand the irony[17])
would yield either a hundred blank stares or the faces of a hundred hungry
animals.

In Luke's parable, the owner has lost a sheep and, in desperation, does
what he can to find it. He is so concerned about the lost sheep that he not
only "leaves" (Gk. *leipo*), but "leaves behind" (*kataleipo*) the others.[18] That
missing one out of one hundred is as important to him as all the others, as
perhaps all congregants are important to their churches or all children are
important to their parents. One hopes he has helpers to watch the rest of
the flock.

And finding, he puts it up on his shoulders; rejoicing.
(Luke 15.5)

Whereas the owner is enormously relieved, whether the sheep cared one
iota about being found is irrelevant to this parable. Nor are most sheep, so
Merino farmers in Australia tell me, all that happy to be carried on a person's shoulders. We might picture a bit of a struggle. For the owner, the important thing is that he has found the sheep, and now his flock is complete.

And coming into the house he calls together the friends and
the neighbors, saying to them, "Rejoice together with me,
because I have found my sheep, the lost one." **(Luke 15.6)**

The setting arranged for the party is not in the barn or the sheepfold, but in the house. The Greek used for the guest list takes the form of the masculine plural, and so women may be included in the invitation (in Greek, as in most gendered languages, the term for a group of thousands of women and one man would be in the masculine). The finder of the lost, who rejoiced when he found the sheep, wants to share his joy. Whether inviting only the guys or including women as well, the host would be expected to provide hospitality—the excitement over the finding of a lost sheep only goes so far. It would not surprise me to learn that at the reception the joyful finder served mutton.

I say to you that likewise there will be more joy in heaven at
one sinner repenting than at ninety-nine righteous, those
who have no need of repentance. **(Luke 15.7)**

With this verse, it is Luke who provides the first interpretation by turning the parable into an allegory. The idea that someone, let alone ninety-nine such someones, "do not need repentance" tends to be overlooked in the church, where the prevailing view is that everyone needs to repent. If there are ninety-nine folks in the neighborhood who have nothing to repent for, we really are in the land of fantasy rather than reality. Also overlooked is how the allegory fails to match the parable. There was no repenting in the story; there was no sin; the sheep did not "come to itself" and find its way home. It was the owner who lost the sheep, and if this losing were sinful, he's not seen repenting.

Luke is not the only one to interpret the parable in a way that requires an allegorical key. Consistent with Luke's suggestion that the one repentant sinner is of greater value than the righteous ninety-nine, in the *Gospel of Thomas* our parable appears in a form that is closer to Matthew's version than to Luke's. In this rendition, "Jesus said, 'The (Father's) imperial rule is like a shepherd who had a hundred sheep. One of them, the largest, went astray. He left the ninety-nine and looked for the one until he found it. After he had toiled, he said to the sheep, "I love you more than the ninety-nine"'" (107).[19] *Thomas*'s shepherd easily notices the missing sheep—it is the largest of the flock. Further, *Thomas*'s shepherd plays favorites. This version offers no challenge, provides no moral lesson, and creates no community. There is no celebration, no feasting, just favoritism.

Beyond those of Luke and *Thomas,* allegorical interpretations abound. Popular today is the claim that Luke's parable, along with Matthew's companion version and John's "Good Shepherd discourse" (John 10), in which Jesus states, "I am the good shepherd. The good shepherd lays down his life for the sheep" (10.11), serves to enhance the role of the shepherd within a Jewish culture that despised laborers. From allegories of repenting and forgiveness to an allegory about inversions of social class, more anachronism and more negative depictions of Judaism emerge.

Commentators first conclude that Jewish listeners, or at least enough of them, would have despised shepherds and therefore seen the parable as challenging social convention by depicting a positive image of shepherds. From both the academic study and the Sunday pulpit, the faithful are told: "Pharisees and scribes would never even have contemplated taking up the task of the shepherd. Shepherds belonged to a class of despised trades";[20] "The rabbis both revered the shepherd of the Hebrew Bible and classed the contemporary shepherd among robbers and thieves, the outcast"[21] (it is almost impossible to read about Luke 15 without encountering the term "outcast" every three of four pages); or the parable "would have caused the Pharisees and scribes, people immensely concerned about cleanness, to imagine themselves involved in a trade they considered unclean."[22] The inevitable pernicious conclusion is: "In contrast to rabbinical contempt for shepherds, . . . Jesus, who has fellowship with the despised and sinners, knows and appreciates them as people."[23]

Such views are nonsense. First, the citations do not match the claim. The usually adduced passages are Philo's *On Agriculture* 61; the Mishnah, *Qiddushin* 4.14; and the relatively late *Midrash on Psalms* 23.1–2. Philo was not a Pharisee, but an upper-class philosopher living in urban Alexandria. His comments are in relation to Joseph's brothers, who explain to Pharaoh that they are keepers of sheep and goats (and so not political or economic threats). Philo first notes that they "are testifying their high opinion of the profession of life which they have adopted, not in honor of themselves alone, but of their father also, as being worthy of all possible care and diligence."[24] He then states, "Such occupations are accounted inglorious and mean among those who are loaded with great prosperity, without being at the same time endowed with prudence, and especially among kings." In other words, the very rich who lack wisdom see shepherds as mean. How these very wealthy ignorant people in Egypt became transformed, by a few biblical commentators, into Pharisees in Galilee is a miracle of exegesis.

In the Mishnah, *Qiddushin* 4.14 is a very long passage expressing the personal opinions of a number of rabbis, and it has nothing to do with shepherds per se. The relevant portion reads:

> Abba Gorion of Zaidan says in the name of Abba Guria: A man should not teach his son to be an ass-driver or a camel-driver or a barber or a sailor or a herdsman [here's the shepherd reference] or a shopkeeper, for their craft is the craft of robbers. R. Judah says in his name: Ass-drivers are most of them wicked, camel-drivers are most of them proper folk, sailors are most of them saintly, the best among physicians is destined for Gehenna, and the most seemly among butchers is a partner of Amalek.[25]

Abba Gorion, a second-century sage, is a snob, but his views are hardly indicative of those of all Pharisees or even any from the late Second Temple period. Further, to draw a general view of shepherds—or butchers, doctors, sailors, and so on—from one rabbi, whose views are immediately contradicted in the same passage, is tantamount to borrowing a comment from one of the church fathers and ascribing the view to Jesus or Paul. One could equally cite, from the Mishnah, *Baba Qamma* 10.9, which speaks of accepting shepherds (the same word, *ro'eh*) as judges. Selective citations from later rabbinic sources retrojected into the first century, set up as indicative of all Pharisaic views, and then used to create a contrast with Jesus result in a nasty game of proof-texting.

On the other hand, the numerous positive comments about shepherds made by Philo, the rabbis, the scriptures of Israel, and the Dead Sea Scrolls all go missing in most of these treatments: the Lord is a shepherd (Ps. 23.1; see also Isa. 40.11; Ezek. 34.11–13, 15–16; 37.24–25; Jer. 23.2–4); Rachel tended sheep, as did Zipporah, and they both made splendid wives; David was a shepherd, as was Moses. From the community eventually associated with Qumran, the Damascus Document (CD) asserts, "He [the Guardian of the community] shall love them [the Congregation] as a father loves his children, and shall carry them in their distress like a shepherd a sheep."[26]

Since rabbinic texts are sometimes adduced to show how "the Pharisees" despised shepherds, it becomes appropriate to cite rabbinic texts, indeed, parables, on how shepherds functioned in storytelling. The midrashic text *Exodus Rabbah* offers a "good shepherd parable" featuring Moses (2.2). The prompt for the parable is Exodus 3.1: "Now Moses was keeping the flock of his father-in-law Jethro." The parable reads:

> The Holy One tested Moses by means of the flock, as our rabbis explained: when *Moshe rabbenu* (Moses our teacher) was tending Jethro's flock in the wilderness, a lamb scampered off, and Moses followed it, until it approached a shelter under a rock. As the lamb reached the shelter, it came upon a pool of water and stopped to drink. When Moses caught up with it, he said, "I did not know that you ran away because you were thirsty. Now you must be tired." So he hoisted the lamb on his shoulder and started walking back with it. The Holy One then said, "Because you showed such compassion in tending the flock of a mortal, as you live, you shall become the shepherd of Israel, the flock that is mine."

I do wonder if there's an edge to this parable. The shepherd is supposed to know if his sheep are thirsty. There may be a warning here to Moses and so to any leader: "You may have the right compassion, but you also require knowledge of the needs of your flock." The parable would have also evoked, for its Jewish listeners, the account in Exodus 17 of the Israelites camped at Rephidim with "no water for the people to drink" (17.1).

Returning to the first parable in Luke 15 and reading it in light of these multiple shepherding images, we find that Jesus, in describing a man who has lost and then found his sheep, is not elevating the role of shepherd. Indeed, the parable no more speaks to the elevation of the so-called despised shepherd than a pastor who refers to his congregation as a "flock" has elevated the role of sheep.

Once we get beyond the common moves to make Jesus look good by making Judaism look bad, and once we recognize that Luke's allegorical reading, which connects the lost sheep with the repentant Christian, is not what the parable's original audience would have concluded, we can begin to see what the parable is actually doing.

The parable presents a main figure—the owner, not the sheep—who realizes he has lost something of value to him. He notices the single missing sheep among the ninety-nine in the wilderness. For him, the missing sheep, whether it is one of a hundred or a million, makes the flock incomplete. He engages in an exaggerated search, and when he has found the sheep, he engages in an equally exaggerated sense of rejoicing, first by himself and then with his friends and neighbors. If this fellow can experience such joy in finding one of a hundred sheep, what joy do we experience when we find what we have lost? More, if he can realize that one of his hundred has gone missing, do we know what or whom we have lost? When was the last time we took stock, or counted up who was present rather than simply counted on their presence? Will we take responsibility for the losing, and what effort will we make to find it—or him or her—again?

Lost Coin

Or what woman, having ten drachmas, if she would lose one
drachma, does not light a lamp and sweep the house and
seek resolutely until she finds? **(Luke 15.8)**

Just as commentators see Jesus as elevating the role of the "outcast" shepherd over and against a Jewish elitist view, so they see him as elevating the role of the "despised" woman within an early Judaism or at least a Pharisaic context that makes the Taliban look progressive.[27] All too familiar are comments such as, "Luke combines parables in this instance in which there could only be negative feelings among Pharisaic critics about the main actors—first a shepherd, now a woman."[28] One popular homiletic commentary observes: "In a patriarchal society where pious men could pray, 'Blessed be God that he [sic!] has not made me a woman,' Jesus's stories with central female characters would be startling, if not offensive."[29]

Apparently, the authors of Esther, Ruth, Judith, Susanna, 2 and 4 Maccabees, *Liber Antiquitatum Biblicarum,* and a host of other Jewish sources never got the message that central female characters are offensive. Yet the commentators still want to find Jews offended by central images of a shepherd and a woman. Rather, perhaps we might find it offensive that Jesus's own context is so negatively portrayed.

Instead of putting the parable on the offensive list, it is better used as one coin among many in the treasury of information about Jewish women in antiquity. This treasury reveals not a population oppressed by "patriarchal Judaism," but a diverse group with various notable social roles.

For example, the woman who has ten drachmas, silver coins, is by no means marginal, outcast, or poor. She's not only relatively well-off; she has her own home and her own set of friends. The parable fits neatly with what other accounts tell us. Our homeowner in Luke 15 confirms what we know from other sources: women have access to their own funds, and Jewish women are hardly the poorest of the poor. All four Gospels, in various ways, describe a woman who anoints Jesus with extremely expensive ointment (Matt. 26.9; Mark 14.5; Luke 7.38–39; John 12.5). According to Luke, Jesus and his followers are supported by the female Jewish patrons

Mary Magdalene, Joanna, and Susanna (8.1–3). Mark (5.26) and Luke (8.43) describe a woman who spent her money on physicians. These same two Gospels record the story of a woman who gives her last two coins, her whole "life" (the same term used to describe what the father of the prodigal divided), to the Temple treasury (Mark 12.42–43; Luke 21.2–3). Other women also appear in the Temple, such as the widow Anna (Luke 2.36–37) and Mary the mother of Jesus (Luke 2.22–39, 46–50). Jesus heals a woman in a synagogue (Luke 13.10–17), where she is not restricted to a balcony or behind a screen. In the parable of the Widow and the Judge, a woman appears in court (Luke 18.2–8). The "daughters of Jerusalem" appear in public to weep for Jesus (Luke 23.28), as does the widow of Nain, whose only son Jesus raises from the dead (Luke 7.11–16). The list goes on. I am not arguing that first-century Judaism was an egalitarian paradise; I am arguing that Jesus was by no means unusual in telling stories about women. Given his Jewish context, it would have been peculiar if he did not.

And when she finds, she calls together (female) friends and (female) neighbors, saying, "Rejoice with me, because I have found the drachma, the one I had lost." **(Luke 15.9)**

Finally, we also learn from the Lost Coin that the "friends and neighbors" our joyful woman invites to celebrate are female, as the form of the Greek nouns tells us. The happy homeowner does not ask anyone's permission to issue her invitation, and there is no reason to think that these friends and neighbors had to ask permission to join in the rejoicing.

As with the Lost Sheep, the parable of the Lost Coin does not need to invent a negative Judaism to surprise and provoke. The second parable sounds the same themes of loss, search, completion, and joy. As the flock of one hundred is incomplete at ninety-nine, so the silver coin collection is incomplete at nine. It is easier to notice one item missing from a collection of ten than one out of a hundred, but it is still difficult to distinguish nine coins from ten in a pile. The woman, like the owner of the flock, counted. When she found a coin missing, she went all out for the search.

The shepherd's urgent search for his lost sheep is replayed in the woman's urgent search—lighting the lamps, sweeping the floor—for her coin. Both shepherd and woman experience the joy of finding, and both share that joy with friends and neighbors.

But there is a subtle shift from the first parable to the second. The guardian of the flock speaks only of "my sheep, the lost one" (15.6). He does not claim responsibility for losing it. The woman mentions "the one I had lost" (15.9); she claims responsibility. We are provoked again. We can celebrate when what we have lost is found, but can we also admit our responsibility in the losing?

Likewise, I say to you, there will be rejoicing before the angels of God at one sinner repenting. **(Luke 15.10)**

Luke does not permit us to ask such questions about responsibility, since Luke insists the parable is about repenting and forgiving. Luke finds no fault with the owner or the householder; for Luke, the focus is on the sheep and the coin, despite the fact that neither took any action. The sheep and coin were "lost" and then "found"; they were passive objects. It is their owners, who first lost, then found, then celebrated, who should be the focus of our attention. They had the problem, and they fixed it. Thus when we turn to the third parable in Luke 15, we might want to pay attention to the father, who comes to realize what he has lost and desperately wants to find and celebrate.

Finally, if readers want to maintain the traditional view that the shepherd in the first parable and the father in the third are meant to represent God, then it is only fair to regard the woman with her coin as divine as well. Augustine already associated her with Christ in his role as the Wisdom (Gk. *sophia*) of God.[30] I don't think Augustine's reading is one that Jesus's first-century Jewish audience would have taken; nevertheless, at least here there is something we might all celebrate.

Sheep, Coin, and Prodigal: Clues in Interpretation

We do not know if Jesus told the parables now found in Luke 15 as a set of three. Matthew and *Thomas* offer only variants on the Lost Sheep and do not present either the Lost Coin or the Prodigal Son. Nevertheless, the three parables are connected in numerous ways: by the themes of loss, and joy and feasting, as well as by structure.

We might think about the three parables, each with its main character (flock owner, householder, father) and something that is lost (sheep, coin, son[s]), as following the folkloric "rule of three." This rule, familiar from "Cinderella and Her Two Stepsisters" or, to use a nonkosher image, "The Three Little Pigs," uses two models to set up a third, and the third creates the variation on the theme. We will find the same "rule of three" operative when we turn to the parable of the Good Samaritan; there, the first two figures, priest and Levite, set up anticipation of the third, but the third, the Samaritan, is quite the variation.

In the first two parables in Luke 15, one of one hundred and then one of ten is lost. We may be surprised that the owner even notices that one of a hundred has gone missing, and even with one out of ten the loss may not be self-evident (as an experiment, one might put ten quarters in a pile, remove one, and see if a quick glance reveals any difference). Yet in the third parable there are only two sons. The father is convinced that the younger, the prodigal, is the one who is lost, and in many respects he is correct. However, we find at the end of the parable that the son who is in fact "lost" is the elder. The owner spots the missing sheep among the hundred, and the woman spots the missing coin among the ten. The father, with only two sons, was unable to count correctly.

In the first two parables, a man and then a woman diligently, if not frantically, search for the precious lost object. In the third, the father does not search for the younger son; the prodigal has taken himself to a "far region," out of his father's purview. Yet we get the impression that the father is waiting for the child's return: when the son is still far off, the father sees him. Perhaps he had been watching the road rather than his estate or his account books. It will turn out that the urgent search will not be for the prodigal, but for the elder brother.

In the first two parables, feasting and rejoicing end the story; in the third, the feasting and rejoicing are left behind as the desperate father tries to make his family whole. The story does not end with the party, but with two men in the field, one urging and comforting, the other resisting, vacillating, or reconciled—we do not know.

In the first parable, the shepherd does not take responsibility for losing his sheep; in the second, the woman admits her fault; in the third, the father does not initially even realize that his elder son is lost; his desperate search then is not for the younger who himself went astray, but for the older, whom he had lost. The first two parables have happy endings; the third leaves us with father and older son in the field. The challenge continues.

～⌒ら

Some man had two sons. (Luke 15.11)

As all biblically literate people know, the beginning words of this parable, "There was a man who had two sons," introduce a literary convention. As these readers also know, we do well to identify with the younger son. However, the story in Luke 15 is a parable, and parables usually do not do what we might expect.

Adam had two sons, Cain and Abel. Granted, Abel, the younger, is dead for most of Genesis 4, but his is the sacrifice that is accepted. The elder, Cain, who committed fratricide, is driven from the soil, hidden from the face of the divine, and made a fugitive and a wanderer (4.14). Abraham had two sons, Ishmael and Isaac. The younger, Isaac, the child of the promise (see Gal. 4.23, 28), inherits Abraham's covenant and is revered as Israel's second patriarch. The prediction for the older son, Ishmael, is: "He shall be a wild ass of a man, with his hand against everyone, and everyone's hand against him; and he shall live at odds with all his kin" (Gen. 16.12). Ishmael and his mother, Hagar, are exiled from Abraham's camp.

Isaac has twin sons, Esau and Jacob. The younger, Jacob, barters a bowl of lentil soup for the elder's birthright and then tricks his father into giving him the blessing that was rightfully Esau's. Jacob, the younger, becomes both the recipient of the vision of the ladder that extends between heaven and earth and the father of the twelve tribes that comprise the nation that bears his new name, Israel.

Jacob's favorite son, Joseph, has two sons, Manasseh and Ephraim. When it comes time for Jacob to bless his grandchildren, Joseph positions the boys so that the elder, Manasseh, is by Jacob's right hand; the younger, Ephraim, stands by Jacob's left. The aged patriarch, in blessing Joseph's children, crosses his hands, so that the younger receives the primary blessing.

The pattern continues throughout Israel's history. David is the youngest of seven; Solomon is the second child born to David and Bathsheba; and so on.

All biblically literate listeners know to identify with the younger son. But those first-century biblically literate listeners were in for a surprise, when the younger son turns out not to be the righteous Abel, faithful Isaac, clever Jacob, strategic David, or wise Solomon. He turns out to be an irresponsible, self-indulgent, and probably indulged child, whom I would not, despite his being Jewish, be pleased to have my daughter date.

And said the younger of them to the father, "Father, give to me the portion of the property that is falling to me. And he divided between them the life." **(Luke 15.12)**

To ask for one's share of an inheritance indicates a potential lack of wisdom, but it is not a sin. It was not particularly unusual then, nor is it even now. Yet numerous commentators, academic and homiletic, insist that by asking his father for his inheritance, the younger son has sinned; he is in violation of the commandment, "Honor your father and your mother" (Exod. 20.12; see also Lev. 19.3; Deut. 5.16; Luke 18.20).[31] He has treated his father as if he were as good as dead is the common interpretation.[32] Jewish legal scholar Bernard Jackson trenchantly observes, "Jewish sources give no support to [the idea] that the prodigal, in seeking the advance, wishes his father dead."[33]

Even those commentators who do see the younger son as violating his father's honor rarely remark on the father's reciprocal complicity. Leviticus

19, the chapter that contains the famous commandments, "You shall love your neighbor as yourself" (v. 18) and, "The alien who resides with you . . . you shall love . . . , for you were aliens in the land of Egypt" (v. 34), also insists on the *mitzvah* ("commandment") of reproach, what is called in Hebrew *tochecha*. Leviticus demands: "You shall reprove your neighbor, or you will incur guilt yourself" (v. 17). If a person is sinning, it is the responsibility of others to stop the sin. Had the prodigal "sinned" in asking his father for his inheritance (and that is unlikely), then the father should have reproved the boy. He did not. Instead, he acquiesced.

Ignoring Ben Sirach, who sagely counseled, "In all that you do retain control. . . . When the days of your life reach their end, at the time of your death distribute your property" (33.23–24), the father in our parable agrees to his son's request. Anticipating King Lear, he provides an example of the Babylonian Talmud's negative view of someone "who transfers his property to his children in his lifetime" (*Baba Metziah* 75b). The events so far may be foolish, but there is nothing to suggest sin, and so no reason to see the parable, yet, as about repenting and forgiving.

That the father is himself prodigal is suggested by the idea that he gave half of his estate to the younger son. The NRSV mitigates the father's staggering foolishness. "Divided his property" sounds at least fiscally appropriate. The Greek is starker: "He divided between them the life (*bios*)." When the widow gives two small coins to the Temple treasury, it is her whole "life" that she gives (Mark 12.44). We should not pass over this phrasing too quickly. The father has, in an ironic anticipation of his son's spendthrift ways, been prodigal: he has given what he has.

One can, and generations have, read the father as God the Father. However, this reading runs contrary to the sense of the parable, for the son is, at least on first reading, just a son, in the same way that the man who had a hundred sheep is just an owner of a flock and the woman who had ten coins is just a householder. Like the shepherd who lost his sheep and the woman who lost her coin, the father is about to lose his younger son.

Dad has divided his property. Deuteronomy 21.17 states, "He must acknowledge as firstborn the son of the one who is disliked, giving him a double portion of all that he has; since he is the first issue of his virility, the right of the firstborn is his." Consequently, the older son should have received a two-thirds share. However, in the first century, fathers determined allocation.[34] By getting half of the estate, the soon-to-be prodigal is doing remarkably well.

We might wonder if this generosity toward the prodigal is designed to remind us of Joseph, just as "the man who had two sons" reminds us of Adam, Abraham, Isaac, and Joseph himself. According to Genesis, Jacob gave to Joseph a double portion by treating Joseph's sons, Ephraim and Manasseh, as equal to each of his other sons (see Gen. 48.13–20). Attentive readers may hear at this point and subsequently in the parable not only echoes of those numerous fathers with two sons, but also, particularly, the Joseph story. The younger son mirrors Joseph in his move to a foreign land, his increasing degradation, and then his elevation to an elite position. We might wonder if this indulged son is the child of the father's beloved wife, as Joseph was Rachel's son.

Up to this point, no one in this family is behaving well. That first-century Jewish audience, already discomforted by their inability to identify with the overgratified son, finds itself increasingly distanced from him, even as the son increasingly distances himself from his father and his land.

And after not many days, gathering together all, the younger son took a journey into a far region, and there he scattered the property through excessive living. **(Luke 15.13)**

What happened during the few days the son remained at home goes unspoken. The father may have been waiting for the son to rethink his venture. He would have been in the process of "dividing his life"—not only selling property in order to provide the inheritance in liquid assets, but also feeling the heart-wrenching pain that comes when the child who is the light of his life is about to leave. The older brother may have been busy exulting in having his own share of the estate, fuming over having been given half rather than two-thirds, or feeling resentful that once again Dad had indulged Junior's ill-conceived request. That he is not mentioned following the opening verse should give readers pause in attempting to ascribe motivation to him. Absence of evidence—his reaction, his views—is not the same thing as evidence of absence. Attempts to condemn the older brother for failing to mediate the relationship between father and prodigal would be fair, if those who find him to have failed also condemned the father for his own prodigality.[35] It is evident at this stage of the parable that the younger son is not doing much thinking at all.

Without a word of leave-taking, the prodigal cuts himself off from his family, friends, neighbors, and homeland, and he heads to a region where love of strangers was not in the law code. There he proves himself prodigal: instead of showing reckless generosity, he scatters (Gk. *diaskorpidzo*) his property in dissolute living (*zoon asotos*). The NRSV's translation, "squander," correctly finds the nuance of the verb. The same term appears in the next chapter, Luke 16.1, where Jesus recounts a parable in which a dishonest manager "scatters" or "squanders" the property of his employer. The son and his counterpart in the next parable are interested only in self-gratification; they are not building food banks or staffing homeless shelters. Not only are they fiscally irresponsible; they are self-indulgent, greedy, and therefore, to say the least, hardly admirable.

They both also involve others in their scattering, and so they are culpable in spreading sin. Philo notes that prodigals destroy not only themselves, but those who enter their sphere: "A life spent on drink and licentiousness (*asotos bios*) is a menace for everyone."[36] Although Luke does not tell us what exactly constituted the prodigal's "dissolute living," the implications are that Junior is engaging in gambling, alcohol abuse, sexual indulgence, and a variety of other activities of which we good folk would not approve.

The younger son's actions may reflect negatively on his father; by failing to discipline his son and by acquiescing to his dishonorable request, the father may be seen as complicit in the son's debauchery. Dad could never get a job as an ecclesial authority, for as the Letter of Titus states, "You . . . should appoint elders (*presbyters*) in every town, . . . someone who is blameless, married only once, whose children are believers, not accused of debauchery (*asotia*) and not rebellious" (1.6). To see the father as God the Father becomes, at least for a nonallegorical reading, increasingly difficult.

And having spent all, there was a strong famine in that
region, and he himself began to be in need. And going, he
became joined to one of the citizens of that region, and he
sent him into his fields to feed pigs. And he was desiring to
be filled from the pods that the pigs were eating, but no one
was giving to him. **(Luke 15.14–16)**

What exactly caused Junior's fall is a matter of cultural understanding.
Readers in the United States, the United Kingdom, Australia, and South
Africa tend to attribute his desperate state to a combination of bad parenting, lack of community values, separating himself from his network, and
personal irresponsibility. One individual in a church-based adult-education
program suggested, when I asked what went wrong with the prodigal so
that he found himself in such a dire condition, that, had Junior experienced
prayer in the public-school system, none of this mess would have happened.

Readers in Russia tend to note neither parental failure nor fiduciary in-
eptitude, but the famine—there was no food to distribute.[37] In a Vanderbilt University seminar on Luke's Gospel, a graduate student from Kenya
proposed that the real problem was lack of generosity, for no one gave him
anything.[38] This reading is particularly commended by the narrative context
of the parable. Junior's yearning to be filled (Gk. *epithymein chortasthenai*) is
the same term used to describe the sick and destitute Lazarus in Luke 16.21.
Whether from personal, familial, natural, or cultural causes, the younger
son is in trouble. He has encountered the perfect storm.

The question then becomes: In a situation of famine, lack of generosity,
and poverty created by personal lack of responsibility, what does one do to
survive? Before we can determine what the prodigal does in answer to this
question, again we need to clean out readings that are mistaken about early
Judaism.

That the prodigal finds himself in non-Jewish territory is evident from
the reference to pigs. Archaeological digs in the lower Galilee reveal no pig
bones; in the Decapolis, where Jesus exorcised the demon-possessed man by
sending his tormentors into a herd of pigs, pig bones appear (see Matt. 8.30;

Mark 5.12; Luke 8.32–33). The Mishnah, *Baba Qamma* 7.7, insists, "No Israelite may raise swine anywhere," and this later ruling appears to have reflected Jewish culture at the time of Jesus, as archaeological studies suggest.

The prodigal's location does not, however, harp on Jewish obsessions regarding purity or xenophobia, two stereotypes that commentators typically import into the parables. For example, one commentator asserts, "Jews would immediately recognize that [the prodigal had gone into] unclean Gentile territory made up of unclean Gentile people."[39] The idea of being in gentile regions—which means everywhere outside Judea, Samaria, and lower Galilee—was not anathema to most Jews, then or now. Jews in the Diaspora welcomed gentiles into their synagogues, worked with gentiles in the marketplaces, talked to gentiles in the public baths. At the time of Jesus, there were probably more Jews living outside Judea and lower Galilee than there were in the Jewish homeland; over a million were in Alexandria in Egypt. The prodigal's problem is that he is hungry, not that he is "unclean" amid the "unclean."

Nor should we charge him, as some commentators do, with apostasy,[40] despite the fact that Leviticus 11.8 states of pigs: "Of their flesh you shall not eat, and their carcasses you shall not touch; they are unclean for you." First, the son ate no ham hocks or pigs' knuckles; if he did, he would not be starving. Second, he was sent to feed the pigs, not to butcher them. Third, the son hired himself out to a citizen; there is no indication that he knew his task would be to feed pigs.[41] Finally, the son did what he did in order to live; Jewish Law is law by which one lives, not by which one dies. The prodigal is in an impossible situation, but the issue is not Jewish xenophobia or purity. The problem is starvation.

And coming to himself, he said, "How many hired laborers of
my father are abounding of bread, but I by famine here am
lost? Getting up, I shall go to my father and I shall say to him,
'Father, I have sinned against heaven and before you; not still
am I worthy to be called your son; make me as one of your
hired laborers.'" And rising up, he went toward his father.
(Luke 15.17–20a)

A proverb from the rabbinic commentary *Leviticus Rabbah* (13.4) notes,
"When Israelites are reduced to eating carob pods, they repent." The son's
comments fall in line with this idea. Junior speaks of his sin and his desire
for restoration to the household, albeit on lesser terms as a day laborer rather
than a beloved son. His rehearsed lines sound contrite. Thus, for many
readers who, influenced by Luke, see the parable as about repenting and forgiving, Junior is understood to have repented.

And yet first-century listeners may have heard not contrition, but conniving. Junior recalls that Daddy still has money, and he might be able to get
more. Unlike the sheep and the coin, he has not been "found." Rather, he
recovers his true nature—he is described as "coming to himself"—and that
self is one who knows that Daddy will do anything he asks. In his planning,
the prodigal and the narrator repeat the term "father": ". . . laborers of *my
father* . . . go to my *father* . . . *Father*, I have sinned . . . went toward his *father*."
Although Junior speaks of being treated as a hired hand, his repeated paternal language suggests that he still thinks of himself as his father's "son."
He is not questioning the relationship. His phrasing "not still am I worthy"
suggests that he still has the title "son."

Further suggesting Junior's lack of remorse is his line, "I have sinned
against heaven and before you." Biblically literate listeners hear an echo of
the empty words Pharaoh mouths in order to stop the plagues: "Pharaoh
hurriedly summoned Moses and Aaron and said, 'I have sinned against
the LORD your God, and against you'" (Exod. 10.16). The prodigal is
no more repentant, has had no more change of heart, than Egypt's ruler.

Homiletician David Buttrick concisely summarizes the prodigal's strategy: "I'll go to Daddy and sound religious."[42]

In his thoughts, the prodigal also puts himself in the company of the self-absorbed figures in other parables. The "rich fool" of the same-named parable thinks to himself, "What should I do, for I have no place to store my crops?" (Luke 12.17). His conclusion is to build more barns, not to distribute his food to the poor. The dishonest manager speculates, "What will I do, now that my master is taking the position away from me? I am not strong enough to dig, and I am ashamed to beg" (16.3). His conclusion is to draw others into his dishonesty. Even the judge who faces the tenacious widow eventually says to himself, "Though I have no fear of God and no respect for anyone, yet because this widow keeps bothering me, I will grant her justice, so that she may not wear me out by continually coming" (18.4–5). All four parables use the device of interior monologue to let listeners know what the characters are thinking, and in all cases what they are thinking leads to at best morally ambiguous action.[43]

And yet when he was far off, his father saw him, and had compassion, and running, fell upon his neck and continually kissed him. **(Luke 15.20b)**

Before the prodigal gets to his rehearsed speech, his dad runs to welcome him. It is possible he was watching for his son. After all, he had divided his life and lost half of it when his beloved son left home. His "compassion" need not be taken as a surprising reaction; there is no reason to expect the father to be a detached patriarch who would show neither care nor compassion. Rather, his compassion should remind us of the Samaritan, who saw a wounded man and reacted with compassion, viscerally, in his gut (Luke 10.33); it is the same reaction Jesus himself has when he sees the funeral procession of the only son of a widow (7.13). The term indicates recognition that one who might be considered dead could become alive.

Despite the father's rejoicing, which should have been anticipated by the joy of the sheep owner and the woman, commentators racing out with him conclude that his actions are at best undignified and even dishonorable. New Testament scholar Luise Schottroff traces this reading to Joachim Jeremias, who saw the father as tossing aside the dignity of an "aged oriental."[44] Another commentator, asserting that "fathers were remote and figures of authority," sees the father's running as not only surprising, but also shocking, for "gentlemen of honor do not run except in cases of emergency."[45] Another suggests that to run, the father would have had to pull up his robes and so expose his legs, "which would have been considered shameful in a Semitic culture."[46] Still another insists, "The father in the parable is playing a role no proper Semitic patriarch would enact. He has left his honor behind, his position, his community standing."[47]

From these already overstated observations, the comments, not unexpectedly, descend into a negative picture of Judaism over and against which Jesus shines ever more brightly. For example, we are told, "A more expected reaction would have been for the father to rend his garments and declare his son disowned."[48] Some commentators even propose that the father had participated in a Jewish ceremony known as *qetsatsah* and so had legally cut the son out of the family[49] or that "it is obvious the father never performed the *common* Jewish ceremony of forever disowning the boy,"[50] and that "the *typical* Jewish father would have forever 'cut off' his son with a formal ceremony."[51] The so-called common tradition, absent from the Mishnah, appears in the relatively late texts *Ruth Rabbah* 7.11 and the Jerusalem Talmud (*Ketubot* 2.10; *Qiddushin* 1.5). Our parable offers no hint of it.

The most extreme of these readings claims that the father ran to protect the son from the ire of the locals who, knowing of the son's shameful behavior, would be likely to stone him[52] and that the father holds a dinner party "as a gesture of reconciliation with the villagers."[53] We thus go from a loving father who desperately misses his son and, like his predecessors who find their sheep and coin, rejoices when he sees him to an intolerant Jewish father and his bloodthirsty Jewish neighbors who cannot wait to stone the son who shamed his father. Exegesis gives way to stereotype at best.

Proverbs, which does come close to being a "Semitic patriarch rule book," presumes that its readers run, both literally and metaphorically: "When you walk, your step will not be hampered; and if you run, you will not stumble" (4.12); "The name of the LORD is a strong tower; the righteous run into it and are safe" (18.10). Isaiah, an "ancient Semitic patriarch," proclaims, "but those who wait for the LORD shall renew their strength, they shall mount up with wings like eagles, they shall run and not be weary, they shall walk and not faint" (40.31). The book of Tobit recounts the angel Raphael's words to his young charge Tobias, "You are aware of how we left your father. Let us run ahead of your wife and prepare the house" (11.3). Running is fine—a potential disciple runs to Jesus (Mark 10.17); Zacchaeus runs to see him (Luke 19.4); Peter runs to Jesus's tomb (Luke 24.12)—the point is, as Paul states, not to "run aimlessly" (1 Cor. 9.24–26).

The father is hardly aimless. He sees the son he thought was lost, was dead, and he reacts with compassion and love. Of course he would be delighted with the boy's return, and of course he would again display his generosity toward him. That is why he kisses him with the same fervor (Gk. *kataphileo*) that the woman who "showed great love" kissed Jesus's feet at the home of Simon the Pharisee (Luke 7.38, 45). In so doing, the father lost no status. Had the father lost his honor, then those who attended his banquet would have lost theirs as well. As for the idea that the locals were seeking to stone the son, the claim constructs, on the basis of no evidence, a retrograde and wrathful Jewish culture over and against which, again, Jesus stands as inventing grace and compassion.

Jewish fathers of the first century were not, at least according to the sources we have (which should be the sources that inform our history), distant or wrathful. In the Sermon on the Mount, Jesus asks, "Is there anyone among you, if his child asks for bread, will give a stone?" (7.9). Thus, children ask fathers for bread, and the dads provide. The popular claim, designed to create a feminist Jesus, that "cash is male, bread is female," and so the father who has "bread enough to spare" is cast in the role of mother,[54] attends neither to the Lord's Prayer, in which one asks the "father in heaven" for "bread," nor to Jesus's example of fatherly concern. We find numerous fathers seeking healing for their children: the synagogue ruler Jairus begs Jesus to heal his daughter (Mark 5.23 cf. Matt. 9.18; Luke 8.41); the father of an epileptic boy entreats first the disciples and then Jesus to heal his son (Matt. 17.14–15; Luke 9.38–42).

Philo, yet another good source for the "Semitic patriarch rule book," remarks

that parents often "do not lose thought for their wastrel (*asoton*) children but
... lavish their kindness on the wastrels more than on the well behaved.... In
the same way, God too ... takes thought also for those who live a misspent life,
thereby giving them time for reformation, and also keeping within the bounds
His own merciful nature." [55] Thus at least this one Jew sees a father as doting
rather than distant, and God as doting rather than distant as well.

As for what "typical oriental patriarchs" might do, today's scholars sometimes derive their models not from ancient sources, but from contemporary
Muslim and Christian informants in the Middle East. One major problem
with such fieldwork approaches is that the questioners sometimes forget to
ask the women. Biblical scholar Carol Shersten LaHurd, reading the parable
with Yemenite women, posed the question: "What would your husband do
if his son returned home after wasting all his money?" The women unani-
mously agreed that the father would lovingly welcome the son, especially if
he were a child of his old age. [56]

Some commentators today, still regarding the father in the parable as the
Father in heaven, want to credit Jesus with inventing a new theology that
rejects the supposed Jewish or Old Testament God of wrath in favor of the
Christian or New Testament God of love, a view popularly espoused by the
second-century heretic Marcion. Therefore, the more surprising they can
make the father's actions, the more they can solidify what is ultimately a
Marcionistic theology. Residual marcionism, the view that God had a personality transplant somewhere between the pages of Malachi and Matthew,
is still alive and well in churches today; it is also still a heresy. There is no
compelling reason in the parable itself to see the father as God, but even if
Jesus's Jewish audience had made this connection, they would have found
nothing surprising. The covenant is still in place; God still loves the wayward, from David to Ephraim to Israel.

Rabbinic literature, to which a number of commentators turn in order
to find their negative depictions of the Prodigal Son's Jewish context, actually offers a contrary view. *Deuteronomy Rabbah* 2.24 recounts a parable
that opens with a citation from Deuteronomy 4.30, "You will return to the
LORD your God." It continues:

> R. Meir said, "To what is the matter like? It is like the son of a king
> who took to evil ways. The king sent a tutor to him who appealed

to him, saying, 'Repent, my son.' But the son sent him back to his father [saying], 'How can I have the effrontery to return? I am ashamed to come before you.' Thereupon his father sent back word: 'My son, is a son ever ashamed to return to his father? And is it not to your father that you will be returning?' "[57]

Pesikta Rabbati 184–85 recounts:

> A king had a son who had gone astray from his father on a journey of a hundred days. His friends said to him, "Return to your father." He said, "I cannot." Then his father sent word, "Return as far as you can, and I will come the rest of the way to you." So God says, "Return to me, and I will return to you."[58]

For the rabbis, the challenge is not in seeing God's love in a new way; the challenge—an inevitable challenge in every religious system—is to get the wayward to return.

Now that we've cleaned out the negative, ahistorical, and at best unfortunate stereotypes, we can get back to the prodigal.

And said the son to him, "Father, I have sinned against heaven and before you; not still am I worthy to be called your son." And said the father to his slaves, "Quickly carry out a robe, the first, and put it on him, and give the ring to his hand and sandals to the feet. And bring the calf, the grain-fed one, sacrifice and, eating, we may rejoice. Because this, my son, was dead, and he came back to life; he had been lost, and was found." And they began to rejoice. **(Luke 15.21–24)**

The prodigal's beginning words to his father are a perfect repetition of what he had planned to say. We might imagine him rehearsing all the way from the pig farmer's house to his own home. Although we could conclude that the son has returned repentant and humbled, with genuine feelings of un-worthiness, his initial address belies that reading. He begins with the word "Father," not "Sir" or "Lord" (*kyrios*) or "Master" (*despotes*). As soon as he speaks the word, he reinstates himself as a son, not a hired worker or slave. Dad had agreed to his earlier request; perhaps, like Jacob with Joseph, Dad has always indulged the younger son, and the son could count on that love continuing.

Whether the son is sincere or not, his father doesn't care, any more than the sheep owner cared about ovine repentance or the woman cared about the emotional state of her found coin. The father preempts the son from reciting the rest of the script he had planned. He is joyful, he wants to celebrate, and he wants everyone to share his joy.

The father then calls for the "first," or best, robe. In a society where most people only had two garments, this family has a closetfull. Its wealth has remained secure, even with the prodigal's profligacy.

The accessorizing also has an ironic textual resonance. Just as the son's words echo those of Pharaoh to Moses, so the ring and the garments given to the young man, who left his wealthy estate, hit bottom, and returned, might remind us of the story of Joseph. His new patron or father figure, Pharaoh, took "his signet ring from his hand" and "put it on Joseph's hand; he arrayed him in garments of fine linen" (Gen. 41.42).[59] The irony is delicious. In both Genesis and our parable, the favored younger son, himself not initially of the most admirable character (Joseph is an annoying twit who tells his family that one day they will all bow down to him, has no problem with his father's favoritism, and tattles on his brothers), finds himself in a foreign land, ini-tially in dire circumstances, in the employ of gentiles, and surviving famine.

However, their situations also create an ironic contrast. Joseph might be both pitied and admired, because he is sold by his brothers into slavery, es-capes dissolute living by resisting the advances of his master's wife, earns his elevation to Pharaoh's court by his wisdom and his recognition of divine sup-port, unites his family, and preserves them from starvation.[60] The prodigal leaves home on his own, does nothing to benefit anyone except himself, and still ends up well accessorized. Whether his family can be united remains to be seen. The prodigal may ultimately be the cause by which father and older brother come to be united, but although he created the circumstances for a possible reconciliation, he did not do so with any intent.

From the father's concerns for food and clothes, several exegetes fatten up the view that the father with "bread enough to spare" is gender-bending or, to put the point directly, "In a way, he is behaving like a mother—kissing, dressing, feeding."[61] The next step is of course to claim, "This father abandons male honor for female shame."[62]

Although they are a good faith effort, the claims ultimately undermine a concern for both women and gender. First, in making the father also the mother, ignored are questions concerning actual women in the family. Did the mother die? Was she, like Anna in the book of Tobit, thrilled at the return of her son? Were the two brothers children of different mothers,[63] the younger perhaps the son of Rachel's beautiful descendant and the older, faithful one the scion of her less loved or possibly hated sister, Leah (Gen. 29.33)? Second, making the dad into a mom presumes that fathers were not, and could not be, nurturing, loving, or invested in their children, and we have seen that this is not the case. Nor, finally, has the father done anything shameful.

The language of resurrection—"was dead and came back to life"—speaks to the father's true joy: he has his son back. There is no reason to move immediately into allegorical reading, despite the resonances with the story of Jesus himself. Were Jesus to have told this parable, his initial audience would have had no clue that he would be proclaimed both dead and resurrected. Moreover, if we take the prodigal as autobiographical, then the older brother becomes completely removed from the narrative.

Such Christological readings that see Jesus as the protagonist of all of his stories are not "wrong"; they are legitimate interpretations in light of church doctrine, and they are often profound. For example, Catholic theologian Henri Nouwen suggests: "I am touching here the mystery that Jesus himself became the prodigal son for our sake. He left the house of his heavenly Father, came to a foreign country, gave away all that he had, and returned through his cross to his Father's home."[64] While Nouwen's reading at least fits the words of the parable, I'm a bit less convinced by the extended version of this allegory, in which we hear that it is Jesus who comes to us "in the guise of the sinner, the debauched, the prostitute, the unclean, the enemy, the unsavory" and so "challenges us to participate in a radical, irresponsible hospitality that turns the rules of polite society upside-down."[65]

Rather, the allegory might function better as a negative exemplar. The prodigal squandered his inheritance; Jesus did not. The prodigal sinned; Jesus did not. The prodigal is thinking about his stomach; Jesus, as Christian tradition tells us, was thinking about the salvation of the world. Contextually, Jesus does not come to us as a lost coin, lost sheep, or lost son. With regard to plot, it is one thing to welcome a "debauched" stranger to our home; it is something else entirely to welcome back a child. Nor does the father turn "the rules of polite society upside-down"; there is no reversal in the welcoming home of a prodigal son. Finally, the heavenly Father in Christological configuration does not have "two sons," but the "only begotten" one. Despite its ingenuity, the reading fits neither the context nor the plot.

Other than the generic "they" who begin to rejoice, the parable says nothing about Junior's reaction to the welcome. Therefore, it is at best generous to conclude that he is "shattered by the offer of grace, confesses unworthiness, and accepts restoration to sonship in genuine humility."[66] That would be nice, but I still have a picture of a manipulative, pampered, and perhaps relieved kid at the fatted-calf buffet.

Before rushing off to allegory, we do well to look at this father as a happy dad whose favorite son has returned. And we do well to notice who is not mentioned as invited to the party.[67] "Some man had *two* sons." Most of us, including the dad in the parable, had lost count.

And his son, the elder, was in the field, and as he, coming, drew near to the house, he heard symphony and chorus. And calling over one of the servants he inquired what these things might be. And he said to him, "Your brother has come, and your father has sacrificed the grain-fed calf, because he received him healthy." And he became angry, and he did not want to go in. **(Luke 15.25–28a)**

At last we meet the older brother, and again expectations are disrupted. He is no Cain, who kills his brother; he is no Ishmael, a "wild ass of a man," or

Esau, who having despised his birthright and being tricked out of his bless-ing, wants to murder his twin. He is not, in other words, a conventional older brother. He is rather a figure for whom we might feel some initial em-pathy. The man who searched for and found his sheep and the woman who searched for and found her coin called their friends and neighbors to cele-brate; no one runs out to invite the older son to the feast. No one noticed he was missing.

We do not know what the brothers' relationship had been, but the tra-dition suggests that it may well have been dysfunctional, for sibling rivalry is another biblical convention: Cain and Abel, Isaac and Ishmael, Jacob and Esau, Leah and Rachel, Joseph and his brothers, Perez and Zerah, Sol-omon and Adonjiah, and so on, even to Luke's Gospel, where Mary and Martha (10.38–42)—sisters who never speak to each other, one who is closer to Jesus and one who is resentful of that closeness—anticipate the prodigal and the elder. Even were the brothers' relationship a good one, the older cannot find it in his heart to rejoice at the news of Junior's return. His own sense of being ignored—by both the reinstated brother and the happy father—counters any possible joy he might have had. As one com-mentator observes, the father indulges the one who slights him and slights the one who indulges him.[68]

The elder brother's anger is not unprovoked—he has been ignored by those who are feasting and celebrating, even as he has also been ignored by numerous readers. His alienation is palpable. Whereas the prodigal comes home to his "father," the older brother approaches the "house." The slave's words reinforce the elder's embeddedness within his family: "your brother . . . your father," but the elder does not, perhaps cannot, acknowledge these relationships.

Perhaps the elder is even legitimately worried that this father is giving to Junior what according to the disposition of his estate should have gone to him. On this matter, Dad will reassure him that his own inheritance is intact.

And his father, going out, comforted/urged him.
(Luke 15.28b)

The father is now in the role of the man searching for his sheep and the woman searching for her coin. He needs to return the lost to the home; he needs to make his family complete. But children are not sheep or coins; they are not property; they are people. Unlike a sheep that can be lifted on one's shoulders or a coin that can be picked up from the floor, returning the lost son to his home proves much more difficult. Children, unlike sheep and coins, have long memories, emotional needs, and a voice of their own.

The father did not know until this moment that the elder was the son who was truly "lost" to him. Once the recognition comes, he does what the shepherd and the woman do: realizing his loss, his lost *son,* the son whom he *loves,* he seeks to make his family whole. He pleads with him. The NRSV translates Luke 15.28, "His father came out and began to plead with him." Though technically correct, the translation misses the nuance of the Greek. The verb here is *parakaleo,* and it has the sense both of pleading or urging and of comforting. Those familiar with John's Gospel may recall references to the "Paraclete," usually translated "Advocate" or "Comforter"; the Paraclete, John's Holy Spirit, remains with the community in Jesus's absence to provide comfort, instruction, and advocacy.

For this parable, the term is apt. The father wants to urge and to plead with the elder to join the celebration, and he wants to provide comfort by telling him that he has always had paternal love. The parable wisely refrains from providing the father's words—no rehearsed speech, no pat lines can rectify a broken relationship. Nor, at this point, would any speech resolve the older son's emotional turmoil. He first needs to express his own resentment.

And answering, he said to his father, "Look, all these years I
am slaving for you, and not one commandment of yours have
I passed by, and for me not one young goat did you give so
that with my friends I might rejoice. But when your son, this
one, the one who ate up your life with whores came, you
sacrificed for him the grain-fed calf." **(Luke 15.29–30)**

Years of resentment have finally boiled over and found expression. The son's
fidelity has been overlooked. Once again, the problem child receives more
attention, or more love, than the prudent and faithful one. By announc-
ing that there is "more joy in heaven" for the one who repents than for the
ninety-nine who need no repentance, Luke reinforces this preference. We
might think of the older son as speaking for those ninety-nine who have no
need of repentance but who appear to bring less joy.[69]

The son's alienation is reflected in his words. In contrast to the narrator's
language of "his father" in connection with him ("And his father, going out,
comforted/urged him. And answering, he said to his father"), the servant's
"your brother" and "your father," and the prodigal's frequent mention of and
address to his "father," there is no relational language in the older son's remarks. Instead, he distances himself from both father and brother by speaking of "your son, this one."

The mention of "whores" (Gk. *pornai*) could be an attempt to sway the
father's opinion against the prodigal, since the parable never made clear that
sexual gratification was the way the younger son lost his money. There is
no notice that Junior sent home a postcard with a picture of the Whore of
Babylon and an inscription, "Having a wonderful time . . ." Then again, such
action would be in keeping with "dissolute living" as well as something that
good sons, according to convention, would avoid. As Proverbs 29.3 states,
"A child who loves wisdom makes a parent glad, but to keep company with
prostitutes is to squander one's substance."

The elder might have gone out of his way to distance Junior from Dad, but
he looks an amateur compared to Luke, who seeks to distance readers from
those grumbling Pharisees and scribes with which the chapter begins. Luke

leads readers to see the elder son as representing Pharisees and scribes who object to Jesus's table fellowship with sinners. Then the commentators run with Luke's prompt and begin to pile up the elder brother's negative traits: he epitomizes works-righteousness; he follows the father's wishes in order to earn the father's love; he is obedient as a slave rather than as a son and so shows the terrible yoke of Torah; he remains faithful because he wants the reward and not because he finds value in the family; he perceives his relationship with his father to be based on "law, merit, and reward" rather than on "love and graciousness."[70] Among Presbyterian pastors, as one survey reveals, "It is the dutiful, religiously obedient, yet joyless, older brother who tends to serve as the emblem of sin."[71]

One commentator even suggests that the son's refusal to join the banquet shames the father and might be expected to result in a beating.[72] Following this view, another suggests that the elder has insulted his father, "not only by refusing to enter the feast, but by addressing him without a title. This insult is even worse than that given by the younger son, for this is public."[73] Who else is in the field aside from perhaps the servant is not clear (everyone is at the buffet), so how the setting can be seen as "public" is but one problem with this reasoning. The scene is intimate, with a focus on family dynamics, not village vengeance. The father "urges" and "comforts" his son to return; he is not the sort of dad who would beat his child into submission.

In a more sympathetic variant on reading the older son as representing restrictive Judaism, New Testament professor Barbara Reid speaks of how, in the context of Luke's community, the narrative may have "addressed the painful issue of incorporating the Gentiles into the people of God."[74] Jesus's original audience would not have heard this message, since there's nothing about the prodigal that suggests he represents the "gentile" nations. Working for a pig farmer is not the same thing as advocating for him. As for the "painful" issue of such incorporation, it would be good to know what exactly was painful. Much Jewish eschatological speculation suggests that, in the messianic age, the gentile nations will come to worship the God of Israel, but they will come as gentiles, not as converts to Judaism; see, for example, Zechariah 8.23, which offers the prediction: "Thus says the LORD of hosts: In those days ten people from nations of every language shall take hold of a Jew, grasping his garment and saying, 'Let us go with you, for we have heard that God is with you.'" The gentiles come with Israel to Zion, but they do not say, "Circumcise us when we get there." Why Jews would find gentiles worshipping the God of Israel "painful" is unclear. Given that gentiles were welcome to worship with Jews in the synagogue and in the Jerusalem Temple, where the outer court was called the Court of the Gentiles, the pain is not self-evident.

In another sympathetic vein, theological ethics professor Nancy Duff compares the elder's attitude to the "self-righteous" in churches today who do not welcome and do not want to be reconciled to fellow church members who promote "the re-imagining conference, the ordination of homosexuals, and abortion."[75] The ends are fine; the means don't work. Those who seek inclusion within the church are not analogous to our prodigal, who is not a representative of inclusiveness. The congregation who hears this sermon will then, likely, associate the unwelcoming attitude with the "Jewish" view and see reconciliation as a uniquely Christian virtue. That is not the intent of the homiletic suggestion, but, given its appropriate connection of the elder brother to fellow congregants, it is a likely result.

More helpful might be the comments LaHurd adduced from Arab women when she asked their views of the elder son. Not only did these women see the elder as expressing the "work level of an older child" in comparison to the younger siblings who were not held to the same standards of responsibility; two women also observed that if the son really felt himself to be a slave, he would not have been able to express his views to his father. For the women, the parable offered a mirror of family dynamics, not an allegory about God, Christians, and Jews.[76]

Before we leave these verses, one final point on their irony. The son spoke of working like a slave. It is possible that there were slaves in the father's household, because it is the slaves who accessorized the prodigal and prepared the feast (Luke 15.22). To a real slave, the comment, "I have been working like a slave for you," on the lips of the elder son and heir, does not quite ring true.

And he said to him, "Child, you always with me are, and
everything that is mine is yours. But it remains necessary
to cheer and to rejoice, because your brother, this one, was
dead, and lived to life, and being lost, even he was found."
(Luke 15.31–32)

Although most English versions begin the father's response with "Son," in
the Greek the father's address to his elder son is *teknon,* better translated
"child." It is the same address Mary uses when she and Joseph, after desperately searching for their lost son, find him in the Temple: "Child (*teknon*), . . .
your father and I have been searching for you in great anxiety" (Luke 2.48).

The endearment "Child" begins the father's attempt to reconcile with his
older son. In stating, "You are always with me, and everything that is mine
is yours," the father makes both an emotional and a technical appeal. Emotionally, the point is correct: in the father's view, the son had never been lost;
he has "always been with" the father. But what the father felt and what the
son felt were two different reactions. Technically, the father had divided his
property between his sons. It is going too far, however, to suggest that the
fatted calf, ring, robe, and sandals presently belonged to the older brother,
and that the father was dipping into the brother's inheritance to equip the
prodigal. The older brother says nothing about to whom the items given to
the prodigal belong. Indeed, he would not have been a good son, had he
taken control of his "share." He complains not that Dad took his property,
but that Dad showed affection to the prodigal that he had never shown
to him.

Perhaps the father's love for the elder son can also be seen in his language.
Although Dad has welcomed the prodigal home, kissed him, and restored
him to his prior status as "son," he never actually speaks to him. Perhaps
there is nothing needed to be said; here, words are all the father has, and he
uses them wisely.

The specifics of his response should, in turn, give pause to those who follow Luke's contextualization regarding the father as the Father and the elder
son as "the Pharisees" or, by extension, "the Jews." The father speaks to his

elder son both of their ongoing relationship and of sharing: "Everything I have is yours." As far back as the second century, Tertullian realized that the allegory could not hold, albeit for less than benevolent reasons. Surely, he thought, God would never have made such a claim about a connection with the Jews and, surely as well, those Jews could not have claimed perfect obedience, never violating any commandment.[77] Tertullian was no fan of Jewish practice, but his rejection of the allegory has merit.

After assuring his elder son of their perpetual bond, the father then attempts to restore, or create, a relationship between the two children. Correcting the elder's phrase "your son, this one" to "your brother, this one," the father reminds his child that the relationship exists between the two of them. Were either brother to be missing, the family would not be whole.

Finally, the father repeats his resurrection language. The missing brother has been restored; he is home; celebration is warranted.

Reconciliations

"It remains necessary to cheer and to rejoice," insists the father, but he and his elder son are still in the field. Now what? Without Luke's allegory of repentance and forgiveness and without the easy equating of the elder son with those grumbling Jews, the parable has no easy or comfortable interpretation.

What would we do, were we the older son? Do we attend the party? What will happen to this family when the father dies and the elder son obtains his inheritance? Will he keep Junior in the restored position to which the father elevated him or will he send him to the stables, to be treated as one of the "hired laborers"? This might be a legally acceptable move, but it is one without honor, mercy, or concern for the father's wishes. When personal resentment overrides familial and cultural values, we all lose.

What do we do if we identify with the father and find our own children are lost? Is repeated pleading sufficient? What would be? What does a parent do to show a love that the child never felt? The parable shows us that indulgence does not buy love, but withholding can stifle it. And so we search, desperately, because our family is not whole. Sheep and coins are easy; children less so.

What are we to make of that younger son? It is neat and tidy to see him as shattered by grace and fully repentant, but I doubt first-century readers would have. I neither like nor trust the younger son. I do not see him doing anything other than what he has always done—take advantage of his father's love. It's hard to get much work done when one is filled with fatted calf. And yet his father loves him, and he is a member of the family. Therefore, he cannot be ignored, and to dismiss him would be to dismiss the father as well.

If the younger son is seen as truly humble, repentant, and recognizing his dependence on the generosity of his family, how will he act now? What can he do to gain back the respect that his adventures have cost him? The father has provided him an initial act of reconciliation, but at some point he will need to prove his own responsibility.

The parable might even be read as resisting Luke's easy interpretations of repentance and forgiveness. In this household, no one has expressed sorrow at hurting another, and no one has expressed forgiveness. When it comes to families, there are factors other than repentance and forgiveness that hold us together. Here the first two parables provide a helpful guide. The sheep and the coin did not repent, but the celebration occurred nonetheless, because the man and the woman were able to rejoice at the finding of the lost and the restoring of the collection to wholeness.

If we hold in abeyance, at least for the moment, the rush to read repenting and forgiving into the parable, then it does something more profound than repeat well-known messages. It provokes us with simple exhortations. Recognize that the one you have lost may be right in your own household. Do whatever it takes to find the lost and then celebrate with others, both so that you can share the joy and so that the others will help prevent the recovered from ever being lost again. Don't wait until you receive an apology; you may never get one. Don't wait until you can muster the ability to forgive; you may never find it. Don't stew in your sense of being ignored, for there is nothing that can be done to retrieve the past.

Instead, go have lunch. Go celebrate, and invite others to join you. If the repenting and the forgiving come later, so much the better. And if not, you still will have done what is necessary. You will have begun a process that might lead to reconciliation. You will have opened a second chance for wholeness. Take advantage of resurrection—it is unlikely to happen twice.

What counts for the family also counts for the world. A father had two sons—Cain and Abel—and so we realize that to kill an individual is not only to kill a brother; it is to kill a quarter of the world's population. We may have written off Cain, but he not only survives; he thrives. We may judge him only as guilty, but even he has a story to tell. Cain committed fratricide, but that is not the sum total of who he is. The mark of Cain is a mark of divine protection; if God can protect him, surely we can as well. Can we find it in our hearts to reconcile him to the human family?

A father had two sons—Isaac and Ishmael—if either is sacrificed, then both are. Today some of the children of Isaac and Ishmael can find themselves at odds or at war, as the Middle East shows us. Yet these two sons reunite at Abraham's death, and together they bury him. Ishmael's hand was to be against his brother's, but Ishmael here proves the prediction wrong. If Ishmael and Isaac can reconcile, perhaps their children can do the same.

A father had two sons—Jacob and Esau—one who stole birthright and blessing and one who vowed murder in revenge. And yet, when Jacob, wounded from his wrestling at the Jabbok River, encounters Esau, the two reconcile.

A father had two sons . . . The details can be filled in, and filled, by any among us. The scriptures of Israel give us hope for the sons in Luke's parable. They should give us hope for our own reconciliations, from the personal to the international. We need to take count not only of our blessings, but also of those in our families, and in our communities. And once we count, we need to act. Finding the lost, whether they are sheep, coins, or people, takes work. It also requires our efforts, and from those efforts there is the potential for wholeness and joy.

CHAPTER 2

The Good Samaritan

And look, some lawyer stood up; testing Jesus, he says, "Teacher, (by) doing what eternal life will I inherit?"

And he said to him, "In the Law, what is written? How do you read?"

And answering, he said, "You will love the Lord your God with all your heart and with all your soul and with all your strength and with all your mind/intention, and your neighbor as yourself."

And he said to him, "Rightly you answered. This do, and you will live."

But he, wanting to justify himself, said to Jesus, "And who is my neighbor?"

Replying, Jesus said, "Some person was going down from Jerusalem to Jericho, and he fell among robbers, who, stripping him, even placed blows, going away, leaving him half dead.

"And by coincidence, some priest was going down that road, and seeing him, he passed by on the other side. And likewise a Levite, coming to the place, even seeing, passed by on the other side.

"But some Samaritan, traveling, came near him and seeing, had compassion. And coming toward (him), he bound up his wounds, pouring oil and wine (on them), and having set him upon his own animal, he brought him to an inn and cared for him.

"And upon the next day, taking out, he gave two denarii to the innkeeper and said, 'Take care of him, and whatever you might spend, I, upon my return, will give back to you.'

"Which of these three a neighbor—does it seem to you—was to the one who fell among the robbers?"

And he said, "The one doing mercy for him."

And said to him Jesus, "Go and you do likewise."

Luke 10.25–37

T hroughout the English-speaking world the term "good Samaritan" is synonymous with charitable do-gooders. Hospitals with the name "Samaritan" appear throughout the United States, from Medstar Good Samaritan Hospital in Baltimore to Good Samaritan Hospital in Los Angeles. The "Samaritans" is "a national charity and the co-ordinating body for the 201 Samaritans branches in the United Kingdom, the Republic of Ireland, the Channel Islands, and the Isle of Man";[1] this organization, which also has branches in the United States, is dedicated to suicide prevention. Samaritan's Purse is "a nondenominational evangelical Christian organization providing spiritual and physical aid to hurting people around the world. Since 1970, Samaritan's Purse has helped meet needs of people who are victims of war, poverty, natural disasters, disease, and famine with the purpose of sharing God's love through His Son, Jesus Christ."[2] Australia has the GSDS, the Good Samaritan Donkey Sanctuary,[3] which does exactly what its name suggests.

The parable of the Good Samaritan is so well known for its message of aiding the stranger that it has become a staple of political discourse. Former U.S. president George W. Bush invoked the parable in his first inaugural address: "I can pledge our nation to a goal: when we see that wounded traveler on the road to Jericho, we will not pass to the other side."[4] Bush's presumption was that the U.S. population—who, in the minds of some of our politicians, are all Christians—would immediately pick up the reference: "wounded traveler" and "road to Jericho" are images from the parable.

I checked with a Jewish friend of mine—a naturalized U.S. citizen who pays more attention to national and local politics than most people I know. She thought the reference might have been to an accident in New York, since she knew there was a Jericho on Long Island. When I noted that the reference was biblical, she wondered if the president was thinking of Rahab, the prostitute from Jericho who aided the spies sent into the land by Joshua.

For President Bush, the parable is about taking care of nations in distress. Nor is he the only politician to invoke the parable in speaking about public policy. Queen Elizabeth II remarked in her 2004 Christmas message that the parable, which tells how a mugging victim is helped by a "despised foreigner," is about "tolerance and respecting others." She summarizes: "Everyone is our neighbour, no matter what race, creed or colour. The need to look after a fellow human being is far more important than any cultural or religious differences."[5] More recently, in the spring of 2013, one of Mrs. Thatcher's successors, Tony Blair, offered his own appropriation. At the opening of a new Baptist Center in Jordan—the Jordan in the Middle East, not on Long Island—Mr. Blair, speaking on behalf of the Faith Foundation, also took the parable again in the direction of aid. In his description, Jesus "extols the virtue of the Good Samaritan, the stranger, over those who were supposedly devout believers."[6]

In the 1970s, I heard a citizen of Sierra Leone interpret the parable as proclaiming that one should take aid from whoever would offer it, even the enemy, and thus Jesus gave warrant for his country's acceptance of aid from the Soviet Union. Although I do not think that this reading is quite the original import of the parable, it at least highlights two important points. It recognizes the role of the Samaritan as enemy and suggests the possibility of interpreter identification with the wounded man rather than the Samaritan who gives aid. The standard reading is the one in which "we" are the Samaritans; "we Samaritans" help "them," the sick, the poor, foreign nationals, and so on.

The parable of the Good Samaritan has come to mean whatever we want it to mean. In one respect, this inevitable appropriation is to be appreciated. Texts should always take on new meaning as they are encountered by new readers from new cultural contexts. However, texts also have their own original context.

The various appropriations and interpretations of the parable heard today are generally good news. What's not to like about helping the stranger and being charitable toward others? But those are not the messages a first-century Jewish audience would have heard. They didn't need a parable to tell them to care for others; they were already commanded to love both the neighbor and the stranger. Those Jews in antiquity would not be thinking of governmental resources or foreign aid; the Samaritan would not have reminded them of a secretary of state or a prime minister. Nor would they have thought of Samaritans as "strangers." To the contrary, they were the all too familiar neighbors and all too hated enemies.

The parable for them would not have been about looking after a fellow human being, and the parable is not, finally, an answer to the question, "Who is my neighbor?" It is more provocative than that. And if we readers identify with the Samaritan—as the politicians and charitable organizations do—we have missed the deeper implications of the parable as well. Worse, the standard identification we readers have today with the Samaritan leads to the standard anti-Jewish interpretations that have infected much of New Testament study. In many Christian contexts, the Samaritan comes to represent the Christian who has learned to care for others or to break free of prejudice, whereas the priest and the Levite represent Judaism, understood to be xenophobic, promoting ritual purity over compassion, proclaiming self-interest over love of neighbor, and otherwise being something that needs to be rejected.

To get an initial hint of the distance between the mind-set of parable's original audience and our own twenty-first-century perspectives, we might begin by reflecting briefly on the term "good Samaritan." Today, we use the term as if it were not peculiar. Yet as far as I am aware, there are no "Good Catholic" or "Good Baptist" hospitals; there are no social service organizations called "Good Episcopalian" or "Good Mexican" or "Good Arab." To label the Samaritan, any Samaritan, a "good Samaritan" should be, in today's climate, seen as offensive. It is tantamount to saying, "He's a good Muslim" (as opposed to all those others who, in this configuration, would be terrorists) or "She's a good immigrant" (as opposed to all those others who, in this same configuration, are here to take our jobs or scam our welfare system), or, as Heinrich Himmler put it to a gathering of SS officers, every German "has his decent Jew"—that is, knows one good Jew—and as far as

Himmler was concerned, even one was too many, because that might create sympathy.[7] The problem with the labeling is not simply a lack of sensitivity toward the Samaritan people—yes, there are still Samaritans. It is also a lack of awareness of how odd the expression "good Samaritan" would have seemed to Jesus's Jewish contemporaries.

What happens when we strip away two thousand years of usually benevolent and well-intended domestication and hear the parable as a first-century short story spoken by a Jew to other Jews?

The Malevolent Lawyer

Jesus's recounting of the parable of the Good Samaritan to a lawyer may have been an actual incident. Similarly, it is possible that Jesus told the parables of the Lost Sheep, Lost Coin, and Lost Sons to a combined gathering of sinners and tax collectors, scribes and Pharisees. But given how these contexts so neatly fit Luke's agenda and how the other Gospels locate similar sayings in different contexts, it is just as likely that Luke has repackaged traditional material. Luke tells us that the parables of the lost are about repenting and forgiving; that message would not be clear from any of the three parables themselves. Luke tells us that the parable about the unjust judge and the importuning widow is about constant prayer. Again, that's unlikely to be what Jesus's original audience heard.

Nevertheless, the encounter between Jesus and the lawyer that forms the context for the parable neatly fits what we can take to be Jesus's own agenda. Here Luke may have developed the context, but it is a context that helps bring the parable's own implications into sharper focus.

~~~~~

And look, some lawyer stood up; testing Jesus, he says,
"Teacher, (by) doing what eternal life will I inherit?"
(Luke 10.25)

Four points, all of which betray Luke's antipathy toward this lawyer and his associates, follow from this single line. The first clue concerns Luke's depiction of lawyers, for Luke's Gospel, anticipating Dick the Butcher, who in Shakespeare's *Henry VI* memorably planned, "The first thing we do, let's kill all the lawyers," holds no affection for those in the profession. According to Luke 7.30, "the Pharisees and the lawyers" reject John the Baptist and so reject "God's purposes for themselves." In Luke 11.45, after Jesus insults his Pharisaic hosts at a dinner party by calling them "unmarked graves," a lawyer in attendance protests: "Teacher, when you say these things, you insult us too." That was Jesus's intent. Jesus, who is not the most polite of dinner guests, responds by accusing him and his fellow lawyers of loading the people with impossible burdens and not lifting a finger to help, of approving of the killing of God's prophets, and of taking away from the people "the key of knowledge." Luke's readers will know that the lawyer in chapter 10 is not among the righteous.

For Jesus's Jewish audience, lawyers would likely have been positive figures and their connection to the Torah a good thing. There is no immediate Hebrew equivalent for the Greek term *nomikos,* translated "lawyer." In the Septuagint (LXX), the Greek translation of the Hebrew scriptures, the term for "lawyer," *nomikos,* appears just once, but not in a translation from any Hebrew text. It occurs in 4 Maccabees, a Jewish text likely contemporaneous with Luke's Gospel and today included in the canons of some Eastern Orthodox communions. The *nomikos,* which has the connotation of "learned in the Law," is a priest named Eliezer, who serves as a leader for the people.

Fourth Maccabees describes the program of forced assimilation begun by Antiochus IV Epiphanes, the Seleucid king who took control of the Jewish homeland in the mid-second century BCE. Jews who refused to sacrifice to the Greek gods or who insisted on retaining their traditions of circumcision and dietary regulations were tortured and then killed for their fidelity. The king, showing a slithery combination of compassion and cruelty, tells Eliezer the lawyer, "Before I begin to torture you, old man, I would advise you to save yourself by eating pork" (5.6). Despite the king's argument that eschewing pork makes no philosophical sense, the lawyer responds that Torah has invaluable merit: it "teaches us self-control, so that we master all pleasures and desires, and it also trains us in courage, so that we endure any suffering willingly; it instructs us in justice, so that in all our dealings we act impartially, and it teaches us piety, so that with proper reverence we worship the only living God" (5.23–24).

This positive view of lawyers continues elsewhere in the New Testament. For example, the Letter of Titus includes the exhortation, "Make every effort to send Zenas the lawyer and Apollos on their way, and see that they lack nothing" (3.13). Here the role of lawyer overlaps with that of missionary.

Luke's second clue regarding the lawyer's negative characterization is his address to Jesus, "Teacher." Today, there are few more honorable callings than "teacher," and as a "teacher" myself I want to provide the term with every positive connotation. However, for Luke's narrative, calling Jesus "teacher" usually suggests that the interlocutor does not fully understand or respect who, for Luke, Jesus really is. Just a few examples. At the dinner party where Simon the host silently objects to Jesus's allowing a woman known to be a sinner to anoint Jesus's feet and then kiss them, Jesus says, "Simon, I have something to say to you." Simon replies, "Teacher, . . . speak" (7.40). When Jesus arrives at the home of a distraught father whose daughter has just died, "someone came from the leader's house to say, 'Your daughter is dead; do not trouble the teacher any longer'" (8.49). Jesus is not being "bothered" by raising the dead child. Although the request of a "man from the crowd" who calls out, "Teacher, I beg you to look at my son; he is my only child" (9.38) sounds respectful, Jesus responds by identifying the man and his associates as a "faithless and perverse generation" (9.41). We've already noted the lawyer at the banquet who addresses Jesus as "Teacher" and then accuses him of insulting those present (11.45). The same pattern of the title coupled with misunderstanding or a lack of respect occurs in Luke 12.13; 18.18; 19.39; 20.21; 20.28; and 21.7. For Luke, the better address to Jesus is not "Teacher," but "Lord" (Gk. *Kyrios*).

The third clue to the lawyer's negative depiction is his rationale for engaging Jesus in conversation. He asks his question not to gain knowledge, but to "test." In Matthew 22, a similar scene is repeated: a *nomikos* (the only use of the term in the Gospels outside Luke) also "stands" to "test" Jesus (22.35), and his intentions are not good either.

The term "test" (Gk. *ekpeiradzon*) is exactly what Jesus's followers pray to avoid: "Lead us not into temptation"; the line, familiar from the Lord's Prayer, is literally, "Do not bring us to the test" (Luke 11.4, just a few verses after the parable of the Good Samaritan). By testing Jesus, the lawyer takes the Devil's role, for it was Satan who had "tested" Jesus in the wilderness. Jesus shuts the Devil up by telling him, "Do not put the Lord your God to the test" (4.12).

The lawyer's question itself is the fourth negative. "What must I do to inherit eternal life?" (NRSV) is the wrong question. The verb "do" is an aorist participle (*poiesas*), a tense that suggests a single, limited action. The lawyer is thinking of something to check off his to-do list: recite a prayer, offer a sacrifice, drop off a box of macaroni for a food drive, put a twenty in the collection plate. If he's efficient, he can inherit eternal life before lunch. He should be thinking of living a life of righteousness, much like the lawyer in 4 Maccabees. But he's a lawyer, and this is Luke's Gospel, so righteousness is not going to be his concern.

Indeed, the question "What must I do to inherit eternal life," when asked by someone seeking to "test," is similar to the other trick questions Jesus's opponents pose.[8] The trick question is a generic form that cannot be answered yes or no. In the Gospels, "Is it lawful for us to pay taxes to the emperor?" (Luke 20.22) is a trick question. To respond "yes" invites the accusation that one is a collaborator; to respond "no," that one is a revolutionary. The Sadducees ask another trick question. In the case of a woman married to seven brothers, whose wife is she in the resurrection (20.29–32)? Because the Sadducees do not believe in resurrection, the question is merely hypothetical. Here the lawyer asks a question that cannot be answered: one does not "do" anything to "inherit" eternal life.

The question presumes eternal life is a commodity to be inherited or purchased on the basis of a particular action rather than a gift freely given. As far as our sources, including the New Testament, indicate, most first-century Jews already believed in resurrection, or eternal life. The Gospels and Acts speak of a group of Jews called the Sadducees, sometimes glossed with the description, "who say there is no resurrection" (Matt. 22.23; Mark 12.18;

Luke 20.27; Acts 23.8). That marker distinguishes them from other Jewish groups. (As we are wont to say in the biblical studies business, the Sadducees did not believe in resurrection, and that is what made them "sad, you see.")

In the account of the raising of Lazarus, Jesus tells the dead man's distraught sister Martha, "Your brother will rise again." Martha, reflecting the predominant Jewish view, responds, "I know that he will rise again in the resurrection on the last day" (John 11.23–24). The point is confirmed in the Mishnah. *Sanhedrin* 10.1 insists, "All Israel has a share in the world to come." Granted the Mishnah then lists the exceptions who do not receive the soteriological benefits of community membership: apostates, those who deny that resurrection is proclaimed in Torah, and Epicureans, who live a life of complete pleasure in the present.

In Luke 18.18–25, a ruler (Gk. *archon*) asks Jesus the same question that the lawyer posed, but his attitude is different. The ruler begins, "Good Teacher," whereas the lawyer simply said, "Teacher." The ruler has the more respectful address, even if it is still limited. His question, however, is just as misguided. Given that Jesus offers a number of parables that begin "There was a rich man who . . ." and then detail the unfortunate fates of the rich, and given that Jesus states, "There is no one who has left house or wife or brothers or parents or children, for the sake of the kingdom of God, who will not get back very much more in this age, and in the age to come eternal life" (18.29–30), the ruler may well have been concerned about his future. He wants assurances.

Jesus confirms what the ruler already knows. Just as the lawyer in the lead-in to our parable cites Torah in response to Jesus's question, so here Jesus cites Torah to the ruler: "You know the commandments: 'You shall not commit adultery; You shall not murder; You shall not steal; You shall not bear false witness; Honor your father and mother'" (18.20). His point is not that following the commandments "earns" the ruler a spot in heaven. Jews followed Torah not to earn eternal life; this was already part of the covenant. They followed Torah in response to the gracious gift of the covenant that God gave them, because to do so prevented sin and because to do so showed how love of God and love of neighbor were to be manifested.

The ruler replies, "I have kept all these since my youth" (18.21). It is likely he had. Not murdering, stealing, or bearing false witness along with the positive act of honoring parents are relatively easy laws to follow (avoiding greed, envy, and lust; loving the neighbor and the stranger; and caring for the poor, the widow, the orphan, and the alien are the more difficult ones). Jesus does not give him the answer or the assurance he wants, and his desire for personal confirmation has not abated.

He wants Jesus to acknowledge that he is fully righteous, despite the fact that he is "a rich man who . . ." Jesus advises: "There is still one thing lacking. Sell all that you own and distribute the money to the poor, and you will have treasure in heaven; then come, follow me." When the ruler hears Jesus's counsel, "he became sad; for he was very rich" (18.22–23). Like that of the lawyer in our parable, the ruler's focus on eternal life leads nowhere; a focus on caring for others might offer a better path.

How far off base is our lawyer? He thinks in terms of a single action rather than a life of righteousness. He thinks of "eternal life" as a commodity to be inherited or acquired rather than a gift freely given. He focuses on eternal life—his own salvation—when he should be, as Judaism teaches, focused on loving God and neighbor, honoring parents, eschewing stealing, and so on. Finally, he is asking obnoxious questions to which he already knows the answers.

Jesus does not directly answer his question. Instead, he uses what is sometimes called the "Socratic method" but which, I think, Jews invented or at least perfected. In typical Jewish fashion, he answers a question with a question.

And he said to him, "In the Law, what is written? How do you read?" **(Luke 10.26)**

By turning the question back on the lawyer, Jesus evades the trick. He may also be appealing to the lawyer's ego: "Surely sir, you know the answer; after all, you are the trained professional." Jesus provides the lawyer an opportunity to display his knowledge to the public.

Mention of the "Law" refers to the Torah, and specifically the Pentateuch (Genesis, Exodus, Leviticus, Numbers, and Deuteronomy, or, as Jesus would have said, Bereshit, Shemot, Vayikra, Bamidbar, and Devarim, the Hebrew designations), or simply the Books of Moses. Actually, the Torah is not much interested in eternal life or life after death. It is much more interested in how to live in the present. Moses exhorts: "Choose life so that you and your descendants may live, loving the LORD your God, obeying him, and holding fast to him, for that means life to you and length of days" (Deut. 30.19–20).

Jesus does not merely ask, "What is written in the Torah?" He glosses that question with the more specific: "How do you read?" The double focus on literacy—what is *written* and how it is *read*—is usually ignored, but to do so misses the historical point. The lawyer is literate, a quality not shared by the majority of the population in antiquity. According to Luke, John the Baptist's father, Zechariah, can read and write. Because he had been struck mute by an angel, he asks for a writing tablet in order to announce his son's name (1.63). Luke also presents Jesus as literate, in that he can locate his synagogue reading in the scroll of Isaiah (4.17). These may be exceptional cases. The claim by the first-century Jewish historian Josephus that the principal care of Jews is to educate our children well[9] cannot be used to determine that all Jewish children were literate.

Most people in antiquity did not own books; there were no lending libraries in Nazareth or Capernaum. Nor did most people have a need to read; there were scribes and lawyers who had the skill. The focus on literacy will return in a few verses. For now, we find that the lawyer's response does not, at least initially, require literacy skills.

⌇

And answering, he said, "You will love the Lord your God
with all your heart and with all your soul and with all your
strength and with all your mind/intention, and your neighbor
as yourself." **(Luke 10.27)**

The lawyer's response is a combination of two verses of the Torah known to all practicing Jews then and now. The first is Deuteronomy 6.5, which is part of Judaism's daily liturgy. The Hebrew *V'ahavta et adonai elohecha, b'chal l'vovcha, u'v'chal nafshecha, u'v'chal meodecha* means, "You shall love the Lord your God with all your heart and with all your soul [your *nefesh*, your very being] and with all your might (or strength)." Luke's text includes a fourth element, "all your mind." The point of both versions is the same: love of God is the ground of one's being and the guide for one's life.

The second verse the lawyer cites is inextricably connected to the first: love of God has to be manifested; to love means to act. "You shall love your neighbor as yourself" is Leviticus 19.18. This too was a well-known verse in early Judaism. According to the great Rabbi Akiva, who was martyred by the Romans about a century after Jesus, "You shall love your neighbor as yourself" is the greatest teaching of the Torah.[10]

The lawyer was right to combine Deuteronomy 6 and Leviticus 19, but he was not original; the two had already been combined in Jewish thought. The ancient text known as the *Testaments of the Twelve Patriarchs* pairs the verses in the *Testaments* of both *Issachar* (5.2) and *Dan* (5.3). The same combination of love of God and love of neighbor appears in different contexts in Matthew 22.37 and Mark 12.29–31, where Jesus summarizes the two verses as the "Great Commandment" and insists: "On these two commandments hang all the law and the prophets [the Torah and the Prophets]." Although the combined verses command love of God and love of neighbor, they do not mean, "Just do some good loving, but forget about dietary regulations, circumcision, Sabbath observance, or Temple sacrifice." They mean that the love commandments become the touchstone by which all other actions are assessed.

The importance of extending these two verses into the rest of Torah is signaled by their contexts. In antiquity, as today, single verses come with contexts. When scripture was read in the synagogue—in the *parshah hashavuah,* the "portion of the week" (comparable to the Revised Common Lectionary)—whole chapters were read. Deuteronomy 6.5, which insists on loving God, is preceded by Israel's essential theological proclamation, "Hear, O Israel, the Lord is our God, the Lord alone." Following the love command are mandates to teach Torah to one's children, to inscribe God's words upon the doorpost of the house (the *mezuzah,* which can be found on the doors of Jewish homes to this day), and to speak of them at all times.

To cite Leviticus 19.18 also invoked the rest of the chapter. Leviticus 19 begins with God telling Moses, "Speak to all the congregation of the people of Israel and say to them, 'You shall be holy, for I the LORD your God am holy.'" It continues with statutes ranging from those commanding reverence for parents and keeping the Sabbath to those forbidding idolatry, stealing, swearing falsely or lying, profaning the divine name, and engaging in improper sexual relations (a list that resembles the Ten Commandments). It also mandates care for the poor, the blind, and the deaf. Thus love must manifest itself in action.

The lawyer knew the commandments, and he would have known the context. Whether he fully understood them is another question.

And he said to him, "Rightly you answered. This do, and you will live." **(Luke 10.28)**

The lawyer got the right answer; good for him. However, he did not quite get the right question, so Jesus changes it for him. Whereas the lawyer asked about "eternal life," Jesus reframes what is at stake by exhorting, "Do this, and you will live." The imperative "do" focuses not on a single action, but on an ongoing relationship. Leviticus 18.5, like Deuteronomy 30, makes the same point: "Do this and live." The point is to "live now" and not be focused on "eternal life."

Were the lawyer wise, he would have thanked Jesus and gone off to show his love. But he's a lawyer in Luke's Gospel, so we know that a humble, compassionate response is unlikely. Instead, he proves his malevolent intent toward Jesus by posing another, even more inappropriate question.

But he, wanting to justify himself, said to Jesus, "And who is my neighbor?" **(Luke 10.29)**

"Wanting to justify himself"—that is, wanting to make himself look "right" (as in "justified margins") in the eyes of anyone listening in—the lawyer asks another question. His concern for self-justification is something Luke's Jesus despises. Later in this Gospel, Jesus condemns the Pharisees, whom Luke portrays, contrary to all other sources, as "lovers of money," with the accusation: "You are those who justify yourselves in the sight of others; but God knows your hearts; for what is prized by human beings is an abomination in the sight of God" (16.15). The lawyer, like the Pharisees according to Luke, is interested in self-aggrandizement, when he should be interested in love of God and neighbor.

His question, "Who is my neighbor?" is on the technical level not a bad one. The Hebrew term usually translated "neighbor" (*rea'*), the term that appears in Leviticus 19.18, has several connotations. In Genesis 11.3, it means "fellow" or "the other guy"; the NRSV renders this verse, which concerns the building of the tower of Babel, "And they said to one another," rather than, literally, "And said a man to his neighbor." Exodus 33.11 uses "neighbor" to describe an intimate friendship between God and Moses. Again, the NRSV misses the technical term by translating, "The LORD used to speak to Moses face to face, as one speaks to a friend"; the term translated "friend" is *rea'*, "neighbor." Deuteronomy 19.14 (also 27.17) defines *rea'* as a person with whom one shares a common border: "You must not move your neighbor's boundary marker." Jeremiah 9.4–5 warns against trusting "neighbors" as well as trusting relatives; here the connotation is others in the community.

The term *rea'* can also mean "lover." Hosea 3.1 reads, "Go love a woman who has a lover"; the Hebrew says, literally, "Go love a woman, the lover of a neighbor." Song of Songs 5.16 is, "This is my beloved and this is my friend"; the term translated "friend" is, of course, *rea'*. The *rea'* in Proverbs 3.29 is someone who "lives trustingly beside you" and therefore against whom no harm should be planned.

The context of Leviticus 19.18 suggests that the "neighbor" is to be distinguished from the "stranger" (KJV) or the "resident alien" (NRSV). The chapter goes on to state, "When an alien (Heb. *ger*) resides with you in your land, you shall not oppress the alien. The alien who resides with you shall be to you as the citizen among you; you shall love the alien as yourself, for you were aliens in the land of Egypt" (19.33–34). The point is developed by Ezekiel, who puts the resident alien on the same footing, and on the same land, as the fellow Israelite. The prophet states that, in the allotment of the land following the return from exile, the inheritance shall not only be for the people Israel, but also "for the aliens who reside among you and have begotten children among you. They shall be to you as citizens of Israel; with you they shall be allotted an inheritance among the tribes of Israel. In whatever tribe aliens reside, there you shall assign them their inheritance, says the Lord GOD" (47.22–23). Thus the alien is necessarily a neighbor, a fellow.[11]

On the home front, I wonder if those folks who want to impose "biblical values" on America today have considered Leviticus 19 in debates over immigration reform. On the international scene, I wonder why those people ranging from some right-wing Jews to some Christian Zionists do not consider Ezekiel 47 in discussions on the Middle East. But those questions require another book.

In the Septuagint, the Hebrew *ger* ("alien") in Leviticus 19 becomes *proselytos,* "proselyte." But the term does not have today's meaning of "convert" in the context of Leviticus. It could not, because the Israelites were not "proselytes" in the land of Egypt; they did not worship Egypt's gods. The "proselyte" is the one who "comes forward" (the literal meaning of the term) by choosing to live among a different people and so to share their lives, their joys and concerns.

Thus, the general meaning of "neighbor," at least for Hebrew speakers, is a person in intimate or legal relationship. Not everyone fits into this category. Leviticus is designed as Israel's Law code; it is not for universal application. Relations with people inside the community will be different from those with people outside the community, just as throughout the world today citizens of a nation or state have certain rights and responsibilities that non-citizens do not.

The lawyer's question has legal merit. One needs to know who are neighbors, and so under the same legal system, and who are not. But in the context of love, his question is not relevant. According to Leviticus, love has to extend beyond the people in one's group. Leviticus 19 insists on loving the stranger as well. Josephus, the first-century Jewish historian, agrees. In his *Against Apion,* a text likely contemporaneous with Luke's Gospel, he asserts, "For I think it will become clear that we possess laws that are extremely well designed, with a view toward piety, fellowship with one another (Gk. *koinonia*), and universal benevolence (*philanthropia*) as well as justice (*dikaiosyne*), endurance in labors, and contempt for death."[12]

For our parable, the lawyer's question is again misguided. To ask "Who is my neighbor" is a polite way of asking, "Who is *not* my neighbor?" or "Who does not deserve my love?" or "Whose lack of food or shelter can I ignore?" or "Whom I can hate?" The answer Jesus gives is, "No one." Everyone deserves that love—local or alien, Jews or gentile, terrorist or rapist, everyone.

The lawyer had not been attending to Jesus's other teachings. In the Sermon on the Mount Jesus states, "You have heard that it was said, 'You shall love your neighbor and hate your enemy'" (Matt. 5.43). The Torah includes no commandment to hate one's enemy; perhaps Jesus is reflecting a saying known from the sectarian group responsible for the Dead Sea Scrolls. The *Rule of the Community* does state: "You shall love all the sons of light . . . and hate all the sons of darkness" (1QS 1.9–11). Enemies are, conventionally, people we hate. If we did not hate them, they would not be enemies, at least from our perspective. And that may be the point. Jesus continues, "But I say to you, Love your enemies and pray for those who persecute you, so that you may be children of your Father in heaven; for he makes his sun rise on the evil and on the good, and sends rain on the righteous and on the unrighteous" (Matt. 5.44–45). Love cannot be restricted. Luke made the same point: "If you love those who love you, what credit is that to you? For even sinners love those who love them" (6.32). The lawyer had not been listening.

According to Jewish law, the lawyer is responsible for loving those like him, and those who are not like him but who live in proximity to him although they are not part of his people, the "children of Israel" as he defined the term. Leviticus does not explicitly require him to love his "enemy" who lives across the border, outside the boundaries of the community. In Jewish thought, one could not mistreat the enemy, but love was not mandated. Proverbs 25.21 insists, "If your enemies are hungry, give them bread to eat; and if they are thirsty, give them water to drink" (Paul cites Prov. 25.21–22 in Rom. 12.20). Only Jesus insists on loving the enemy: "Love your enemies and pray for those who persecute you." He may be the only person in antiquity to have given this instruction.

Given this concern for loving the enemy, the focus on literacy in the lead-in to our parable provokes another possible reading. In Hebrew the words "neighbor" and "evil" share the same consonants (*resh ayin*);[13] they differ only in the vowels—but ancient Hebrew texts do not have vowels (if this sounds odd, think of text-messaging). Both words are written identically.

When Jesus asks the lawyer, "How do you *read*?" he is therefore asking, "Dear sir, are you able to see, in the very words of the Torah, the equation of enemy with neighbor and thus the command to love both?" The lawyer has read the words in the Hebrew, but he cannot see their full meaning.

Not only does our lawyer fail to interpret the Law in its fullest meaning; he is about to become the recipient of a parable. We know, from the parables told by Jotham and Nathan, that if a parable is directed to a particular individual, the individual is likely to come to an unwelcome realization. The lawyer asks, "Who is my neighbor?" In response, Jesus is about to bring him to the test.

Replying, Jesus said, "Some person was going down from Jerusalem to Jericho, and he fell among robbers, who, stripping him, even placed blows, going away, leaving him half dead." **(Luke 10.30)**

The opening of the parable efficiently sets the scene. The person (Gk. *anthropos*) lacks identification; he could be rich or poor, free or slave, priest or lay, nice or naughty. He may have been coming home from offering sacrifice in the Temple; he may be a healer on his way to a sick person in Jericho; he may be a tourist. His profession is irrelevant. The man is "some man" or everyone. Jesus's listeners would have had no trouble identifying with the victim; they may have been victims of attack themselves.

The road from Jerusalem to Jericho was an eighteen-mile rocky path that descended from about 2,500 feet above sea level to Jericho's 825 feet below. The Romans paved the road in the late 60s CE so that the Tenth Legion could move its siege engines toward the doomed Jerusalem. Even those who had never traveled the road, were they biblically knowledgeable, knew about its dangers, and its possibilities. It was on this road that David fled from his rebellious son Absalom (2 Sam. 15.23–16.14); it was here that King Zedekiah escaped his Chaldean pursuers (2 Kings 25.4).

And it is here that the commentators leave the road for detours into imagination. For some of the church fathers, who were engaging in an allegorical interpretation that would have mystified a first-century Jewish audience, the fellow in the ditch is a sinner in need of salvation. Predictably then, the priest and the Levite, representing the Law and the Prophets, are those who cannot save; the good Samaritan is Jesus himself; his two coins represent baptism and the Eucharist; and so on.[14]

Continuing this negative image of Judaism are modern commentators, whose interpretative key is not allegory, but sociology. Increasingly popular is the view that Jesus's audience would have had little sympathy for the man in the ditch. One scholar classifies the poor fellow as a "despised tradesman."[15] Why Jews would "despise" people in trades is unclear; Pharisees, for example, typically held day jobs (e.g., Paul was a leather worker). Another adds: "Traders were notoriously dishonest, and their itinerant lifestyle and constant interaction with all sorts of people make it impossible for them to observe even the most basic laws concerning food preparation and purity. For that same reason, the wounded man would not have evoked the lawyer's empathy."[16] Thus we get the impression that the Jewish audience would find the eating of a ham sandwich damning, but would not care about a violent physical attack.

I heard one explanation saying that the man was of the school of Shammai, since he was attacked by bandits. How does this follow? The Mishnah, *Berakhot* 1.3, presents a discussion of whether to stand up or lie down when reciting the Shema. The school of Shammai states, "In the evening everyone should recline in order to recite and in the morning they should stand, as it says, 'When you lie down and when you rise.'" The citation is from Deuteronomy 6.7, the same section that contains the love commandment. The Mishnah then quotes Rabbi Tarfon: "I was coming along the road in the evening and reclined to recite the Shema as required by the House of Shammai. And in doing so I placed myself in danger of being attacked by bandits." Aha, say commentators, he is mugged because he was praying at the wrong time.

The parable says nothing about the man's position at the time of attack. The fellow in the ditch is just a fellow, a victim of a violent crime, period.

Not only do some scholars engage in blaming the victim, and not only do they add gratuitous points about purity laws; they also sympathize with the robbers. Common today is the view that the robbers are Jewish Robin Hoods (picture *Men in Tights and Tzitzit*) who, displaced from family lands by overtaxation and urbanization, protest their socioeconomic disenfranchisement by taking from the rich and giving to the poor. Thus the robbers are "roving terrorists staging their own form of protest against various types of official and unofficial exploitation of the poor."[17]

The robbers are not merry men dropping off their gains with the "Good Samaritan Society" or the United Jewish Appeal. Nor is there reason to presume that the man waylaid by robbers was wealthy; were the man wealthy, his lack of bodyguards is inexplicable.

The reasons for rejecting the Robin Hood model are numerous, but I'll just note the reason that comes from a close reading of the ancient sources. The term the parable uses for the robbers, *lestai,* is used by Josephus over forty times; it appears fifteen times in the New Testament, and nine times in the Septuagint. The basic meaning is "member of an armed gang." As early as Homer, the term referred to both highwaymen and pirates who act without mercy. In 2 Corinthians 11.26, Paul speaks of his "frequent journeys, in danger from rivers, danger from bandits (*lestai*), danger from my own people, . . . danger in the wilderness," and so on; the *lestai* are not his friends either.

These negative connotations continue in the Gospels. Those who make the Temple "a den of robbers (*lestai*)" are not dispossessed peasants robbing from the rich (Mark 11.15–19). According to John 10.7–8, Jesus states: "I am the gate for the sheep. All who came before me are thieves (*kleptai* [whence "kleptomaniac"]) and bandits (*lestai*); but the sheep did not listen to them." In John 18.40, Barabbas, the guilty one set free when the innocent Jesus goes to his death, is a *lestes*. In Mark 15.27 and Matthew 27.38–44, but not in Luke, the men crucified on Jesus's left and right are *lestai*. Yes, we could see the crucified men as freedom fighters executed by Rome; we could also see them as murderers, thieves, or, as Luke describes them, "criminals" or "evildoers" (Gk. *kakourgoi,* from *kakos* and *ergon;* 23.33).

So the robbers are the bad guys, as we note also from their violence. The traveler is stripped, beaten, and left half dead in a ditch. He is robbed not only of his possessions, but also of his dignity, his health, and almost his life.

Luke describes him as having "wounds" (Gk. *traumata,* hence "trauma"). The lawyer had asked about eternal life—he should rather be worried about those left half dead. So should commentators.

And yet half dead is still alive; the man is, despite being naked (as would be a corpse before shrouding) and prostrate, alive. Listeners, identifying with him, can only hope that rescue will come. And because they identify with him, their question—and so our question—is: "Who will help *me?*"

<hr />

And by coincidence, some priest was going down that road, and seeing him, he passed by on the other side. And likewise a Levite, coming to the place, even seeing, passed by on the other side. **(Luke 10.31–32)**

Just as the fellow in the ditch is revictimized by being labeled a despised merchant or a bad Jew, so too the priest and the Levite receive their share of negative interpretations that go well beyond the justified critique of their failure to act. Again, stereotypes get in the way. Here are the two most common misreadings and why they are unhelpful.

First, a number of scholars talk about the peasant dislike of the "priestly elite."[18] This view comes more from contemporary distaste for religious hierarchies than it does from Luke's text or Jesus's context. There is nothing that makes a priest and even less a Levite part of the "elite." Priests and Levites may have had neither wealth nor status. In Judaism, the priesthood is not a vocation; it is an inherited position. The priestly line descends from Aaron, the brother of Moses. One is a priest if one's father was a priest. Levites, who form a lesser category of priests, also receive their role according to their paternal line; they are descended from Aaron's ancestor Levi, the third son of Jacob. All other Jews, except Jews by choice, are descended from Jacob's other children; they are Israelites.

These lines continue in Judaism to this day. The term for "priest" in Hebrew is *kohen,* and Jews with the last name Cohen or Kane may well be from the priestly line. Similarly, Jews with the last name Levi, Levine (like me), or

Lewis may well have levitical ancestry. But neither the name nor the priestly role says anything about wealth or community status.

Josephus, who was himself an elite priest, mentions other priests who were poverty-stricken. According to his *Antiquities,* the high priest Ananias, who served from about 47 to 52 and who, according to the book of Acts (22–23), tried Paul in Jerusalem, sent his servants to the Temple threshing floors, where they "took away the tithes that belonged to the priests by violence, and did not refrain from beating such as would not give these tithes to them . . . so that [some of the] priests that had previously been supported with those tithes died for lack of food."[19] There are "priests," and then there are "high priests"; the social positions of the two groups should not be confused.

The priest in the parable enters Luke's Gospel with fine precedent. Zechariah, the father of John the Baptist, is a priest, and John's mother is from a priestly family. It is Zechariah who recalls how God had promised "that we would be saved from our enemies, and from the hand of all who hate us . . . to give light to those who sit in darkness and in the shadow of death" (Luke 1.71, 79). The man in the ditch and those who identify with him have reason to hope.

As for the distinction among the priestly ranks, Luke invariably describes the priests involved in Jesus's death as "*chief* priests" or the "*high* priest." Our priest is an ordinary priest who does what is all too ordinary: he fails to act when he should.

The second, more common, and just as misguided explanation for the priest's and Levite's failure to help is that they are following Jewish Law. From both classroom and pulpit comes the claim that the priest and the Levite pass by the man in the ditch, because they are afraid of contracting corpse contamination and so violating purity laws. A few examples demonstrate the pervasiveness of this view.

A 2005 book with the optimistic title *The Wide, Wide Circle of Divine Love: A Biblical Case for Religious Diversity* states: "If the traveler were already dead, or he died while they were attending him, then they would have become unclean, contaminated, because they touched a dead body. This would have made it necessary for them to seek ritual cleansing before they could resume their responsibilities."[20] What "ritual duties" the priest and the Levite would have had is unclear, since the parable explicitly notes that the priest is going "down" (*katabaino*) from Jerusalem, not up to the Temple. Why ritual cleansing is a problem is unstated.

The popularity of this view is confirmed by its appearance in *The Harper-Collins Study Bible* for Luke 10.32. The annotater claims, "Both [Levite and the] priest may have been concerned about impurity from contact with a corpse (see Num. 5.2; 19.11–13)."[21] Numbers 19.10b–13 states, "Those who touch the dead body of any human being shall be unclean seven days. They shall purify themselves with the water on the third day and on the seventh day. . . . All who touch a corpse, the body of a human being who has died, and do not purify themselves, defile the tabernacle of the LORD; such persons shall be cut off from Israel." There is nothing impure about touching a person who is "half dead." Nor is there any sin involved in burying a corpse; to the contrary, the Torah expects corpses to be interred.

The better background for our priest is not Numbers 19, but Leviticus 21. This chapter, addressed to "the priests, the sons of Aaron," mandates, "No one shall defile himself for a dead person among his relatives, except for his nearest kin" (vv. 1–2). Yet even here, this is only half the story. To follow Torah, the priest should have checked to see if the man was alive and, finding him alive, should have helped him. Should he have discovered a corpse, he should have covered it and then immediately gone for help.

Walter Wink, in an article entitled "The Parable of the Compassionate Samaritan," offers the possibility that, were the priest to have come within four cubits to check on the man in the ditch and if it turned out that the man was dead, the priest "would be defiled and was liable to disciplinary flogging (*b. Sot.* 44a–44b)."[22] The very late Talmudic passage states, "A dead body affects four cubits with respect to communicating defilement." There is nothing about flogging.

Biblical scholar Richard Bauckham proposes that the priest in the parable "cannot get close enough to tell without risking defilement from the corpse if that is what it turns out to be. This is because, in first-century Jewish thought about such matters, corpse-impurity travels vertically through the air. If any part of the priest's body were to be above any part of a corpse, he would contract impurity."[23] Had the parable only been about a priest, the argument would be more compelling.

The presence of the Levite makes the priestly concern irrelevant. This distinction between priests and Levites in observance of purity laws continues to this day. *Kohanim,* "priests," will remain outside the cemetery gates unless the funeral is for an immediate relative; Levites as well as other Jews will step onto the cemetery grounds. Further, Samaritans were also bound by laws concerning corpse contamination; just as the Samaritan found the question irrelevant, so should we in our attempt to understand the parable.

Even the parable itself undercuts the possibility that the motive of priest and Levite stems from purity regulations. Had the priest been going up to Jerusalem (one always goes "up" to Jerusalem; one could be on the moon and still go "up" to Jerusalem), where he would be engaged in Temple activities, he may well have been concerned about purity. However, the parable obviates that explanation immediately; it tells us that the priest is going "down" from Jerusalem. Thus, he need not be in a ritually pure state.

The Law, rather, required that both men attend to the fellow in the ditch, whether alive or dead, for one is to "love the neighbor" and "love the stranger" both. Regarding corpses, Jewish Law requires that a dead body be treated with utmost respect. The point is perhaps best seen in the book of Tobit; the book's titular hero, a Jewish male Antigone, risks his life by attending to unburied corpses (1.16–20). Philo writes in his *Hypothetica* that among the precepts Jews follow are those that say, "No one shall keep anyone from performing funeral honors to the dead, but shall even throw upon them so much earth as if sufficient to protect them from impiety; that no one shall violate or move, in any manner or degree whatever, the graves, or tombs, or memorials of those who are dead."[24] Similarly, in his *Against Apion,* Josephus writes, "There are other things which our legislator ordained for us beforehand, which of necessity we ought to do in common to all men; as to afford fire, and water, and food to such as want it; to show them the roads; and not to let anyone lie unburied. He also would have us treat those that are esteemed our enemies with moderation."[25] The connection of this passage to Luke's parable and frame is remarkable. Josephus sees Jews as expected to attend to a corpse on the roadside, not to pass it by.

The Mishnah, *Nazir* 7.1, reads: "A high priest or a Nazirite [a person under a vow of utmost purity] may not contract uncleanness because of their dead [relatives], but they may contract uncleanness because of a neglected corpse." The Babylonian Talmud is even stronger: "As long as there are no other people to look after the burial of a corpse, the duty is incumbent on the first Jew that passes by, without exception, to perform the burial" (*Nazir*

43b; Jerusalem Talmud, *Nazir* 56a). Judaism still takes this mandate seriously. That is why Jews stood vigil at Ground Zero until every corpse was recovered. Burying the dead is one of the highest *mitzvot,* most important commandments in Judaism, for it is one of the few acts that cannot be repaid by the person who benefits from it.

Finally—and one would hope that these numerous reasons are sufficient to put this focus to rest—Luke does not seem interested in purity concerns here, although such concerns surface elsewhere. When Luke wants to make a point about purity, Luke mentions Pharisees and scribes.[26] None appears in our parable.

Arguments that read the parable in terms of "uncleanness" or "purity" are made by modern Christians, not by Jesus or Luke. Neither gives the priest or Levite an excuse. Nor would any excuse be acceptable. Their responsibility was to save a life; they failed. Saving a life is so important that Jewish Law mandates that it override every other concern, including keeping the Sabbath (see, e.g., 1 Macc. 2.31–41; 2 Macc. 6.11; Mishnah, *Shabbat* 18.3). Their responsibility, should the man have died, was to bury the corpse. They failed here as well.

The best explanation I've heard for the refusal of the priest and the Levite to come to the aid of the man in the ditch comes from Martin Luther King Jr., who preached: "I'm going to tell you what my imagination tells me. It's possible these men were afraid. . . . And so the first question that the priest [and] the Levite asked was, 'If I stop to help this man, what will happen to me?' . . . But then the Good Samaritan came by, and he reversed the question: 'If I do not stop to help this man, what will happen to him?'" King went on, "If I do not stop to help the sanitation workers, what will happen to them?"[27] King then went to Memphis, and it was there he was assassinated. There are bandits on the road.

Whatever the motives of the priest and the Levite, King is correct. They, like the lawyer, thought only about themselves, not about the man in the ditch.

So if the issue is not priestly purity, why did Jesus speak explicitly of a priest and Levite? The duo anticipate, in good folkloric fashion, the appearance of the third figure. We have already seen the "rule of three" in our study of the parables of the lost: the first two set up the third. For the Good Samaritan, the rule works even better, for in its usual function the first two figures fail and the third will succeed. Examples include the decidedly nonkosher "Three Little Pigs" and the equally nonkosher suitors for Portia's hand in the *Merchant of Venice*. Name two, and the third comes automatically. For a more modern analogy, to say in a church context, "Father, Son, and . . ." evokes the third, "Holy Spirit." Or, for a less theological albeit Jewish example, "Larry and Moe" evokes "Curley."

For Jesus's audience, and for any synagogue congregation today, the third of the group is obvious. Mention a priest and a Levite, and anyone who knows anything about Judaism will know that the third person is an Israelite. Ezra 10.5 speaks of the "leading priest, the Levites, and all Israel"; Nehemiah 11.3 states that "in the towns of Judah all lived on their property in their towns: Israel, the priests, the Levites . . ." Both priest and Levite should have stopped to help. The audience, surprised at this lack of compassion, would have presumed both that the third person would be an Israelite and that he would help.

However, Jesus is telling a parable, and parables never go the way one expects. Instead of the anticipated Israelite, the person who stops to help is a Samaritan. In modern terms, this would be like going from Larry and Moe to Osama bin Laden.

⌒‿⌒

But some Samaritan, traveling, came near him and seeing, had compassion. And coming toward (him), he bound up his wounds, pouring oil and wine (on them), and having set him upon his own animal, he brought him to an inn and cared for him. **(Luke 10.33–34)**

As the parable turns to the good Samaritan, its structure changes. As spare as the earlier descriptions of priest and Levite were, the text now lavishes attention on the Samaritan's actions. The robbers steal and wound, while the Samaritan tends with his own goods. The bandits leave the man half dead, while the Samaritan returns him to life. Whereas the priest and the Levite go out of their way to distance themselves from the victim, the Samaritan literally "goes up to him" and shows him "compassion." Luke had already used the term, which carries the connotation of a visceral reaction (i.e., he felt it in his guts), to describe Jesus's response to seeing the widow of Nain at her son's funeral procession (7.13), and it describes the reaction of the father to the return of his prodigal son (15.20). In all three cases, the reaction is a response to a presumed death or loss; it signals the drive to restore wholeness.

The Samaritan's compassion then becomes, for many of today's interpreters, the hook by which the sermon functions. In a number of settings, the parable serves as a warning against prejudice; for example, the two who walk by are a pastor and a choir director, while the Samaritan is a gay man, an "illegal immigrant," a person on parole, or any other victim of bigotry. The point in this reading is that "they" are really nice, that "we" sometimes fail in our obligations to help, and that "we" too should "have compassion" on those who are mistreated.

We even have so-called Good Samaritan laws designed to protect people who aid accident victims. Had the parable been set in New York rather than Judea, our lawyer likely would volunteer to represent the man in the ditch, sue the Samaritan for improper medical treatment, and take thirty pieces of silver for the settlement.

But to understand the parable as did its original audience, we need to think of Samaritans less as oppressed but benevolent figures and more as the enemy, as those who do the oppressing. From the perspective of the man in the ditch, Jewish listeners might balk at the idea of receiving Samaritan aid. They might have thought, "I'd rather die than acknowledge that one from that group saved me"; "I do not want to acknowledge that a rapist has a human face"; or "I do not want to recognize that a murderer will be the one to rescue me."

According to the Bible, Samaria had an earlier name, Shechem. It was at Shechem that Jacob's daughter Dinah was raped (readers of the novel *The Red Tent* would do well to read the original, Genesis 34). The second reference to Shechem/Samaria is Judges 8–9, the story of the false judge Abimelech, who murders his rivals. It is to him and his supporters that Jotham tells his parable of the Trees. Thus, to Jesus's Jewish audience as well as to Luke's readers, the idea of a "good Samaritan" would make no more sense than the idea of a "good rapist" or a "good murderer."

As the Bible recounts, the Samaritan people originated after the twelve-tribe United Monarchy ruled by David and then Solomon split into two independent states. The Southern Kingdom, Judah, with its capital in Jerusalem, retained a descendant of David on the throne; the Northern Kingdom, Israel, with its capital in Samaria, was ruled by a series of charismatic leaders (see 1 Kings 12). According to 1 Kings 16.32, Ahab, the husband of the infamous Jezebel, constructed an altar to the Canaanite god Baal in Samaria. Slightly later, the slightly more virtuous King Jehu turned Baal's shrine into a latrine (2 Kings 10.18–27).

The Northern Kingdom, called both Israel and Ephraim (after Joseph's son; see, e.g., Isa. 7.9; Jer. 31.9), was conquered by the Assyrians in 722 BCE, and many of its citizens were carted off to places unknown (see 2 Kings 17.1–16, which attributes the destruction of Israel to the apostasy of its population). Assyrian records contain an inscription from Sargon II claiming that 27,290 were exiled, but political figures then, as now, are often inflated. The Assyrians then moved residents from other conquered nations into the region. According to 2 Kings 17.24: "The king of Assyria brought people from Babylon, Cuthah, Avva, Hamath, and Sepharvaim, and placed them in the cities of Samaria in place of the people of Israel; they took possession of Samaria, and settled in its cities." The resulting population took its name from the capital, and so the Samaritans as a nation were born.

During the next century, Babylon conquered Assyria and then in 587 BCE conquered the Southern Kingdom, Judah, and took the remaining Davidic king as well as many of the country's leading citizens into exile in Babylon. In 538, Cyrus of Persia conquered Babylon; one of his acts was to repatriate the Judahites to their homeland. Some stayed in Babylon; others returned, and they did so with plans to rebuild not only their nation, but also their Temple. It was over the construction of the Temple that a new enmity between Jews who had returned from Babylon and Samaritans would develop. According to Nehemiah 4.1–8 (see also Ezra 4.7–11):

> When Sanballat [Samaria's governor] heard that we were building
> the wall, he was angry and greatly enraged, and he mocked the
> Jews. He said in the presence of his associates and of the army of
> Samaria, "What are these feeble Jews doing? Will they restore
> things? Will they sacrifice? Will they finish it in a day? Will they

revive the stones out of the heaps of rubbish—and burned ones at that?" ... But when Sanballat and Tobiah and the Arabs and the Ammonites and the Ashdodites heard that the repairing of the walls of Jerusalem was going forward and the gaps were beginning to be closed, they were very angry, and all plotted together to come and fight against Jerusalem and to cause confusion in it.

In the early fourth century (ca. 388), the Samaritans constructed their own temple on Mt. Gerizim, and following the conquests of Alexander the Great in 333 Samaria was rebuilt as a Greek city (*polis*). Enmity with the Jews in the south continued. The Jews who rebelled in 165 BCE against the assimilationist policies of the Seleucid king Antiochus IV Epiphanes and his allies in the priestly establishment resented the Samaritans for not coming to their aid. The Jewish king John Hyrcanus attacked Samaria in 128 BCE and burned down the Samaritan Temple on Mt. Gerizim.[28] It was rebuilt by Herod the Great, who also rebuilt the Jerusalem Temple.

From the Persian period in the late sixth century BCE to the time of Jesus, Jews and Samaritans remained at odds. Each claimed the true descent from Abraham, true understanding of Torah, the correct priesthood, and the right form of worship in the proper location.

To look at the Samaritans only through the perspective of the biblical tradition is to tell only half the story. The Samaritans' own self-designation is *Shamerim*, meaning "guardians" or "observers" of the Law. Jewish readers may know the Hebrew equivalent, *shomer*, as in *shomer shabbas*, or "Sabbath observant." An alternate, external etymology is found in 1 Kings 16.24, which states that the name came from a fellow named Shemer, who originally owned the property on which the Samaritans lived.

Samaritans traditionally view themselves as descendants of Joseph, and thus of his sons Ephraim and Manasseh, and as possessing the correct interpretation of Torah, which had been promulgated at the Northern sanctuary in Shechem. As for the Jews, according to ancient Samaritan tradition, they got off track at the time of Samuel, when the priest Eli set up a heretical sanctuary at Shiloh. Errors continued, from Solomon, who, incorrectly in their view, erected a temple in Jerusalem; to Ezra, who in their view rewrote the Pentateuch with a Judean bias; to Rabbi Hillel, who corrupted the tradition with his innovations regarding the interpretation of the Torah. They further suggest that the Jews got off track by adding to the Pentateuch additional books, those texts today called the Prophets and the Writings.

The enmity between the two groups waxed and waned depending on the time, but for the most part relations were not warm. The Jewish king Herod the Great took a Samaritan woman named Malthace as one of his wives (he had nine, according to Josephus); she was the mother of Herod Antipas (the tetrarch responsible for the death of John the Baptist) and Herod Archelaus as well as of a daughter named Olympias.[29]

According to the Gospel of John, Jesus meets a Samaritan woman at a well (4.1–42). Biblical readers know the scene, because it recapitulates the meeting of Abraham's servant and Rebekah, Jacob and Rachel, and Moses and Zipporah. That Jesus had earlier been identified as a "bridegroom" (3.29) solidifies the convention: Jewish man meets a woman at a well, object matrimony. Although the Samaritan woman, married many times, is not the expected Jewish virgin, a wedding of a sort ensues, as through the woman the Samaritan village comes to accept Jesus's messianic claim.

In the course of the story, John makes clear how unexpected the relationship is. Jesus says to the woman, "Give me a drink," and she responds, "How is it that you, a Jew, ask a drink of me, a woman of Samaria?" The evangelist secures the impression of enmity by adding, "Jews do not share things in common with Samaritans" (4.7, 9). In that same chapter, the Johannine Jesus, unsympathetic to religious pluralism, responds to the woman's question about the location of true worship, "You worship what you do not know, we worship what we know, for salvation is from the Jews" (4.20–22).

The Fourth Gospel is not the only text to indicate problems between Jews and Samaritans. According to Matthew, Jesus enjoins his disciples, "Enter no town of the Samaritans" (10.5). Luke even ensures that readers unfamiliar with local politics understand the enmity. In the chapter preceding our parable (9.51–56), Luke recounts that a Samaritan village refused Jesus hospitality "because his face was set toward Jerusalem." The apostles James and John, at their apostolic best and recalling the prophet Elijah in 2 Kings 1.10, then propose to call down fire from heaven to destroy the village. Jesus has to explain that dropping bombs is not the proper response to a lack of hospitality.

Josephus, no friend of the Samaritans, confirms the enmity. Not only does he claim that Samaritans would affiliate with the Jews when it was politically advantageous, but declare themselves a distinct group when it was not;[30] he also describes direct Samaritan attacks on Jews. According to his *Antiquities,* at the time of the Roman governor Cumanus (ca. 48–50) it was the "custom of the Galileans" to travel through Samaria on their way to the pilgrimage festivals in Jerusalem. Samaritan residents in a village called Ginea attacked the Galileans and massacred a number of them. Other Galilean Jews sought the governor's help in punishing the murderers, but, as Josephus recounts, the Samaritans bribed Cumanus to do nothing. A number of Galileans, "much displeased," ignoring the warnings of saner voices, and opting for vigilante justice, "plundered many Samaritan villages." The Samaritan leaders accused the Jews not only of plunder, but also of setting their villages on fire. The political crisis, which arose in part because of both Jewish and Samaritan reaction to Roman rule, ultimately required the emperor Claudius's intervention.[31]

Rabbinic sources debate the status of Samaritans, given the ethnic, theological, and religious connections between Samaritans and Jews. Early Tannaitic texts (e.g., Babylonian Talmud, *Qiddushin* 75b; Jerusalem Talmud, *Ketubot* 3, 1, 27a; minor tractate *Kutim* 1.1) regard Samaritans as Jews. After the Bar Kokhba revolt (132–35 CE), later rabbinic sources begin to show anti-Samaritan ideas.[32]

New Testament scholars tend to cite these negative statements as normative for the time of Jesus. A number of commentators note for this parable, and even more frequently for John's story of the Samaritan woman at the well, that "the Jews" considered "Samaritan women menstruants from the cradle and so perpetually unclean."[33] The reference, which is usually not given, is the Mishnah, *Niddah* 4.1: "The daughters of the Samaritans are [deemed unclean as] menstruants from their cradle." Missing from the discussion, almost invariably, is citation of the next passage: "The daughters of the Sadducees, if they follow after the ways of their fathers, are deemed like to the women of the Samaritans" (*Niddah* 4.2). Thus the Mishnah cannot possibly reflect the view of "all Jews."

Because the Mishnah goes on to describe how Samaritan women do observe the laws of family purity—the Samaritan Pentateuch replicates the menstrual injunctions in the Hebrew text—the rabbis wonder how could they be unclean (Babylonian Talmud, *Niddah* 31b). Finally, a third rabbinic text, the Tosefta (lit. "Additions," a volume that adds to Mishnaic teaching) states: "A Samaritan is like a non-Jew, according to the opinion of Rabbi [i.e., Judah ha-Nasi, the codifier of the Mishnah]. Rabbi Shimeon ben Gamliel [his father] says, 'A Samaritan is like Israel in all respects.'"[34] Selective citation of rabbinic literature in service of making Jesus look better than "Judaism" is not a helpful exegetical procedure.

On the American Bible Society's website dedicated to understanding this parable, one commentator notes: "Some scholars have cited a rabbinic tradition that says that Jews who accept aid from a Samaritan will delay the redemption of Israel. If, then, the wounded traveler was Jewish, the story becomes an open attack on first-century Jewish theology and piety. It seems to point out the foolishness of tying Israel's redemption to such a bigoted idea."[35] No rabbinic reference is given, and the Bible Society never contests the point; for it, the idea of Jewish xenophobia was a given. I contacted the author to ask about the source. He responded, "I found the reference in E. Juengel, *Paulus and Jesus,* 3rd ed. (Tübingen, 1967), p. 174, but he never cited the rabbinic tradition and I could not find it elsewhere in the book."[36] Klyne Snodgrass solves the mystery of the citation. The claim is "based on the misuse of a late tradition in *b. Baba Batra* 10b and comments in Str-B 4/1, pp. 538 and 544."[37] Str-B is the abbreviation for Hermann L. Strack and Paul Billerbeck's 1922 *Kommentar zum Neuen Testament aus Talmud und Midrash,* a compendium of connections the authors saw between the New Testament and all of rabbinic literature.

There is one more level of our investigation about how this incorrect citation made its way into New Testament studies. It apparently entered through the work of Walter Grundmann,[38] the director of the Nazi program entitled Institute for the Study and Eradication of Jewish Influence on German Church Life (*Institut zur Erforschung und Beseitigung des jüdischen Einflusses auf das deutsche kirchliche Leben*).[39] Again, anti-Jewish material is repeated, because no one questions it.

Finally, with the rise of postcolonial and liberation-theological readings, negative stereotypes of Jewish-Samaritan relations coupled with negative stereotypes of Jewish purity laws combine. When biblical interpretation functions to enfranchise people, name systems of oppression, or inspire change for the better, this is all to the good. When, however, the means by which these concerns are facilitated include negative stereotyping, then the ends are compromised. For example, in his "'Dalit Theology' and the Parable of the Good Samaritan," M. Gnanavaram maps the Dalit (untouchable) onto the Samaritan, and the priest and the Levite correspond to the "high-cast non-Dalits." The Samaritan is the "outcast," although the only person cast out in the Gospel in relation to Samaritan issues is Jesus, who was refused lodging in a Samaritan village (Luke 9.53); the Samaritan is "oppressed," although according to the parable he has freedom of travel and economic resources.[40] Readers will need to determine if the end, the passionate call for liberation, justifies the means, if the means turn out to be a negative caricature of Jewish culture.

Finding the Better Intertext

Rather than understand the parable through negative stereotype, we do better to understand it as, in part, a resurrection of an earlier biblical incident. Along with the accounts of Dinah and Shechem in Genesis 34, Jotham and Abimelech in Judges 9, and the fate of the Northern Kingdom, there is another biblical account of Samaria, one that presents a different form of relationship. According to 2 Chronicles 28.8–15, the Samaritans—here identified as "the people of Israel"—captured two hundred thousand Judean "women, sons, and daughters; they also took much booty . . . to Samaria." A prophet named Oded then condemned the Samaritan army:

> Because the LORD, the God of your ancestors, was angry with
> Judah, he gave them into your hand, but you have killed them in a
> rage that has reached up to heaven. Now you intend to subjugate
> the people of Judah and Jerusalem, male and female, as your slaves.
> But what have you except sins against the LORD your God? Now
> hear me, and send back the captives whom you have taken from
> your kindred, for the fierce wrath of the LORD is upon you.

A number of the Samaritan leaders, chastened, agreed with the prophet. Their actions anticipate the imagery found in the parable of the Good Samaritan:

Then those who were mentioned by name got up and took the captives, and with the booty they clothed all that were naked among them; they clothed them, gave them sandals, provided them with food and drink, and anointed them; and carrying all the feeble among them on donkeys, they brought them to their kindred at Jericho, the city of palm trees. Then they returned to Samaria.[41]

The cycle of violence can be broken.

For the person in the ditch or the listener who identifies with him, 2 Chronicles 28 offers a necessary lesson. Those who want to kill you may be the only ones who will save you.

And upon the next day, taking out, he gave two denarii to
the innkeeper and said, "Take care of him, and whatever
you might spend, I, upon my return, will give back to you."
(Luke 10.35)

In 1980, British prime minister Margaret Thatcher claimed: "Nobody would remember the Good Samaritan if he had only good intentions. He had money as well."[42] Mrs. Thatcher overstates; the parable would still convey its basic message, had it stopped at the previous verse. Thus her comment at best serves to prompt another question: What does Luke 10.35 contribute to the parable?

First, the verse makes clear, despite numerous sermons to the contrary, that the Samaritan is not a social victim. He has money, freedom of travel, the ability to find lodging (more than what Jesus found in the Samaritan village), and some leverage with the innkeeper. The parable, in its original setting, is not about the type of prejudice that creates people on the margins; it is about hatred between groups who have similar resources.

Second, a benevolent reading of the Samaritan's final actions understands him as providing not one-time aid, but long-term care. Thus the sense of loving neighbor means continual action, not something to check off the to-do list. The Samaritan's offering the innkeeper what amounts to a blank check fits within Jesus's overall concern for generosity. Moreover, his trusting the innkeeper to care for the wounded man echoes the trust the wounded man had to have had in him. By trusting the innkeeper, he provides confirmatory evidence that we make our neighbors; that trust is essential for life.[43]

More cynical interpreters, aware of how Jesus's Jewish audience likely felt about this Samaritan hero, might see an ominous implication in the Samaritan's final actions. The Samaritan promises to return, and should he be displeased with the innkeeper's ministrations, he will repay in kind. The Samaritan made the choice to care for the man in the ditch; the innkeeper's motives to continue the care—benevolence, financial incentive, fear of retaliation—go unspoken. In the long run, at least as far as the victim is concerned, they may not matter. Of ultimate import is not our motive, but our action.

The parable proper ends here. But Jesus is not done with the lawyer, and neither are we.

⁓

"Which of these three a neighbor—does it seem to you—was to the one who fell among the robbers?" And he said, "The one doing mercy for him." And said to him Jesus, "Go and you do likewise." **(Luke 10.36–37)**

The lawyer asked Jesus, "Who is my neighbor?" Jesus reframes the question. As Martin Luther King Jr. so eloquently revealed in his sermon, asking the right question is of utmost importance. The issue for Jesus is not the "who," but the "what," not the identity but the action. The lawyer is unable even to voice the hated name "Samaritan." He can only say, "The one doing mercy for him."

The parable spoke about compassion, but the lawyer read the action as one of mercy. His rephrasing the issue is apt: compassion can be felt in the gut; mercy needs to be enacted with the body. The term may come from Luke, who uses it extensively, but only in the infancy materials, where mercy is an attribute of the divine: "His mercy is for those who fear him" (1.50); "He has helped his servant Israel, in remembrance of his mercy" (1.54); "Her neighbors and relatives heard that the Lord had shown his great mercy to her" (1.58); "Thus he has shown the mercy promised to our ancestors" (1.72) and, finally, "by the tender mercy of our God, the dawn from on high will break upon us" (1.78).

For the lawyer, and for Luke's readers, the Samaritan does what God does. The divine is manifested only through our actions. Therefore, Jesus responds to the lawyer's observation not with a question and not with a parable, but with an imperative: "Go," he says, "and you do likewise." To speak of loving God and loving neighbor does not require theological precision; it does not ask for a particular location of worship (Gerizim, Jerusalem, Mecca, the Ganges, or Ssogoréate . . .); it does not speak to a particular book (the Torah, the Samaritan Pentateuch, the Christian Bible, the Qur'an, or the Book of Mormon . . .). Loving God and loving neighbor cannot exist in the abstract; they need to be enacted.

We do not know what the lawyer did following this parable. Nor do we know if the parable was actually spoken to a lawyer, or if Luke has provided both the opening and closing frame. All we can know is what we, upon hearing this parable in its narrative frame, will do.

The Parable in Today's World

For a final sense of the profundity of the parable, we need only look from ancient texts to present contexts. The parable of the Good Samaritan is one of the few that makes an almost perfect translation to today's situation.

Samaria today has various names: the West Bank, Occupied Palestine, Greater Israel. To hear the parable today, we only need to update the identity of the figures. I am an Israeli Jew on my way from Jerusalem to Jericho, and I am attacked by thieves, beaten, stripped, robbed, and left half dead in a ditch. Two people who should have stopped to help pass me by: the first, a Jewish medic from the Israel Defense Forces; the second, a member of the Israel/Palestine Mission Network of the Presbyterian Church U.S.A. But the person who takes compassion on me and shows me mercy is a Palestinian Muslim whose sympathies lie with Hamas, a political party whose charter not only anticipates Israel's destruction, but also depicts Jews as subhuman demons responsible for all the world's problems.

The parable of the "Good Hamas Member" might be difficult for people in support of Israel's existence. Were Jesus a Samaritan, we'd today have the parable of the "Good Jew," told in the streets of Ramallah. If people in the Middle East could picture this, we might have a better vision for choosing life.

Can we finally agree that it is better to acknowledge the humanity and the potential to do good in the enemy, rather than to choose death? Will we be able to care for our enemies, who are also our neighbors? Will we be able to bind up their wounds rather than blow up their cities? And can we imagine that they might do the same for us? Can we put into practice that inauguration promise of not leaving the wounded traveler on the road? The biblical text—and concern for humanity's future—tell us we must.

CHAPTER 3

The Kingdom of Heaven Is like Yeast

> Similar to the kingdom of heaven is leaven that a woman, taking, hid in three measures of flour until was leavened all.
>
> **Matthew 13.33**

Of all the parables, this one received the highest number of "red" votes from the Jesus Seminar, a gathering of scholars who seek "to renew the quest of the historical Jesus and to report the results of its research to the general public, rather than just to a handful of gospel specialists. Initially, the goal of the Seminar was to review each of the sayings and deeds attributed to Jesus in the gospels and determine which of them could be considered authentic."[1] According to the seminar's website:

> Like the mustard seed, the parable of the leaven makes light of an established symbol. Leaven was customarily regarded as a symbol for corruption and evil. Jesus here employs it in a positive sense. That makes his use of the image striking and provocative. . . . To compare God's imperial rule to leaven is to compare it to something corrupt and unholy, just the opposite of what God's rule is supposed to be. This reversal appears to be characteristic of several of Jesus's sayings, such as "The last will be first and the first last." The Fellows included the parable of the leaven in that small

group of sayings and parables that almost certainly originated
with Jesus.[2]

The seminar's goal of determining what Jesus said is a worthy one; its concern to locate Jesus in his own historical context is similarly worthy. However, it is also essential to study that historical context, and here all the good
intention in the world cannot compensate for indigestible results. When
heard in its own context, the parable of the Leaven can be subversive, but
what it subverts is not the image of the holy.

The Leaven should get a rise out of its hearers, but in order to experience
this, we need to clean our palates of both the bland, white-bread interpretations and the toxic ones as well.

Initial Crumbs, Both Tasty and Not

Most interpretations of the parable of the Leaven, like interpretations of
most parables, are obvious and uninteresting. For this parable, we hear comments such as: "Out of the most insignificant beginnings, invisible to human
eye, God creates his mighty Kingdom, which embraces all the peoples of the
world";[3] or "As yeast works to leaven the dough, so the growth of the kingdom is inevitable"; or "Just as few converts, like yeast, can work to convert
the entire population"; or "God's rule, like yeast, working in a hidden way,
will pervade one's life, giving it a new quality."

We do not need a parable to tell us that the divine kingdom is "mighty,"
and there are better ways of assuring us that the kingdom will come. Leaven
is not, in fact, "invisible"; leaven in antiquity is what we today call sourdough
starter. Nor is it insignificant—it is essential for baking. The idea of the
leavened dough as embracing all peoples creates for me a mixed metaphor in
which I picture Strega Nona's spaghetti pot overflowing into the streets and
choking the population. The idea of the divine rule as permeating one's life is
good, albeit with an individualistic focus that runs contrary to the concerns
of Jesus as best as they can be determined, given his interest in community.
Nor does the reading give any sense of either what this internal rule is or
how it manifests itself. If the parable says that "acknowledging God means

you'll be a better person," again, the point may be true, but it is by no means shocking.

Although the various allegorical moves—the dough represents the entire world; the dough represents the individual—are all plausible, none is compelling. Such interpretations leave little to chew on or to savor. Rather than catch in the throat—a matter that really is something of life and death—bland interpretations slide easily down the gullet and pass quickly through the body.

Such white-bread servings can already be made tastier by attention to how else bread functions in Jesus's teachings. "Give us this day our daily bread," the phrase from the Lord's Prayer or the "Our Father" (Matt. 6.11; cf. Luke 11.3), speaks to several Jewish concerns, from the view that as God fed us in the wilderness with manna (Exod. 16; Num. 11; Deut. 8), so God will continue to provide for our needs, to the image of the world to come as a giant banquet, in which "people will come from east and west, from north and south, and will eat in the kingdom of God" (Luke 13.29; cf. Matt. 8.11). The term translated "daily," Greek *epiousion,* has a connotation of "for tomorrow" or "for the future," and that complements the idea of the eschatological or heavenly banquet.

This Jewish idea of feasting in the world to come permeates the stories of Jesus, and permeates his own mission as well. Luke's story of Jesus opens with his being placed in a "manger," that is, a feeding trough. What more delicious symbolism could there be for the person who would compare his body to bread? Jesus feeds thousands, in recollection of how the ancient prophets Elijah and Elisha provided food and in both an anticipation of and a present enactment of the kingdom of heaven.

Jesus consistently meets people at table, dines indiscriminately, is continually associated with food—imagery made most memorable at the Last Supper. He tells a desperate gentile mother who is seeking a healing for her daughter, "Let the children be fed first, for it is not fair to take the children's food [i.e., his healing ministry] and throw it to the dogs," but she convinces him to act by cleverly reheating his words: "Sir, even the dogs under the table eat the children's crumbs" (Mark 7.27–28; cf. Matt. 15.26–27).

Paul, who wrote his letters before the evangelists produced their Gospels, describes the institution of the Eucharist:

> For I received from the Lord what I also handed on to you, that
> the Lord Jesus on the night when he was betrayed took a loaf of
> bread, and when he had given thanks, he broke it and said, "This
> is my body that is for you. Do this in remembrance of me." In the
> same way he took the cup also, after supper, saying, "This cup is
> the new covenant in my blood. Do this, as often as you drink it, in
> remembrance of me." (1 Cor. 11.23–25)

By the time we get to John's Gospel, Jesus has become the "bread of life" (6.35) and "the living bread that came down from heaven" (6.51).

Any parable with a reference to leaven, dough, or bread brings with it all this appetizing accompaniment, and it makes the parable much more nourishing. There is thus necessarily more going on in the parable than a lesson on "the growth of the kingdom."

The plain and palatable are, however, better than the indigestible or poisonous. Some pastors or homilists still drag out the standard view that whatever Jesus said must somehow relate to how morbid or moribund his early Jewish context had become. Thus we still hear comments like: "The yeast is mightily permeating the dead lump of religious Judaism,"[4] or "The Kingdom arrives as a negation of the established temple and cult and replaces them with a sacrament of its own—a new and leavened bread."[5] According to the founder of the Jesus Seminar, Robert Funk, the parable shows how Jesus wielded his "herculean wrecking bar" in order to "precipitate the loss of the perceived world of Judaism. . . . The world in which the scribes and Pharisees were at home was shattered upon a new world designed for the poor and destitute, the tax collectors and sinners. The righteousness of the Pharisees was devalued as confederate paper."[6]

Matthew, in whose Gospel our parable appears and who insists that the righteousness of the followers of Jesus must "exceed" that of the scribes and Pharisees (5.20), would have found this an odd comment. So would Jesus's initial followers—all Jews living a Jewish life in a Jewish world. So would other Jews, who blessed, broke, and ate leavened bread, their daily bread.[7] Interpretations that insist on constructing a pervasive, official Judaism that establishes categories of the "religiously disinherited" and that is antithetical to "the destitute, the maimed and the blind,"[8] may seem tasty at first—but they poison the food and therefore poison the recipient.

To appreciate the parable, we must attend to the elements, such as the cultural understanding of yeast and the amount of bread that three measures of flour would yield. We need to recognize how the parable draws upon images from the scriptures of Israel as well as how it matches flavors with the numerous references to bread in the Gospels themselves. We need to correct the translations that have the woman "mixing" the yeast into the dough, because that is *not* what the Greek says. And we do well to see what the combined imagery of women and dough, hiding and ovens would have suggested to people living in the first century.

Yeast

The term for "yeast" (Gk. *zume*) refers to sourdough starter and not to those little red packets of cultured yeast that sit in refrigerator doors. This starter is created when water mixes with the naturally occurring yeast spores that end up in flour when it is ground, and then the yeast's enzymes break down the starch in the flour and convert it into glucose; the starter serves as the leavening agent when it is subsequently mixed in with more dough. Anyone who has ever made starter can watch the decomposition process. Recipes instruct bakers to place the starter in a bowl, cover the bowl with a dishcloth, and let the mixture sit in a warm, breezeless place, such as a dark oven. As the mixture sits, the fermentation process takes place. The starter is ready when what the recipe books call a "pleasant sour smell" develops and the mixture has bubbles.

Granted, I come from a long line of women whose skills were never well displayed in the kitchen; my mother was a mediocre cook, and I am a domestic disaster. Nevertheless, the idea of sour smell combined with a bubbly mixture created by the process of fermentation—that is, enzyme decay— does not immediately strike me as palatable. To the contrary, there's an "ick" factor at play. The process, with its possible negative connotations, was already known in antiquity. Plutarch mentions that yeast is the "product of corruption" and that "the process of leavening seems to be one of putrefaction."[9] Whereas *zume* is required to produce bread, and there are few things more appealing than the aroma and taste of freshly baked bread, the starter is utilitarian at best.

This brief foray into the culinary arts complements the view of yeast that we find in Jesus's cultural (pun intended) world. The comparison of the kingdom to yeast might well have been surprising to a first-century Jewish audience, since yeast, especially when used metaphorically, could have a negative valence. Metaphorically speaking, there is good yeast and there is bad yeast, and Jesus appears to have used the metaphor in its negative sense.

One need not be a Bible scholar or an expert in Greek to recognize this fact; all one needs is a concordance. In addition to appearances in Matthew 13.33 and Luke 13.21, the term "yeast" or "leaven" shows up eleven times in the New Testament, and each occasion hints of something whose taste is a bit off. Following the scene traditionally known as the Feeding of the Four Thousand (Matt. 15.32–38; the title is a demographic understatement, given that "those who had eaten were four thousand *men,* besides women and children"), Jesus and the disciples cross the Sea of Galilee into a region called Magadan. The disciples, who are not the sharpest knives in the drawer, realize that they had forgotten to bring any bread. This should not have worried them, as Jesus has amply demonstrated, twice, providing food is not a problem.

Picking up on their worry, Jesus turns the conversation into a metaphoric warning: "Watch out, and beware of the yeast of the Pharisees and Sadducees" (Matt. 16.6; see also Mark 8.15; Luke 12.1). The disciples consistently misinterpret his comment; they think he is annoyed because they had forgotten to bring bread. Many things annoy Jesus—hypocrisy, injustice, lack of concern for the poor, failure to love God and neighbor. Forgetting a snack does not make his top-ten list.

Moreover, at least as far as Matthew is concerned, Jesus is capable of fasting for forty days (4.2). Immediately after the baptism, the Spirit leads Jesus to the desert, where Satan tempts him. It is during this "temptation" that the imagery of bread first appears in the Gospel. Satan cajoles the starving Jesus, "If you are the Son of God, command these stones to become loaves of bread." Jesus responds by quoting Deuteronomy 8.3: "One does not live by bread alone, but by every word that comes from the mouth of God" (Matt. 4.4). With this comment he does not dismiss the importance of bread, for hungry people must be fed. Rather, he makes clear that his focus is not only on bread, but also on the divine word. The same chapter of Deuteronomy from which Jesus quotes makes the point: "Therefore keep the commandments of the LORD your God, by walking in his ways and by fearing him. For the LORD your God is bringing you into a good land ... where you may eat bread without scarcity" (8.6–9). Matthew, likely coming from a Jewish context, may well have anticipated that readers would bring knowledge of the rest of the chapter to bear on their understanding of Jesus's response.

The disciples in Matthew are not thinking about Deuteronomy, Jesus's miracles, or even the use of metaphor; they are thinking with their stomachs. Jesus rebukes them by accusing them of having "little faith" and then by reminding them about the feedings of the multitudes. Finally, exasperated, he asks, "How could you fail to perceive that I was not speaking about bread? Beware of the yeast of the Pharisees and Sadducees!" (16.9–11). "*Then*," says Matthew, the disciples realize that Jesus was not talking about "the yeast of bread," but about the teachings of his opponents.

This use of leaven to suggest something negative, such as misleading teaching, bubbles up in Paul's language as well. In 1 Corinthians 5.6–8, Paul uses the metaphor of "yeast" to describe the negative effects of boasting; such displays of self-importance in the community can ferment and so lead to a breakdown in the communal body. Paul complains, "Your boasting is not a good thing. Do you not know that a little yeast leavens the whole batch of dough?" (see also Gal. 5.9, where Paul uses the same metaphor to describe the ill effects on the congregation of a competing gospel). The modern analogy would be, "One bad apple spoils the whole bunch."

Paul then develops the metaphor by appealing to the association of the holiday of Passover with unleavened bread. The image, from the book of Exodus, is a Jewish one, but those gentile followers of Jesus to whom Paul writes would have known it; the Septuagint (LXX), the Greek translation of the scriptures of Israel, was their Bible as well. He tells his congregation, "Clean out the old yeast so that you may be a new batch, as you really are unleavened. For our paschal lamb, Christ, has been sacrificed" (1 Cor. 5.7). With one sentence, he manages to reinforce the negative connotations of yeast, associate Jesus with the paschal offering that saves from death, and associate the congregation with *matzoh,* unleavened bread, which the Israelites ate during the exodus and which Jews to this day traditionally eat instead of leavened bread on the eight days of Passover. Paul reinforces the negative connotations of leaven with his concluding sentence, "Therefore, let us celebrate the festival, not with the old yeast, the yeast of malice and evil, but with the unleavened bread of sincerity and truth" (5.8).

The term "yeast," used metaphorically in the New Testament, has a negative connotation. Yet at least in the Gospels, it is *particular* leaven that is the problem. The leaven "of the Pharisees" is to be avoided, but not the leaven that Jesus offers. This distinction between different forms of leaven appears in patristic treatment. In his *Epistle to the Magnesians,* the early second-century bishop of Antioch, Ignatius, alludes to Paul's metaphor: "Put aside then the evil leaven, which has grown old and sour, and turn to the new leaven, which is Jesus Christ. Be salted in him, that none among you may be corrupted, since by your savor you shall be tested." Ignatius then, anticipating the indigestible anti-Jewish readings of the parable, concludes, "It is monstrous to talk of Jesus Christ and to practice Judaism."[10] There is no milk of magnesians to coat this metaphor.

Picking up Ignatius's crummy conclusion, some biblical scholars further misconstrue leaven's metaphorical register by associating it with the category "impurity"; they then extend the misconstrual by associating it with various forms of moral corruption. Even more problematic, they go on to equate moral corruption with patterns of first-century Jewish life or with Jewish views of holiness. For example, Robert Funk proposes that "the Kingdom comes as an inversion of what everybody takes to be the case with the sacred" and concludes that the parable could signal the entry of "tax collectors and harlots," but not Pharisees, into the kingdom.[11] I'm not seeing much of a "last shall be first and first shall be last" in the parable; "all leavened" means exactly that: all is leavened. There's no division in this story, and there's no need to import into it questions of sacrality.

Extending this (unnecessary) connection between leaven and corruption, another commentator proposes that "the parable opposes traditional understandings of the holiness and purity of the people of God" and "a 'corrupting' of the people of God through the inclusion of outcasts."[12] This study, published in 1988, is now available online at a website designed to promote the role of women in Roman Catholic settings.[13] The ends (a concern for women's inclusion) do not justify the means (an ahistorical reading of the parable by presenting Judaism as a system creating "outcasts"). In like manner, a homiletics professor proposes in an essay on preaching the parable, "The presence of a 'contaminating' element fundamental to the reign of God might serves as an illustration of Jesus's welcome of the outcast."[14] The parable has much to commend it, but it says nothing about "outcasts." Even Paul, who does want to bar people from his churches (the very same letter in which Paul uses the metaphor of leaven exhorts, "But now I am writing to you not to associate with anyone who bears the name of brother or sister who is sexually immoral or greedy, or is an idolater, reviler, drunkard, or robber. Do not even eat with such a one" [1 Cor. 5.11]), does not associate leaven with casting out *people*.

Similarly, Jesus Seminar scholar Bernard Brandon Scott connects both the woman and the yeast to impurity; he notes, correctly, that although "it is not true to say that in general women were viewed as unclean and men clean, it is true that in religion, especially purity codes, women were at a disadvantage."[15] He then concludes that the yeast represents "moral corruption" and that Jesus deconstructs the purity codes: "All those who were unable for one reason or another to observe the purity code would be leaven and that would be most folks."[16] In like manner, Barbara Reid finds that the parable "proclaims that God's realm thoroughly incorporates persons who would have been considered corrupt, unclean, or sinners according to the prevailing interpretations of the Jewish purity regulations" and finally concludes that the parable disrupts the xenophobia of "Jewish Christians," because it implies the mixing of gentiles into the dough of the church.[17] Suddenly the parable has become a countercultural manifesto designed to subvert a negatively stereotyped Judaism that creates outcasts of pretty much everyone.

Contributing to this unpalatable approach is the frequent narrow reading of the scriptures of Israel and rabbinic texts. One scholar insists, "Leaven in the Bible, without exception, is used as a symbol of corruption by unclean or sinful things. . . . Throughout the Hebrew scriptures, leaven is a symbol of the unholy, indeed, of the ungodly!"[18] The inevitable conclusion is: "Leaven is a symbol of sin, of evil, of rank unbelievers," and the parable has to do with the "exclusion of the impure from God's anticipated kingdom in first-century religious thought."[19] Who knew?

Problems here proliferate. First, the parable says *nothing* about purity, outcasts, or gentiles. Leaven is not itself "impure"; if it were, Jews would not have had to remove it from their homes at Passover, because they would not have used it in the first place. Throughout the scriptures of Israel, "leaven" is used primarily to speak of the products that need to be removed during the Passover holiday. The commandment, "You shall remove leaven from your houses" (Exod. 12.15) indicates that other than the week of Passover, leaven is a staple product. One does not enjoin the removal of something that is not present.

If yeast were impure, bread would be too; that very point should demonstrate why purity is the wrong category. The Temple, the ultimate place of purity, is also the place where *leavened* bread serves as an offering to God. Leviticus 7.13 provides the following instruction for the "thanksgiving sacrifice of well-being": "You shall bring your offering with cakes of leavened bread" (Heb. *chometz;* Gk. *artois zumitais*). Amos 4.5 speaks similarly of the "thank offering of leavened bread." The positive valence of the term "flour" confirms the positive view of the (leavened) bread; "flour" is used most often in the Bible in relation to Temple offerings.

As a modern analogy, I doubt that Jews who recite the traditional grace before meals, "Blessed are you, O Lord our God, sovereign of the universe, *who brings forth bread from the earth* (*ha-motzi lechem min ha'aretz*)," are associating leavened bread with the unholy or the ungodly.

Finally, Leviticus 23.17, in setting out instructions for offerings to God, states: "You shall bring from your settlements two loaves of bread as an elevation offering, each made of two-tenths of an ephah; they shall be of choice flour, baked with leaven (*zumoo*), as first fruits to the LORD." The holiday for which these instructions serve is the spring harvest festival, known as *Shavuot* ("Weeks") in Hebrew; for the Jewish community, the holiday commemorates the receiving of the Torah on Mt. Sinai. The church baptizes this holiday into the celebration of Pentecost, the time it proclaims that the Holy Spirit descended on Jesus's followers (see Acts 2).

Yeast is not impure or "unclean"; neither is mustard seed, the principle image in the parable that both Matthew (13.31–32) and Luke (13.18–19) juxtapose to this parable.[20] Jesus is comparing the kingdom to leaven that a woman used in preparing bread; he is not saying, "The kingdom of heaven is like a piece of bacon or road kill." Indeed, the image of "leaven" or "yeast" in the literature at the time of Jesus spanned the positive to the negative.[21] The first-century Jewish philosopher Philo remarks that leaven functions symbolically in two ways: "Leaven . . . stands for food in its most complete and perfect form, such that in our daily usage none is found to be superior or more nourishing" and "everything that is leavened rises, and joy is the rational elevation of the soul."[22] Also giving leaven positive connotations, Rabbi Jehoshua ben Levi said: "Great is peace, for it is as the leaven to dough. If the Holy One had not given peace to the world, sword and beast would devour up the whole world, as it is written, 'And I will give peace in the land'" (*Derekh Eretz Zuta;* the biblical citation is Lev. 26.6). Moving toward the negative image is Rabbi Abahu's reflection that God took responsibility for human evil: "It was I that put the bad leaven in the dough, for 'the inclination of a person's heart is evil from his youth'" (*Tanhuma Noah* 4; the comment is a gloss on Gen. 8.21). Thus, there is no reason why any reader in antiquity would equate the term with impurity; whether the term is positive or negative needs to derive from context.

Next, as far as women's impurity goes, the commentators overstate (at best). Given the late onset of menstruation, the early onset of menopause, frequent pregnancies, and the likely cessation of the menstrual cycle during lactation, it may well have been the case that men—who are impure after ejaculation—were more often impure than women. Somehow, this point never finds its way into sermons. I similarly doubt that most Jewish women who gave birth or men who ejaculated thought to themselves, "Damn. I'm in a state of ritual impurity."

Most damning to this view of yeast as suggesting impurity is the fact that there is no historical basis for the claim that Judaism made outcasts of people who did not observe the purity laws or the related claim that the purity laws themselves were an impossible burden on the poor. Archaeological investigation of the Galilee shows numerous *miqvaot* (ritual bathing pools); stone vessels, which do not convey impurity; Sabbath lamps; and an absence of pig bones. Jesus and his fellow Jews observed the purity laws; it was easy for them to do so, both because of what was available in their environment and what was not. The same point holds for Jews throughout the centuries who to this day continue these observances.

Jesus did not do away with purity laws, and neither did his immediate followers. There would be no reason for them to do so within a Jewish environment. Purity practices are not a form of social marginalizing. To the contrary, they are a recognition of the boundaries between the sacred and the profane, then as now. Going to the Temple should not be the same thing as going to the market. Attending to the birth of a child or the burial of a corpse should not be followed immediately by a return to the world of business as usual, but should require taking the time to recognize the power of life and death. By engaging in distinctive practices concerning diet and immersion, Jews recognize the importance of the body. For those early Jews, the practices not only manifested their participation in the covenant; they also affirmed their identity as Jews within the wider Roman Empire. We might think of purity concerns as an ancient form of what we today call "multiculturalism" or "identity formation." As soon as "purity" gets on the menu of certain forms of New Testament exegesis, the taste is predictably a bad one, and the food is again spoiled.

Although it is correct to claim that the connection between yeast and the kingdom might be unexpected, especially given its uses in the New Testament, it is too much to conclude, as others have done, that "the very beginning of the parable with the simple word 'leaven' would throw an audience off guard and maybe into a panic,"[23] or that in thinking of yeast we might think of the swelling of a "decomposing corpse,"[24] given an association with fermentation or even a cancerous breast tumor.[25]

Hearing that the Romans are invading would cause the people to panic. I doubt that same reaction would be prompted by a metaphor, especially when that metaphor is couched in all sorts of positive images, such as women baking and three measures of flour. Cursing the name of the divine is blasphemous; claiming there is more than one God is blasphemous; eating a bagel made with yeast is not (although eating a bagel with mayonnaise comes close). A decomposing corpse would be a major source of impurity, but Jews surely can tell the difference between a cadaver and a crumpet. In thinking of fermentation, I am more inclined to associate yeast with beer making or more broadly with fermentation of grapes into wine. A malignant tumor is a tragedy, but it has nothing to do with fermentation, yeast, bread, or Jewish purity laws. Finally, the parable has nothing to do with the Temple, an institution in which leavened bread—showbread—was part of the daily offering. In like manner, the yeasty hot-cross buns sold at the church bazaar every Easter are not attacks on the Eucharist or the Roman Catholic Church.

Yeast *need not* have a negative connotation, but it *might* have one. If the Pharisees and opposing teachers have a bad form of leaven that taints whatever it touches with hypocrisy or incorrect doctrine, then the leaven Jesus provides would have the opposite effect: it permeates "all" the good dough it has infused and gives rise to something nutritious. For our parable then, the image of leaven requires at least an initial assessment: Is this good leaven or bad? Is something bad being turned into something good, or do we pay attention to the potential of its power, for good or ill? The symbolism, at least initially, is indeterminate.

The Woman and What She Did

Jesus tells parables with female characters: an importuning widow, a woman who loses and finds her coin, five wise and five not so wise virgins awaiting a bridegroom. There is nothing surprising about women appearing in stories—they've been doing so since, well, Eve (or, if you prefer, Tiamat, Isis, Astarte, or Gaia). As long as there have been women, there have been stories told about and by them.

Women, and feminine images in general, have been connected with the sacred: Woman Wisdom of Proverbs and the Wisdom of Solomon; the Shekhina, the feminine presence of the divine; the prophets Miriam, Deborah, Huldah, and their sisters, including Philip's four virgin daughters; and so on. Given the numerous positive women figures in early Judaism, the idea that the kingdom of heaven can be compared to a woman who bakes is no more shocking than the idea that it can be compared to a fellow who plants seed or a fellow who seeks a lost lamb.

In the biblical tradition, women have also been connected with the not so sacred, from Ben Sirach's assertion, "From a woman sin had its beginning, and because of her we all die" (25.24), to the Whore of Babylon in the book of Revelation. Thus we cannot, simply from the reference to the woman in the parable, tell anything about her status. Given that she is engaged in something relative to the kingdom of heaven, we are justified in seeing what she does in a positive light.

The extent to which we focus on the woman herself is up for debate. One could make the argument that it is not the woman who is the focus, but the leaven: "Similar to the kingdom of heaven is *leaven* that a woman . . . hid." But I would not want to dismiss the woman as the main actor.[26] Her presence is accentuated in the version of this parable presented by the *Gospel of Thomas*. This collection of sayings, which looks much like the hypothetical

Q source, is preserved not in Greek or even Aramaic, but in Coptic. In this version, "Jesus said, 'The Father's imperial rule is like [a] woman who took a little leaven, [hid] it in dough, and made it into large loaves of bread. Anyone here with two ears had better listen!" (*Thomas* 96).[27]

Thomas compares the kingdom not directly to the yeast, but to the woman who took the yeast. Had Matthew's parable read, "The kingdom of heaven is like a woman who hid yeast in dough," perhaps we'd find stained-glass windows of female chefs in many churches to go along with the windows of Jesus the sower, Jesus the Good Shepherd, and Jesus the bridegroom.[28] Then again, there are very few stained-glass windows of women seeking lost coins, despite the fact that the windows portray the shepherd seeking his sheep as Jesus and the one who welcomes the prodigal as God the Father.

The greater problem with the parable is not the woman, but what she does. According to most major English translations, the woman "mixed" the yeast with three measures of flour. The problem is that the Greek does not say "mixed." The Greek term is *enkrypto,* which comes from a root meaning "hide," as in cryptology, or secret-code making, or, to be closest to the Greek, "encryption." Thus, she is literally doing something secretly with an ambivalent or multivalent substance that works by processes of decay.

Whereas the parable of the Leaven is the only place in the New Testament where this verb is found, the cognate verb *krypto*—that is, the verb without the prefix—is common. In many cases, it refers not only to something that is hidden, but to something that should or must be uncovered. In Luke 8.17 (Mark 4.22), Jesus insists, "Nothing is hidden that will not be disclosed, nor is anything secret that will not become known and come to light." In the Sermon on the Mount, Jesus tells his disciples, "You are the light of the world. A city built on a hill cannot be hid" (Matt. 5.14). Whether the Gospel of John sought to correct this association of the disciples with light or to complement it by having Jesus claim, twice (John 8.12; 9.5), that *he* is the light of the world, remains an open question. In either case, again, what is hidden must be made manifest.

Matthew reinforces the idea that what is hidden is something precious that belongs to Jesus and his followers by depicting Jesus as thanking God for having "hidden" information about Jesus himself as well as the final judgment from "the wise and intelligent," but revealing it to "infants," that is, the trusting church (11.25). Two chapters later, just a few verses after the

Leaven parable, Matthew explains that Jesus spoke in parables "to fulfill what had been spoken through the prophet"; Jesus says, "I will open my mouth to speak in parables; I will proclaim what has been hidden from the foundation of the world" (13.35). The reference is to Psalm 78.2, which in the Hebrew reads, "I will open my mouth in a parable (*mashal*); I will utter riddles (*chidot*) from ancient times." The Septuagint (Psalm 77.2) provides a different version, which appears to underlie Matthew's quote: "I will open my mouth in parables; I will utter riddles (*problemata* [whence "problems"]) from the beginning." The citation is more likely Matthew's conclusion than Jesus's own self-description, but it does fit the general view that Jesus revealed mysteries previously unknown or at least unarticulated.

The term "to hide" appears in Luke 18.34 and 19.42 in reference to the truth of Jesus that was, temporarily, unavailable to those who encountered him. Colossians 3.3 proclaims that the lives of Jesus's followers are currently "hidden with Christ in God," but will be revealed when Jesus is made manifest. According to 1 Timothy 5.25, "Good works are conspicuous; and even when they are not, they cannot remain hidden."

Whatever that woman is doing, its results will come to light. What is hidden is only hidden so that it can be brought forth, and in that revelation the original is somehow transformed: the infants gain special knowledge; the disciples, new insight; the faithful, a new way of being; the world, more good works than it had ever known. "Hiding," like "yeast," can have a negative valence, but in this parable it is a hiding that will lead to something wonderful.

This hiding, together with images of three measures of flour and of a woman baking, should send readers to the scriptures of Israel. Like hiding a baby Jesus in a king cake for Mardi Gras, so the parable hides in its words an allusion to an ancient narrative.

Three Measures of Flour

Three measures, in first-century terms, is not synonymous with three cups. Three measures of flour is somewhere between forty and sixty pounds. The dough would be far too much for one woman to knead on her own, and the yield would be far too much for one person to consume. The image is one of extravagance, or hyperbole. We might be reminded of many other New Testament images of food in abundance, from the wedding at Cana, with its sixty gallons of good wine (John 2.1–11), to the feeding of the five thousand, in which five loaves and two fish yielded twelve basketfuls of leftovers (e.g., Matt. 14–20).

We should also be reminded of the places in the scriptures of Israel where the phrase "three measures of flour" as well as cognate references appear. Genesis 18 locates Abraham sitting at the entrance to his tent "in the heat of the day." He's hot, he's had to deal with the difficult relationship between his first wife, Sarah, and his other wife, Sarah's slave Hagar, and he's just completed not only his own circumcision, but also that of every male member in his household. It's been a long week. Suddenly, Abraham looks up and sees "three men standing near him." In classical Christian tradition, the three men represent the Trinity; in Jewish thought, they are God and two angels; for secular biblical scholars, the event probably never actually happened, but the story is of import.

Abraham, displaying the hospitality for which he will become famous, runs from his tent, prostrates himself before the strangers, and invites them to lunch. "Let me bring a little bread," he tells them. Then he tells his wife, "Make ready quickly three measures of choice flour (Heb. *kemach solet;* Gk. *semidalis*), knead it, and make cakes" (Gen. 18.6). A *little* bread from three measures? Were my husband to run out into the street, invite three strangers to lunch, and then tell me to make sixty dozen biscuits, at least one of us would need counseling. Then again, given my culinary inabilities, he never would make such a request.

Not only do the three measures make a connection to our parable; so does the term for the "cakes." The Hebrew term for "cake" is *ugot,* and there is nothing unusual about it. But the Septuagint translates the Hebrew as *enkrypsias.* The term, which refers to a cake that is baked on hot stones, is a cognate of our own *enkrypto,* save that instead of the Greek letter *pi* it uses the letter *psi.* The two words come from the same root. The connection between the parable and the passage from Genesis is secure.[29]

What the connection means, however, is another matter. The three visitors inform Abraham that his wife Sarah, who is well past menopause, will have a son. Sarah, overhearing the message, laughs to herself and thinks, "After I have grown old, and my husband is old, shall I have pleasure"—despite centuries of modest interpretation that insists she is anticipating the joy of having a long-awaited child, Sarah is thinking of sexual pleasure. The term in Hebrew for "pleasure," *edna,* is a cognate of the word Eden (the verse in question is Gen. 18.12, for which the best mnemonic device is to recall Tchaikovsky's *1812 Overture,* in which the cannons go off and the earth moves).

Other possible references to "three measures of flour"—whether implicit or explicit—are less nourishing as intertexts, but they may also be used to garnish the parable. For example, a second possible but remote allusion appears in 1 Samuel 1.24. Here Hannah, who had finally conceived and given birth to Samuel, the son for whom she prayed, is prepared to dedicate her child to divine service. "When she had weaned him, she took him up with her, along with a three-year-old bull, an ephah of flour, and a skin of wine. She brought him to the house of the LORD at Shiloh." An *ephah,* as biblical scholars usually note, is the equivalent of three "measures" (Heb. *se'ah*). Here the connection to our parable is through the combined mentions of the amount, the flour, and the woman. That the pericope is also about childbirth may, as we shall see, also have some bearing on how we see the parable functioning.

Another, more remote connection can be located in Judges 6. In this account, Gideon prepares a meal that includes not only a calf (recollecting the menu of Abraham's meal in Gen. 18.7), but also an *ephah* of flour. However, Gideon's cakes are unleavened; he did not have the time to allow the dough to rise. The context concerns Israel's security against the larger, more powerful Midianite forces; the consuming of the meat and bread by a supernatural fire functions as a sign to Gideon that he will be able to deliver Israel, despite the fact that, as he states, "My clan is the weakest in Manasseh, and I am the least in my family" (6.15). The connection to the parable here is the theme of a small beginning yielding a major result.

We can now return to the parable, for now we have enough information to chew on.

Tasty Morsels

Might the message be that we should reevaluate the meanest of domestic materials, that what we see as negative or simply utilitarian may have spiritual potential? The kingdom can be associated with pearls, but also with yeast, with banquets, but also with mustard seeds, with kings, but also with shepherds.

Or perhaps the parable might inspire us to think of the women in antiquity, who did much of the baking.[30] If we think of leavened bread, we should also think of the people who maintained the sourdough starter, kneaded the bread, and watched it while it baked to be sure it did not burn.

To extend this possibility, perhaps the parable has something to do more specifically with women's bodies. Back during the time of Homer, women's bodies were analogized to the ground. Granted, the image of being plowed is not a pleasant one, but at least the view prevailed that women's bodies, like the earth, nurtured the seed planted in them. By the time of Jesus, the imagery had changed. Women's bodies now were compared to ovens, as in that charming expression still heard today, "She's got a bun in the oven." Ovens do not provide nutrients; they do not nurture; they are simply incubators.

And yet Genesis 18, underlying the parable of the Leaven, is a story about an unexpected, miraculous, mysterious pregnancy.[31] The idea of hiding yeast and of the dough rising on its own can suggest insemination and then pregnancy. The idea that this parable hides an image of pregnancy and parturition is not just a feminist fantasy; it is supported as well by the common metaphor that associates pregnancy and childbirth with the messianic age. Second Esdras 4.39–40, in answer to the question about when the final judgment will occur, reads, "Go and ask a pregnant woman whether, when her nine months have been completed, her womb can keep the fetus within her any longer." In Romans 8.22, Paul draws upon the same image: "We know that the whole creation has been groaning in labor pains until now." Perhaps the parable tells us that, like dough that has been carefully prepared with sourdough starter or a child growing in the womb, the kingdom will come if we nurture it.

Lest readers conclude that my feminist inclinations or my hormones are seeing pregnancy where there is none, I offer one more possible intertext. The Babylonian Talmud, *Ketubot* 10b, reads, "As the leaven is wholesome for the dough, so is blood wholesome for a woman. And one has [also] taught in the name of Rabbi Meir, Every woman who has abundant blood has many children."[32]

Or, to change the subject, given the enormous yield that would result from forty to sixty pounds of flour, perhaps the parable speaks to the importance of extravagance and generosity. Perhaps it suggests we adapt our lives in light of the kingdom and do something that might seem foolish or wasteful to people on the outside. Imagine inviting three strangers to lunch. Imagine setting up a food pantry that stocks more than one family could eat. Imagine baking bread for those who have none and who wonder about all those well-fed folks who pray, "Give us this day our daily bread."

I did hear one wag suggest that the parable proclaimed the kingdom of heaven to be present when women were in the kitchen, barefoot, pregnant, and baking. One could, conceivably, adopt this view. The Mishnah (*Ketubot* 5.5) does prescribe bread making as one of the seven forms of labor the wife is to perform for her husband along with grinding flour, doing the laundry, cooking, feeding the children, making the bed, and working in wool. It is, however, unlikely. This woman is doing something cryptically rather than in an up-front manner that can be controlled; she's going to produce more bread than a single person can eat; she might even be in the position to determine who gets the bread. Jesus asks his disciples, "Is there anyone among you who, if your child asks for bread, will give a stone?" (Matt. 7.9). With this fellow, perhaps stone soup might be on the menu.

Or finally, perhaps the parable tells us that despite all our images of golden slippers and harps and halos, the kingdom is present at the communal oven of a Galilean village when everyone has enough to eat. It is present, inchoate, in everything, and it is available to all, from the sourdough starter to the rain and the sunshine. It is something that works its way through our lives, and we realize its import only when we do not have it. To clean out the old leaven allows us to make room for the new, to start again, and again to feast.

CHAPTER 4

The Pearl of Great Price

The kingdom of heaven is like a man, a merchant, seeking
fine pearls; on finding one pearl of extremely great value,
he went and sold all that he had and bought it.

Matthew 13.45–46

I n the academy, the parable of the Pearl of Great Price is typically read as
a Christian allegory of discipleship, and the focus is on the person who
chooses to seek the kingdom.[1] The merchant is the "metaphorical model
for the disciple of Jesus,"[2] and the pearl is the gospel, the good news of the
kingdom.[3] The merchant is not only making an investment in the good
news; he is "sacrificing" everything he has in order to obtain it. Thus, his action is "radical"[4] (a term requisite for New Testament interpretation today).
For these academic commentators, Jesus himself is the teller of the parable,
but not its referent.

For pastors who spend more time in pulpits than at lecterns, the interpretation is still based on allegory, but the focus tends to be less on the person
doing the seeking than on Christ as both subject and object of the search.
For these interpreters, "The man who is searching for the pearls is, of course,
Jesus himself. He is the sower who went out to sow. He is the one who scattered the sons of the kingdom throughout the world, as he tells us. He is the
one who planted the mustard seed in the field."[5] Or, "Christ is the Pearl of
Great Value, and we are the merchant seeking for happiness, for security, for
fame, for eternity. And when we find Jesus, it costs us everything."[6]

The more homiletic readings also tend to veer away from a direct focus on Jesus and instead sound the themes of sin and redemption. One pastor proposes, "Perhaps I am the Pearl of Great Price," a point reinforced by the fact that the "pearl is born in great suffering and pain, when a foreign speck of sand enters the environment of the shell," and this image "is used as a picture of sin coming into the environment of our world and like an annoying, irritating foreign substance caus[ing] harm."[7] In another variant, we are told: "The pearl here is the Church. We are strangers here on this earth, but God is transforming us into the image of His Son. We, as His Church, have been purchased with the blood of Christ. There is great pain involved in producing the pearl, as Christ went through great pain to produce the Church."[8]

All of these interpretations are viable. The text, especially detached from its literary and historical contexts, opens to multiple views. Allegorical readings can speak to eternal truths and ultimate longings. Yet the point these allegorical interpretations make is also obvious. Such readings rarely produce a challenge and rarely offer a surprise; rather, they confirm standard Christian views.

A second problem with the traditional allegories, beyond their confirmatory rather than challenging messages, is that they cannot convey what a parable would have meant to its original audience. Allegories require keys, so that readers know that the elements given in the tale correspond to very particular elements on the outside. As these allegories were developed much later, that original audience would not have had the key.

With this parable, the allegorical interpretations create yet a third problem. They threaten to turn the kingdom to which the merchant and pearl are compared into a commodity or an obsession. For some readers, the kingdom, like the pearl, can be "bought," usually through sacrifice; this makes the kingdom a commodity. Others concentrate on the seeking and make the pearl, and so the kingdom, an obsession.

Resisting the immediate move to allegory—a resistance perhaps suggested by the failure of the allegorical readings to agree with one another—we investigate what the merchant and the pearl suggest with regard, respectively, to social roles and objects of value. Recognizing both the merchant's search for multiple pearls and his unexpected decision to purchase only one, we might find a reading that allows us to recognize what is of ultimate importance for ourselves as well as for our neighbors. Realizing that once the merchant obtains his pearl of utmost value, he is no longer a merchant, we might discover a challenge to our own identity.

A healthier way of reading the parable begins by deallegorizing both the merchant and the pearl, persists by recognizing the exaggerated absurdity of the merchant's actions, and addresses how the parable raises questions of surprise, identity, and ultimate concern.

A Person, a Merchant

Despite most English translations, Matthew 13.45 in Greek does not state, "The kingdom of heaven is like a merchant." Matthew's initial identification of the protagonist is not "merchant," but "a person (*anthropos*)."⁹ Thus we have the redundant appositive, "a person, a merchant" or, in the more mellifluent gendered terms, "a man, a merchant." The simplest interpretation of this normal Greek expression is that the second term delimits the person to a merchant category. Yet the phrasing also opens the initial interpretation to any person. It also subtly suggests that the protagonist is not God seeking us or even Jesus seeking his own. Finally, and even more subtly, it shows the fellow's identity to be potentially unstable. He is a person, but that he is a merchant is a secondary category. He will stay a person, but he may not stay a merchant.

The appositive formulation is common Matthew's parables. The person who sowed weeds among the wheat in the earlier parable is "an enemy, a man" (13.28)—and so, at least for the parable, not the Devil or an evil spirit. In 13.52, Jesus states that a scribe trained for the kingdom of heaven is like "a man, a householder" (the NRSV offers "master of the household"; the KJV comes closer to the Greek with "a man that is an householder").

In 18.23 Jesus compares the kingdom to "a man, a king, who wished to settle accounts with his slaves." The same formulation appears in several other parables: 20.1 (the landowner in the parable of the Laborers in the Vineyard), 21.33 (the landowner whose tenant farmers kill his servants and his son), and 22.2 (the king who gave a wedding banquet for his son). Each usage resists the allegory. The parable has a meaning beyond itself, as most if not all stories do. But not every householder or king need immediately be seen as a cipher for God, not every merchant is the disciple, and not every pearl is the Christian gospel.

Our man is a "merchant"; the underlying Greek is *emporos,* whence the English "emporium." The Greek term has the connotation of a wholesaler, and perhaps one who markets through agents items consumers do not need at prices they cannot afford. Whereas in the previous parable the man who serendipitously finds treasure in the field (13.44) could be any lucky person, the "merchant" is not just "everyone"; he has a profession, and he is already engaged in that profession by his seeking of merchandise. The parable could be cast with a different protagonist, for example, a king who gives up his throne in order to win a larger kingdom, a warrior who trades his sword for a sharper blade, the widow who sells a stand of fruit trees in order to purchase a vineyard. The general structure or form (or potato) might be the same— seeking, finding, focusing, risking, selling, buying—but the connotations necessarily differ.

In today's English, "merchant" has a generally positive connotation, which may be surprising given the at-best ambivalent character of the most famous "merchant" in English literature, Shylock, who is usually incorrectly identified as the "merchant of Venice" (the title character is Antonio). We think of "merchants" as socially respectable, perhaps a step up from "salespeople" and two steps up from "peddlers." We like the idea of "merchandise," which sounds better than "stock." The term also has a bit of a nostalgic ring to it—merchants were the independent shopkeepers who formed the "chamber of commerce."

Such positive connotations all but disappear when the term is heard in its biblical context. Just as comparing the kingdom to yeast, which has negative connotations in the rest of the New Testament, might have gotten a rise out of the audience, so comparing the kingdom to a merchant of any sort might have been a tough sell.

Granted, biblical word studies are often tedious; they are frequently the contributions of nervous graduate students who, lacking imagination, nevertheless have the capability of using a concordance. Frequently the word studies serve to show the nuances of a term; even more frequently, the results are uninteresting. With our merchant, a bit of an interest is maintained, since the term in the Bible, and elsewhere in antiquity, generally has negative connotations.

The only other place *emporos* appears in the New Testament is in the book of Revelation, and the description is not complimentary. Depicting the Roman Empire as a whore, Revelation 18.3 connects the "kings of the earth" who have "committed fornication with her" to the "merchants of the earth" who "have waxed rich through the abundance of her delicacies." These same merchants "weep and mourn" for Rome, since "no one buys their cargo anymore" (18.11; see also 18.15–23). These *emporoi* are decadent; they are not related to the "kingdom of heaven" save by being very far removed from it.

Merchants receive similarly dismissive treatment in the Septuagint. Aside from a few neutral references to the appropriate setting of prices (e.g., Gen. 23.16), *emporoi* sell Joseph into slavery (Gen. 37.28), fill Solomon's over-extended coffers (1 Kings 10.15, 28; 2 Chron. 1.16), sell other Israelites into slavery (1 Macc. 3.41; 2 Macc. 8.34), and epitomize transgression. As Sirach 26.29 states, "A merchant (*emporos*) can hardly keep from wrongdoing, nor is a tradesman (*kapelos*) innocent of sin." Merchants are not to be trusted to provide honest responses (Sir. 37.11), although the sage does state that one should not be ashamed of taking profit from them (42.5).

The bulk of the other references concern foreign traders (e.g., Isa. 23.8; Bar. 2.23; Ezek. 27 passim; 38.13). The merchant is thus a boundary crosser, with all the ambivalence that that activity creates—he can be trespassing, or he can be forging alliances. He is socially suspect. He deals in what is not *truly* of value; his trade is not in land or family or truth; his trade is in moveable, fungible property.

Not only are merchants regarded with some suspicion; the entire enterprise of high-end trade receives a negative verdict in the biblical tradition. The Greek term for "marketplace" is *emporion*, "business" is *emporia,* and "doing business" is *emporeuomai;* it is almost impossible to find a positive biblical connotation to any of these terms. According to John 2.16, Jesus thrusts all the merchants out of the Jerusalem Temple, and as he does, he tells "those who were selling the doves, 'Take these things out of here! Stop making my Father's house a marketplace!'" For similar negative uses, see Deuteronomy 33.19; Isaiah 23.17; and Ezekiel 27.3.

In Matthew's parable of the Wedding Banquet, one of the guests who refuses the king's invitation to the banquet does so for his business connections: "But they made light of it and went away, one to his farm, another to his business" (*emporia;* 22.5). The Septuagint agrees; all eleven uses have negative connotations (Isa. 23.18 (twice); 45.14; Ezek. 27.13, 15, 16, 24; 28.5, 16, 18; Nah. 3.16).

Even the doing of high-end business is suspect. James 4.13 condemns those "who say, 'Today or tomorrow we will go to such and such a town and spend a year there, doing business (*emporeuomai*) and making money.'" Similarly, 2 Peter 2.3 warns against those who "in their greed . . . exploit (*emporeuomai*) you with deceptive words. Their condemnation, pronounced against them long ago, has not been idle, and their destruction is not asleep."

The Septuagint follows suit. The verb is used for the deceptive dealings of Shechem with Jacob and his sons, following the rape of Jacob's daughter Dinah (Gen. 34.10, 21). In Genesis 42.34, Joseph uses it to test his brothers to see if they will deliver Benjamin to him. Second Chronicles 1.16 and 9.14 employ the term in speaking of Solomon's coffers. Hosea 12.1 and Ezekiel 27.13, 21 utilize *emporeuomai* to describe exploitative international trade, including slavery. The most famous use is in Amos 8.6, where the prophet accuses the wealthy of "buying the poor for silver and the needy for a pair of sandals, and selling the sweepings of the wheat." It is only in Proverbs 3.14 and 31.14 that the verb has positive connotations, but in these passages is it predicated of Woman Wisdom. Perhaps only in the wise hands of a supernatural woman is engaging in high-end trade a good thing.

Despite these negative uses, a few commentators nevertheless insist, "Merchants were generally held in high regard by Jews."[10] However, the rabbinic sources used to support the claim are late and the references are less to wholesalers than to rabbis who are engaged in local trade. The high-priestly families who were engaged in such business ventures were by no means held in high regard by the majority of the population; to be obscenely wealthy was not likely to win popular support, a point confirmed by all the parables that begin, "There was a rich man who . . ."

Joachim Jeremias—whose *Jerusalem in the Time of Jesus* was written in the 1960s—provides most of the data on merchants from which contemporary commentators and homilists draw. The problem is that his timing is anachronistic. Jeremias proposes to discuss "trade in Jerusalem before AD 70,"[11] but he offers no contemporaneous sources for how Jews understood merchants. Discussing "the merchant himself" from our parable, his primary sources are *Lamentations Rabbah,* the Tosefta, and the two Talmuds.

His references to wholesalers are from *Pesikta Rabbati, Exodus Rabbah,* and *Lamentations Rabbah.* These texts range from about 250 through to 700 or even 800 CE. Although they may well contain material dating to Second Temple times, the argument needs to be made, not presupposed. Nor is there anything in these contexts about "high regard" per se. Perhaps Jeremias took the "high regard," or in his words "great respect," from the notice that "even priests engaged in commerce."

In my more cynical moments, I do wonder if Jeremias, who was so assured that Jews at the time of Jesus appreciated commerce, was reflecting his own stereotypes rather than assessing ancient sources. Then again, such thoughts on my part would be uncharitable.[12]

The ten references to *emporoi* in *Antiquities* and *War* conform generally to the Septuagintal uses. The same usage holds for the dozen or so references in Philo. Josephus mentions one "merchant," a certain Ananias, who teaches the women of the court of Adiabene according to the ancestral ways of the Jews[13] and so confirms the association of merchants with people who work outside the land of Israel.

"The kingdom of heaven is like a merchant . . ." Funny business at best; bad marketing for a parable. Jesus has caught my attention, but I'm not sure I'm going to like the product he is selling.

Fine Pearls

In the allegorical readings, the pearl is the most desirable thing one could have and thus it must symbolize the Christ, or the gospel, or the kingdom itself. That is not quite what the parable says. The "kingdom of heaven" is not compared to the pearl, it is compared to the merchant who, seeking fine pearls, sells all he has for one fabulous item. To restrict the analogy to the pearl eliminates the provocation of the parable.

To regard pearls as just a very fine type of jewelry also sells the parable short. The parable does not describe the merchant as searching for "fine jewels"; it is specific in the item sought. Pearls are not like any gem; they have unique properties that the parable may well exploit.

According to Pliny, pearls held the "topmost rank among all things of price."[14] Their price was, literally, above rubies. They are jewels that the majority of the population of the Roman Empire would never have seen, save in artistic depictions. The rich man who ignored Lazarus may have had a few pearls (they look nice on purple); the Whore of Babylon likely had more. But a shepherd or a carpenter, or the population of Nazareth—no pearls.

Yet Pliny's statements on pearls could be informative for our parable. For example, Pliny, and following him a number of other Latin writers, recounts that Cleopatra wagered her lover Marc Antony that she could consume ten million sesterces (today more than million dollars) at one banquet. For the desert course, her servants put before her a single plate with a pool of vinegar on it. Taking off one of her matching set of pearl earrings, she put the jewel into the vinegar, watched it dissolve, and then swallowed the residue. The Latin satirist Horace recounts a similar story: "The son of Aesopus [a famous actor of Cicero's day] took a fine pearl from the ear of Metella and dissolved it in vinegar, with the apparent intention of swallowing a million sesterces in a lump. How is he any saner than if he were to throw that sum into a swift river or a sewer?"[15] Conspicuous consumption—the accurate use of this term—holds for swallowing a pearl. I'm surprised that biblical scholars have not cited this story in order to form a contrast to Jesus's feeding the five thousand with a few pieces of bread.

Aside from price and use by the uberwealthy, several other attributes of pearls could contribute to an interpretation that took the specificity of pearls seriously. For example, pearls are produced from oysters, a nonkosher animal, although the pearl itself would not be forbidden to halakhically ob-servant Jews. This may be one of the reasons they are not mentioned in the scriptures of Israel, while other precious stones, such as rubies (Isa. 54.12; Ezek. 27.16), emeralds (e.g., Ezek. 28.17; 39.10), and sapphires (e.g., Exod. 24.10; 28.18), are. There are no undisputed references to pearls in either the Masoretic text or the Septuagint. The NRSV translates Job 28.18, part of a paean to Wisdom, as, "No mention shall be made of coral or of crystal; the price of wisdom is above pearls," but the Hebrew term rendered "pearls" (*p'ninim*) means "jewels." The Septuagint removes the reference to any jewel.

Second, pearls are among the few jewels produced from a living creature (coral is another). With this focus, the parable could speak to the impor-tance of the natural world, or of creativity, or of how a creature so small and so distinct from human beings—and yet so alive—could create an object of such beauty. Oysters can naturally produce a pearl; human beings cannot.

Third, pearls are formed when the oyster, to protect itself from a foreign object such as a grain of sand lodged between its mantle and shell, coats the object with nacre, the same substance that creates the expanding shell. The analogy of the creation of a pearl to the shedding of tears is thus apt. Considering the means by which the pearl is formed, interpretations could move toward the valuation of certain forms of suffering, the indifference of others to it, or even schadenfreude. Rarely however do biblical scholars comment on the source of the pearl, perhaps because the ancients did not; Pliny suggests that pearls are the children of shells.[16] These matters rest rather in the hands of homilists, such as those who see the grain of sand as sin or as testing on this earth.

Pearls do appear elsewhere in the Gospel tradition, but their relevance to the understanding of the parable beyond the matter of value is negligible. The Sermon on the Mount exhorts, "Do not give what is holy to dogs; and do not throw your pearls before swine, or they will trample them under foot and turn and maul you" (Matt. 7.6). Readers might therefore see the pearl in the parable as comparable to what is holy, and so the allegorical readings do receive some support. Yet rarely is the connection between the Sermon on the Mount and the parable developed. If the pearl is the kingdom or eternal life, then it cannot be "given" by one person to another. If the pearl is the gospel message, then it has to be proclaimed to all (Matt. 28.19) and so should not be withheld. Moreover, the parable's plot resists connection of the parable in Matthew 13 to this warning in Matthew 7, for the merchant in the parable is not about to throw away his one magnificent purchase.

For a second New Testament reference, 1 Timothy 2.9 instructs, "Women should dress themselves modestly and decently in suitable clothing, not with their hair braided, or with gold, pearls, or expensive clothes." Not only does this verse confirm the already potentially negative image of the merchant; it also suggests that those who sell pearls (i.e., merchants) are not living according to the ideals of the kingdom. In 1 Timothy, the pearl is just an ostentatious piece of jewelry and as such has the power to prompt sin. No wonder this same letter notes, "For the love of money is a root of all kinds of evil, and in their eagerness to be rich some have wandered away from the faith and pierced themselves with many pains" (6.10).

The same negative view of accessorizing with pearls appears in Revelation, and there in conjunction with the merchants of the earth. Revelation

18.12–13 details the "cargo of gold, silver, jewels and pearls, fine linen, purple, silk and scarlet . . . and human lives" for which the merchants will weep. Revelation 18.16 describes Babylon the Whore, the "great city . . . adorned with gold, with jewels, and with pearls." Whereas in the final New Testament reference, pearls are described as adorning the heavenly Jerusalem (21.21), these heavenly pearls are no more comparable to the pearls known on earth as is the gold that paves the new Jerusalem's streets: "The twelve gates are twelve pearls, each of the gates is a single pearl, and the street of the city is pure gold, transparent as glass."

The Seeking Merchant

Along with the potentially negative connotations of both merchants and pearls, the merchant's action should also be assessed. On the one hand, he differs from the "person" (*anthropos*) in the previous parable, the Treasure in the Field, in that he was actively seeking something. He may already be closer to the kingdom in that he recognizes there is something he wants or needs, but he does not at present have. The merchant, unlike the fellow in the field, is not satisfied with the status quo.

However, *how* as well as *what* the merchant seeks is also of relevance to the interpretation of the parable. In his seeking, the merchant is not an obvious epitome of wisdom. First, he changes course midstream: seeking fine pearls, he gives up his quest not when he has a sufficient number of pearls, but when he finds only one. Thus it is incorrect to state, "He finds exactly what he is looking for"[17] or to read the parable in light of people who are "terribly earnest about finding an ultimate meaning for their lives, and they may spend years and substantial resources in their quest."[18] The merchant was not looking for "meaning"; he is looking for a commodity that he will remarket. Nor is he looking for that one special pearl. Rather, once he finds the magnificent pearl, he liquidates his holdings and buys it.

Whether his "seeking" is necessarily positive is another issue commentators typically do not address. In Matthew 6.33, Jesus says to his disciples, "Strive first for the kingdom of God and his righteousness, and all these things will be given to you as well." However, the first verb would be better translated "seek" (*zeteo*); it is the same verb that opens the description of the merchant: he is "seeking" (*zetounti*). Next, in 7.7–8, Jesus assures his disciples, "Seek (*zeteite*), and you will find . . . for . . . everyone who seeks finds." Although the Sermon on the Mount does not make explicit what the disciples are to seek, the context suggests that the object is the kingdom of heaven (cf. 7.21: "Not everyone who says to me, 'Lord, Lord,' will enter the kingdom of heaven, but only the one who does the will of my Father in heaven").

The merchant both seeks and finds. But the merchant is seeking pearls, not the kingdom. He wants a commodity he can purchase, not an ethic by which to live, a Christology through which to worship, or a soteriology by which he can be assured of salvation. Like the disciples, he invests all of his resources to obtain what he seeks; unlike the disciples, he does not give to the poor or forsake his former life; rather, he sells "all he has" (*panta hosa eichen*) to purchase one pearl of great value. Nor does he end up with what he was initially seeking: he finds one pearl of great value, not lots of pearls.

The phrase *panta hosa eichen,* which also appears in Matthew 13.44 and 18.25, suggests that the merchant sold more than just his merchandise. It indicates all possessions—his home, food, clothing, provisions for his family if he had one. As Matthew 18.25 states regarding the unforgiving servant: "His lord ordered him to be sold, together with his wife and children and all his possessions (*panta hosa eichen*)." The unforgiving servant's possessions go to pay off a debt; the merchant's go to purchase a pearl. The former case concerns the needs of others; the latter concerns only the merchant's own desire.

Our merchant has obtained his desire: a beautiful object, but one that cannot nourish, shelter, or clothe. R. T. France is one of the few commentators who gets this point: "Unlike the man in the previous parable, who could presumably live off his treasure once he had secured it, this dealer, though initially a man of some substance, is apparently impoverishing himself to acquire something supremely valuable which he could admire and display but could not live off unless he sold it again."[19]

Claims that the merchant acts to obtain the pearl "in a serious and reasonable way"[20] and that because he is "uniquely sensitive to the value of the pearl," he "wisely invested all he has to purchase it"[21] are correct only if taken to mean that the merchant does whatever he needs to do to obtain what he wants. Whether it is *reasonable* or *wise* to liquidate everything he owns is another issue. New Testament scholar M. Eugene Boring understates in suggesting that what the merchant did "may not have measured up to everyone's understanding of common sense."[22] Reading the merchant as involved in what might be called venture-capital or market speculation, theology professor Pheme Perkins states, "Most of us cannot imagine taking such risks."[23] The modern analogy would be to put all one's eggs in a single basket, but at least an egg can be breakfast. Then again, there is nothing in the parable that suggests the one pearl is obtained as an investment.

A later rabbinic tale, known popularly as "Joseph Who Honors the Sabbaths," suggests that what the merchant has done is foolhardy rather than reasonable or prudent. The Babylonian Talmud, *Shabbat* 119a, recounts how a certain wealthy gentile heard from Chaldean fortune-tellers that "Joseph-who-honors-the-Sabbaths" would come to obtain all his property. To protect his personal wealth, the gentile *"went, sold all his property,* and *bought a precious stone"* with the proceeds, which he set in his turban. As he was crossing a bridge, the wind blew his turban off and cast it into the water, where a fish swallowed it. The fish was subsequently caught and brought to market late on the Sabbath. The fish seller brought the fish to Joseph-who-honors-the-Sabbaths, who bought it. Opening the fish, Joseph found the jewel, which he sold "for thirteen roomfuls of gold denarii." The moral: "He who lends to [i.e., expends money for] the Sabbath, the Sabbath repays him."[24] Again the merchant is associated with a gentile, and again the merchant's actions are risky, if not foolish.

Readers familiar with the Jesus tradition will hear in this rabbinic account an echo of another story, that of the miraculous payment of the Temple tax. In Matthew 17.27, Jesus advises Peter that "we" should not give offense to others by refusing to pay the annual half-shekel tax to the Jerusalem Temple. To obtain the money for the payment, Jesus advises Peter: "Go to the sea and cast a hook; take the first fish that comes up; and when you open its mouth, you will find a coin; take that and give it to them for you and me." This is a lesson that in literal terms is not likely to be repeated.

Back to our merchant. Whether what he does is risky or wise, foolhardy or dedicated, he has gained a pearl of enormous value. In the gaining, he has not only fulfilled a desire he did not know he had; he has also changed his identity. He had been looking for fine pearls, but he buys only one. By finding that pearl of ultimate worth, the merchant stops being a merchant. Thus he redefines himself, and we must see him anew as well. What is he? What do we make of his example? What does a former merchant "do" with a pearl? How do we locate ourselves in the parable?

Commentators rush in to provide answers and so to tidy up a very messy story. The following are a series of settings into which the merchant and the pearl have been placed or, better, mounted.

A Setting for the Pearl: Knowledge

The version of the parable in the *Gospel of Thomas* begins the domestication: "Jesus said, 'The Father's imperial rule is like a merchant who had a supply of merchandise and then found a pearl. That merchant was prudent [*or* shrewd]; he sold the merchandise and bought the single pearl [*or* the pearl alone] for himself.' So also with you, seek his treasure that is unfailing, that is enduring, where no moth comes to eat and no worm destroys" (76).[25] The advice does work on the literal level: pearls do not decay. It also controls the allegory: the treasure is not something physical; it is the Gnostic ideal; the pearl/treasure is eternal. Finally, this merchant is less prodigal than his Matthean counterpart in that he sells his "merchandise" and not "everything." For so-called Gnostic texts, in which a pearl can be special knowledge, as epitomized by the "Hymn of the Pearl" in the *Acts of Thomas,* the reading is expected; the parable, with its potential to challenge, humor, and surprise, has become an obvious allegory.

A Second Setting for the Pearl: Sacrifice

Modern commentators also domesticate the parable by constraining its meaning to a recognizable Christian value. One of the more popular tropes academic interpreters employ for describing Matthew 13.44–46, the parables of the Treasure in the Field and the Pearl of Great Price, is that of sacrifice. Commentator Craig Blomberg says: "Quite simply, *true disciples are those who recognize that God's kingdom is so valuable that it's worth sacrificing whatever it takes to be its citizens.*"[26] This approach takes seriously the merchant's full liquidation of his assets as well as the parable's interest in finances. But immediately full liquidation becomes charitable donation. For example, in discussing this parable, Blomberg begins with an account of students at St. Petersburg Christian University in Russia who pooled resources in order to help a classmate pay for passage to return home for a funeral. Then these analogies begin. The merchant is the true disciple, his goods are sacrificial offerings used to aid a fellow disciple, and the pearl is the railway ticket, the gratitude of the recipient, or whatever is seen to promote Christian virtue.[27]

The language of "sacrifice" is not culturally part of the merchant's repertoire; neither financial investment nor commercial liquidation is necessarily a sacrifice. Matthew states that the merchant sold his goods, not that he suffered any loss. "The price paid is not a sacrifice, but an exchange of something lesser for something greater."[28] Had the parable suggested that the merchant felt a sense of loss over what he exchanges, the language of sacrifice would be present. Had the parable indicated that the merchant suffers want by going without, again, sacrificial language might be appropriate. From a theological perspective, had the parable indicated that the sacrifice was on behalf of another or designed to establish or restore relationships or had served to mark a holiday, expiate guilt, or offer thanksgiving, again, the metaphor of sacrifice would fit. But the parable offers none of these prompts, and the *emporos* does not conjure up sacerdotal or sacrificial connotations. The language of "investment" rather than sacrifice could have also been applied to the merchant's action, but that has a less positive connotation when it comes to religious values.

A Third Setting for the Pearl: Anything but Economics

Other commentators assure us that the interpretation of the parable has nothing to do with money, or the mundane, at all. Repeatedly, we hear: "Metaphors aren't meant to be pressed down to every last detail, and analogies all break down at some point. Most people, in fact, don't give up anywhere close to everything that they have in order to enter the kingdom."[29] Ironically, the quote already presumes an interpretation related to full divestment, since it speaks of those who "give up . . . everything." Even as commentators affirm that the merchant as well as the fellow who found treasure in the field "take a radical step in order to obtain something of greater value," they also affirm "if the two parables meant to challenge listeners to renounce their own possessions (sell everything you have; see Matt. 19.21), they would be bizarre."[30] Somehow, when Jesus really is being "radical," we conclude he cannot be saying exactly what he seems to be saying. Thus the parable cannot mean anything literal with regard to economics. Allegory enters again: "We have an infinitely valuable pearl," which amounts to "great knowledge of scripture and the hope for God's kingdom, the 'new covenant' (Matt. 26.28)."[31] Although not importing the language of sacrifice, this move away from economics is also a move away from the parable, which is replete with economic indicators.

Digression into Another Field

> The kingdom of heaven is like treasure hidden in a field,
> which a person found and hid; then in his joy he goes and
> sells all that he has and buys that field. (Matt. 13.44)

Noting that Jesus addresses the Pearl of Great Price as well as the immediately preceding parable of the Treasure in the Field, or the parable of the "Lucky and Potentially Dishonest Man" (13.44) only to the Twelve (13.36), other commentators see in the two parables the theme of discipleship. The connection to discipleship is by no means impossible, but it is Matthew's contextualization that evokes it, not the parable itself. Like the *Gospel of Thomas,* Matthew's Gospel too has begun the interpretive process.

Whether Jesus told the parables together or Matthew combined them cannot be determined. The combination, however, makes logical sense, and Matthew is a logical editor. The parables share common ideas, characterizations, and results. Both depict a person who sells all that he has to purchase something desired. Both also present a gap between the desire and the fulfillment.[32] The man in the first parable has to sell his goods in order to purchase the field where the treasure is hid. The merchant is seeking pearls; upon finding one special pearl, he liquidates his assets to purchase it.

However, the distinctions between the two parables should not be ignored. For example, the first parable focuses on the logical actions of *any* person who finds a treasure; the actions are in the present tense. The second parable begins with any person, but then delimits that person to one particular man, and it presents his actions in past tenses: aorist, imperfect, and perfect.[33]

Most readers can identify with the man in the field in the first parable; identifying with the merchant requires more effort. We can all be the person who, serendipitously, finds a treasure; indeed, more than a few of us perhaps dream of being this person (those who purchase weekly lottery tickets or play bingo may be particularly amenable to this connection). As far as we know, the man who obtains the lucky find had not been spending his life seeking "treasure." But few of us are wholesalers seeking fine pearls, and fewer still would sell everything in order to buy one of them.

Differences between the Treasure in the Field and the Pearl of Great Price continue when the two parables are read in relation to other comments in Matthew's Gospel. This text, like the *Gospel of Thomas,* had already begun the interpretation, and the domestication, of Jesus's words. Attentive readers will associate the good fortune of the man in the field with Jesus's warning in the Sermon on the Mount, "Do not store up for yourselves treasures on earth, where moth and rust consume and where thieves break in and steal; but store up for yourselves treasures in heaven, where neither moth nor rust consumes and where thieves do not break in and steal. For where your treasure is, there your heart will be also" (6.19–21). A buried treasure is an earthly treasure; it can be lost.

Matthew then reinforces the allegorical interpretation for the first parable. The association of treasure and kingdom of heaven that began in the Sermon on the Mount is repeated at the end of the parables discourse: "Therefore every scribe who has been discipled for the kingdom of heaven is like a person, a master of a household, who casts out of his treasure what is new and what is old" (13.52). This last line of the discourse returns readers to the practical and so the economic. It is an echo of Matthew 12.35, "A good person out of his good treasure casts out good, and an evil person out of his evil treasure casts out evil." It is also an echo of the parable of the treasure, both with its redundant "a person" and by its concern for an image with economic weight. The term "cast out" also requires assessment. For Matthew, one does not store up in the treasury or the treasure; one "casts out" (*ekballo*) from it. As with a demon—the term is technically used in exorcisms—possessions on earth are to be cast out, not stored up.

For Matthew, the two parables are about discipleship, just as for *Thomas* the pearl is about knowledge. Allegory again prevails, and the literalness of the parable, with its focus on a merchant, merchandise, and selling and buying, becomes overshadowed.

In the effort to remove the two parables from having any substantive interest in economics, let alone from suggesting that total divestment is commendable, commentators often adduce Matthew 19.16–29 along with the story of Zacchaeus in Luke 19.1–10 to argue that Jesus does *not* expect people to abandon everything. The first set of verses offers Matthew's take on a story we have already seen in Luke: the account of the potential disciple who seeks from Jesus information on eternal life. For Luke's Gospel, the man's questions provide resonance to the opening frame of the parable of the Good Samaritan; Matthew's version, in a different narrative context, has different implications.

In Matthew 19.16, a person asks Jesus, "What good deed must I do to have eternal life?" (see the discussion of the same wrong question that elicits the parable of the Good Samaritan in Chapter 2). Jesus corrects the questioner by moving his focus from "eternal life" to entering "into the life" and then from the singular deed to the plural: "Keep the commandments." When the interlocutor persists, "Which ones?" Jesus responds with the second half of the Decalogue as well as Leviticus 19.18 on loving neighbors.

The interlocutor claims to have fulfilled all these commandments but, still dissatisfied, asks a third question, "What do I still lack?" Although some interpreters see the young man as infected with a neurotic works-righteousness that has him attempting to pile up good deeds in order to earn his heavenly reward, more productive would be to query the young man's insistence that he really does "love his neighbor as himself." Were he to do this fully, he might not be economically rich, because he would have used more of his funds to help the poor or set up his house as a place of refuge for the homeless. More productive also would be to recognize that Jesus does suggest a possible next step. Jesus again refocuses the man's attention: he advises, "If you wish to be perfect, go, sell your possessions, and give the money to the poor, and you will have treasure in heaven; then come, follow me" (19.21).

"Aha," think not a few commentators, "*only* to this young man does Jesus issue his call to perfection with its attendant divesting." Zacchaeus, the chief tax collector, does not give up his home or wealth (so Luke 19.1–9),[34] nor does Martha sell her home (Luke 10.38–42). Ignored in these apologia is the fact that Matthew promotes such perfection: "Be perfect, therefore, as your heavenly Father is perfect" (5.48). Moreover, this perfection may well relate to divesting. Just as the merchant sells all he has to purchase the pearl, so Peter and his associates "have left everything and followed" Jesus (19.27). Their profit margin is enormous, for in response to this initial investment, they will sit on thrones, serve as judges over all Israel, "receive a hundredfold, and . . . inherit eternal life" (19.29). Similarly, Paul states, "For we rejoice when we are weak and you are strong. This is what we pray for, that you may become perfect" (2 Cor. 13.9).

Jesus did not tell all his followers to sell what they have and join the ranks of the destitute. Nevertheless, he appears to have found this lifestyle the best way of laying up treasure in heaven. Just as Paul did not mandate that all followers of Jesus be celibate, as he was, he advised that celibacy, including continence in marriage, is the preferable behavior, given that "the present form of this world is passing away" (1 Cor. 7.31). So also Jesus: divesting is not required, but it is preferred.

The merchant in the parable does what the young man cannot, but the disciples can—he divests from everything he owns for the new treasure whose value perhaps only he can see, since no one else has found, or bought, or held on to this pearl. (What the pearl's original owners did with the funds the merchant provided them is not the concern of the parable; perhaps this excess of cash prompted them to give to the poor as well, but I doubt it.) Moreover, he purchases that pearl, just as the man in the previous parable purchased the field. Had the parable talked about barter, serendipitous find, or unexpected gift, the economic focus would not be as strong.[35]

The Gospel tradition does not expect everyone to sell all they have, but it does expect some to do this. Jesus appears to have set up a two-tiered system: some of his followers divest all; others keep their own finances, but dedicate them to the concerns of the mission (feeding the hungry, clothing the naked, providing hospitality to the apostle, etc.).

Perhaps the parable really does speak to the use of money. Much of the rest of the tradition does. So does the prevailing negative use of words dealing with merchandising.

A Fourth Setting for the Pearl: Detachment

Along with the move to allegorize the parable away from the economic, another domesticating move is to understand Matthew 13.45–46 in terms of "detachment," defined as "the essence of Christian spirituality."[36] The merchant in this interpretation finds "freedom from absorption in the attractions, pleasures, and concerns of this world—not because these are bad in themselves, but because believers have been caught by a vision of God's love and God's future that simply relativizes all these things."[37] I am not seeing in the merchant's quest a vision of divine love or a focus on the future, but perhaps I am too literal. He is looking for pearls and he finds something beyond the normal pearl. If he's looking for love, he's looking in all the wrong places. Nor am I seeing a "relativizing" of items other than the pearl; divesting is not relativizing. Although reading the parable for what it says about relativizing is probably better than reading it with a view toward sacrifice, this interpretation still fails to get at the challenge of the text even as it risks devaluing the pearl.

Other commentators resist the merchant's unexpected purchase long enough to provide closure to the parable. At the same time that he correctly observes that the merchant's "extraordinary commitment [to] dispose of all that one has to buy the pearl is to make a drastic and life-changing act,"[38] commentator Arland Hultgren also assures readers that he "will probably sell [the pearl] on the retail market and make a good profit."[39] David Buttrick similarly notes, "In order to survive he will have to sell the pearl anyway."[40] The parable stops with the purchase of the pearl, and we should leave it there. Unlike the story of the prodigal and his brother, there are no lingering questions or unresolved relationships. There is no reason to engage in what Klyne Snodgrass calls a "violation of narrative time" in order to find meaning or challenge in the parable.[41] Our merchant was in search of fine pearls; he found the one that surpassed all the rest, and he bought it. He changes his focus from the many to the one, and he stops looking.

To conclude that the pearl is only of value if it is resold and thus that it has no "ultimate value" is to read the pearl only as a commodity. To conclude that the kingdom's "corrupting power is the desire to possess it"[42] is again to commodify the kingdom, even as the reading resists the claim.[43]

The kingdom is not the pearl, and it is not the merchant. The kingdom is what comes after "it is like": the kingdom is like a merchant who seeks pearls and who, upon finding what he was not expecting—the greatest of the great—makes every effort to attain it. To reduce the kingdom of heaven to a thing, whether the pearl or the merchant, is also an act of commodification. To commodify the kingdom is to dismiss the import of an individual's ultimate concern. The merchant has found what he wanted, although until the moment of the find, he did not realize his true desire. He has reconceptualized both his past values and his future plans; the "magnitude of the life change" is paramount; he is no longer what he was.

Sometimes a Pearl Is the Key to the Kingdom

When it comes relating the parable of the Pearl of Great Price to the kingdom of heaven, we have a man in the wrong profession. We have the wrong target of his initial search—a luxury item that few can afford; it has lachrymose and nonkosher origins; its purchase requires a use of funds that could have been given to the poor. We have the wrong result of the search—the merchant finds something he was not seeking. He thought he wanted "fine pearls"; it turns out, he had incorrectly assessed his desire and his goal. To obtain his pearl he engages in a risky and seemingly foolish venture of divesting. We have the wrong result—the merchant has spent everything he has on a pearl, an item with no practical value. Once he purchases it, he is no longer a merchant. And therein lies the challenge.

By the standards of the status quo—whether in first-century Galilee or twenty-first-century America—the merchant has acted in a reckless manner. The merchant, however, sets up alternative standards not determined by society, but determined by something else, whether his own desires or a heavenly prompt. He really is "countercultural." He defines his treasure in his own terms. He is able to recognize what for him has true value, and he can do what he needs to do in order to obtain it. The pearl the merchant obtains is not simply the best of the lot, the one among the many. It is qualitatively different, singular, exemplary; it points beyond the concept of "pearl" to something new, something heretofore unseen and unknown. There is a transcendent quality, a mystery, to this pearl. And so the parable provokes.

Our erstwhile merchant first raises questions of our own acquisitiveness.[44] We are continually seeking, whether the object is fine pearls, a new job, another degree, or spiritual fulfillment. But each time we find our goal, it turns out to be ephemeral. There is always a new necklace, a new career, a new form of study, a nagging sense that we have not done what we need to do. We flit from desire to desire, never permanently fulfilled, always somewhat discontent. The merchant's actions show that knowing one's pearl obviates all other wants and desires.

Will we know what we truly want when we see it? The merchant has removed himself from the realm of buying and selling, seeking and finding, wanting and wanting more. Not only can the cycle be broken; the merchant demonstrates that one can step out of it entirely.

Second, and of greater challenge, should we be, indeed can we be, like the erstwhile merchant, who is, to use another economic term, willing to go "all in," not for a gamble but for an ultimate concern? His is an act not of sacrifice, because we do not know the extent to which he previous valued what he sold (note: "sold," not "gave away"), and we do not know if he suffered any loss. Nor has he sacrificed in any religious sense. Nor again does he demonstrate the relative value of all his other possessions; he does not simply place the one pearl ahead of everything else. The issue isn't relative value; it's all or nothing. Thereby, the parable asks: Can we assess what is of ultimate value in our own lives, not simply in terms of relativizing, but in terms of ultimate concern? More, it asks: Are we willing to step aside from all we have to obtain what we want?

Third, we know what is of value for the erstwhile merchant, who now, no longer a merchant, might be called "the man who possesses the magnificent pearl." Along with challenging all readers to determine our own pearl, the parable asks if we know what is of ultimate concern to our neighbors.

On Monday evenings during the school term, I either teach or facilitate a Divinity course at Riverbend Maximum Security Prison, where Tennessee's death row is located. The first year I taught at Riverbend, the class—twelve Riverbend inmates and twelve Vanderbilt students—studied the Gospel of Matthew; after all, Matthew's Gospel contains the parable of the Sheep and the Goats, which talks about visiting people in prison.

When discussing Matthew 13.45–46 with my students—some candidates for ordination, others serving life sentences—I asked: What is your pearl of supreme value? For what would you sell everything you own? To use Hultgren's words, for what would you "make a drastic and life-changing act"?[45] The divinity students mentioned the church. But the commentators are correct: most people do not sell everything they have for the sake of the church. Despite the plausible claim that Matthew's Gospel encourages such perfection, the Gospel also recognizes two types of disciples, the itinerants who take to the road and the householders who provide them support.

One student in the Graduate Department of Religion mentioned the doctoral degree. The desire for a Ph.D. was for her an irritant of sorts. She had already earned a Master's of Divinity and had planned to go directly for the Ph.D. in New Testament, but life intervened. She married a pastor, had children, and served as the minister's wife (a professional role). She continued her education whenever she could—seeking pearls on Amazon, the History Channel, or in online courses. Her husband discouraged her; he already had a Doctorate of Ministry (D.Min.) and felt that one doctor in the family was sufficient. She persevered. Seeking more information, she came across the website of Vanderbilt's Graduate Department of Religion and decided to apply. Not only was she accepted; she was awarded funding.

For various and very good reasons, entering the program coincided with the end of her marriage. That night she explained, and here I paraphrase: "I never expected to find myself here, but when the graduate-school offer came, I did what I needed to do to accept it. I gave up my home and my status as 'minister's wife'; I took out loans; I took back my original name. I do not know what will happen at the end of this program, but that does not matter. I am doing what is right for me. I have my pearl." Most of us, I suspect, would not have had the courage to change our lives, our identities, for the sake of what we most want; we may not even know what the final goal is. This student showed the daring, the courage, that many of us might lack. She redefined herself.

One of the Riverbend students responded with the single word, "Freedom." He would do what it takes—confession to rather than denial of his crime, anger management courses, psychological tests, and so on—in order to increase his chances of parole. He realized what he wanted, freedom, only when he realized he did not have it. When and if he obtains it, he intends to break the cycle of crime and incarceration. With his sentence flattened or pardon granted, he is no longer the "insider" or the "criminal," but the "free man" who needs to form his own new identity. When I drove home that evening, with the searchlights and the barbed wire reflecting in my rear-view mirror, I realized that this student's "pearl" is something I take for granted.

Another Riverbend student said, "Safety." He will invest all he has in order to ensure that he will not be knifed in the chow line or attacked in the shower. Again, his pearl is something that I had not considered.

And a third said that when he came into prison, he lost all that he had—his property, his clothing, but also his identity, his dignity. He had to construct his own pearl, layer by painful layer, tear by tear, and see what was really important.

Here is one final interpretation. I do not think it is quite what Jesus had in mind, but it does fit the question of ultimate concern. The word for "pearl" in Greek is *margarita,* a recognition that can bring new meaning to the expression "pearly gates." When I mentioned this translation in class, one of my students, a recovering alcoholic, explained how the margarita, the drink, was her pearl of complete value. She sold everything—home, food, family—for the drink. And so we ask: Do we take stock of our priorities? What is our image of the kingdom? What, really, do we want? The parable consequently asks us if searching for pearls, searching for commodities or multiples or stuff, is worth pursuing. It is good to know that there may be something out there, beyond our imagination, that demands our recognition of its ultimate value. It is good to know if our definition of what constitutes the kingdom of heaven is healthy or harmful. Not all pearls on the market are cultured; some are fake, although their cost can be exceptionally high as well.

Jesus, the historical Jesus, cared about prioritizing. In light of the in-breaking of the kingdom of heaven, which is already here as his followers found manifested in his presence and yet to come as manifested by the full presence of justice, we are forced to act. We are forced to determine what we must do to prepare for this new reality. What do we keep and what do we divest? How would we live if we knew ultimate judgment was coming on Tuesday? What are our neighbors' ultimate concerns, and what are ours? Once we know that material goods will only collect rust or dust, and once we know that the only thing that counts is treasure in heaven, surely we must find a new way to live.

Attending to the anomalies of the story, refusing to allegorize in order to domesticate, challenging our acquisitiveness and our sense of what is truly of value, the parable disturbs. That is what parables should do.

CHAPTER 5

The Mustard Seed

How shall we compare the kingdom of God, or with what parable might we put it? It is like a mustard seed, which, when sown upon the ground, the smallest is of all the seeds on earth. And when sown, it rises up and becomes the greatest of all vegetables, and it makes large branches, so that are able under its shadow the birds of the heaven to dwell.

Mark 4.30–32

Like is the kingdom of the heavens to a mustard seed, that taking, some person sowed in his field. The smallest, on the one hand, it is of all the seeds, but when it has grown, greatest of the vegetables it is, and it becomes a tree, so that when come the birds of the heaven, even they dwell in its branches.

Matthew 13.31–32

To what is like the kingdom of God, and to what should I make it like? It is like a mustard seed, which taking, a man casts in his garden, and it grew, and became a tree, and the birds of the heaven dwelled in its branches.

Luke 13.18–19

Jesus told a parable that had the following elements: a small mustard seed, branches, and birds taking shelter. Whether he told the parable in various ways—one time with a garden and another with a field; one time with the seed growing into a large vegetable and another with the seed growing into a giant tree—or whether each evangelist took the building blocks of the parable and constructed his own details cannot be known. Because we do not know if details present in only one Gospel—from Matthew's explicit mention of a person having "sowed" the seed "in his field" to Luke's seeing the seed as "cast" or "tossed" into a "garden"—belong to the original parable, it becomes impossible to determine if these details hold the key to the parable's interpretation.

Such difficulty has never stopped biblical scholars, however, from determining an original reading, one that goes back to Jesus and one that, at least for many scholars, inevitably demonstrates his political savvy or social radicality. From such tiny details, giant trees grow. But, to continue the metaphor, many of those roots are not deep at all.

The parable of the Mustard Seed has put forth so many branches of interpretation that the birds of heaven could build multiple nests and still have room for expansion. Of these branches, two major ones stand out. The first sees in the parable the theme of the contrast between small seed and large, or large enough, plant (whether tree or impressive vegetable). The second, and more speculative, concentrates not on size, but on the details of the imagery: the symbolic value of mustard, tree, birds, and branches. Both branches in turn give rise to distinct leaves.

For traditional commentators, the smallness of the seed suggests the miraculous growth of the kingdom, whether in one's heart, in the church, or in society. One leaf on this branch emphasizes Christology, in the contrast between Jesus's negligible effects in Galilee and the influence his teachings will have in the future and in the world: "The parable sets forth a message of encouragement. . . . The seemingly insignificant acts of work and witness by the disciples of Jesus are of ultimate importance."[1]

Another leaf has a soteriological marker: the small seed leads to universal redemption, as the birds of the heaven, representing the gentile nations gathered into Israel,[2] take shelter in the boughs of the church. From this branch, followers can have "confidence in the little gospel."[3] This reading receives enhancement from the Gospels' other reference to the same plant, in which the contrast of small to large also appears. In Matthew 17.20, Jesus states, "For truly I tell you, if you have faith the size of a mustard seed, you will say to this mountain, 'Move from here to there,' and it will move; and nothing will be impossible for you." Luke 17.6 offers the variant: "If you had faith the size of a mustard seed, you could say to this mulberry tree, 'Be uprooted and planted in the sea,' and it would obey you."

Nearby is yet another leaf; this one finds the growth of the church to be part of natural development, for the church inevitably grows as the seed inevitably germinates. As Barbara Reid astutely notes, "This interpretation of the slow, but inevitable growth of the Church as the locus of the reign of God was most popular in the nineteenth century with the rise of evolutionary science."[4] Darwinism, or natural selection, turns out to support Christianity, according to this parable.

And yet another leaf on this same branch, fertilized by other seed metaphors in the New Testament, leads to the suggestion that the parable has something to say about eternal life. This reading uses the "small beginning to large ending" model to emphasize not only a grander ending, but one that is different in kind from the original. Mustard seed does not grow into giant trees; such growth would be miraculous (at this point, Darwin would have nothing to say). Similarly, the seed sown of human flesh becomes transformed into something distinctly new and distinctly glorious. For example, in 1 Corinthians 15.36–38, Paul uses the image of a seed to describe the nature of the resurrected body: "What you sow does not come to life unless it dies. And as for what you sow, you do not sow the body that is to be, but a bare seed, perhaps of wheat or of some other grain. But God gives it a body as he has chosen, and to each kind of seed its own body." Similarly, in John 12.24, Jesus states, "Very truly, I tell you, unless a grain of wheat falls into the earth and dies, it remains just a single grain; but if it dies, it bears much fruit." Therefore, read within John's shadow, the parable is about the mystery of the resurrection.[5]

When we turn to the second branch, we find leaves from edgier commentators whose focus tends to be on politics rather than piety; this second branch, perhaps one unnaturally grafted onto the parable, displays the transgressive aspect of the kingdom by focusing not on size, but on the elements of the parable. In these readings, the mustard seed is taken to be a "'despised and rejected' weed,"[6] a symbol of "proverbial noxiousness"[7] that proclaims the demise of empire. The mustard is a "dangerous" weed that threatens to "destroy" the garden by taking it over.[8] The garden is the status quo, or the empire, or Judaism, or everything that is not in agreement with the gospel.

Another leaf on this transgressive branch plays home to the birds the mustard attracts, for the birds are destructive to the cultivated field. For this leaf, the birds, who could have been cast by Alfred Hitchcock, serve as warnings to "the upper classes who live off the toil of the poor cultivator" since their "ventures pose a challenge to oppressive systems of power just as mustard run wild can overtake cultivated fields.[9] The mustard takes over and the birds move in, and so the upper classes have no place to lay their heads.

This same branch also contains a number of leaves that regard the mustard seed placed in a garden as a violation of Jewish laws concerning planting a plot of land with two types of crops.[10] That only one version of the parable mentions a "garden," and that version is from Luke's Gospel, the Gospel with the least information on or interest in Jewish legal concerns, is a point to be gently swept aside. From this now expected theme of "the parables show how bad Jewish Law is" comes the assertion that the mustard seed is an apt image for describing Jesus's "association with the unclean"[11] and for his kingdom as welcoming the "unclean" gentile nations into the church. The mustard seed here becomes a symbol of impurity (despite its being entirely kosher, as anyone who has had a decent kosher hot dog with the requisite mustard can attest) and a symbol of the gentile nations (lime Jell-O or a BLT perhaps might serve this symbolic function; mustard, unlikely). A variant on this view is that "Jesus depicts a kingdom not of the righteous but of the impudent rule-breaking sinners. . . . The kingdom of God will be open to the undesirable."[12]

Still another leaf sees the parable as "a restructuring of Jewish expectation," given that the kingdom "does not come with a glorious bang and the defeat of Rome," but rather enters with an insignificant seed.[13] This argument continues by suggesting that the parable is a parody of ancient empires. Ezekiel 31 compares Assyria to a cedar of Lebanon in which the birds nest, and this mighty tree is now fallen (see also Ezek. 17). Jesus's kingdom, which will not fall, is not a mighty cedar, but a lowly mustard plant.[14] Perhaps, proposes Luise Schottroff, the mustard bush "is meant to indicate the different quality of God's cosmic majesty in contrast to the imperial world powers."[15] In a riff on this view, commentator Joshua Garroway sees the story of the erstwhile demon-possessed man, once named "Legion," as reflecting the mustard seed: "The invaded becomes the invader as the cured demoniac, like a solitary mustard seed, reenters the community from which he has been expelled and preaches a message that rapidly proliferates."[16]

That Mark speaks of a vegetable rather than a tree and of the birds as nesting in the "shadow" rather than the branches must then be Mark's misunderstanding of the imagery. That the demon-possessed man in Mark 5.1–20 was not "expelled" from the community; rather, he refused to be contained by it. Mark does not tell us anything about his missionary work, but this omission too is a minor irritant to be ignored in favor of the bigger picture.

The first branch, which grows from the contrast between the small seed and the giant tree, is stunted both by the lack of evidence of the proverbial smallness of the seed and by the generally obvious if not banal conclusion that the kingdom grows. Extensions, such as the connection of the seed to resurrection, stretch the allegorical possibilities of the parable. The second branch frequently becomes deformed by misreadings of mustard as a noxious weed rather than a valued medicinal plant, of Jewish customs regarding planting and purity, and of the mustard seed in terms of empire.

The pruning of these branches begins by clearing out the leaves of convention and polemic. The fertilization of the plant then proceeds by showing how the parable poses challenges to Jewish readers and at the same time treats distinct Jewish practices with respect.

Starting Small and Growing Large

Mustard seed is not, contrary to what Jesus states, the smallest of seeds; orchid and cypress seeds are smaller. Moreover, mustard seeds do not grow into giant trees. The *brassica nigra,* or "black mustard," seed sprouts into a plant that can grow, given perfect agricultural conditions, eight to ten feet; therefore scholars frequently presume this is what Jesus is talking about. To describe it as a "tree" is generous. The *salvadora persica,* also found in the land of Israel, produces a modest bush growing no more than a foot in height.

Interpreters who want to read the Bible as a book about science and agriculture take extra care to bring the parable into conformity with nature. Some resort to explanations that limit the comparison base: mustard seed is the smallest seed that would be planted *in particular locations,* such as vegetable gardens,[17] or the smallest of the seeds one could find *in the land of Israel.* Others play with grammar. The term used in the parable, traditionally translated as the superlative, "smallest," is really the comparative, "smaller" (Gk. *mikroteron,* as in the English term "micro"); they thus suggest that the parable is not really saying "smallest"—that the comparison with "all" the other plants is just then a technical aggravation. We can all grant that the seed is small, even if we can't agree on whether the Bible is a scientific textbook and therefore botanically unassailable.

More problematic for the branch of interpretation that derives its major points from the discrepancies in size between small seed and giant tree is the fact that the smallness of the mustard seed is not proverbial in Greek, Roman, or Jewish culture—at least as far as we know. Neither the Tanakh nor the Septuagint mentions mustard or mustard seed. Further, the term "mustard seed" (Gk. *kokkos sinapeos*) appears nowhere we can locate prior to its use in the Gospels. From Greek and Roman sources that do refer to mustard seed and mustard, notice is taken of its sharp taste, its medicinal benefits, and its rapid growth, but not of the size of the seed.

Only in later rabbinic documents does the smallness of the seed attain attention (Mishnah, *Niddah* 5.2; Babylonian Talmud, *Berakhot* 31a). According to one of the more obscure comments in the Mishnah, "[If] one were eating a heave offering and felt his limbs tremble, he holds on to the penis and swallows the heave offering. And they are made unclean by any amount [of discharge] at all, even though it is like a grain of mustard [Heb. *ayin hardal;* lit., an "eye of mustard"], and less than that." This seminal image—one does wait for an opportunity to use that metaphor correctly—is matched by a menstrual one in the Talmud: "What is an example of a halakhic decision which admits of no discussion? Abaye said: 'Such a one as the following of R. Zeira; for R. Zeira said: "The daughters of Israel have undertaken to be so strict with themselves that if they see a drop of blood no bigger than a mustard seed, they wait seven [clean] days after it."' " In other words, minor spotting is considered in determining when a wife can again engage in conjugal relations.

Although smallness is certainly a factor in the two rabbinic uses, images of both sexuality and sterility outweigh the focus on size (that things other than size are important in the broader conversation of sexuality is not news, but it is good to know). Given that these rabbinic uses postdate the New Testament, one might well wonder if the rabbis are having a bit of fun with the Gospel citations. For the Gospels, mustard seed is related to faith; for the rabbis, it is related to genital discharge.

The parable necessarily makes a comparison: the smallest (or, technically, smaller) seed creates a home for the birds. What we do with this comparison still remains an open question. There is no challenge in hearing that from small beginnings come great things; there is no provocation in the point that Jesus's message grew over time. There is no reason to presume that the seed must represent faith, the gospel, or the Christ; there is no necessary reason for seeing the tree as the church or the birds the nations of the world. Perhaps the seed, the plant, and the birds are exactly that.

Branches Unnaturally Grafted

While some readers struggle to make the parable of the Mustard Seed into a treatise on botany, others emphasize that what the parable teaches is contrary to nature, and what is contrary to nature is a theological as well as political good. To some extent, interpretations of parables that challenge the status quo are commendable; parables should serve to "afflict the comfortable" or at least to provoke reflection. *That* a parable is challenging should not be an issue; the issues are better framed in terms of *what* the parable challenges and *how* it does so.

For a number of commentators, the "kingdom" in the parable is transgressive: the parable presents a genetic mutation of the mustard plant into a tree, and thus nature is subverted; the parable describes a violation of Jewish purity codes, and thus Torah or at least its prevailing interpretation is subverted; the parable compares the kingdom to a weed or it parodies ancient metaphors of empires, and thus the notion of empire is subverted. In each case, however, the claims are shaky at best.

Mark notes that the seed grew into a vegetable (*laxanon*) or what the NRSV translates "shrub." Were translators to take this reading of "vegetable" more seriously, the tendency to interpret mustard as a weed or as something noxious would likely die on the vine. No one I know interprets Romans 14.2, "Some believe in eating anything, while the weak eat only vegetables (*laxana*)" as a reference to consuming noxious weeds. Had Jesus intended to speak of a weed, he could have used the term (as he does in the parable of the Weeds in the Wheat, Matt. 13.24–30). Matthew offers the plant an upgrade: the seed becomes a vegetable (*laxanon*) and then a tree (*dendron*). A miracle has occurred; the mustard seed has become something otherwise nonexistent, a mustard tree. For Luke, the seed "becomes a tree" (*egeneto eis dendron*) without going through the vegetable stage.

At this point, scholars seek to establish the original wording of the parable. The focus on the *ipsissima verba* ("the very words"; the expression does sound more profound in Latin) has a utilitarian value: if we can determine what words Jesus actually used, we might be able to determine more precisely the cultural resonances and so the allegorical meaning the parable holds. Not surprisingly, those who want to take the parable as subversive find the original to be Luke's version and see Mark as missing the point of the parable by changing the image from a tree to a shrub.[18]

The exercise in finding the exact wording is, as we have seen, a lesson in futility; each version has its proponents, and each can be understood as redacted by the evangelist. Claims that the Q version[19] (the version found in the Gospels Matthew and Luke) is more original than the one in the Gospel of Mark falter in part on the lack of secure evidence for a Q source in the first place. They also falter on the claim that Jesus told the parable only one way, with one set of words, and then the church corrupted everything he said. Good storytellers, and Jesus was certainly a good storyteller, adapt their stories to their audiences and to their immediate circumstances. Viewing Jesus as some sort of automaton who had to make each of his pronouncements the same yesterday, today, and forever robs him of his humanity and his narrative genius.

Jesus told a parable about a small mustard seed, a sprouting of some sort, and a growth that is large enough to shelter birds. Whether the detail of the mustard is of issue—if the focus of the parable is from the small to the great, then whether the plant is mustard or orchid or sesame need not be relevant—remains an open question. Whether the detail of the tree as opposed to the plant is of issue—descriptions can be generous; the point of the tree may be a Q upgrade of an original—also remains an open question. Finally, whether the birds are simply avian nesters or whether they are to represent the nations of the world also remains an open question. It is from these details and questions that interpretations should be extracted.

We do not need genetic mutation to see the parable as provocative. Neither do we need to import the category of Jewish purity laws. Despite the fact that no parable directly addresses purity, save for the pigs in the parable of the Prodigal Son, where the uncleanness of pigs is taken for granted rather than challenged, some commentators continue to see purity as the major issue Jesus tackles, and they see Jesus as challenging the purity system. That is, they see him as challenging one of the major concerns of Torah, of Jewish identity, and of the very practices that have kept Jews Jewish over the past two millennia. This is a misreading of the parables, and a misreading of Jesus.

Here's how this misplaced purity focus works. First, several scholars insist on interpreting the Mustard Seed parable according to the same terms by which they interpret the parable of the Leaven, and they insist that the parable of the Leaven is about uncleanness and impurity. Although Matthew and Luke place the two parables together, neither Mark nor the *Gospel of Thomas* (20) does. Mark pairs the Mustard Seed with the parable of the Seed That Grows Secretly (Mark 4.26–29: "The kingdom of God is as if someone would scatter seed on the ground, and would sleep and rise night and day, and the seed would sprout and grow, he does not know how. The earth produces of itself, first the stalk, then the head, then the full grain in the head. But when the grain is ripe, at once he goes in with his sickle, because the harvest has come"). *Thomas* surrounds the parable with comments on discipleship. Thus the parable of the Mustard Seed should have interpretations neither controlled by nor constrained by the parable of the Leaven.

Second, and more damning to the purity patrol, the parable of the Leaven is, as we have seen, not about purity. If we want to interpret Seed and Leaven together, then we need a different interpretation. What they share is, first, size: yeast and seed are small, and the tree and the yield are large. Second, both play on the theme of secrecy: the yeast is "hidden," and the seed grows out of sight, in the earth, as the related parable of the Seed That Grows Secretly emphasizes. Third, the Mustard Seed and the Yeast are both about the necessities of life: bread and shelter. Finally, each shows that a single person's actions have a possible impact on life outside the immediate context; that is, the people who will come to eat the enormous amount of bread the woman has produced, and the birds that will nest in the branches of the tree.

Cleaning out the "Leaven is impure and therefore Mustard Seed is impure" leaf, which extends to the idea that the mustard seed is a transgression of laws against planting two types of seeds in the same plot, requires another step. Any appeal to the rabbis for determining the meaning of a Gospel passage is a fraught issue: rabbinic sources are later than the New Testament, generally prescriptive (what should be done) rather than descriptive (what is actually being done), often in contradiction with each other since they preserve minority as well as majority opinions, and not necessarily, or in some cases even likely, indicative of anything practiced in the late Second Temple period in the Galilee.

Nor are most New Testament scholars trained to use rabbinic literature. Typically, we rely on the works of our predecessors, themselves untrained, and, typically again, we cite the same texts repeatedly without necessarily or even often checking their original contexts.

The argument for the mustard as representing an impurity that is transgressive runs as follows. First, laws against mixing of diverse kinds, from mixing linen with wool in textiles to planting two types of crops in a field, are adduced from Leviticus as well as select rabbinic sources. For example, Leviticus 19.19 states, "You shall not let your animals breed with a different kind; you shall not sow your field with two kinds of seed; nor shall you put on a garment made of two different materials." The Torah is concerned with taxonomy. Categories of sacred and profane, such as the Sabbath and the rest of the week, female and male, Israel and the nations, kosher and not kosher, all serve to mark the covenant community as a distinct people.

Next, the commentators take Luke's "garden," Greek *kepos,* to represent Jesus's original wording as well as to be the Greek equivalent of the Hebrew *argula*, a term not appearing in the Tanakh, but present in the Mishnah (only in *Kilaim* 3.1–2; *Shabbat* 9.2), where it appears to mean "garden bed."[20] Then they conclude that "planting mustard seed is proscribed in Palestinian custom"[21] and that the parable, which describes the mustard as either planted in or tossed into a garden, presents a mixing of kinds that "pollutes the garden, makes it unclean."[22]

Ostensibly confirming this reading, scholars further argue that the mustard is a "weed." To make this final case, they quote the first-century Roman naturalist Pliny the Elder, who describes mustard as follows: "It grows entirely wild, though it is improved by being transplanted; but on the other hand when it has once been sown it is scarcely possible to get the place free of it, as the seed when it falls germinates at once."[23] Thus is it uncultivated, in violation of purity laws, out of place, deviant, and so on.

Although appearing sound, arguments for the transgressive and impure nature of mustard seed have no roots. First, the Mishnaic evidence for the illegal presence of mustard in a garden with other plants is not as secure as is frequently asserted. Although *Kilaim* 2.8 states, "They do not flank a field of grain [with] mustard or safflower," it goes on to note, "they flank a field of vegetables [with] mustard or safflower." Luke's garden (*kepos*) may well be a vegetable garden, given that the same term appears in the Septuagint to describe the vegetable garden King Ahab wanted to plant in place of Naboth's vineyard (1 Kings 21.2; cf. Deut. 11.10). Mustard in a vegetable garden: no problem.

Next, the rabbis debate where mustard can be planted. *Kilaim* 2.9 quotes Rabbi Meir (early second century CE) as prohibiting more than three patches of a field with mixed plants to be planted with mustard "for [then the field as a whole] looks like a field of mustard," but the sages immediately counter, "Nine patches are permitted, ten are prohibited." The mustard in the parable is looking increasingly kosher. Finally, the Tosefta (*Kilaim* 2.5) "explicitly permits surrounding the vegetables in a garden bed with mustard or safflower."[24] Therefore, when we read that "mustard plants were not popular in ancient Palestine,"[25] we might wonder why, given mustard's healing properties and tasty flavor and given the extensive rabbinic commentaries on where it can be planted.

As for the location of the seed in the parable, Luke's "garden" is only one of several variants. Matthew has the mustard planted in a "field," and planting mustard in a field is not a legislative problem. Indeed, Luke may have mentioned the "garden" in order to make the parable more familiar to his gentile readers.

The only other uses of "garden" (*kepos*) in the New Testament are in John 18.1, 26, and 19.41. The first two references are to the location the Synoptics call Gethsemane, the place where Jesus was arrested. The third reference concerns his burial: "Now there was a garden (*kepos*) in the place where he was crucified, and in the garden (*kepos*) there was a new tomb in which no one had ever been laid." The Septuagint also associates gardens with tombs (e.g., 2 Kings 21.18 states, "Manasseh slept with his ancestors, and was buried in the garden [*kepos*] of his house, in the garden of Uzza"). I do not think vegetable gardens are intended with these references; one does not usually tiptoe over the cucumbers and peppers to pay one's respects. Thus, I am not inclined to put too much weight on the import of the location for the parable. The seed goes where seed goes—into the ground.

Finally, on the question of illegality: it is clear from the rabbinic evidence that some Jews were planting mustard seed. That is all the parable notes— that it was planted. The parable mentions nothing about other crops in the garden. Since mustard can be planted, and since mustard has medicinal and gastronomical benefits, there is no reason to see anything untoward, let alone transgressive or impure, about the seed in the garden. Had Jesus wished to speak of the seed among the other vegetables, as he does with the weed among the wheat, he could have done so. The lack of reference to other plants in this plot or field or garden also uproots the claims of impurity or halakhic violation.

The citations from Pliny are even less convincing when it comes to the idea that mustard requires a warning label, lest its transgressive property become toxic. First, Pliny does not regard mustard as noxious or even clearly as a weed. He recognizes that mustard grows wild, but he focuses his account on the wild crop transplanted to an intended location, whether garden or field he does not specify. Thus his concern is its domestication. Both rabbinic texts and pagan sources generally regard mustard as a cultivated plant.[26] They do not generally speak of the mustard as taking over (let alone conquering or colonizing) the garden. If a minister today told a parable about a buttercup or a dandelion, I do wonder if the congregation would immediately think of military incursion. Moreover, anyone who "plants" a seed might be expected to tend the garden.

Pliny also states that mustard is "extremely beneficial for the health" and helpful in the treatment of "snake and scorpion bites, toothache, indigestion, asthma, epilepsy, constipation, dropsy, lethargy, tetanus, leprous sores," and other illnesses.[27] Thus, even his notice of its "pungent taste and fiery effect"[28] is unlikely to suggest transgression. To the contrary, mustard is exactly the type of crop one wants.

Like beginning with yeast and ending up with bread, the movement from seed to plant produces something desirable and something that is more than the sum of its parts. With yeast and seed, one can do little, but with the bread and the plant much can be gained.

A Little Bird Suggested . . .

The parable, however, has more than just seed and tree; it also has birds. Thus commentators, who cannot find mustard in the scriptures of Israel, go bird hunting. "Birds of the heaven" (Heb. *of ha-shamayim;* Gk. *peteinoi tou oranou*) fly through the Tanakh almost fifty times, starting as early as Genesis 1.26, where God states of humanity, "Let them have dominion over the fish of the sea, and over the birds of the air, and over the cattle, and over all the wild animals of the earth, and over every creeping thing that creeps upon the earth." To have a more convincing intertext, however, a connection between birds and trees is in order.

The connections do appear. Several times these same scriptures associate the birds with sheltering in trees, and the parable can be read in terms of any of these associations. Psalm 104.12, 16–17, the paean to divine greatness that begins, "Bless the LORD, O my soul," affirms, "By the streams the birds of the air have their habitation; they sing among the branches. . . . The trees of the LORD are watered abundantly, the cedars of Lebanon that he planted. In them the birds build their nests." With this intertext, the parable hints not only of divine greatness, but also of humanity's participation in that greatness even if we do not realize it.

However, it is not to the benevolent sheltering trees that commentators go in search of understanding the mustard seed. Instead, they go to Ezekiel 31 and Daniel 4, both of which associate birds and trees with fallen empires. Ezekiel, writing in the context of the Babylonian exile, advises: "Consider Assyria, a cedar of Lebanon, with fair branches and forest shade, and of great height, its top among the clouds. . . . All the birds of the air made their nests in its boughs; under its branches all the animals of the field gave birth to their young; and in its shade all great nations lived" (31.3, 6). Given that readers then, and now, knew that Assyria fell to Babylon—the empire that destroyed Ezekiel's Jerusalem and took the prophet into exile—the tree's demise is not unexpected: "Therefore thus says the Lord GOD: 'Because it towered high and set its top among the clouds, and its heart was proud of its height, I gave it into the hand of the prince of the nations; he has dealt with it as its wickedness deserves. I have cast it out'" (31.10–11). Deserted by its human inhabitants, Assyria's ruins are home only to the wild creatures: "On its fallen trunk settle all the birds of the air, and among its boughs lodge all the wild animals" (31.13).

Daniel echoes the prophecy. According to the story, King Nebuchadnezzar of Babylon had dreamt of the cutting down of a tree "visible to the ends of the whole earth. . . . The animals of the field found shade under it, and the birds of the air nested in its branches, from it all living beings were fed" (4.11–12). Daniel explains to Nebuchadnezzar: "It is you, O king. You have grown great and strong. Your greatness has increased and reaches to heaven, and your sovereignty to the ends of the earth" (4.22).

Once the trees are compared to fallen kingdoms, it is an easy step to the popular view that the parable is a burlesque of empire.[29] In Jesus's retelling, it is the tenacious mustard plant and not the mighty cedar that represents the kingdom of heaven. The interpretation is appealing, particularly given twentieth- and twenty-first-century consciousness of the perils of empire.

Making this reading even more attractive to present-day interpreters is the connection of the birds to the gentile nations. With this conclusion, the parable shows that God's empire is multicultural, but it arrives via natural process and not nuclear power.

Whether these readings would have occurred to first-century Galileans is another matter. Unlike the image of the vineyard, which had become a conventional image of Israel, birds nesting in a tree was not a conventional image for empire. Had Ezekiel described his mighty cedar as a "tree" (Gk. *dendron*), then we might be more sanguine about a connection at least with Luke's version of the parable. Had the parable mentioned a cedar or noted the destruction of the tree, the connection to imperial burlesque would have stronger roots.

Nor are the birds of heaven quite the image of gentiles, as is often claimed. The expression "birds of the heavens" (what the NRSV typically renders "birds of the air") shows up forty times in the earlier scriptures, both the Tanakh and the Deuterocanonical (Old Testament Apocrypha) texts. Rarely does it even come close to a connection with gentiles. Mostly, the birds are exactly that, birds: being named by the first human in the Garden of Eden (Gen.

2.20), entering Noah's ark (7.3), devouring the flesh of corpses (e.g., 1 Sam. 17.44, 46; 2 Sam. 21.10; 1 Kings 14.11; Ps. 79.2; Jer. 7.33); representing the animal world (Job 12.7; Ps. 8.8; Jdt. 11.7). Even in other sayings of Jesus, the birds are exactly that, birds. For example, in the Sermon on the Mount, Jesus instructs: "Look at the birds of the air; they neither sow nor reap nor gather into barns, and yet your heavenly Father feeds them. Are you not of more value than they?" (6.26). In speaking to a would-be disciple, he says, "Foxes have holes, and birds of the air have nests; but the Son of Man has nowhere to lay his head" (Matt. 8.20). In like manner, not every reference to a chicken has a Christological focus, despite the imagery in Matthew 23.37 and Luke 13.34; there is no poultry messianism.

The focus of the parable is not on the contrast to other types of trees, but—if a contrast is to be foregrounded—it is on the size of the seed versus the growth or size of the result of its germination. The image of birds nesting in trees is common in scripture, but the connection to the demise of empires is relatively rare. In Luke 17.6, Jesus speaks of faith the size of a mustard seed that can uproot a mulberry bush, but there is no good reason to think that the mulberry represents Rome. Finally, there is no immediate reason to think that the birds of the parable are anything more than birds; the allegory is not needed for the parable to have meaning.[30] Not all egrets are Egyptians or sparrows Spartans. Sometimes a seed is just a seed, a bird is just a bird, and a tree is just a tree.

From a Single Seed Come Multiple Readings

The parable need not be read as about empire; it should not be read as teaching about the problems with Jewish purity laws. To focus on the "noxious" aspect of the mustard is no more helpful than to read the parable of the Leaven as being about impurity. No one in the cultures of the time, whether Jewish or pagan, regarded either mustard or leaven as a bad thing. Each had great utilitarian value; each was commonly available; each brought good things to those who served it.

The parable does mark a contrast between small and great. It may well be read in light of the parables of the Leaven and the Seed That Grows Secretly. It has something to say about seeds and birds, growth and shelter. These are the component parts of the parable, and it is from these that meanings may best be drawn.

To speak of the parable as demonstrating that great outcomes arrive from small beginnings is correct, but it is banal. To note *what* outcomes might occur provides better provocation. Mustard is a curative, and one available to anyone. It is part of the good world God gives us; like the sun, which insists on shining, the seed insists on growing, to be used by anyone who finds the plant. Like the vast amount of bread the woman baked, the mustard plant offers more than a single person can use. The invitation to partake is a universal one, as the birds so neatly demonstrate. Instead of looking at the plant as a noxious weed, we might be better off seeing it as part of the gifts of nature; something so small, allowed to do what it naturally does, produces prodigious effects.

The concern for nature continues with the avian references. The birds of the heavens find shelter wherever it is available, whether in the mighty boughs of the cedar or on its fallen trunk. The parable is less about the fall of empire than it is the ability of God's creatures—feathered or flesh—to survive, to make do with whatever is available. The message may be less one of imperial critique than of ecological adaptation and survival.

Snodgrass suggests that one of the markers of the seed is its insignificance.[31] Granted, this reading serves both Christological and ecclesiological functions: Jesus's initial ministry was not broadly recognized among his fellow Jews, but it took root and spread especially among the gentiles; the church began with just a small group in Jerusalem, but became a global force. However, the parable speaks of the significance of the seed, that one seed grew into a plant. Thus no seed is, or should be, seen as insignificant; each contains life within it.

The transformation of yeast and dough into bread and of seed into plant opens another interpretation. What we see now is potential, but that potential needs to be actualized. The yeast has to be placed into the dough; the seed has to be planted. Even small actions, or hidden actions, have the potential to produce great things.

In addition, from both plant and dough we learn yet at least three more lessons. First, some things need to be *left alone*. Keep fiddling with the dough and it will not rise; keep exposing the seed to air and it will not germinate. Not everything, or even everyone, needs our constant attention. We are part of a larger process, and although we may start an action, once started, it can often do quite well on its own. Second, sometimes we need to *get out of the way*. We are not always the focus; sometimes we are the facilitator for something bigger than ourselves. The woman hides the yeast in the dough; whether people knew she did the baking or not remains unstated. The man plants, or even tosses, the seed. Who sowed it is much less important than the tree into which the seed grows. The final image is not a focus on the human actor, but on the results of the action.

Finally, both images are of domestic concerns: the seed parable is set in a garden or local field; the yeast parable is set at a village oven. The kingdom of heaven is found in what today we might call "our own backyard" in the generosity of nature and in the daily working of men and women. We need not adopt an "anti-empire" image here. Better would be the notion that the "lust for big-time success"[32] is misplaced. The challenge of the parable can be much homier: don't ask "when" the kingdom comes or "where" it is. The when is in its own good time—as long as it takes for seed to sprout and dough to rise. The where is that it is already present, inchoate, in the world. The kingdom is present when humanity and nature work together, and we do what we were put here to do—to go out on a limb to provide for others, and ourselves as well.

CHAPTER 6

The Pharisee and the Tax Collector

And he even said to some of those believing in themselves that they are righteous and despising the rest this parable:

"Two people went up to the Temple to pray, the one a Pharisee and the other a tax collector. The Pharisee, standing, by/to himself, these (things) prayed, 'O God, I give thanks to you that not am I like the rest of people, greedy, unrighteous, adulterers, or even like this tax collector. I fast two times of the Sabbath [i.e., each week]; I give a tenth of whatever I acquire.'

"But the tax collector, at a distance standing, did not wish to raise the eyes to the heaven, but he beat his breast, saying, 'O God, be merciful to me, a sinner.'

"To you I say, descending to his house, this one is justified, alongside that one. Because everyone who exalts himself will be humbled, and the one who humbles himself will be exalted."

Luke 18.9–14

Two fellows go up to the Temple to pray—one righteous and one sinful; one honored as a popular leader and respected teacher, and one despised as a collaborationist with the Roman government. One, who has an abundance of good deeds, prays a prayer of thanksgiving, and the other, a self-identified sinner, simply asks for mercy. We have here two conventional types, the upright and the fallen. Because Jesus's story is a parable, and because parables do the unexpected, we might expect the un-subtle points that the sinner turns out to be a saint and the saint turns out to be satanic. And that is how the parable has traditionally been understood. Ironically, however, this expectation is in part what the parable thwarts. The saint is not a sinner, the sinner is not a saint, and our conventionally unconventional reading about a reversal of status in the long run gets us nowhere.

The Expected Anti-Jewish Stereotypes

If the conventionally unconventional winds up missing the provocation of the parable, the standard readings in the Christian settings miss it all the more. For many Christian readers, the Pharisee—the one who in his own context would be seen as righteous and respected—is a negative figure wallowing in hypocritical sanctimoniousness. Conversely, the tax collector, the sinful collaborationist, is the justified hero.

This reading matches the traditional views of the Prodigal Son, with which this parable is often paired. The Pharisee in the Temple, like the elder brother in the field, is understood as engaging in works-righteousness and refusing to accept the repentant sinner (or gentile); the prodigal and the publican are regarded as both saved by grace and just darling. Augustine extends this reading by making the Pharisee the "Jew" and the tax collector the "Gentile [Christian]."[1] The message of the parable then becomes that it is better to be a repentant tax collector than a sanctimonious Pharisee, and better to be a Christian saved by grace than a Jew who despises others and teaches salvation by works.

In more recent times, readings that begin with the works-righteousness versus grace interpretation extend this false dualism by seeing the parable as functioning to "undermine the authority of the redemptive media," that is, the Temple.[2] For this approach, the Temple is a system based on works, not grace; it serves to prop up the empire rather than enfranchise the peasant; it is a "domination system" that Jesus comes to destroy. Thus the parable serves to subvert "the metaphorical structure that sees the kingdom of God as temple."[3] Once again, Jesus emerges less as a first-century Jew than as Young Man Luther, the Pharisee and the Temple represent (bad) Judaism, and the sinful tax collector is the redeemed (gentile) Christian. Once again, Jesus wept.

Such views of the Temple, Pharisees, and Judaism rely on negative stereotypes, not on what the parable says or what the sources of the period indicate. Such stereotypes also thwart the genre of Jesus's storytelling, because in this parable, this *story,* the Pharisee and the tax collector are not typical members of either group. Both men are caricatures.[4]

Neither Pharisee nor tax collector behaves in the manner that a first-century Jewish audience would expect. Listeners would be surprised that a Pharisee would be dismissive of others in the community; they would be surprised that a tax collector can be repentant. And they would be provoked, as we all should be, by the implications of the relationship between the two men.

That first-century audience would also be befuddled by the modern idea that the Temple system did not work or that it was primarily a domination system designed to pacify the peasant and mystify the power of the ruling authority. Even after the First Revolt against Rome began in 66, Jewish pilgrims continued to come to the Temple. To suggest that every pilgrim who went to the Temple, every worshipper who found it a particular site of holiness, every Jew who participated in ancestral traditions was misguided, ideologically complicit in imperial, colonial control, or otherwise unaware of how this institution was manipulating the peasantry, is to impose on these earlier worshippers a modern, anti-institutional, generally Protestant view of ritual. It is to deny the Jewish connection to the Temple, a connection shared by Jesus's followers, who continued to worship there. Such claims also misunderstand the ongoing Jewish connection to the Kotel, the Western Wall of the Jerusalem Temple, which remains the holiest site in Judaism.

The parable does not critique the Temple. To the contrary, the Temple is the place that welcomes both Pharisee and tax collector, and it is the place where both find justification. How they both find justification is the surprise, and the challenge, of the parable.

And he even said to some of those believing in themselves
that they are righteous and despising the rest this parable.
(Luke 18.9)

As with the prodigal and prudent brothers, Luke has provided a literary context in which negative images of Pharisees and, for some later Christian readers, of Jews in general drive the interpretation. Luke begins the tradition of interpreting the parable in terms of Pharisaic sanctimoniousness and publican saintliness; the opening line, from the hand of the evangelist, provides the interpretive frame of self-righteousness. What often goes missing is the audience Luke gives to the parable. "Those believing in themselves" need not refer to the Pharisees; it may well refer to Jesus's own disciples, last mentioned in 17.22. The parable is part of a longer discourse in which Jesus gives his followers, directly as well as through several other parables, instructions on their role. Thus although the parable does speak about regarding others with contempt, the charge is one that could fit any listener.

As for "believing in themselves" or "trusting in themselves," that is not the problem. Personal trust is not a bad thing, and one's knowledge of one's own ability may be the sign of a healthy approach to life. Jews could be proud about their fidelity to Torah, just as Christians may well be pleased when they attend church, participate in a mission trip, visit people in prison, feed the hungry, and so on. Paul himself states that "as to righteousness under the law" he was "blameless" (Phil. 3.6), and he does not find such a statement to be sinful. Personal recognition does not detract from love of God or from repentance.

Nor does personal recognition that one has behaved well speak directly to concerns with "works-righteousness," that is, the idea that we have to pile up good works in order to be judged worthy of salvation. The Pharisee is in relation to God because he is a Jew under the covenant, not because he does "good works." Indeed, his performance of good works is his way of enacting the covenant with God. He does not do good works to earn a place in heaven; he does good works because that is how he understands what

God wants him to do. The problem with his prayer is not in his personal religiosity; it is in his negatively judging someone else. The Pharisee has the information to speak to his own status, but he cannot and therefore should not judge the hearts of others.

The parable of the Pharisee and the Tax Collector may well have been spoken by Jesus and then contextualized by Luke. Yet here Luke helps us by having the parable addressed to disciples; thereby, Luke shows us that negatively judging others is not a trait that signals "Jewish" values; it is, rather, a human trait, and one to which the followers of Jesus themselves may fall prey.

Two people went up to the Temple to pray, the one a Pharisee and the other a tax collector. **(Luke 18.10)**

We are now in the eighteenth chapter of Luke's Gospel, and we have met numerous unlikeable Pharisees and a number of quite darling tax collectors. When we read the Gospel, our sympathies are with the tax collector and not at all with the Pharisee. This is exactly the opposite stance from which a first-century Jewish audience would have heard the parable.

Tax Collectors

For Luke, tax collectors are invariably sinners on their way to becoming righteous.[5] They come to John for baptism (3.12; 7.29); they heed Jesus (15.1) and dine with him (5.29–30 cf. 7.34); a tax collector named Levi becomes one of Jesus's apostles (5.27); another, a chief tax collector named Zacchaeus ("Mr. Righteous"), seeks to see Jesus and becomes his host (19.2). Luke's ideal readers would identify with the tax collector. For readers today, however, the tax collector stands for "people today who suffer the stigma of being considered second-class citizens, even by some Christians—teenage moms; single or divorced parents of whatever age, the physically challenged, foreigners, particularly of Middle Eastern nationalities; the poor; the home-less; and so on."[6]

First-century Jews would beg to differ. The tax collector is the agent of Rome and not the agent of God, and the two can be seen as being at cross-purposes. The tax collector would have been presumed to be corrupt, as we see with Zacchaeus, who despite his righteousness is despised by the people in his town. The tax collector is not the repentant hero; he is likely dishonest, likely to overcharge the population. Hence the Baptist's exhortation, "Collect no more than the amount prescribed for you" (Luke 3.13). Tax collectors, at least according to Luke, were rich (19.2), well connected, and ostentatious enough to host banquets (5.29).

Thus our tax collector does not, as a few commentators insist, occupy "a marginal position within society." His problem is not that he was "without power, wealth, or status . . . sinned against, oppressed, and marginalized";[7] his problem is that he is a sinner, probably rich, an agent of Rome, and, as a tax collector, has likely shown no mercy to others.

The presence of the tax collector in the Temple is therefore unexpected. He was a traitor to his people; the government for which he worked, the Roman Empire, used the Temple as its personal bank. Josephus writes that Pontius Pilate "spent money from the sacred treasury in the construction of an aqueduct to bring water into Jerusalem, intercepting the source of the stream at a distance of 200 furlongs. The Jews did not acquiesce in the operations that this involved, and tens of thousands of men assembled and cried out against him." A riot ensued, with Pilate's soldiers, upon his orders, "punishing alike both those who were rioting and those who were not."[8]

Claims that Temple and the Roman taxation system were in competition and that the tax collector's "very vocation robbed the Temple of its dues, by forcing the faithful to pay taxes rather than tithes, thus supporting the hated Roman occupation rather than the sacrificial system"[9] overstate. Somehow the Jewish population paid both the Roman and the Temple tax; neither system was exorbitant.

From such details, first-century Jews might well have been interested in the attitudes of the tax collector toward the Temple. The tax collector works for the government that abuses the Temple system. Will he abuse it as well by making it his own personal bank, with an automatic withdrawal of forgiveness? Is he like the prodigal, going home to his support base, with plausible anticipation that he will be well received? Would he be regarded as expressing genuine humility, or would he be seen as craven and his sense of having to supplicate the divine inappropriate, for gods do not need such supplication?[10] Jewish auditors may have been surprised that the tax collector's prayer does not end in an expression of hope, as do the penitential Psalms (24, 50, 77, 78), the Prayer of Manasseh, and other such supplications.[11] Acknowledging sin and asking for mercy are both commendable actions, but if they are not accompanied by a resolve to stop sinning, they prompt cheap grace.

Our tax collector is in the Temple, praying. Jesus has given us an image that unsettles.

Pharisees: A Brief History

Like the quest of the historical Jesus, there is also a quest of the historical Pharisees, for ironically the only self-identified Pharisee from whom we have written records is Paul of Tarsus. Thus, in order to understand the Pharisees, we need to look at literature written by outsiders to their group, including Josephus, the Dead Sea Scrolls, the later rabbis, Paul himself, and some of the early followers of Jesus with whom they were in competition for reception by the broader Jewish community in the land of Israel.

Since members of this group are most familiar to modern readers because of their New Testament portraits—the term "Pharisee" is still seen as synonymous with "hypocrite," a connection made by the New Testament (see especially Matt. 23)—we start here. And we start, given our parable, with Luke's portrait.

Unlike the invariably positive tax collectors in the Gospel tradition, Luke's depiction of Pharisees is more ambivalent, albeit ultimately negative. Pharisees do have their good points. Some invite Jesus to dine with them (7.36; 11.37), and they do ask him questions that need not be perceived as hostile (17.20). Their warning to Jesus, "Get away from here, for Herod wants to kill you" (13.31), can be seen as benevolent, although it could also be read as an attempt to prevent Jesus from entering Jerusalem and so to abort his mission. Finally, the Pharisees drop out of Luke's Passion narrative, so at least they are not directly responsible for Jesus's death.

Pharisees are also pictured in Acts in a generally positive light. The Pharisee Gamaliel speaks on behalf of Peter and John after they were arrested by the Sanhedrin (5.34–39); Paul acknowledges his Pharisaic connections (26.5; cf. Phil. 3.5). At the Jerusalem Council, held to debate the requirements for gentiles in the church, Pharisees appear as members of the Jesus movement, albeit on the wrong side of the debate (15.5).

However, the majority of Luke's references to Pharisees are not complimentary. Unlike the tax collectors, Pharisees reject John's baptism and so God's purposes (7.30). Jesus condemns them for greed and elitism (11.38–44; 16.15), and Luke adds the generic insult that they were lovers of money (16.14). Primarily they serve as negative foils who complain about Jesus's dining with those tax collectors and their sinning friends (5.30; 7.39; 15.2); fuss over his claiming the ability to forgive sin (5.17–26); complain about his disciples' plucking grain on the Sabbath (6.1–5); condemn Jesus's healing on the Sabbath (6.6–11); seek to silence his disciples' praise of him (19.39); and attempt to trap him rhetorically (11.53–54; 14.1–6).

For the majority of Jesus's Jewish audience, the Pharisees would have been respected teachers, those who walked the walk as well as talked the talk. Josephus, a priest who found the Pharisees' voluntary organization in competition with his own inherited priestly status, mentions their interpretations of Torah designed to make ancient teachings relevant to the society of their day: "On account of which doctrines, they are able greatly to persuade the body of the people; and whatsoever they do about divine worship, prayers, and sacrifices, they perform them according to their direction; insomuch that the cities gave great attestations to them on account of their entire virtuous conduct, both in the actions of their lives and their discourses also."[12]

The New Testament's comments on the "traditions of the elders" may have some connection to these Pharisaic updatings. For example, Mark 7.3 states that the "Pharisees, and all the Jews, do not eat unless they thoroughly wash their hands, thus observing the tradition of the elders." Jesus rejects some of these teachings; instead, on what appears to be more an ad hoc than systematic basis, he develops his own interpretation of Torah. We can see his own version in his comments on Sabbath healing (Matt. 12.10–12) or in his extension of the commandments regarding murder and adultery to love of enemy and forbidding lust (5.27–28, 43–44).

Pharisaic interpretations of Torah distinguish the Pharisees not only from Jesus, but also from the Sadducees, a point the New Testament also notes. Josephus explains:

> The Pharisees have delivered to the people a great many obser-
> vances by succession from their fathers, which are not written
> in the laws of Moses; and for that reason it is that the Sadducees
> reject them, and say that we are to esteem those observances to be
> obligatory which are in the written word, but are not to observe
> what are derived from the tradition of our forefathers. And
> concerning these things it is that great disputes and differences
> have arisen among them, while the Sadducees are able to persuade
> none but the rich, and have not the populace favorable to them,
> but the Pharisees have the multitude on their side.[13]

In Paul's view, his being a Pharisee was a marker of distinction (Phil. 3.5).

Following the destruction of the Jerusalem Temple in 70 CE, members of the Pharisaic movement, along with scribes and others, came to compose what has come to be known as rabbinic literature. The rabbinic texts, more or less contemporaneous with the ante- and post-Nicene fathers, include the Mishnah, a compendium of Jewish law written down around 200 CE; the *Bavli,* or Babylonian Talmud, and the *Yerushalmi,* or Jerusalem Talmud (commentaries on the Mishnah, finally redacted after the fifth century); and the equally late midrashic collections (running commentaries on biblical books, such as *Genesis Rabbah* and *Ruth Rabbah*).

There are connections between first-century Pharisees and the later rabbis. For example, both groups are concerned with Sabbath observance, dietary regulations, ritual purity, and promoting correct understanding and following of Torah.[14] Thus the Pharisees could be seen as "proto-rabbis." However, there are also distinctions, just as there are in every party that lasts for several centuries and faces new circumstances including, in the case of the rabbis, the destruction of the Jerusalem Temple, the disastrous Second Revolt against Rome in 132–35, and the growing prominence of the rabbinic community in Babylon (present-day Iraq).

Nor can we go directly from rabbinic literature to the earlier time of Jesus. Rabbinic literature is generally prescriptive—it details the way the rabbis would like to see Jewish life lived—rather than descriptive—it is not a direct window into actual practices. Moreover, rabbinic literature is often a series of disagreements among rabbis rather than a definitive code; the rabbis debate everything, from the circumstances under which divorce can be granted to the determination of what constitutes work on the Sabbath. Consequently, as we've seen throughout these studies of the parables, it is highly problematic to take a rabbinic statement, unsupported by any other text of the first century, and understand it to be representative of practices at the time of Jesus.

We may be on safer historical ground by looking at rabbinic storytelling. Whereas laws must be adapted and should be debated for the health of a society, stories can remain stable over the generations. Rabbinic parables may well reflect earlier views, especially since they tend to be connected to a biblical passage; the laws are more likely to be adapted.

With regard to their sphere of influence, Pharisees were substantially village- rather than Temple-based. The Temple was the center of priestly power. Josephus recounts how Pharisees sought to influence Temple practice; that is the meaning of "and whatsoever they do about divine worship, prayers, and sacrifices, they perform them according to their direction" in the earlier quote. We might compare attempts by lay Catholics to determine the celebration of the Mass. Thus the Pharisees were not on home turf, but they were in a place whose operation and leadership would have been of great concern to them.

Although some scholars suggest that the Pharisee of our parable was a "retainer" in the Temple system and that "through the network of synagogues, the Pharisee and his faction participated in efforts to enforce the collection of tithes,"[15] the ancient sources do not support the claims. Tithes were collected by regional Temple representatives, not Pharisees. Second, Pharisees do not run synagogues; synagogue rulers (such as Jairus) do. Nor, by the way, do the later rabbis run synagogues; rabbinic literature locates them primarily in the schoolhouse or academy.

Equally incorrect, albeit probably as popular, is the insistence that Pharisees "believed that God's blessing, most notably ridding the land of the Romans, was contingent upon their achieving a significant measure of obedience among themselves and among the population as a whole," that they were "very nationalistic and fueled an intense hatred of Gentiles," or that they insisted that at "minute obedience to their detailed laws" was necessary in order to "stay saved."[16] Again, we do not have direct information on what the Pharisees believed. The New Testament portraits give no indication that the Pharisees were ultranationalists or that they fueled an intense hatred of gentiles. Those who claim that Paul, the (former) Pharisee, was a political firebrand take their case from Galatians 1.14, where Paul says, "I was far more zealous for the traditions of my ancestors." However, to be zealous for his tradition does not make him a political "zealot" seeking liberation from Roman domination.

It is easy to compare them to whatever population of the congregation is seen to be judgmental, parochial, bigoted, stuck-in-the-mud, or otherwise unable to see the "newness" of the "good news," as the pastor so understands it. The problem is that the "good news" should not be based on bad history; nor should the reaction of the congregation be, "Thank God, I'm not like those Pharisees (baa baa baa)."

Were Jesus to have told this parable to a group of Jews, they would have begun with the impression that the Pharisee was pious and righteous and the tax collector sinful and self-interested. It turns out, the parable would have confirmed these views. And yet it still provokes. The question, and so the location of how Jesus tells a story that can challenge, is determining what the provocation is.

Going Up to the Temple

For both Jesus's original audience and for Luke's gentile readers, going to the Temple to pray would be seen as entirely commendable behavior.[17] The Temple was not a "domination system" in the way many New Testament commentators describe it. It was not a place known for overtaxing the population, exploiting the poor, in full collaboration with Rome, or profaning the covenant. It did not function to suggest that people who worshipped elsewhere were precluded from receiving mercy.[18]

Such negative views of the Temple, which have permeated many a Christian congregation, begin with an initial misreading of the Gospels. Mark 11.17 depicts Jesus as teaching, "Is it not written, 'My house shall be called a house of prayer for all the nations'? But you have made it a den of robbers."

Uninformed readers then presume that the Temple therefore must have been both xenophobic and exploitative. Both views are incorrect.

Against the claims for a Temple-disseminated xenophobia, gentiles were welcome in the outer court, the Court of the Gentiles, just as they were welcome to participate in synagogue gatherings. The Temple was thus already a "house of prayer for all nations." The phrase comes from Isaiah 56.7, an eschatological vision of the gentiles worshipping the God of Israel.

Although the Temple was built, as were most temples in antiquity, with ascending degrees of sacrality—Court of the Gentiles, Court of the (Jewish) Women, Court of the (Jewish) Men, Court of the Priests, Holy of Holies—and thus gentiles were prohibited from certain areas, this does not make the building a place of xenophobia. Perhaps Matthew and Luke dropped the phrase "for all nations" from their versions of the Temple scene (Matt. 21.13; Luke 19.46), because they knew this internationalism was already operative.

"Den of robbers" is not a place where robbers rob. The term "den" (Gk. *splaion*) really means "cave," and the better modern rendition would be "hideout." A den of robbers is a place where robbers go with their ill-gotten gains to feel safe. The phrase comes from Jeremiah 7.11, and the context is the prophet's distress that the people sin and then presume that God, operating on automatic, will forgive them if they offer the right prayers and sacrifices. The prophet's words ring loudly to this day:

> Will you steal, murder, commit adultery, swear falsely, make offerings to Baal, and go after other gods that you have not known, and then come and stand before me in this house, which is called by my name, and say, "We are safe!"—only to go on doing all these abominations? Has this house, which is called by my name, become a den of robbers in your sight? You know, I too am watching, says the Lord. (7.9–11)

The people visiting the Temple are sinful, but that doesn't make the Temple a place where sin is encouraged.

Nor again was the Temple, according to "the normative reading of reality," the only place where forgiveness of sin or reconciliation with God could be found.[19] Nor had it failed in its calling to be the "centre of boundless salvation,"[20] as we see from the continuation of pilgrimage even after the First Revolt broke out.

It was a place of restoration, pilgrimage, worship, and inspiration. For example, the Temple was the place where proclamation of a regained state of purity following skin disease was found, since only the priest had the authority to proclaim someone "clean"; that is why Jesus sends the man he healed from leprosy to the priest (Matt. 8.4; Mark 1.44). It was also the place where one made sacrificial offerings, and the Temple made the offerings on behalf of all the people. But God was omnipresent: in the village and on the farm, at the family table and the synagogue, as well as in the Jerusalem Temple.

Although associated with sacrifices of repentance—as well as of thanksgiving, peace, and purity—the Temple was not the only place in which people could repent or find forgiveness. Josephus insists, "God is easily reconciled to those that confess their faults, and repent of them."[21] He does not insist that such reconciliation requires Temple sacrifice. Philo makes a similar point about how Jews pray with trust in "the compassionate nature of that Being who will have forgiveness rather than punishment."[22]

What Jesus himself was protesting in the Temple, in that scene so familiar from Hollywood recreations, remains an open question. In John's Gospel, he says nothing about a house of prayer or a cave of thieves. There he finds "people selling cattle, sheep, and doves, and the money changers seated at their tables"; running them out with a whip of cords, he charges, "Take these things out of here! Stop making my Father's house a marketplace!" (John 2.14, 16). The allusion is to Zechariah 14.21, where the prophet envisions the time when "there shall no longer be traders in the house of the LORD of hosts on that day." For John, the focus is not on gentile worship or exploitation; it is on the placement of the vendors, which in Jesus's view disrupted the sanctity of the site. One might compare it to a beautiful cathedral with a gift shop in the narthex.

From xenophobia to exploitation, commentators have developed a host of sins they perceived the Temple system as committing. One popular view is that people who did not pay the half-shekel Temple tax "faced social ostracism, shunning, and vilification by Temple authorities. It was this situation that seems to have created a growing class of peasants, artisans, and other rural workers known as the *am-ha-aretz,* or 'degraded dirt farmers.'"[23] Such charges, made without any primary source references, find no purchase in historical analysis. "Temple authorities" would have had no means of determining if a worshipper had paid the Temple tax, in the same way that the "authorities" at the National Cathedral have no means of determining if worshippers are in good standing with their hometown churches or even whether they have a hometown church.

The term *am ha'aretz,* the "person of the land," appears first in Genesis 23.7, in reference to the Hittite residents of Canaan before whom Abraham bows. In Exodus 5.4, Pharaoh uses it to describe his Egyptian population. Leviticus 4.2–27 uses the expression for the common people as opposed to the priests. The phrase, used fifty-two times in the scriptures of Israel, does not connote the "degraded" or the shunned. In rabbinic sources, it comes to mean those who do not heed rabbinic dictates, for, as we have noted, rabbinic teaching was initially prescriptive rather than descriptive. But even here the idea of the "degraded dirt farmer" is absent.

The Mishnah, *Demai* 2.2, states that one who tithes all his produce should avoid the hospitality of an *am ha'aretz,* because one cannot tell if all his foodstuffs are tithed. On the other hand, Rabbi Judah says in the same passage that "one who accepts the hospitality of an *am-ha'aretz* is trustworthy." Nothing here about Temple ostracism (nor would there be; the Temple had been destroyed a century and a half earlier); nothing here about degradation.

The Babylonian Talmud (*Berakhot* 47b) offers the classical rabbinic definition:

> We have been taught, Who is an *am-ha'aretz*? He does not eat
> profane food in ritual cleanness. So said R. Meir. But the sages say:
> "Anyone who does not tithe his produce in the proper way. Our
> masters taught: Who is an *am-ha'aretz*? He who does not read the
> *Sh'ma* morning and evening—such is the opinion of R. Eliezer.
> R. Joshua said: Anyone who does not put on *tefillin* [phylacteries].
> Ben Azzai said: Anyone who has not *tzitzit* [fringes] attached to
> his garments. R. Nathan said: Anyone who has no mezuzah at his
> doorway. R. Nathan ben Joseph said: Anyone who has sons, but
> does not bring them up to the study of the Torah. Others say: Even
> if he has read scripture and studied Mishnah, but has not attended
> upon disciples of the wise, he is an *am-ha'aretz*.

The focus on post-70 rabbinic interests is evident. The lack of focus on economic as opposed to ritual practice should also be evident. As David A. Neale points out after an exhaustive discussion of the *am ha-aretz* in rabbinic sources, "to attempt to establish a sociological profile of the general Jewish public through the lens of rabbinic pronouncements on the *'ammei ha-aretz* is not only poor methodology but profoundly misleading."[24]

For both men in this parable, the Temple is a place of prayer. It is a place where God is found; where fidelity can be celebrated and reconciliation found, without precluding other sites for such celebration and reconciliation; where Jewish distinction can be proclaimed over and against Roman insistence on assimilation. It is this same place where Jesus's followers continued to worship after his crucifixion.

The Pharisee, standing, by/to himself, these (things) prayed,
"O God, I give thanks to you that not am I like the rest of
people, greedy, unrighteous, adulterers, or even like this tax
collector. I fast two times of the Sabbath [i.e., each week];
I give a tenth of whatever I acquire." **(Luke 18.11–12)**

Luke's Greek underlying 18.11 has been translated in various ways, from the relatively neutral "The Pharisee, standing by himself, was praying thus" (NRSV), to the more negative self-absorbed "stood and prayed thus *with* himself" (KJV), to the idolatrous "took up his position and spoke this prayer *to* himself" (NAB[25]). Those who do opt for seeing the Pharisee as praying *concerning himself* or *to himself*[26] exacerbate the Pharisee's negative depiction. The phrasing is ambiguous in the Greek, so we readers must choose just how obnoxious we find the Pharisee to be. The Pharisee's distance may indicate his sense of elitism, a desire to commune personally with his God, or that he seeks to shame the tax collector.[27] How we assess the Pharisee may well tell us more about ourselves than about him. Yet whatever we conclude, we should note that the address is still to God and the gratitude is still expressed to God.

The view that the Pharisee was engaged in a "deliberate separating of himself from his neighbor, the publican"[28] by his "standing by himself" overstates. So too is the claim that the Pharisee stands by himself because of his concern for ritual purity.[29] Were the Pharisees so obsessive about purity, they could have moved to Qumran; instead, they are continually in contact with Jesus, including inviting him, at least three times, to banquets in Luke's account. If they were so obsessive, it is unclear how they could be the teachers of the masses, respected by them, and at the same time eschew any contact with them.

As for the content of the prayer, some commentators label it "astonishing" in that it is "disingenuous, self-deceptive, and mean-spirited"; the Pharisee "implicitly considers himself an autonomous agent of moral virtue; he is hardly dependent upon God for anything."[30] The prayer is distinctive, but not for those reasons. First, the Pharisee thanks God for his state and thus shows his dependence. As for being an autonomous agent of moral virtue, Pharisees did believe in a combination of fate and free will. To some extent, his moral stance is of his own doing: he resisted temptation; he chose to follow Torah. At least the first part of the prayer is perfectly fine, for it is another way of saying, "There but for the grace of God go I."[31]

Other commentators do not see the prayer as astonishing at all, because they begin with the presupposition that Jewish prayers are commonly elitist, derogatory toward others, and self-satisfied. Common in both popular and lay sources is the comparison of the Pharisee's prayer with the Babylonian Talmud, *Berakhot* 28b: "I give thanks to thee, O Lord my God, that thou hast given me my lot with those who sit in the seat of learning, and not with those who sit at the street corners; for I am early to work, and they are early to work; I am early to work on words of the Torah and they are early to work on things of no moment."[32]

This prayer does set up distinctions. But it should be seen not as about self-import, but about gratitude. It is God who provided the supplicant with the opportunity to study rather than have to work to earn money. It is God who allows the supplicant to see what is truly important or, perhaps, to have his "pearl of great price." Thus the Pharisee's prayer might be compared to Deuteronomy 26.1–15, especially vv. 12–14. As professor of Old Testament Fredrick C. Holmgren observes, "The worshiper stands before God, and in this holy moment he speaks *to God* of the kind of person he is.

He confesses that he has done what God expects of him; he has been sincere and responsible."[33]

Additional possible parallels scholars have adduced to the Pharisee's prayer include 1QH[a] 15:34, the ever popular Tosefta, *Berakhot* 6.18 (with parallels in Babylonian Talmud, *Menachot* 43b; Jerusalem Talmud, *Berakhot* 9.1), and the Babylonian Talmud, *Berakhot* 28b;[34] the prayers from the Tosefta and from *Berakhot 28b* may be the most cited rabbinic prayers in Christian contexts, simply because they seem to confirm the stereotype that Jews are elitist or misogynist and Jesus a populist and a feminist. Often they are cited to make Jesus or Paul look better than their "Jewish" or "rabbinic" context.

The first prayer, from the Qumran *Thanksgiving Hymns,* reads, "[I give you thanks,] Lord, because you did not make my lot fall in the congregation of deceit, nor have you placed my allotted territory in the council of hypocrites, but you have called me to your kindness, to your forgiveness." There is nothing sanctimonious or hypocritical in this prayer; there is gratitude for God's grace toward the supplicant. Just as Pharisees believed in a combination of fate and free will, so the Essenes, with whom the Qumran scrolls can be associated, believed everything was determined by God. Thus the composer thanks God for the grace that allows him to be a faithful worshipper.

The prayer from the Tosefta, *Berakhot* 6.18, reads:

> R. Judah says, "A man must recite three benedictions every day:
>
> > 'Blessed be You, Lord, who did not make me a gentile.
> > 'Blessed be You, Lord, who did not make me uneducated.
> > 'Blessed be You, Lord, who did not make me a woman.' "

Rabbi Judah was responsible for the codification of the Mishnah around 200 CE. This text is from about half a century later. To claim the prayer was recited by all Jews in the first century is a stretch. Second, the prayer praises God that the supplicant is in a position to know and so to follow all the commandments. Gentiles were not under Torah and so were not expected to follow it. The uneducated do not know all the rabbinic commentary and so are unable, in Rabbi Judah's eyes, fully to understand the practices and the rationales. Women were exempt, in the rabbinic system, from many time-bound commandments, since the rabbis realized that their time was not their own; domestic duties, child care, and so on would have precluded their saying certain prayers at certain times.

When my son Alexander attended the Orthodox Jewish Day School in Nashville, which at the time had a Chabad rabbi as its director, he was taught this prayer, known as the *she'lo asani* (Heb. "Who did not make me"). I asked him why he would give thanks for not being made a gentile, uneducated, or a woman. In his best five-year-old way, he explained that sometimes it is important to thank God for things that we may not feel thankful for, because God knows what's good for us. Gentiles are not responsible for following all the commandments that Jews have, the uneducated do not follow them because they do not know them, and women are more naturally good than men are. Therefore, he was to thank ha-Shem for making him a Jew, educated, and a man, because all three combined put on him greater responsibility to behave appropriately.

I do not find such contemporary explanations convincing. However, I do understand how the tradition attempts to limit the negative implications. I also understand how this particular prayer, despite its frequent citation by New Testament scholars (and hence my need to address it here) has *nothing* to do with the parable.

Finally, his prayer is not, contrary to yet another theory, based on a Galilean proverb, "Better a tax collector than a Pharisee self-righteous before God."[35] There is no such proverb. Galileans were as dedicated to the Temple as Judeans, and we do not have any evidence that first-century Galileans despised Pharisees.

As for those readers who want to see Jewish prayers as divisive and Jesus as inventing the all-embracing liturgy, we might compare Jesus's own prayer: "I thank you, Father, Lord of heaven and earth, because you have hidden these things from the wise and intelligent and have revealed them to infants" (Matt. 11.25). Or we might cite the rabbinic teaching: "I call heaven and earth to witness: whether Jew or Gentile, whether man or woman, whether servant or free, they are all equal in this: that the Holy Spirit rests upon them in accordance with their deeds!" (*Seder Eliyahu Rabba* 10). But here I am proof-texting.

What is astonishing about the prayer is not the list of good acts per se. It is astonishing both because it negatively judges the tax collector rather than attempts to bring him into a better religious purview and because, as the next line shows, it attests supererogatory work that no Pharisee was expected to perform.

Fasting and Tithing

Deuteronomy 26.12–15 states:

> When you have finished paying all the tithe of your produce in the third year (which is the year of the tithe), giving it to the Levites, the aliens, the orphans, and the widows, so that they may eat their fill within your towns, then you shall say before the LORD your God: "I have removed the sacred portion from the house, and I have given it to the Levites, the resident aliens, the orphans, and the widows, in accordance with your entire commandment that you commanded me; I have neither transgressed nor forgotten any of your commandments: I have not eaten of it while in mourning; I have not removed any of it while I was unclean; and I have not offered any of it to the dead. I have obeyed the LORD my God, doing just as you commanded me. Look down from your holy habitation, from heaven, and bless your people Israel and the ground that you have given us, as you swore to our ancestors— a land flowing with milk and honey."

Our Pharisee has done what was commanded, even to his use of the first person in his prayer, and much more.

The Pharisee has gone beyond even the strictest of strict understandings of Torah. No text requires that *everything* be tithed. Jesus comments on how Pharisees "tithe mint, dill, and cummin" (Matt. 23.23), and the most even the Mishnah suggests is a tithe on figs bought in the marketplace and eaten at home (*Masserot* 2.1). Our Pharisee does more; he is speaking of all his possessions: home, clothing, animals. "In sum, the Pharisee's prayer is a caricature, and might have brought a smile even on the faces of real Pharisee bystanders."[36] He is as good as one could be; he is like another Abraham, who gave Melchizedek "one-tenth of everything" (Gen. 14.20).

Nor is there any requirement for twice-a-week fasting. The practice, used for mourning, repenting, or personal discipline, was not designed for asceticism. The dominant Jewish view was one of enjoying the good world that God provided. By such rigorous fasting practices, the Pharisee may be further distinguishing himself not only from rogues and murderers, but also from everyone else, given the importance of table fellowship. To fast by oneself is to withdraw from the community rather than to be part of it. However, more likely his fasting as well as his tithing locates him within the community. Both would be considered meritorious acts performed on behalf of and so in solidarity with the rest of the covenant community. He may even be "vicariously [making] atonement for the sins of the people by fasting twice a week."[37]

Despite the Pharisee's meritorious conduct, he makes no comment explicitly about purity laws. This silence is then filled in by commentators, who continue to regard the Jewish purity system as something negative. To see the Pharisee and the tax collector as "one more incompatible pair, the clean and the unclean"[38] is to misconstrue Jewish purity laws. The parable is set in the Temple, and anyone who enters has to be ritually pure. There is no reason to see the tax collector outside the Temple as any more or less impure than the average Jew; inside the Temple, he is necessarily ritually pure. Moral impurity is not the same thing as ritual impurity. The tax collector sold out his people to the Roman government; he did not, as far as we know, either have a ham sandwich or ejaculate immediately before entering the Temple.[39]

For first-century Jews, Jesus's description of this particular Pharisee would have been taken as a humorous representative of a character type, the "saint," and not a representative of popular scorn, regional dislike, obsessive purity codes, or Temple domination. He is also a character type about to be disabused of his distinction from the tax collector. What he does not realize is that his supererogatory practices, coupled with the Temple sacrificial system, will lead to the tax collector's justification as well as his own.

But the tax collector, at a distance standing, did not wish to
raise the eyes to the heaven, but he beat his breast, saying,
"O God, be merciful to me, a sinner." **(Luke 18.13)**

Our tax collector has positioned himself "far off" or "at a distance" (Gk. *makrothen,* the same term used in Mark 15.40 to describe the women at the cross and in Luke 16.23 to explain the distance between Lazarus in heaven and the rich man in Hades). Although the parable does not answer the question "distance from what," seeing the tax collector as standing apart from the Pharisee and from other worshippers would not be an incorrect reading. He may have feared that fellow worshippers would shun him or worse, given his traitorous behavior. Perhaps he felt himself even unworthy to come before God. Perhaps he is indicating his own sense of isolation.

Not surprisingly, commentators again evoke their negative stereotypes of purity laws to explain the tax collector's position by claiming that he was "most likely ostracized by other worshippers because of his suspected ritual impurity"[40] or that "because the tax collector entered the homes of unclean people, touched unclean objects, and handled unclean money, he would be considered ceremonially unclean."[41] There is nothing in the parable about other worshippers "ostracizing" him; it is the tax collector who stands apart, not the other worshippers. Nor does the parable say anything about purity; it need not do so, since Jesus's Jewish audience would already know that one needed to be ritually pure in order to enter the Temple. Handling money is something the Temple itself did, as the money changers converted coinage from throughout the empire into Tyrian shekels. Moreover, money itself is not "unclean"; if it were, there would be no monetary offering. The publican's problem is his profession, not his purity.

Another scholar appeals to the Mishnah, *Tamid* 4.6, in suggesting that certain Temple officials made "the unclean stand by the Eastern Gate."[42] The passage is irrelevant to the parable, because, again, the parable has nothing to do with purity. The "unclean" described in *Tamid* 4 may be a reference to those whom priests had pronounced as healed of their leprosy, who would need to wait for the appropriate time to make their offering; it may refer to priests in states of ritual impurity (e.g., because of ejaculation), who did not want to appear as if they were not doing their jobs.

Just as commentators frequently take a negative view of anything the Pharisee does, so they are inclined to see value in every action the tax collector takes. A few scholars enhance the tax collector's humility by observing that his "beating his breast" is an action associated not with men, but with women at funerals.[43] I doubt Jews across the spectrum from Orthodox to Reform who "beat their breasts" during the recitation of the litany of sins (Heb. *al chet*) see themselves as getting in touch with their feminine side. The same point holds for the witnesses to the death of Jesus described in Luke 23.48: "And when all the crowds who had gathered there for this spectacle saw what had taken place, they returned home, beating their breasts." The tax collector is atoning, something not associated only with women.

His prayer, "Be merciful to me" (Gk. *hilaskomai;* lit., "pardon, be propitious"), may contain a faint echo of 2 Chronicles 6.29–30, Solomon's invocation: "Whatever prayer, whatever plea from any individual or from all your people Israel, all knowing their own suffering and their own sorrows so that they stretch out their hands toward this house; may you hear from heaven, your dwelling place, forgive [Gk. *hilase*], and render to all whose heart you know, according to all their ways, for only you know the human heart."

Dennis Hamm, professor of New Testament at Creighton University, notes that the term is connected to the Tamid service,[44] described in Exodus 30.16 and mentioned in Hebrews 2.17 regarding atonement. It goes too far to conclude that the Pharisee and tax collector came to the Temple precisely at the time of the sacrifice,[45] but the connection of the setting and the language to atoning sacrifice cannot be missed. It is in the Temple that the tax collector believes he can find atonement, and he is correct.

We have no reason to doubt the tax collector's sincerity. He bravely entered the Temple, where he knew that other worshippers might regard him as a collaborationist, an extorter, or a rogue. He admits his sin and his need for mercy. Commentators who insist, "There is no way at this point that the tax collector, on the basis of his prayer alone, can receive forgiveness,"[46] or that, for Jesus's Jewish listeners, "at the very least their expectations of what ought to happen in the temple area are challenged, even shattered"[47] limit the mercy of God, the value of community merit, the trust of the tax collector, and Jewish theology.

A first-century Jewish audience would not presume such limitations. Rather, they would be forced to allow for the possibility that a tax collector could be righteous. Those listeners might hear even more provocative, more disturbing messages about both personal righteousness and divine mercy, but select Christian theology and English translations that follow from it hide the point.

⸺⸺⸺

To you I say, descending to his house, this one is justified, alongside that one. Because everyone who exalts himself will be humbled, and the one who humbles himself will be exalted. **(Luke 18.14)**

According to today's translators, Jesus ends the parable with an explanation: "I tell you, this man went down to his home justified *rather than* the other; for all who exalt themselves will be humbled, but all who humble themselves will be exalted" (18.14). Numerous problems beset this verse, from its initial connection to the parable, to its translation, to its interpretation.

First, the comment about those who humble themselves and those who exalt themselves is a floating statement, easily tacked onto any story. The same line appears in Luke 14.11 as a conclusion to Jesus's instructions about behavior at banquets and in Matthew 23.12, a set of instructions on how disciples are to behave. There is no necessary reason for thinking it traveled initially with our parable, and Luke may have attached it to the parable to control the meaning of the story, just as Luke provides an opening frame to limit the parable's meaning to those who would aggrandize themselves.

Second, from Luke's zero-sum game of the humble and exalted and as well from Luke's depictions of good tax collectors, with whom readers are to identify, and bad Pharisees, from whom they should distance themselves, then flow the assessments of the judgment Jesus offers. The standard reading is that the tax collector receives the gift of grace, while the Pharisee, shackled by his view that following Torah is what earns divine love, "finds no justice or favor."[48] Others go as far as to suggest that the Pharisee, who asked for nothing, received nothing. The problem with this view is that it prompts exactly the same type of dualistic, judgmental system that Jesus speaks against, for it suggests the response, "Thank you, God, that I am not like that Pharisee." Once we negatively judge one character and promote the other, the parable traps.

Luke leads us into such temptation by appending the floating saying. Jesus was a much more challenging teacher. Jesus and his fellow Jews were not bound in their thinking by the social-science insistence upon limited good; they knew that the God of Israel was generous. In their view, there is enough grace for Pharisee and tax collector both.

They knew that the tax collector could be justified. The problem was, they would not have liked the idea. Nor would they have liked how this justification took place. Were we in their system, neither would we—and that is the punch of the parable.

And so we come to the simple preposition, on which one of the challenges of this parable hangs. Biblical scholars generally presume that the Greek preposition *para,* used to refer to the Pharisee, means "rather than" that one. They see the tax collector as justified, and the Pharisee as not. This is a legitimate translation. However, that preposition can have multiple translations. Commentator Timothy Friedrichsen comes close to complicating this claim in his suggestion that *para ekeinon* [rather than / along side that one] "is Luke's addition to an original ending that did not offer full resolution."[49] More intriguing and truer to the provocation of the parable is his proposal that the phrase be taken in an inclusive sense: "*Para* + accusative can mean 'because of' or 'on account of.'"[50] Thus the last line could be understood as suggesting that the tax collector received his justification on account of the Pharisee.

That pesky Greek preposition *para,* as in "paradox," "parallel," "Paraclete," and "parable," can mean "rather than"; it can also mean "because of." Another meaning, and the one most familiar from the use of the prefix in English, is "to set side by side." Its primary connotation is not one of antagonism ("rather"), but one of juxtaposition ("next to"). Therefore, without Luke's tag line about those who humble themselves, the parable should conclude, "This man went down to his home justified alongside the other" or even "because of the other." Why is it that so many interpreters find both compelling and congenial readings that damn figures identified with Jews and Judaism?

The translations of "along side" and "because of" make greater sense in historical context, and they also prompt the greatest challenge of the parable. Judaism is a communitarian movement in which people pray in the plural ("Our Father . . . Give us . . . Forgive us . . ."), and in which each member of the community is responsible for the other. (We saw this concern in our discussion of the prodigal's father, who does not rebuke his younger son.) To this day, in the liturgy for Yom Kippur, the Day of Atonement, the entire congregation recites a public confession, while "beating our breasts." This concern for community responsibility means that the sin of one person can negatively impact everyone else.

At the same time, it means that the good deeds of one person can have a positive impact on the lives of others. For example, Jewish tradition speaks of what is commonly translated "merits of the ancestors" (Heb. *zechut avot*); *zechut* is better understood as "desert" or "juridical innocence"[51] or more colloquially, "stored-up protection." The idea is that even if we sin, and we will, the benefits of the good deeds of Abraham, Isaac, Jacob, and the other "fathers" could be transferred to us.

We have seen that the Pharisee has more good deeds, a greater store of protection, than he could need. First-century Jews then might conclude that the tax collector has tapped into the merit of the Pharisee as well as, given the location and his use of atonement language, the communal aspect of the Temple system. Just as one person's sin can create a stain on the entire community, so one person's righteousness can save it. It is precisely by this transfer of good deeds that, in one way of understanding Jesus's death, the cross works for salvation: Jesus's faithfulness (the "faith of Christ," subjective genitive, Gk. *pistis christou*) is what allows others to be justified.

Divine Pedagogy

At the end of the parable, we are left without full resolution, which is what a good parable should do. Is the Pharisee praising God or praising himself? Is the tax collector trusting in the divine or not? Will he keep his day job and continue to sin, or will he make restitution for his sins and find another line of work? With whom are readers to identify, the Pharisee who does so much more than is expected, and perhaps is a bit self-satisfied in the process, or the tax collector who, as far as we know, has done nothing for the benefit of the community, but who at least seems sincere in his request?

We cannot fully identify with either the Pharisee, who will continue to behave in a righteous manner far beyond what most people will do, or the currently repentant tax collector, who may continue to do the wrong thing. Once we judge one better than the other, we are trapped by the parable. And if we dismiss them both, we are also trapped, for most of us are neither as supererogatory as the Pharisee nor as sinful as the tax collector.

But we do see again through the parable ideas that we already, somehow, knew but did not want to acknowledge. We see that divine grace cannot be limited, for to limit this grace would be to limit the divine. This unlimited generosity is something many of us find problematic. We are quite happy when *we* are saved; we are less happy when this salvation is extended to people we do not like, especially when our dislike is bolstered by seemingly very good reasons such as, "He's a sinner."

The type of generosity shown by a God who makes the sun shine on the just and the unjust alike, the type of generosity that allows the tax collector to tap into the collective repentance of the Temple system and the good deeds of the Pharisee, is what we want for ourselves, but what we don't want others to have. And we know, deep down, that our sense of "justice" here is limited.

To give an up-to-date reading of how the parable works, and so the genius of Jesus's teaching, we need a modern example. Here's what the parable sounds like in a twenty-first century context.

The story of the tax collector's ability to tap into the merit of the Pharisee and the encompassing, communal grace of the Temple system is the ancient version of the middle-school group project. This assignment, perhaps now more familiar through reality television, puts together, in classical terms, the smart one, the one who is good at art, the one who is able to provide provisions (e.g., coffee, donuts, Scotch), and the one who both literally and figuratively brings nothing to the table. Three do their fair share, and more, since they cover the fourth's work as well. The project receives an excellent grade. The fourth, who may show up at the meetings with all sincerity but who contributes nothing, benefits from the work of others. In middle school, where I was the "smart one," I found this system unfair. I was justified (I got the "A"), but alongside me, indeed because of me, so was the slacker.

My sense of justice then was too narrow, my sense of generosity too constrained, my sense of self-import too great. But that fourth person believed in the system; that fourth person, whom we dismissed as lazy, as stupid, or as unable to contribute, may well have done what he could. He may have felt himself unworthy; indeed, we three others may have signaled to him that we were disappointed he was assigned to our group. He trusted in us; he trusted in the system. Had we been more generous with him rather than resentful, we would have learned more as well.

And what if he didn't care at all? What if he depended on us, even thought we were fools for doing his work for him? What we do is still worthwhile. We can afford to be generous. There are other systems of justice (e.g., test grades, a final judgment) in which his contributions or sins will be assessed.

We are all our brother's, and sister's, keeper, and living in a community is another form of group work. We all have something to contribute, even if what we give is the opportunity for someone else to provide us a benefit. If we take more seriously this necessary interrelationship, we might be more inclined to consider others, because our actions, whether for ill or for good, will impact them. And if our good deeds aid someone else, rather than begrudge them, why not celebrate all who are justified?

CHAPTER 7

The Laborers in the Vineyard

For is like the kingdom of the heavens to a man, a householder, who went out in the morning to hire workers for his vineyard. And agreeing with the workers for the denarius of the day, he sent them into his vineyard.

And going out around the third hour, he saw others standing in the marketplace, without work. And to those he said, "You go, even you, into the vineyard, and whatever is just, I will give you." And they went.

And again, going out around the sixth and also the ninth hour, he did likewise.

And around the eleventh, going out, he found others standing, and he says to them, "Why here are you standing all the day without work?"

They say to him, "Because no one has hired us." He says to them, "You go, even you, into the vineyard."

When evening came, says the lord of the vineyard to his steward, "Call the workers and give to them their wage/reward, beginning with the last ones to the first ones."

And coming, those around the eleventh hour, they received each a denarius.

And coming, the first, they thought that more they would receive. And they received each a denarius, even they. And receiving, they were grumbling against the householder. They were saying, "These last ones one hour did, and equal to us them you have made, to the ones having borne the burden of the day and the burning heat."

And answering one of them he said, "Friend, not do I harm you. Did not for a denarius you agree with me? Take what is yours and go. And I wish to this one, to this last one, to give as even to you. [Or] is it not permitted to me what I wish to do with what is mine? Or is your eye evil because I am good?"

Thus will be the last first and the first last.

Matthew 20.1–16

The parable describes a householder who went out early in the morning to hire workers for his vineyard.[1] At about 6:00 A.M. he contracted with a group of workers for a denarius, what in most translations reads "usual daily wage." He subsequently hires more workers at 9:00 A.M., noon, 3:00 P.M., and finally 5:00 P.M. When evening arrives, he orders his manager to pay the workers, beginning with the last hired. The manager gives the last hired the "usual daily wage." The first hired believe that since they had worked longer hours, they would receive more pay. Yet they are paid the same amount. Distressed, they grumble that the householder has been unfair. The householder strikes back: "Take what is yours and get out." The parable wraps up with the floating saying, "So the last will be first, and the first will be last."

Despite the fact that the parable has multiple characters (householder, workers, manager), multiple settings (vineyard, marketplace), and multiple elements (timing, moves from vineyard to market and back, the moment of payment), the traditional title of the parable is "The Laborers in the Vineyard."

Titles are always deceptive; they necessarily focus on one aspect of a story and so deemphasize or mask the importance of others. They already slant the interpretation, for good or for ill. The title "The Laborers in the Vineyard" or sometimes "The Workers in the Vineyard" highlights first the workers and second the location. It encourages interpreters to associate with the laborers and not the landowner; this focus in turn allows the easy allegory that the landowner is God, and the parable becomes a lesson in how we are to understand the divine. Once allegory enters, the real world is left behind,

as well as any concern the parable—and Jesus, its teller—might have for issues of economics, employment, and the relationship between managers and
employees.

The emphasis on the vineyard is another move away from the real world
of managers and marketplaces, let alone of possible sources of the cash and
the labor. It is not needed to identify the parable. The parable of the Complaining Day Laborers would have been sufficient, as would the parable of
the Surprising Salaries. The focus on the vineyard moves the parable into allegory, since vineyard is already in the Jewish culture the metaphor for God's
property. Jesus's Jewish auditors were familiar with God as the vineyard
owner, and Israel as the vineyard, as Isaiah 5.7 and Jeremiah 12.10 suggest.
If Jesus tells a story about a vineyard and an owner, the cultural repertoire
of his audience presumes the association of Israel with the vineyard and the
owner with God.[2] Once we are here in God's vineyard, the parable then becomes, for most readers, a message about salvation.

What happens, however, if we change the title? Whereas commentator
Robert Fortna's early suggestion of "The Humane Capitalist" is both anachronistic and uneasily applied to the parable, given that the householder is
not shown making any profit, but rather pays out more than he might have
been expected to expend on the last hired, at least he notices the economic
aspects of the parable.[3] The verses could equally be labeled "The Consci-
entious Boss," "The Last Hired Are the First Paid," "How to Prevent the
Peasants from Unionizing," "Debating a Fair Wage," or even "Lessons for
Both Management and Employees."

What happens if we change the theological focus? The parable could be
about salvation, but Jesus was more interested in how we love our neighbor
than how we get into heaven. Might we rather see the parable as about real
workers in a real marketplace and real landowners who hire those workers?
The vineyard can still be "Israel," the ideal community that God intended
and that Jesus attempted to call into being in anticipation of the messianic
age. But in this reading, a reading seeking the voice of Jesus the storyteller,
the message is not about eschatology, but economics; it is not about salvation
in the world to come, but the even more pressing question about salvation in
the present.

To those who ask today, "Are you saved?" Jesus might well respond, "The
better question is, 'Do your children have enough to eat?' or 'Do you have

shelter for the night?'" This parable helps us ask those more pressing, more visceral questions. But before we can get to the provocation of the parable, once again, we have to clear the vineyard of the anti-Jewish weeds that have sprung up among the grapes.

Traditional Readings: Jews and the People Jews Reject

For generations, interpreters have viewed the householder as a symbol for God, a figure of "extraordinary forgiveness and grace."[4] In the patristic period, from Origen on, it became common to hear that the first called was Adam, then subsequently Noah, Abraham, Moses, and finally Jesus and the gentiles.[5] Already the seeds of supersessionism are also sowed in this vineyard, since the church fathers regard the ones hired as indicating a progression in salvation history, from the lack of Law in Eden, to Mosaic Law, to Gospel.

Despite changes in allegorical equivalences through the centuries, the Jews still lose. Today, the first-hired workers are usually seen to be those stereotypical recalcitrant, always grumbling Jews, or at least their Pharisaic representatives, who sought to be judged by their "works" and in particular by their toiling under the demanding yoke of the Law, which is how their claim to have "borne the burden of the day and the scorching heat" (Matt. 20.12) was understood. Not a few commentators assert, "There can be little doubt that these grumblers represent the Pharisees and their attitude towards Jesus and his ministry."[6] The last hired are the "tax collectors and fishermen, without any prolonged period of rehabilitation, [who] were brought into the full assurance of God's merciful forgiveness."[7] Jeremias summarizes the earlier consensus: God is depicted as acting like an employer who has compassion for the unemployed and their families. He gives to publicans and sinners a share, all undeserved, in his kingdom.[8] Thus scholars find in the parable a lesson of legalism versus grace, and they see it as a correction to the Pharisees' "impenetrable legalistic understanding of" life in the kingdom as "grounded in the effort to secure their own security."[9]

In a variant of that allegorical reading, the first hired are still Jews, but this time they are Jews who are among the followers of Jesus who rejected the entry of gentiles into their group, especially since those gentiles had not been "toiling under the yoke of the Torah." This view has a long legacy. John Wesley claims the "primary scope" of the parable is "to show, That many of the Jews would be rejected, and many of the Gentiles accepted."[10]

A variation of this reading presents the parable depicting the householder/ God as a proponent of affirmative action, as a gracious God who welcomes new members into the household. José David Rodríguez, in "The Parable of the Affirmative Action Employer," a challenge to his own church, identifies the first hired as Pharisees and then equates them with his coreligionists who reject multiculturalism in the church: "The Black, Asian, Hispanic, and Native Americans who are a part of the Evangelical Lutheran Church in America (ELCA) are just as precious in God's eyes and just as important as sisters and brothers in the faith as any others, even if these others have been part of the Lutheran Church for a longer time span and in far greater numbers."[11] That's a splendid message. The problem, however, is that it presumes, again, that the last hired are of a different ethnic group than the first hired. The message to the people in the pew is not only the (good) message of racial inclusivity; it is also the (bad) message that their sense of Jewish xenophobia is confirmed.

Or, for yet another equally problematic allegory, there is the view that the parable "probably served to defend [Jesus's] association with those conventionally branded 'tax collectors and sinners' (cf. 9.10–13)."[12] Suddenly the workers are job-seeking Roman agents, thieves, or murderers. Again, who knew?

Regardless of whether "the Jews" were followers of Jesus, Pharisees, or Israelites at Sinai, for the traditional interpretation of the parable, they are the negative foil. One scholar summarizes: "Whether one thinks of Gentiles or other excluded classes, recognizing the exaltation of the socially, ethnically, or morally excluded fits Jesus's emphasis elsewhere."[13]

The last hired, who basically get their payment simply for showing up, are of course the ones whom "the Jews" would have rejected. They are the "poor" or the "impure" who are rejected by Jewish culture but treated fairly, indeed graciously, by God, the Householder. Or they are the gentiles who enter the vineyard of Israel by grace. Neat and tidy, the traditional interpretation finds a parable proclaiming a message of ecclesial inclusivity, Jewish xenophobia, and Jesus's invention of divine generosity.

At the same time, this reading allows the parable to escape any practical economic message. Common are claims such as: "The parable surely does not make an economic prescription,"[14] and the "parable is not a lesson in corporate economics or an example of how employers, even Christian ones, are to treat their employees."[15] Readings that deny economic realities and use negative stereotypes of Jews to make a soteriological case are both standard, and poor, and we should put no stock in them.

Revisionist Readings: Jesus Meets Paulo Freire and Michael Moore

Today a number of scholars are seeing Jesus's parables as not about, or not only about, salvation, but about practical issues such as how we get along with our neighbors, engage in labor relations, or address economic or political matters. This is all to the good. However, these alternatives to the traditional view sometimes wind up reinscribing the same negative views of Judaism and the same positive view that Jesus was the only Jew who cared about justice.

In some circles today, the landowner is not a symbol for the divine, but for the despot. He is a member of the exploitative (Jewish) elite who have robbed the peasants of their land and then impoverished them by demanding that they pay exorbitant tithes to the Temple. In cahoots with the Romans, he has no concern that the empire's taxation system is also squeezing people already on the edge of starvation. He represents the class that keeps them impoverished by imposing on them various purity laws that they cannot follow. When the parable is seen as about exploited marginals and the degraded, the householder can only be seen as the enemy. He is not the constrained contractor; he is certainly not the representative of the divine.

In this rereading, the presence of the workers in the marketplace indicates the extent of impoverishment and a "situation of high unemployment."[16] These workers are impoverished by the landowners, who took their land and who now humiliate them by making them work for a wage on what was once their property. The last hired represent the outcasts, the expendables, the surplus population. They are one step away from social banditry (or perhaps from robbing travelers on their way from Jerusalem to Jericho), and it is on their behalf that Jesus speaks.

Jesus's point, in this rereading, is to help workers recognize how the householder is both exploiting them and preventing them from uniting to protest his unfair practices. Now politically aware, they find, in the householder's insistence that the last hired be the first paid and in his paying all the workers the same amount, the abusive capitalist who sows discontent among the workers and so prevents them from unionizing. The parable then becomes a revelation to the workers, who now sense their own manipulation: "Once the *oikodespotes* [landowner] can be seen as a member of an oppressing elite class, his actions and words are open to scrutiny."[17]

The reading is ingenious. Whether it is anything that first-century Jews would have heard is another matter. I do not want to dismiss the concerns of day laborers, then or now. Nor am I suggesting that all first-century Jewish labor issues were ideal. I am, however, questioning this popular understanding of Jesus's context.

First, the presence of day laborers need not indicate high levels of poverty. Even areas with good economic indicators have day laborers and temporary workers. A 100 percent employment rate with all receiving a living wage really would be the kingdom of God.

Not only does the parable lack indication of severe economic distress; so also Jesus's Galilee was not, as far as we know, generally destitute. Archaeological studies not only of Sepphoris and Tiberias, but also of Cana, Capernaum, Gamla, and Yodefat as well as cites in the Decapolis and Caesarea Maritima show flourishing communities, both urban and rural. The two cities built by Antipas lack the massive scale that would have drained the countryside of resources. That Antipas built Sepphoris and Tiberias does not tell us anything about the status of laborers, other than that construction creates jobs. How did Antipas finance his cities? Cash crops such as dates and balsam? Increased taxes? Tolls or levies? Euergetism?[18] We do not know.

Nor again does the Jesus tradition suggest a situation in which the majority population lives on the edge of starvation. Jesus does not address famine conditions: to the contrary, the lilies of the field are doing just fine, as are farmers with their wheat (despite the weeds some enemy may have sown). The five thousand men (not including the women and the children) whom Jesus miraculously feeds have, at least according to the text, the ability to purchase food; as Mark 6.36 describes, the disciples are concerned about the hunger of the people, and they advise that Jesus, "Send them away so that they may go into the surrounding country and villages and buy something for themselves to eat." Jesus expects his followers will receive hospitality from the houses that they visit. In Matthew 10.12–14, Jesus instructs his disciples, "As you enter the house, greet it . . ."; Mark 6.10 offers the variant, "Wherever you enter a house, stay there until you leave the place." Hospitality could be counted upon to be provided.

What if we looked at the parable *not as about* Temple, taxation, and purity—a possible move, given that these concerns are never mentioned in the parable? What if we saw the parable not as about exploitative landowners and workers facing extreme poverty, but as dealing with labor relations in a relatively prosperous period? What if we saw it as about what God would have us do not to earn salvation, but to love our neighbor?

For is like the kingdom of the heavens to a man, a
householder, who went out in the morning to hire workers
for his vineyard. And agreeing with the workers for
the denarius of the day, he sent them into his vineyard.
(Matthew 20.1–2)

The landowner is, in the Greek text, an *oikodespotes*. The term, which does not appear in the Septuagint, is a compound noun formed from two words: *oikos,* meaning "house" (related to the term "ecumenical," which has the connotation of being in the same house or under the same roof; it is also related to the term "economy"),[19] and *despotes,* which means "master" (the origin of our term "despot"). Although the NRSV's translation, "landowner," is viable, the term has a connotation closer to "householder." In the New Testament, it appears only in the synoptic Gospels, and there most often has a connection with a home, not a swath of property.

For example, according to Matthew 13.52, at the end of the chapter on parables, Jesus states, "Therefore every scribe who has been trained for the kingdom of heaven is like the *oikodespotes* who casts out of his treasure what is new and what is old." The NRSV here translates the term "master of a household." For Matthew 13, the *oikodespotes* is the faithful follower, not God.

In Matthew 24.43 (also Luke 12.39), Jesus issues an eschatological warning about remaining vigilant: "If the *oikodespotes* had known in what part of the night the thief was coming, he would have stayed awake and would not have let his house be broken into." Here the NRSV offers yet a third translation, "owner of the house." The same translation appears in Mark 14.14 (also Luke 22.11), where Jesus instructs his disciples to find the place where he would celebrate his Last Supper. They are to follow a man "and wherever he enters, [they are to] say to the owner of the house (*oikodespotes*), 'The Teacher asks, Where is my guest room where I may eat the Passover with my disciples?'"

The NRSV translates *oikodespotes* as "master of the house" for a reference to scribes who interpret texts correctly and as "owner of the house" for the fellow who provides an eating place for Jesus and his disciples, and yet it translates "landowner" in this parable. This translation decreases the possibility that English-speaking readers will understand the protagonist of the parable to be a person and so increase the possibility that they will, as they have traditionally done, see the householder only as a figure for God. This same possibility of seeing the *oikodespotes* as a real householder and not (only) as a symbol for the divine can also inform the other passages where the term appears, such as Matthew 13.27 (the parable of the Weeds in the Wheat), Matthew 21.33 (the parable of the Wicked Tenants), and Luke 14.21 (the parable of the Great Dinner).

The term *despotes* itself also does not necessarily have to have a connotation of the divine; not every master is a representative of God. For several New Testament texts, the *despotes* is the master whom slaves are to obey (1 Tim. 6.1–2; Titus 2.9; 1 Pet. 2.18). Nevertheless, the possibility that the *oikodespotes* in our parable is a symbol for God should not be dismissed completely. Not all kings or vineyard owners in parables represent the divine, but some do.[20]

The term *despotes* on its own generally in the New Testament has that connotation. Simeon, after seeing baby Jesus, prays, "Master (*despotes*), now you are dismissing your servant in peace, according to your word" (Luke 2.29). According Acts 4.24, the followers of Jesus, gathered in Jerusalem, "raised their voices together to God and said, 'Sovereign Lord (*despotes*), who made the heaven and the earth, the sea, and everything in them . . . .'"[21]

Our householder *may* be a representative of the divine, but at this point in the parable, he is simply an employer in search of labor to harvest his vineyard. We shall have to determine if he is God or acting like God in the "vineyard of the Lord." Jesus, good storyteller that he is, leaves the determination up to us.

The householder goes out at 6:00 A.M. to contract with his workers. A number of commentators think this is odd—as one states, "no elite would perform such a chore" as going out to the marketplace to hire laborers[22]—but ancient Jews may have found nothing here strange at all. Often figures in parables do the unexpected, as this householder will do, but hiring workers isn't an unexpected move. The Mishnah (*Baba Metziah* 7.1) states: "He who hires workers and tells them to begin early and finish late cannot force them to it if beginning early and finishing late does not conform to the custom of the place. Where the custom is that they be fed, he is obligated to feed them; where it is that they be served dessert, he must serve them dessert. Everything goes according to the custom of the place."

We might linger on this Mishnaic statement, in part because it sets up a possible context for understanding the parable and in part because Emmanuel Levinas did, and he has become one of the current go-to Jews for Christian theologians.[23] Glossing this passage, Levinas writes:

> Our text teaches that not everything can be bought and not everything can be sold. The freedom to negotiate has limits which impose themselves in the name of freedom itself. It matters little that the limits formulated here are not the same as those demanded by modern trade unions. What matters is the principle of limits imposed on freedom for the greater glory of freedom. It is the spirit in which the limits are set: they concern the material conditions of life, sleep and food. Sublime materialism! . . . For the nature of the limits imposed is fixed by custom and evolves with custom. But custom is already a resistance against the arbitrary and against violence. Its notion of a general principle is tribal and somewhat childish, but it is a notion of a general principle, the root of the universal and the Law. Sublime materialism, concerned with dessert.[24]

Levinas points to a Mishnaic law that is grounded in custom, and the custom itself is what creates a fair system. The rabbis are not overriding the custom; they are sanctioning it. They recognize that different places have different ways of doing things, and according to Levinas when it comes to worker-management relations, the customs the rabbis detail are fair ones.

Had the householder followed the customs of the time, which is what the phrase "usual daily wage" (*ek denariou ten hemeran,* lit., "denarius of the day" [Matt. 20.2]) means, he is constrained. There is a usual wage; there is a payment that workers would expect to receive. Our best estimate is that the Roman silver *denarius* would supply a family with three to six days of food.[25] The payment was fair, but not exorbitant.

The householder cannot offer less than the going rate. He is not "free" to do what he wants. Perhaps this direct hiring placed landowner and worker in a contractual relationship and thus mitigated any arbitrary conscription of the underclass by the elite. Matthew 20.2 states that the landowner and the workers "agreed" upon the payment. The agreement is precisely that; the Greek is *symphoneo,* whence "symphony" (cf. Matt. 18.19, "If two of you agree on earth about anything you ask, it will be done for you by my Father in heaven"). We can make the claim that the workers had no choice, that the "usual daily wage" was an offer they could not refuse. But this is a parable about a householder for whom we have no evidence of a Mafioso backstory; he is a householder, not Don Corleone.

As for the claim that the householder is more "godfather" than God the Father, we even find the argument that his choice of crop represents his exploitative nature. Thus we read, "Vineyards were most likely owned by elites because they produced a crop that can be converted into a luxury item (wine), monetized, and exported."[26] Missing here is the notice that all crops can be converted into monetized commodities. Missing as well is the notice that wine was also a staple of poorer classes. Had wine been so associated with exploitative monetization, then we must wonder why Jesus made wine the feature of his fellowship meals, analogized his blood to it, and entered into its mass production at Cana. It would be odd to have Jesus so associated with wine if it were an elitist luxury item designed to be monetized.

So far, we have a householder, a group of laborers, a wage on which all agreed, and a vineyard that required harvesting. Nothing abnormal yet.

And going out around the third hour, he saw others standing in the marketplace, without work. And to those he said, "You go, even you, into the vineyard, and whatever is just, I will give you." And they went. **(Matthew 20.3-4)**

Things become a tad strange in these next verses. The owner, having gone first to the market at dawn, goes out again at 9:00 A.M., and he finds more workers. The NRSV's "others standing idle" is not quite right. The Greek *agroi* means, literally, "without work." Standing idle suggests milling around or wasting time. "Without work" can have the better connotation of "wanting work, but not able to find it." Our presumption here, as it was with the first hired, is that the householder has employed all he found. The parable gives no indication that any workers were left out.

At 9:00 there is no discussion of either "agreement" regarding the payment or the daily denarius. It has been suggested that the owner takes "advantage of an unemployed workforce, to meet his harvesting needs by offering them work without a wage agreement."[27] Although this suggestion holds for today's unscrupulous employers who hire undocumented workers not in a position to report abuse, it is less likely in antiquity. Were this householder, who is operating in the public square in his hiring practices, untrustworthy, he would have no future workers. He is also constrained by local custom, as the aforementioned *Baba Metziah* 7.1 indicates.

Rather than dismiss our householder as an ancient Gordon Gekko, we might take him at his word. The NRSV translates: "I will give you whatever is right." "Right" is *diakaios,* which has the connotations of "just," "fair," and "proper." Beneath this term is the Hebrew root *tz-d-k,* which connotes both charity and righteousness. Again, the language suggests that the householder is, if not (yet) seen as an image for God, at least a moral exemplar. The parable gives us no reason to distrust him.

And again, going out around the sixth and also the ninth
hour, he did likewise. And around the eleventh, going out,
he found others standing, and he says to them, "Why here
are you standing all the day without work?" They say to him,
"Because no one has hired us." He says to them, "You go,
even you, into the vineyard." **(Matthew 20.5–7)**

Matters are becoming increasingly peculiar. Managers usually know how much labor they need; the same is the case with landowners. That our householder returns to the market over and over against suggests either that he is clueless about the number of workers he needs, that he has an insufficient number of workers although he has hired everyone available, or that he has another agenda. The last possibility is most likely; what that agenda is, however, remains as yet a mystery.

The householder continues to go to the market, but the parable makes no explicit mention of the *need* for more labor.[28] Unclear as well is why these other individuals are in the marketplace, but not hired. We do not know if they had been there since dawn, but were not chosen in the first several rounds of employment, or if they arrived later. They may have already worked another job. Perhaps they were sons and daughters taking care of aging parents or little children. Perhaps they had come from a neighboring village where employment was lacking.

Commentators generally suggest that the last hired were the old and the infirm, but again, there is nothing in the parable that suggests this. To the contrary, the householder's query as to why they were not working suggests that they were capable of doing so. Although the householder's question could be taken as reproachful, it is just as likely to indicate surprise—these workers *should* have been hired.[29] At harvest, there is more than one field and so more than one employer. We might also query how likely it would be that workers would be in the marketplace at 5:00 P.M. Were they hoping for extra work after finishing a full shift elsewhere? Their response to his query also discourages the idea that they were physically incapable of doing the job: they respond not "because we are old and infirm" but "because no one has hired us."

Given that there is no reason to see the last hired as somehow less desirable employees, the standard allegorical readings of the last hired fail to find purchase. Despite the common views that the last hired represent either Jewish "outcasts" who fail to keep the purity laws or the gentile nations, nothing in the parable offers this view. The workers are all part of the same labor pool, they are all found in the same place, they all go into the same vineyard. As far as we know, the first hired worked alongside those who arrived at 3:00 and at 5:00. There is no indication that Judah said to Simeon, "You cannot work next to us because you are in a state of ritual impurity"; nowhere does Susanna say to Procla, "You cannot work here because you are a gentile." The parable makes no qualitative distinction between those hired early and those hired late in the day—it is only the interpreters who import such concerns into the text.

Finally, the householder does not provide any details as to the payment schedule. Perhaps the last hired had heard his negotiation with the first group;[30] perhaps they had heard his promise of a fair wage or that would pay what is "just."

When evening came, says the lord of the vineyard to his steward, "Call the workers and give to them their wage/reward, beginning with the last ones to the first ones." And coming, those around the eleventh hour, they received each a denarius. And coming, the first, they thought that more they would receive. And they received each a denarius, even they. And receiving, they were grumbling against the householder. They were saying, "These last ones one hour did, and equal to us them you have made, to the ones having borne the burden of the day and the burning heat." **(Matthew 20.8-12)**

Although the vineyard owner is first called an *oikodespotes* (20.1), a "householder,"[31] v. 8 calls him the "lord of the vineyard" (Gk. *kyrios tou ampelonos*) and so intimates the identification between householder and divine. For this verse, the NRSV translates *kyrios* not as "lord," but as "owner," and so masks the theological implication.

However, the householder need not *only* be a reference to God, for what God does is often what those who claim to follow God should also do. We can see in this householder a description of how ordinary householders do act or even should act. Therefore, we should be prepared to identify this householder both with God and with our position, as scribes trained for the kingdom of heaven and as prudent stewards who are prepared for eschatological judgment.

Whether seen as divine or domestic or both, the "lord" behaves, yet again, in an unexpected manner. The traditional reading, which takes the "lord" to be a representative of the divine and which also takes the workers to represent different groups of people, concludes that the "parable addresses the resentment felt by those who had spent long years in faithful observance to Torah at the welcome and acceptance Jesus gave to those who appeared to come so late to any sense of conversion."[32] Once Jewish Law becomes equated with "bearing the burden of the day and the scorching heat," we are no longer listening to the Jewish Jesus talking to fellow Jews. When Jewish practice or Jewish society becomes the negative foil to Jesus or the church, we do well to reread the parable.

If we do not read the *oikodespotes* as a representative of the divine, a more modern impression emerges. Today, for a number of commentators, the householder's instructions regarding payment make him both "unjust and arrogant"[33] and render the situation "now not only one of exploitation but also of arbitrariness and injustice."[34] Or the householder is seen as taking from the poor to give to the poor, and so is not displaying any compassion.[35] If we identify with the first hired, we may well agree with these condemnatory interpretations. Our sympathies may well be with those who worked harder than the more recently hired. A feminist reading might advocate even more strongly for the first hired. Their story finds a contemporary analogy in the woman who settles for a set wage in doing factory work, only to find that men hired after she began her job received the same amount of money for doing less work.[36] We may even conclude that in setting up the first hired to resent their coworkers, the householder has engaged in an early form of union busting; he has prevented the workers from uniting and so from protesting their exploitation. Homiletician William Brosend, extending the parable beyond its ending, finds sympathy with the workers. He suggests that the next time the owner heads to the market, no one will respond to the 6:00 A.M. call.[37] I doubt, however, Jesus's initial audience would have heard any of this.[38]

First, it is possible that they already knew about what we today call unions. The Roman world had numerous voluntary associations, so individuals had the voice of a group if they needed to express protest regarding working conditions. According to the Tosefta, *Baba Metziah* 11.24–26:

> The wool workers and the dyers are permitted to say, "We will all be partners in any business that comes to the city." The bakers are permitted to establish work shifts amongst themselves. Donkey drivers are permitted to say, "We will provide another donkey for anyone whose donkey dies." . . . The shipmasters are permitted to say, "We will provide another ship for anyone whose ship is destroyed."

In other words, the Tosefta recognizes the guild (voluntary association, collegium) structure. Had the workers in the parable taken a cue from the local bakers, they could have set up a system to work for all. They choose not to do that. They are interested in receiving their own payment, not in whether the other workers have enough food.

A rabbinic parable with the same plot line—the worker who toils fewer hours gets paid the same, or more, than those who put in a whole day— raises the same question of what the first hired see as "just," and it similarly questions their notion of "justice." Snodgrass adduces, from the Jerusalem Talmud, R. Zeira's eulogy for Rabbi Bun bar Hiyya in *Berakhot* 2.7:

> To what [story] may [the life of] R. Bun bar Hiyya be compared? [To this story.] A king hired many workers. One worker was excellent in his work. What did the king do? He took him and walked with him back and forth [through the rows of crops and did not let him finish his day's work]. Toward evening, when all the workers came to be paid, he gave him a full day's wages along with [the rest of] them. The workers complained and said, "We toiled all day, and this one toiled only two hours, and he gave

him a full day's wages!" The king said to them, "This one worked [and accomplished] more in two hours than you did in a whole day." So R. Bun toiled in the study of Torah for twenty-eight years, [and he learned] more than an aged student could learn in a hundred years.[39]

A similar story appears in several other rabbinic sources, including *Ecclesiastes Rabbah* 5.17 and *Midrash Tanhuma Ki Tissa* 110.[40]

The midrash also shows that, for the rabbis, what God wants is not necessarily what "we" think is appropriate. In its version of the Laborers in the Vineyard, it is the king who prevents the excellent worker from putting in his time. In this configuration, the system is not wage labor, but piece work; the workers are compensated not for quantity of time served, but for quality of work done. In the rabbinic parable, the workers did not consider what the king wanted; they were judging him according to their own standards or their own view of what constituted "work." They had a sense of what was fair based on quantity; the king had a sense of what was right, important, or valuable based on quality. The same structure holds for the Matthean parable. The workers seek what they perceive to be "fair"; the householder teaches them a lesson by showing them what is "right."

As for what will happen the next time the householder goes to the market? Nothing that has not already happened. A wage is a wage, and to refuse to work leads to the loss of a paycheck. Given the patron-client system and honor/shame cultural codes (both overdone in New Testament scholarship, but why not use them when they work?), the first hired will not gripe in public; they have nothing to complain about to the owner. The householder has fulfilled his contract with them; he did not cheat them. The only thing they can do is to testify to his generosity, and that might encourage more laborers to want to work for him. Nor would those hired at 3:00 and 5:00 likely turn down another offer of employment by our householder.

The narrator tells us that the workers expected to be paid more; their initial concern is the money gained. Their complaint shifts the focus. Now they are distressed because the last hired "have been made equal" to them. For some commentators, their question can be rephrased: "What is the point of hard work, of going early to the street corner where day laborers must wait to be hired, of diligence and perseverance, if all of this does not serve

to distinguish us from those who are lazy and shiftless?" Yet there is no indication that the last hired were any more or less lazy and shiftless than the
first hired.

The first hired do not want to be treated equally to the last; they want to
be treated better. It is the commentators who provide the last hired with the
negative characteristics.

And answering one of them he said, "Friend, not do I harm
you. Did not for a denarius you agree with me? Take what
is yours and go. And I wish to this one, to this last one, to
give as even to you. [Or] is it not permitted to me what
I wish to do with what is mine? Or is your eye evil because
I am good?" Thus will be the last first and the first last.
(Matthew 20.13–16)

The householder has the last line just as he was featured in the opening
verse, and so it is his perspective that the parable foregrounds. Here, the
householder makes his case by condemning the grumbling workers; his address, "Friend," shows his dismay, if not his anger, rather than his kindness.
Matthew uses "friend" three times in his Gospel, each time ironically. In
addition to 20.13, "friend" (*hetairos*) appears in the parable of the Wedding
Banquet, in which the king asks, "Friend, how did you get in here without
a wedding robe?" (22.12)—this "friend" is then tossed into the outer darkness. In Gethsemane, Jesus says to Judas, "Friend, do what you are here to
do" (26.50).[41] Thus the grumblers are connected with eschatological punishment and betrayal.

The Septuagint offers the same connotations to the term. "Friend"
(*hetairos*) describes the Philistines who opposed Samson (Judg. 14.11, 20);
Amnon's friend Jonadab, who sets up the rape of Tamar (2 Sam. 13.3);
Hushai, David's adviser involved in the machinations concerning Absalom's
rebellion (2 Sam. 15–16); and the friends of King Belshazzar of Babylon,
who feasted with the Temple vessels and saw the "handwriting on the wall"

(Dan. 5.1–2). The word does not always have a negative connotation, but the possibility is strong that it might. Robert Fortna may well be right in suggesting, "But even to respond coolly is to treat the workers with a kind of respect."[42]

The householder's reference to the "evil eye" may similarly be seen as at least a possible excuse for the grumbling. The "evil eye" possesses an individual. To regard the grumbler and his buddies as struck by jealousy, and so not fully in possession of their good sense, gives them a possible out. The householder has not lost his temper.

The householder, moreover, has a point. The first hired were not treated unfairly. They "agreed" (*symphoneo*) for the going rate. That the householder considers himself in the right is more strongly indicated in the Greek than in the NRSV's "I am doing you no wrong." The Greek *ouk adiko se* can mean "I am not unjust to you," which is another way of saying, "I have treated you justly" or "righteously." The term echoes the fourth verse of the parable, "I will pay you whatever is right" (*dikaios*). Thus it is not the householder, but the workers, who have broken their own sense of community. The householder treated them equally; the first-hired resented that treatment.[43]

Yes, the workers are disgruntled, but the householder has the last word. This householder is no evil tyrant or elitist exploiter. It is the laborers—who do not want the last hired to have a living wage—who are in the wrong.

The last line of the parable is likely not original to it; the saying about the last being first and the first being last contradicts both the notice of equal pay and the grumblers' complaint that the householder has made all the laborers "equal." Rather, the line, which floats around in various Gospels and various settings (Mark 10.31; Luke 13.30; Matt. 19.30), seems to have been imported by the plot: the last hired are the first paid, and the first hired the last paid. It cannot, however, serve as the "moral" of the parable.[44]

The householder gives what had been generously contracted to every worker, regardless of time the employment began. New Testament scholar Brad H. Young proposes, "The laborers should have been happy about the good fortune of their coworkers who, because of the generosity of the landowner, would now have enough provision for their families."[45] Indeed, they should have been, and with this note we may be getting to the provocation of the parable.

Better Dividends

If the shock of the parable, at least to this point, is not that the latecomers, allegorized as gentiles or sinners, are invited, where's the surprise? And if it's not about exploited workers and despotic employers, what's the message?

Maybe Jesus's parable *has* to do with economics after all. Such a focus would be consistent with Jesus's teaching, and it would neatly fit within a first-century context.

Arland Hultgren states that the parable's "outcome is untypical of ordinary life, and that is what makes it so memorable."[46] The outcome may be memorable, but it is not atypical. According to Josephus, when the Jerusalem Temple was completed and the eighteen thousand–plus workmen were in want, "If any one of them did but labor for a single hour, he received his pay."[47] What commentators have insisted is "not a lesson in corporate economics" or denied to be a "model of good management-labor practices" may well be both. Maybe the concern is to work within the localized system and provide, if resources allow, funds so that everyone has enough food.

Given that a number of Jesus's teachings evoke Israel and given his other invocations of David, a connection of our parable to 1 Samuel 30.21–25 is also possible. David insists, "The share of the one who goes down into the battle shall be the same as the share of the one who stays by the baggage; they shall share alike" (v. 24); and the narrator states, "From that day forward he made it a statute and an ordinance for Israel; it continues to the present day" (v. 25). Or, for another example, in his *Life of Moses,* Philo describes the sharing of spoils among those who did the fighting and those who stayed in the tents:

> And Moses praised Phinehas their general, and those who had
> served under him for their good success, and also because they had
> not been covetous of their own advantage, running after booty and
> thinking of nothing, but appropriating the spoil to themselves,
> but because they had brought it all into the common stock, so that
> they who had stayed behind in the tents might share in the booty.[48]

If the landowner pays everyone a living wage, and if the workers can be content with what is right rather than what they perceive to be fair, then a soteriological message can also be adduced. The soteriological view of equal pay for unequal work is also known in Jewish contexts. *Semachot de Rabbi Chiyah* 3.2 asks:

> How do the righteous come into the world? Through love, because they uphold the world through their good deeds. How do they depart? Also through love. R. Simeon b. Eliezar told a parable. To what may the matter be compared? To a king who hired two workers. The first worked all day and received one denarius. The second worked only one hour and yet he also received one denarius. Which one was the more beloved? Not the one who worked one hour and received a denarius! Thus Moses our teacher served Israel one hundred and twenty years and Samuel only fifty-two. Nevertheless, both are equal before the omnipresent.

Midrash Psalms reads: "Solomon said to the holy one, blessed be he: Master of the Universe: When a king hires good laborers who perform their work well and he pays them their wage, what praise does he merit? When does he merit praise? When he hires lazy laborers and still pays them their full wage."[49]

Hence the householder is both analogous to God and a model for followers of Jesus. This association is no Mary Daly–esque view that all householders should be seen as divine; it is instead a warning to the owners that they should act as God does, rather than as "some rich guy" (e.g., Luke 12.16; 16.1, 19, 22).

Dismissing the parable's practical implication is to make the parable safe and so to lose its challenge. Jesus "encouraged landowners" to enact the graciousness of God by "speaking of a vineyard owner who generously assisted some impoverished day laborers."[50] The owner is the role model for the rich; they should continue to call others to the field and righteously fulfill a contract whose conditions are from the beginning to pay "what is right"—and what is right is a living wage. If it turns out that the last hired really were too weak to work, then we might conclude with regard to fairness that the owner has requested from each according to his ability and given to each according to his need. The equality of his payment and thus his treating all the workers "equally" derives from a sense of justice keyed into what people need to live.

The householder not only fulfilled his contract with those he first hired; he also paid a full wage to those who might not have expected it. With these two moves, he proved himself sufficiently clever as to foreclose, in the honor/shame and patron-client system, any harm to himself. The only point that the workers could make about him was that he was generous to others. And in making that point, the workers learned their own economic lesson: the point is not that those who have "get more," but that those who have not "get enough." One does the work—in the labor force, in the kingdom—not for more reward, but for the benefit of all. The next day, perhaps the first will be last, and those who grumble in the evening about bonuses will be desperate in the morning for any job at all.

Although we can see the laborers as "among the poor for whom the kingdom of God would bring change,"[51] the parable does not promote egalitarianism; instead, it encourages householders to support laborers, all of them. More than just aiding those at the doorstep, those who have should seek out those who need. If the householder can afford it, he should continue to put others on the payroll, pay them a living wage (even if they cannot put in a full day's work), and so allow them to feed their families while keeping their dignity intact. The point is practical, it is edgy, and it a greater challenge to the church then and today than the entirely unsurprising idea that God's concern is *that* we enter, not *when*.

Jesus is neither a Marxist nor a capitalist. Rather, he is both an idealist and a pragmatist. His focus is often less directly on "good news to the poor" than on "responsibility of the rich." Jesus follows Deuteronomy 15.11, "Since there will never cease to be some in need on the earth, I therefore command you, 'Open your hand to the poor and needy neighbor in your land.' " However, there is regulation: the rich who fail to open their hand will receive eschatological punishment.

Jesus is not an individualist, and his address presumes a corporate (yes, that is the word) personality. Just as God "makes his sun rise on the evil and on the good, and sends rain on the righteous and on the unrighteous" (Matt. 5.45), so the righteousness of one person or group benefits not only that group, but others as well. Each group needs the other: the workers need the money, and the owner needs the labor. But the corporate point is even stronger.

The prodigal son benefits from the work of the elder brother; the sinful tax collector benefits from the righteousness of the Pharisee; in Christian tradition, sinful humanity benefits from the righteousness and sacrifice of Jesus. In this parable, the last hired benefit from the contract made with their coworkers; they benefit from an employer who pays a just wage to those who labor; they benefit from an employer who is generous with his money. Thus, not only do householder and laborer need each other, the work of some laborers benefits the lives of others. In the end, all have enough to eat, and the rich recognize their responsibility to those who are less well off, a responsibility that includes not simply giving a handout, but hiring "workers" who can thus preserve their dignity.

If we take away the complacent anti-Judaism that so marks parable interpretation, we can keep Jesus in his own social context. If we refocus the parable away from "who gets into heaven" and toward "who gets a day's wage," we can find a message that challenges rather than prompts complacency. If we look at economics, at the pressing reality that people need jobs and that others have excess funds, we find what should be a compelling challenge to any hearer. And in that story, we learn what is means to act as God acts, with generosity to all. And that is what parables are supposed to do.

CHAPTER 8

The Widow and the Judge

And he said a parable to them concerning their necessity always to pray and not to become discouraged, saying,

"Some judge was in some city; God was he not fearing, and people was he not respecting. And a widow was in that city. And she kept coming to him, saying, 'Avenge/grant me justice against my adversary.'

"And not did he wish at the time. But after these things, he said to himself, 'If even God I do not fear nor people do I respect, yet on account of the trouble this widow causes, I will avenge her, so that not into the end, coming, she will wear me out/give me a black eye.'"

And said the Lord, "Hear what the unjust judge says. And will not God make vengeance to his elect, those who cry to him day and night, and will he be patient upon them? I say to you that he will avenge them swiftly. Nevertheless, when the Son of Man comes, then will he find faith upon the earth?"

Luke 18.1–8

Biblical widows are the most unconventional of conventional figures. Expected to be weak, they move mountains; expected to be poor, they prove savvy managers; expected to be exploited, they take advantage where they find it.[1] Tamar, the Bible's first official "widow" (Gen. 38.11); Naomi, Ruth, and Orpah; Abigail (1 Sam. 27.3; 30.5; 2 Sam. 2.2; 3.3); the wise woman of Tekoa (2 Sam. 14.5); the widow of Zarephath (1 Kings 17; cf. Luke 4.26, where her actions go missing); Judith—all manifest agency, and all defy the convention of the poor and dependent woman. The so-called importuning widow of Luke 18 similarly shatters the stereotype, even as she epitomizes the strength, cleverness, and very problematic motives of many of her predecessors.

Yet Luke's feisty widow has been domesticated. The message she gives, at least according to the evangelist, is that of the "need to pray always and not to lose heart" (18.1). No independent woman who badgers a judge until she gets what she wants, she becomes one of those elect who "cry . . . day and night" (18.7). In Luke's concluding image she is more "a woman on her knees" than "a woman with a fist."

Luke has neatly tucked her in with other conventional images of poor, dependent, or powerless widows. The first we meet is Anna, the eighty-four-year-old widow who "never left the temple but worshiped there with fasting and prayer night and day" (2.37), and she sets the agenda for Luke's widows: she prays, she fasts. She does not, however, speak; she does not engage the public; she will not cause any trouble. From Anna Luke moves to the "many widows in Israel" who were starving during the famine and the widow of Zarephath whom Elijah helps; this widow's own verbal jousting and tenacious advocacy for her son do not bear mention (4.25–27). Then come the widow of Nain, upon whom Jesus has compassion and whose son he raises from the dead (7.11–16); the widows preyed upon by venal scribes (20.47); the woman, married to seven brothers and widowed seven times, about whom the Sadducees ask, "Whose wife will she be in the resurrection?" (20.27–33); the Hellenist widows overlooked in the church's daily distribution of food (Acts 6.1); and the widows mourning the death of Tabitha, who may have been their patron (9.39, 41). The widow has become conventional, and the parable has lost its challenge.

Jesus's parables give women agency: the woman with the lost coin along with her female friend and neighbors, the wise and foolish virgins, the widow who encounters the judge. Similarly, Jesus himself engaged with women who were not restricted to prayer and fasting: the woman who anoints him, Martha and Mary (who would dare so restrict Martha?), the Samaritan woman at the well, the Syro-Phoenician woman, and so on. That the parables come from Jesus and not Luke is already suggested by the distinction drawn between Luke's narrative placement of parables and the details of the parables themselves.

Luke is not the only one to domesticate the widow of the parable. Even readers who recognize her dismantling of the stereotype find in her story a tidy theological or ethical message. In a profound study that reads the Gospel in light of the struggles of the women in the diocese of San Cristóbal de las Casas in Chiapas, Mexico, Barbara Reid describes our widow as "more like Ruth and Tamar, widows who take bold steps for their own well-being and who advance God's plan for good for the whole of the people. . . . [She] is an icon of godliness."[2] This is a helpful political reading. It is also generous. Ruth and Tamar's motives are not expressed; it is the tradition, not the narrator, that ascribes to them the advancement of the divine plan. Similarly, Abigail manipulates her relationship with both Nabal and David, the wise woman of Tekoa plays the widow's role as a political ruse, and Judith is also a lying, seductive assassin. Widows, like all women, like all humans, have complex personalities and not always transparent motives. We readers choose how to understand them. And we readers tend to give widows the benefit of the doubt.

Parables are designed to shake up one's worldview, to question the conventional. If a manager can be dishonest, a tax collector righteous, a landowner generous enough to provide a living wage to everyone in the marketplace, and a judge neither God-fearing nor respectful toward the people, surely a widow can be vengeful. What she sees as justice may be something that we or her legal adversary would see as a perversion of justice. For the parable to do its work, for it to challenge all our views rather than reinforce normative gender and class constructs, another look at the widow is necessary.

Importuning Widow and Unjust Judge, or Antagonist and Victim?

How we identify this parable already determines how we understand it. The traditional designation, the parable of the Importuning Widow is not inaccurate, for her case creates the reason for the story; her actions prompt the judge's reactions. But "importuning," aside from being antiquated, conveys weakness through its sense of "begging." Titles such as "Persistent Widow," "Tenacious Widow," or even "Nagging Widow" provide her more agency.

"Persistent" suggests something positive; "tenacious" can be either positive (the tenacious scholar who tracks down every footnote) or negative (the tenacious pit bull); "nagging" tends to evoke negative reactions. She is perhaps exasperated, perhaps rude—she omits any title of respect for the judge.[3] Then again, the judge has no concern for honor, so she shows him none.

For most interpreters, "the main character of the parable is the oppressed woman, the neglected widow. She earns this focal attention because she is unfortunate and because she tries to remedy her bad fortune."[4] Following Luke's cues and biblical stereotypes, we readers tend to presume the widow's cause is just and that the judge models unrighteousness. We root for this woman, because we are conditioned from certain biblical and cultural stereotypes to see widows as not only helpless and needy, but also exploited and abused. We also root for her because we do not like the judge; not only does he lack appropriate religiosity and respect, but also Luke tells us that he is "unjust" (18.6). We want him to lose, and for him to lose, in our zero-sum mentality, therefore the widow has to win. We conclude, "The only decent figure [in the parable] is the woman."[5]

So much for the parable as a genre designed to surprise or provoke. Not all parables have "decent" figures.

Our judgment is determined before all the facts of the case are in. Not only has Luke presented the woman as role model for constant prayer; the English translations have also contributed to her domestication. Most translations have the widow seeking "justice," but the Greek term behind the English does not use the term "justice" (*dikaiosyne*). Rather, she is asking to be "avenged" (*ekdikeo*). The language is juridical; it is standard in legal papyri, where it has the connotation of "to set things right"[6] or "to be vindicated,"[7] so it could be positive or at least morally neutral.

The ambivalence of the term fits the lack of details of her request. Does she want money from her adversary? Access to property? Or does she want her opponent thrown into jail, or to suffer,[8] or to be executed?

Luke offers us not a legal contract, but a parable colored by biblical resonances. The widow's desire is comparable to the vengeance (Gk. *ekdikesis*) executed upon Egypt's firstborn sons (Exod. 7.4 [NRSV: "great act of judgment"; Heb. *mishpat gedolim*]; 12.12), by Israel against the Midianites (Num. 31.2–3), by Samson against the Philistines (Judg. 15.7; 16.28), and by Judith against Holofernes (Jdth. 9.2).[9] Given these resonances, the widow is not interested in coming to terms quickly with her opponent, but in punishing him. We cannot get back behind Luke's Greek to Jesus's Aramaic; we do not know if Jesus himself told this or any other parable. But the ambivalence of the Greek does hint at a parable that, if not by Jesus himself, does sound like him or whoever else told these tales.

The NRSV's mild suggestion that the widow will "wear out" the judge is another taming of the widow. The Greek uses a boxing term: the judge is concerned that the widow will give him a black eye. Whether we take this expression literally and see the woman as threatening violence or metaphorically and see the woman as suggesting humiliation or mortification will impact how we assess her character.[10] As New Testament scholar John Dominic Crossan pointed out long ago, "I look at the widow and I don't consider her right or good. Maybe her adversary is right, but more polite."[11] Our widow, in the Greek, sounds less like Ruth amid the alien corn and more like Leona Helmsley fighting a hostile takeover.

The title parable of the "Unjust Judge" is also popular; the story begins and ends with him, and his interior monologue takes up the majority of the words.[12] To title the parable by mentioning the woman first is to displace the judge. Already we are trapped. Do we foreground the widow or the judge? Who is the protagonist? With whom, if anyone, are we to identify?

Despite the popularity of the title "Unjust Judge," it is also misleading. The judge is "unjust" only according to v. 6, which is the narrator's comment: "And said the Lord, 'Hear what the unjust judge says.'" The parable proper describes the judge only as not fearing God and not having respect for people. Whether these are good or bad traits and what relation they have to the question of justice still need to be sorted out.

Other titles are possible, although I've found none. There are no advocates for the parable of the "Soon to Be Punished Widow's Opponent," although the opponent is also part of the story, and he, like the judge, will suffer because of the widow's demands. But he, and so his suffering, goes ignored, because most readers presume that the widow's case is just and that the opponent deserves whatever the court inflicts upon him.

The parable of the "Vengeful Widow and the Co-opted Judge" is accurate, but that doesn't preach as well. Perhaps that very difficulty in making an easy transition from text to sermon should be a starting point for understanding a parable. If the parable cannot be domesticated, if it cannot be turned into something that neatly fits our preconceived notions of religion or morality, if it discombobulates us—then we may be on the right track.

Luke's Additions and Subtractions

Luke 18.1–8 has a long and intractable history of debates over how much of the parable the evangelist received from the tradition and how much betrays an editorial hand. Religiously conservative scholars are wont to see all eight verses as bearing the stamp of the historical Jesus; those on the more liberal or less confessional side are more willing to see Luke's hand in creating a narrative frame. Almost all agree that 18.2–5 is the core of the parable, and that these four verses originate with Jesus himself.[13] In this view, Jesus told a very short story about a judge and a widow, both with problematic characteristics; the judge is not inclined to grant the widow's request, but because of her persistence and her threats, he does. That's it.

There are various good arguments for why the other verses are additions, and others have already made them.[14] Whether we take the verses surrounding Luke 18.2–5 as from Jesus, the early oral tradition, Luke's special source, or the hand of the evangelist, the core text is a proper parable. As always, interpretation is in part a thought experiment, an act of imagination. If the original parable started with "In a certain city there was a judge" and ended with "so that she may not give me a black eye by continually coming," then what might its audience have made of it?

The Good Widow Oppressed by All

And a widow was in that city. And she kept coming to him,
saying, "Avenge/grant me justice against my adversary."
(Luke 18.3)

All readers come to a text with presuppositions, and all come embedded in cultures where certain words necessarily evoke particular associations. References to a "vineyard," as in Matthew 20.1–16, necessarily suggest a connection to Israel. A story that starts, "There was a man who had two sons," immediately recollects Adam, Abraham, Isaac, and Joseph. Mention of a "priest" and then a "Levite" sets up the expected third to be an Israelite. So too the term "widow" comes with a collection of connotations.

The first association is that widows are in God's special care. Vulnerable, in need of support and protection, they are generally figures to be aided rather than emulated. They are not themselves role models; those who care for them are the role models.

Exodus 22.22 begins this convention: "You shall not abuse any widow or orphan." Because no one should abuse another, the specifics of the mandate tell us that widows, like orphans, were especially vulnerable; lacking a husband who would traditionally provide for them, they are at the mercy of the broader society.

Deuteronomy 10.18 (cf. 24.19–21) continues the theme by providing the preferential option for the widow and orphan along with the stranger: God "executes justice for the orphan and the widow, and who loves the strangers, providing them food and clothing." Similarly, Deuteronomy 27.19 requires economic care for the "alien, the orphan, and the widow," and includes the threat: "'Cursed be anyone who deprives the alien, the orphan, and the widow of justice.' All the people shall say, 'Amen!'" Amen, indeed! According to the Septuagint, the curse is upon anyone who literally "bends away a legal judgment (*ekkeline krisin*)," an accurate translation of the Hebrew *mate mishpat*.

The Torah's concern for the widow, presumed to be poor and exploited, extends to the Prophets and Writings. Isaiah 1.17 equates seeking justice (*mishpat*, a correct judgment) with rescuing the oppressed, defending the orphan, and pleading for the widow (the widow does not plead on her own behalf). Jeremiah 22.3 (cf. 7.6) both equates oppressing the alien, orphan, and widow to the shedding of innocent blood and contrasts this oppression with the command that all "act with justice [Gk. *kresin*, Heb. *mishpat*] and righteousness [Gk. *dikaiosyne*, Heb. *tzedakah*], and deliver from the hand of the oppressor anyone who has been robbed." Job speaks of his care for the widow and the orphan along with the poor (31.16–19); the Psalms locate the widow together with the stranger and the orphan as individuals in vulnerable circumstances (94.6; 146.9). The same themes sound in Ezekiel (22.7; 44.22), Zechariah (7.9–10), Malachi (3.5), and elsewhere.

One scholar reads the widow in light of Proverbs 25.15, "With patience a ruler may be persuaded, and a soft tongue can break stone."[15] I missed the widow's "soft tongue" or the notion of the judge's being "persuaded," unless we think of the widow's threat as creating an offer he couldn't refuse (if so, I picture her dating the householder in the parable of the Laborers in the Vineyard).

Whereas Sirach attributes to widows some agency—"He will not ignore the supplication of the orphan, or the widow when she pours out her complaint" (35.17)—he sees the widow less as demanding justice from her oppressors than as complaining to God about her circumstances. Thus the widow of this Deuterocanonical text finds a sister in Luke's depiction: she continues to beg for what she needs. The judge also finds his allegorical match: as God does not ignore the widow, so the judge (eventually) stops ignoring her as well. Nevertheless, for Sirach the widow is primarily a pathetic figure about whom he insists, "Do not the tears of the widow run down her cheek as she cries out against the one who causes them to fall?" (35.18).

Consistent with this heart-tugging depiction are the claims about the status of widows in first-century Israel. Many commentaries insist that in Jewish society a widow had no legal rights to her dead husband's estate, and so she would be forced out of her house and onto the streets, where she'd have no choice but to beg. They assert that there were "frequent court cases in which a family contested a widow's right to inheritance because, after all, she was no longer 'family.'" Some posit that the widow is lacking a male who would be "pleading her case, as would be his role," but also that "perhaps it is he who is bilking her of her rightful property."[16] Another suggests that the widow "has a lawsuit against one of the heirs of her husband's property, or perhaps she is being evicted from her home, as widows sometimes were (cf. 20.47)."[17] None of this is mentioned in our parable; none needs to be presumed by it.

One scholar claims a "well-known topos of the widow who struggles with a corrupt judicial system for her rights,"[18] although if the topos of the widow who pleads her case were so conventional, there'd be much less shock in our parable. There is some documentation of widows seeking their rights; there is some documentation of people in most every group seeking their rights.

The widow's characterization then becomes completely pathetic. One scholar describes her as "almost resourceless . . . probably illiterate and [she] clearly lacks political influence."[19] Another invokes the image of the "enraged bag lady."[20] A third sees her as "the victim of a man who undermined the economic foundation of her life,"[21] for although "the parable gives no indication that the widow is an exception to the rule of social reality, the majority of the population was poor, and the majority of widows were extremely exploited and oppressed on account of their class *and* gender."[22] A fourth goes as far as to call her an "outcast,"[23] and a fifth sets her in the "ugly and oppressive socio-legal world of first-century Palestine."[24]

The negative characterization of Jesus's Jewish context is, I fear, almost inevitable. For Jesus to look good, it seems that Jewish society must appear to be bad. We move from the "ugly and oppressive" setting to the claim that Jesus's Galilean audience would have seen women, or widows, as "weak, foolish, silly, impotent, chattering, useless."[25] No sources are cited.

Another Look at the Widow

How we would know that the "majority of widows" in either Jesus's or Luke's purview were "extremely exploited and oppressed"[26] in relation to the legal system remains an open question. In his "Helpful Primary Source Material," Klyne Snodgrass offers no such examples of widows being sued for property; he does, however, present the details of a pleading woman who so sufficiently annoys Philip of Macedon that he agrees to hear her case and a few papyrus records of widows engaged in court cases.[27]

In speaking of the parable of the Laborers in the Vineyard, I made clear that I do not want to dismiss the very real concerns of day laborers. Neither do I want to dismiss the very real concern of poor widows. But I do want to question the stereotype. Not all widows are poor, without agency, and completely dependent on the goodwill of others within an "ugly and oppressive" Jewish system.

Widows in what has been termed the "ugly and oppressive socio-legal" situation of Jewish society did have several social safeguards. Whether rabbinic law was applicable to late Second Temple contexts cannot in most cases be known. That the Mishnah is more prescriptive than descriptive—that it details how the rabbis saw their ideal society, not what was necessarily happening—has already been mentioned. In the case of the widow, rabbinic law did prevent widows from inheriting in certain cases, but the rabbis distinguish between inheriting and bequeathing (see Mishnah, *Baba Batra* 8.1).[28] Women could receive bequests of property, land, businesses, material goods, and so on.[29] Women could also bequeath property, as the Mishnah indicates.

Moreover, and here we can be more confident in historical settings, Jewish widows would have had a means of receiving support from the marriage contract (the *ketubah*). We have examples of these contracts dating as early as the fifth century BCE from Elephantine in Egypt. The *ketubah* would have had stipulations for her own finances, including her dowry. The Mishnah indicates that the contract may also have had her claims for alimentation (*mezonot*; see Mishnah, *Ketubot* 4.12, "[If he had not written for her], 'You shall dwell in my house and receive maintenance from my goods, so long as you remain a widow in my house,' he is still liable [thereto], since this is a condition enjoined by the court . . .").[30]

Regarding women's social roles in Jewish settings, the personal documents of Babatha of Maoza, the early second-century twice-widowed woman whose records were preserved in the Cave of Letters, attest, among other things, that she seized her deceased second husband's property in Ein Gedi, petitioned the Roman courts to gain guardianship of her son by her first marriage, and was sued by Miriam, that second husband's co-wife over the estate.[31]

The Jewish widows we know from legal documents were necessarily neither helpless nor cast into the street. The same point holds for widows who were among the followers of Jesus. The Pastoral Letters seek to domesticate widows who, now independent of their husbands, had charge of their own finances, as 1 Timothy 5 shows.[32] As New Testament scholar Carolyn Osiek has demonstrated, the churches sought to make widows dependent on bishops and deacons.[33]

Some widows no doubt were destitute, but to conclude that widow abuse was the dominant pattern is to overstate the case, even as it is to prejudge how the parable would have sounded to its first-century auditors. The parable gives no indication of the widow's economic status. She may be poor and perhaps lacks money to bribe the judge;[34] on the other hand, she has access to the court, and she does not invoke poverty as a reason for her appeal.

Another potential clue to her economic status might be her location: the parable is set in an unnamed "city." This setting evokes Luke 7.37, where a certain woman in the city shows tenacity and achieves what she wants, to the distress of the man in charge of the setting. The woman in Luke 7.36–50 is by no means poor, as her high-end alabastron indicates. However, this connection of the widow to the woman in Luke 7 is Luke's contextualization and not necessarily one that helps with what the parable's original audience would have heard.

A third clue might be her persistence. The woman "kept coming" (the verb is in the imperfect tense and so indicates continual action). Time to continue to visit the judge is a luxury that those who work in a subsistence economy do not usually have. The parable does not suggest that her persistence or her presence in court—if that is where she is bothering the judge; she could equally well be bothering him in the marketplace, the synagogue, or his home—is odd. Whereas Roman moralists found women's appearances in courts inappropriate, that they fulminated so against such public presence does suggest they had examples provoking their disgust.[35]

The widow might well be destitute, oppressed, and desperate. She may also be wealthy, powerful, and vengeful. Or she may be somewhere in between. Once we stereotype her, we can ignore the challenge of the parable, and so ignore the challenge to our stereotypes.

The Judge

Some judge was in some city; God was he not fearing, and people was he not respecting. . . . And not did he wish at the time. But after these things, he said to himself, "If even God I do not fear nor people do I respect, yet on account of the trouble this widow causes, I will avenge her, so that not into the end, coming, she will wear me out/give me a black eye."
(Luke 18.2, 4–5)

Just as the vengeance-seeking widow becomes the model supplicant in Luke's narrative frame and the justice-seeking exemplar in scholarly reception, so the judge receives separate roles in the parable proper, the frame, and the reception. In the parable proper he is not the epitome of righteousness, nor is he clearly corrupt. In the immediate narrative frame, Luke labels him "unjust." In the broader frame, he is the negative version of the deity; the argument proceeds from the lesser to the greater (in rabbinic literature, this type of argument, called a *qal v'homer* ["light to heavy"] is well known) suggests that if an unrighteous judge will grant justice, surely the Righteous Judge will do the same. In the progressive scholarly tradition, the judge represents systemic evil and institutional corruption.

According to the parable, the judge "neither feared God nor had respect for people" (18.2). He confirms this description by interior monologue: "Though I have no fear of God and no respect for anyone . . ." (18.4). He is exactly as described; what we see is what we get.

Questions concerning how this judge was appointed, where he sat, and whether his role corresponds to any known practice have no necessary bearing on the parable's meaning.[36] The parable itself establishes the relevant cultural expectations.

Following Jill Harries's study of Roman court systems, New Testament professor Wendy Cotter proposes that the judge acts as he would be expected to act, for the "judicial system was a closed circle of ambitious elites whose attentions were trained on amassing greater wealth and increasing personal prestige."[37] This is not what happens in our parable. No money exchanges hands. Nor is the judge concerned about prestige.

Luke's own composition and words attributed to Jesus indicate a distaste for the role of judge, whether taken professionally or metaphorically. Luke 6.37 exhorts, "Do not judge" but rather "forgive" (two activities both figures in the parable fail to do). In 12.14, Jesus refuses the role of judge; in 12.58 he describes the threat of being dragged before a judge. Like Jesus, the proconsul Gallio eschews the role of judge (Acts 18.15), and Paul, perhaps facetiously, speaks of Felix as "judge over this nation" (24.10). When judges in Luke-Acts do their jobs, the verdicts are harsh, as Luke 11.19, 19.22, and Acts 10.42 suggest. Luke may even be warning readers to avoid the courts. Whereas Matthew 5.40 states, "If anyone wants to sue you and take your coat, give your cloak as well," Luke 6.29 simply reads, "If anyone strikes you on the cheek, offer the other also; and from anyone who takes away your coat do not withhold even your shirt." Judges are dangerous and to judge unadvisable.

Whether the judge in the parable is unjust, as Luke's narrative frame states, is an open question. In fact, just as we do not know if the widow is righteous or not, so we do not know, finally, how to judge our judge. Is he unjust by denying the widow her cause or by granting her what she wants?

Some commentators view him as "a tragic figure, a thoroughly honest man who permits himself to be corrupted for his personal convenience."[38] Richard Ford, a psychotherapist, proposes that the judge "reenacts with the widow the sequence he learned to expect as a child," namely, that "whenever he tried to get recognition from those on whom he depended, he was regularly shamed," and to "defend himself against such anticipated humiliation, he long ago determined never to depend on anyone; by never extending trust, he would never again be humiliated."[39] Others, while recognizing that his initially unattractive attitude prevents him from being tragic, nevertheless have some sympathy for him. Still others insist that he is "ruthless by any human estimation."[40]

To lack fear of the divine is not the same thing as to be unjust. It is unwise, given that "the fear of the LORD is the beginning of wisdom" (Ps. 111.10; cf. Prov. 1.7). It could signal lack of moral compass (cf. Gen. 20.11, "Abraham said, 'I did it because I thought, There is no fear of God at all in this place, and they will kill me because of my wife'"). And it goes against Jehoshaphat's charge to the judges of Judah, "Let the fear of the LORD be upon you" (2 Chron. 19.7). Biblical law insists, "You shall fear your God" (Lev. 19.14, 32), but not fearing God is not the same thing as being corrupt.

The judge's lack of "respect" can indicate a refusal to defer to a person of higher status; such lack of respect would put the judge outside the patron-client system. He is beholden to no one. Therefore, the proposal that the judge refused the widow justice because he accepted bribes from her opponent[41] does not neatly follow from the details the parable provides. A bribe would anticipate some degree of reciprocity, and this independent judge shows no interest in being in anyone's pocket. More, the parable says nothing about bribery.

His independence can be seen as a commendable trait, as Wisdom 6.7; Sirach 4.22; 32.12; Job 32.21 (LXX); and Deuteronomy 1.17 (LXX) on the ideal impartiality of judges suggest.[42] Conversely, he holds others in contempt, which is not an attractive characteristic.[43] Luke uses the term *entrepo* to describe the judge's lack of respect for others (18.2, 4); the term places him in the same category as the wicked tenants who do not "respect" (*entrepo*) the son of the vineyard owner (Matt. 21.37; Mark 12.6; Luke 20.13): this is not good company in which to be. We might even compare this judge who cares neither about God nor other people to the (equally dislikeable) prodigal son, who speaks of having sinned against heaven and against this father (Luke 15.18, 21).[44] First-century auditors would have seen the judge as a negative figure.[45]

Thus the judge is a good match for the widow, who is no moral exemplar either. At least at the start, they are well matched, for her insistent pleas prompt his equally consistent refusal: "For a while he refused" (18.4, an imperfect tense, to match her "coming"). She does not respect his verdict, because it is not the verdict she wants; he does not respect her or care whether she respects him.

She, however, bests him. The NRSV, blandly, quotes the judge as saying to himself: "Because this widow keeps bothering me, I will grant her justice, so that she may not wear me out by continually coming" (18.5). The Greek is sharper on three points. First, "bothering me" is literally "causing me labor," or colloquially "giving me work." It is the same term that appears in Luke 11.7, where the householder initially refuses his friend's midnight plea for food: "Do not give me work; the door has already been locked, and my children are with me in bed; I cannot get up and give you anything."[46] The widow and the friend at midnight share annoying tenacity, but the widow is no friend of the judge. Whereas the friend sought food, the woman seeks vengeance.

Second, "wear me out" is a boxing term, with the better English translation being "beat me up," "strike me in the face," "do violence to me,"[47] or "give me a black eye."[48] Elsewhere in the New Testament, it appears only in 1 Corinthians 9.27 (the NRSV reads "punish"), Paul's reference to the severe treatment he accords his own body. The cognate noun appears in Proverbs 20.30, which, as an ironic intertext to our parable, reads, "Blows that wound cleanse away evil; beatings make clean the innermost parts." For our parable, the threat of the blow pushes the judge into a decision based on expedience, not justice.

The most the judge can muster in response to the woman is interior monologue; he does not speak with her directly, any more than Martha speaks to Mary or the elder brother to the prodigal. His interior monologue puts him

in some very problematic company. Other Lukan parables in which a protagonist uses interior monologue include the Rich Farmer (12.16–21), the
Unfaithful Servant (12.42–46), the Prodigal Son (15.11–32), the Dishonest Manager (16.1–8a), and the Wicked Tenants (20.9–16).[49] The judge is at
best morally ambiguous.

Third, "grant her justice" literally means "avenge her." The widow will get
what she wants: vengeance. The judge, whether we find him sympathetic or
not, is co-opted by and so complicit in the widow's schemes. When he ac-
cedes to her request, he facilitates her vengeance. His problem is not that "he
turns out to be vulnerable to embarrassment and to a threat to his privileged
place in the society,"[50] that he is concerned she will "defame" him,[51] or that
"although he is clear about his role as judge, he still has to wear the mantle of
justice in public and keep the cover story alive."[52] His cover is already blown.
Both the narrative voice and his interior monologue indicate his lack of concern for public honor. His motive is that he is tired and threatened, not that
he is about to be dishonored.

The parable proper ends with the judge's decision and so it ends as a story
about corruption, violence, and vengefulness. Stereotypes of judges and
widows both fall. Justice is not clearly rendered. Has the widow made the
judge "just" by convincing him to rule in her favor, or has she corrupted
him? What would the widow's opponent think? What do we think?

Luke's Initial Domestication of the Parable

And he said a parable to them concerning their necessity
always to pray and not to become discouraged. . . . And said
the Lord, "Listen to what the unjust judge says. And will not
God make vengeance to his elect, those who cry to him day
and night, and will he be patient upon them? I say to you that
he will avenge them swiftly. Nevertheless, when the Son of Man
comes, then will he find faith upon the earth?" **(Luke 18.1, 6–8)**

Luke cannot abide a topsy-turvy world (pace Acts 17.6). For Luke, our parable is about the "necessity always to pray and not to become discouraged"

(18.1). The problem is that this interpretation is an allegory—there is no reason to think that a widow's badgering a judge would be understood by an initial audience as about prayer to God. Whereas to "pray without ceasing" (1 Thess. 1.2; 2.13; 5.17; 2 Tim. 1.3) is commendable, as David Buttrick states, "The notion that, repeatedly, we must bang on the doors of heaven if we are to catch God's attention is hardly an appropriate theology of prayer."[53]

Luke then additionally interprets the parable by adding a warning at the end: the concern that the "Son of Man" may not find faith on earth (18.8). The story of the widow and the judge does not suggest anything about messianic expectations or worries. That judge is not about to develop faith, and other than faith in her own perseverance, there's no indication in the parable that the widow has any religiosity. It is Luke who places the parable in a context that has apocalyptic elements. The addition of 18.8 on the Son of Man evokes the previous chapter, with Jesus's comment, "The days are coming when you will long to see one of the days of the Son of Man, and you will not see it" (17.22). Luke's comments on delay of the Parousia (Second Coming) in 17.22 conflict with the claim of the swift justice in 18.7. The frame doesn't work externally, and it doesn't help the parable either.

Luke's Further Domestication of the Parable

Along with awkwardly casting the parable as having to do with prayer in light of the delay in Jesus's return, Luke also provides it an interpretation that matches prevailing Roman cultural values by containing and constraining women. Luke is no great friend of independent women. Aside from the infancy materials, which may be additions to a Gospel that originally began with the preaching of John the Baptist,[54] Luke restricts women to ancillary roles. Simon's mother-in-law (perhaps a widow) requires Jesus's rescue (4.39) and responds with service. Luke 8.1–3 restricts women to patronage positions: they support Jesus and the apostles, who do the important work of preaching the word; they respond to Jesus not because of their independent assessment of his message or a divine revelation, but, Luke suggests, in gratitude for his healing their bodies.[55] In Luke 8.19, Jesus's mother (here perhaps also a widow; Joseph goes unmentioned), not identified by name, seeks to see him, but he dismisses her concern, "My mother and my brothers are those who hear the word of God and do it" (8.21).

Although Martha (10.38–42) can be read in the same context as Simon the Pharisee (7.36–42) and other householders whom Jesus criticizes for inappropriate manifestations of hospitality,[56] she is nevertheless put down in favor of her silent sister Mary. Jesus also critiques or, at least corrects, women who publicly express their admiration of him. To the woman who praises the womb that bore him and the breasts that nursed him, Jesus responds that more blessed are those who do the will of God (Luke 11.27–28). Women's biological gifts are fine, but they do not compare with Jesus's agenda. To the daughters of Jerusalem who weep for him, Jesus gives cold comfort in telling them rather to weep for themselves (23.27–28). That marvelous Canaanite/Syro-Phoenician woman, perhaps another widow (Matt. 15.21–28; Mark 7.24–30), has gone missing, and the Samaritan woman at the well (John 4; perhaps a five-time widow?) makes no appearance.

The widows in Luke-Acts are similarly domesticated. They are, in order: Anna (2.36–38), the widow of Zarephath and her contemporaneous Israelite sisters (4.25–26), the widow of Nain (7.11–17), the multiply married levirate widow (20.28–33), widows whose houses scribes devour (20.47), and the widow who puts her coins in the Temple treasury (21.1–4).[57] In light of the rereading of our active, probably vengeful, certainly morally ambiguous widow of the parable proper, these widows have a different story to tell.

Anna, the prophet in the Temple (2.37–38), anticipates the widow of 18.1–8 by praying always and not losing heart. According to Luke 2.36–37, "She was of a great age, having lived with her husband seven years after her marriage, then as a widow to the age of eighty-four. She never left the Temple but worshiped there with fasting and prayer night and day." Although Luke does grant that she is a prophet (2.36) and that she praised God and spoke about the child "to all who were looking for the redemption of Jerusalem" (2.38), he does not accord her any words of her own, as he does with Simeon the prophet. By introducing her as "the daughter of Phanuel, of the tribe of Asher" (2.36), Luke could be understood as subtly infantilizing the prophet; although eighty-four, she is still a daughter.

And yet, perhaps beneath Luke's editorial activity is a much more active widow. Her tribal recognition means that she represents the Northern tribes taken into exile, and taken from history, in 722 BCE.[58] She represents the tenacity of holding on to her identity. Her husband goes unnamed, and thus she, like Mary, emerges as the more important member of her spousal relationship. She is not simply identified by her father's name, but, unlike everyone else in the text save for Jesus via Joseph's genealogy, she receives an explicit connection to one of the tribes of Israel.

Like the widow Judith (16.22), Anna did not remarry.[59] This connection to Judith makes Anna less the frail prophet and more an echo of an ancient warrior. Her interest in "the redemption of Israel" nicely follows from this observation, since the Hebrew version of the phrase appears on Bar Kokhba's coinage.[60] Given these resonances, Anna is no quiet prophet; she is a vocal and visual symbol of Israel's hopes.

Luke next introduces widows in Jesus's synagogue sermon: "There were many widows in Israel in the time of Elijah, when the heaven was shut up three years and six months, and there was a severe famine over all the land; yet Elijah was sent to none of them except to a widow at Zarephath in Sidon" (4.25–26). In Luke's account, the widow is helpless and requires Elijah's aid. Again, Luke has domesticated a woman, for 1 Kings 17 depicts a feisty mother who first matches Elijah in verbal jousting and then demands that the prophet cure her son. The story itself deconstructs. In 1 Kings 17.9 God states, "I have commanded a widow there to feed you," but the widow, apparently, has not heard the command. Elijah has to talk her into providing for him by promising that he will provide for her. This widow is not one who prays daily and has hope. Instead, she states, face-tiously: "As the LORD your God lives, I have nothing baked, only a hand-ful of meal in a jar, and a little oil in a jug; I am now gathering a couple of sticks, so that I may go home and prepare it for myself and my son, that we may eat it, and die" (17.12).

The widow in 1 Kings 17 again criticizes Elijah when her son becomes ill. The NRSV offers: "What have you against me, O man of God? You have come to me to bring my sin to remembrance, and to cause the death of my son!" (17.18). However, the Septuagint does not read "sin" (*hamartia*), but "unrigh-teousness" (*adikias*), the same term Luke uses to describe the judge (18.6). With regard to gender and structural position (supplicant and grantor), the widow of the parable matches the widow of Zarephath. And if the widow of 1 Kings 17 is unrighteous, then the virtue of the parable's widow is again called into question. The judge of the parable is in this analogy cast as the prophet Elijah, to the credit of neither. Elijah, seen in light of the judge, is condemned for not aiding the widows in Israel.

The widow of Nain models the convention: she is a pathetic figure, introduced in the funeral procession of her only son (Luke 7.12). Seeing her, Jesus has "compassion" for her (7.13). The term evokes the good Samaritan, who "had compassion" for the man in the ditch (10.33), and the father of the prodigal, who was "filled with compassion" upon seeing his son return (15.20). These are the only three times in Luke-Acts that the term appears; each refers to the return of an individual from death to life. Thus the woman, not the son, is compared to the "half-dead" (10.30) injured traveler and the ignoble prodigal who "was dead and is alive again" (15.24); without her son, she too is dead.

To the widow of Nain, Jesus issues the negative command, "Do not weep" (7.13); she, unlike Anna, has given up hope. She, unlike the widow of Zarephath, did not demand that the prophet heal her only son. The dead son, upon being raised, "began to speak" (7.15), but the mother, like her fore-sisters in the Gospel, the widow Anna and the widow of Zarephath, says not a word.

Intertextual readings provide her a voice. First, the woman's weeping (7.13) can register not simply as mourning, but also as protest; the same point holds for the weeping of the daughters of Jerusalem in 23.28. Luke's beatitudes anticipate both the widow of Zarephath and the widow of Nain: "Blessed are you who are hungry now, for you will be filled" describes the former; "Blessed are you who weep now, for you will laugh" suggests the latter (6.21). Since the beatitudes continue with the threats to those currently full and laughing, they also, but more subtly, anticipate the widow of the parable, who seeks vengeance. Her opponent will have no reason to laugh. Finally, the widow of Nain, unlike the man in the ditch or the prodigal, not only receives compassion, but also receives the opportunity to act upon it. The final verse of her story indicates that Jesus gave the resuscitated son to his mother (7.15). She will care for him, not he for her. Luke gives no indication that she is in need of additional help; she does not appear oppressed or exploited.

Luke retains the Sadducees' question concerning the widow married to seven brothers (20.28–33; cf. Matt. 22.23–28; Mark 12.19–33). This woman, with no agency of her own, is property inherited by one brother after another. The NRSV delicately states that "the seven had married her" (Luke 20.33); the Greek more bluntly states that "the seven had her as wife." "Had" is the operative term. However, the woman's agency is only removed in the Sadducees' question, not in Jesus's response: "But those who are considered worthy of a place in that age and in the resurrection from the dead neither marry nor are given in marriage (20.35). The anticipated age rejects the idea not only that women need to marry, but also that they are "given." Lest readers conclude that the Sadducees' question confirms that early Judaism treated women as chattel, the question itself belies the argument. Sadducees, as we have seen, do not believe in resurrection, so the question is for them entirely hypothetical. Further, by the first century the tradition of Levirate marriage appears no longer to have been practiced, so again, the question is hypothetical and not a window into social history.

Luke's next reference to widows is Jesus's warning: "Beware of the scribes, who . . . devour widows' houses" (20.46–47; cf. Mark 12.40). Widows are, according to the conventional depiction, victims. On the other hand, these widows *have* houses. More intriguing, the widows are in the same position as the *father* of the prodigal, to whom his older son exclaims, "But when this son of yours came back, who has devoured your property . . ." (15.30). The connection does not "rescue" these widows; it does, however, together with the other stories regarding widows, show that the scribal threat can be avoided. The widow in our parable thus can be a role model, but I don't think Luke wants to make that point.

Finally, immediately after the reference to the widow's houses, Luke retains from Mark the short account of the widow who puts her two coins in the Temple treasury (21.1–4). Of the "poor widow" Jesus states, she "has put in more than all of them; for all of them have contributed out of their abundance, but she out of her poverty has put in what she had, her whole life" (21.3–4). Despite tendencies to read the story as one of Jewish leaders exploiting widows and of the Temple as a "domination system" that sucks the last coins out of the hands of those on fixed incomes, the juxtaposition of the widow references in chapters 20 and 21 together with the material adduced above suggests an alternative reading. The widow of 21.1–4 retains her own income and chooses how to spend it; she has not had her house stripped from her by scribes. Unlike the rich ruler of 18.18–25 and the foolish rich men in parables (e.g., 12.16–21; 16.19–31), she is not attached to her coins;

she gives generously, and Jesus praises her for it. The woman epitomizes what the Gospel exhorts. She is comparable to the disciples, who have left everything for a higher cause (Luke 5.11, 28; cf. Matt. 19.27; Mark 10.28).

Once the widow of the parable is de-domesticated, she opens the possibility for a rereading of the other widows. She grants them both agency and individuality. Luke may want to constrain widows, or women in general, to ancillary roles or pathetic characterizations. Real widows, then and today, resist these stereotypes. Telling a widow in a church today that she is helpless, oppressed, or needy may not be good news. It may also not be accurate.

Provoking Observations

Klyne Snodgrass states of Luke 18.1–8: "I consider this one of the more difficult parables. . . . The parable itself (vv. 2–5) is brief, and without its explanation (vv. 6–8) there is little indication of its intent."[61] Many readers choose to accept Luke's contextualization, regard the parable as about prayer, and take one or both of its main characters as exemplars (whether positive or negative); the parable then becomes a tidy story comprehensible only through allegory.

We choose how to read, and in doing so we harness the parable's ambiguity and the ambiguity of the lives it depicts.[62] This parable disturbs. At the very least, it calls into question stereotypes of widows and judges. Widows may be powerful and vengeful and exploit their positions; judges may be unjust (nothing new here), but their lack of justice may be prompted not by greed or even a preferential option for one class or another, but by irascibility, self-protection, or simply not wanting to be inconvenienced. Once our stereotypes are shattered, we can begin to look at people as individuals rather than as social roles. Stories, whether ancient or modern, hold our interest because people do what they are not expected to do. Women hide yeast in dough, Samaritans show compassion, tax collectors recognize their sinful state.

The parable also disturbs by preventing readers from a positive assessment of either character. Neither judge nor widow is a moral exemplar; neither is even likeable. And yet many of us struggle to find their good qualities; most readers, starting with Luke, want to rescue the widow. Here is a lesson about our own values. We resist the image of evil and seek good qualities. Or we resist ambiguity and force figures into opposites—good and bad, righteous and sinful, "us" and "them"—when we are all part of the same human community.

The parable disturbs again because the only form of closure it creates is that in which widow and judge—and so readers—become complicit in a plan possibly to take vengeance and certainly not to find reconciliation. We may resist that complicity and so opt out of the system that promotes it. We may decide that court cases are not worth our time, that compassion is less time consuming and less corrupting than vengeance. Our task may be to resist the parable rather than rescue it.

Barbara Reid, critiquing the reading that sees the judge as the negative exemplar of the divine—if he can be worn down, how much more so can the deity?—offers a "far simpler" understanding: "It is the widow who is cast in the image of God and who is presented to the disciples as a figure to emulate," for she represents "godly power in seeming weakness."[63] The gender disruption, where the (male) disciples see themselves as widows, is a nice thought, but it also strikes me as anachronistic, at least for both Jesus and Luke. More, I'm not convinced that an allegorical leap, let alone to the divine, is needed for the parable to provide a helpful critique of a worldview, whether that worldview is based in the first or the twenty-first century. Finally, I am wary of any reading that reinforces gender stereotypes, even in the attempt to dismantle them. The widow is not "weak," any more than Tamar, Ruth, Abigail, or Judith is "weak." Widows in biblical narrative rarely are. To live in a patriarchal system is not the same thing as being weak. The author of the 1 Timothy knew that, which is why 1 Timothy 5 wants to control widows.

Although Reid is correct that the widow achieves her goal without "resorting to violence,"[64] she nevertheless threatens the judge, or at least he perceives himself to be threatened. A punch thrown by a widow may be weaker than a punch thrown by Muhammad Ali, but a punch is still a punch, and a threat of violence is still a threat.

And yet the threat creates a relationship. The judge had no relationships—no fear of God and no concern for humanity; had he at least the latter, he might have attended the widow rather than ignored her. The ignoring grates (cf. Matt. 15.21–28). A negative response may be better than no response at all (I think Job would agree). The widow forces the judge to interact with humanity, and not by an objective stance; he has to interact with the widow because she has gotten to him. She has forced him into relationship. If there is a *qal v'homer* lesson here, a lesson moving from the lesser example to the greater, perhaps it is that if interaction is to come—and it will—it is better to engage it than to be forced into it. Then again, paradox sets in: he needs to interact with her in order to stop her from interacting with him.

On the other hand, the judge acts in order to protect himself, and that may not be a bad lesson either. He, like the widow, does what he feels he must do for his own benefit. One commentator, Donald Capps, goes as far to suggest that the judge is "perversely appealing as a pastoral image."[65] Do we admire both judge and widow? Both eventually get what they want. Is that a good thing? If it is, then what is the value of justice, or revenge?

Luise Schottroff offers another appealing reading. For her, the widow is the symbol of resistance. She is a positive symbol and also unmasks the sexism inherent in the "slander [of] women by accusing them of being violent" in that the widow threatens the judge with physical harm.[66] Schottroff, like Reid, is more generous than I. Women can be violent, we can kill, we can rape, we can seek vengeance. This point cannot be ignored either; it would be sexist to do so.

And yet we also learn from this depiction. The widow's behavior is consistent: a person who seeks to be avenged against her opponent is not a person who "loves her enemies." We readers resist the idea; we like to think of widows not only as in need of our protection and as just, but also as nonviolent. The parable destroys this stereotype, and destruction of negative stereotypes is not a bad thing. Rather than see the office or the social role, the parable insists we see the person. Rather than regard widows as weak, we may want to see them as (capable of being) violent. This is a more honest reading.

William Herzog sees the story as about systemic oppression and collusion of those trapped by it.[67] His general point about conscientization, a political interpretation in which people recognize their entrapment in injustice and so can work to change the system, is helpful. On the other hand, telling people that judges can be corrupt, uninterested, or selfish is not news. Nor does the widow do anything to change the system. Whether this reading leads to liberation is yet another issue. If the "good news" is that we collude in our own oppression, this is not news, and it is not good.

But this reading too opens to new possibilities. In the parable, vengeance rules. It is the desire for vengeance that drives the widow; this desire may be, especially in relation to law courts, more pressing than the desire for justice. I note this point as one who has taught for the past ten years in a maximum security prison in Nashville. My students at Riverbend well understand the drive for vengeance, because many of them and others incarcerated at Riverbend are recipients of it. It is the drive to vengeance that leads to the carrying out of the death penalty and, often, the refusal to grant parole even after a man has served forty years in prison and is, according to all the psychological tests, not any threat to society. Were I or a member of my family the victim of the crimes for which these men are in prison, I might very well be on the side of those who want vengeance. And the parable would challenge me: do I want to be in the widow's company?

The widow's desire for vengeance will prompt her violent approach to the judge, and the judge, perpetuating the system of vengeance, will prompt violent action against the opponent. The system then continues: the widow's opponent may well countersue, and nothing is achieved. Indeed, the "opponent" (*antidikos*) appears in Luke 12.58 to show not only the problems of involvement in the courts at all, but also the increasing violence that suits create: "When you go with your accuser (*antidikos*) before a magistrate, on the way make an effort to settle the case, or you may be dragged before the judge, and the judge hand you over to the officer, and the officer throw you in prison." The widow does not follow this advice, and everyone suffers.

All the figures in the parable, and we readers as well, have become enmeshed in, if not colluded with, this system set up at best for a "justice" whose legitimacy is never determined, a justice that by any other name constitutes vengeance. The problem is not ultimately the court. The court is only a system of the larger systemic concern: the human desire for vengeance, a desire that knows no gender or class boundaries, a desire that sucks everyone into its wake. Thus true systemic evil is revealed—and of course readers seek to deny it.

There is no easy closure to the widow's story; there is no closure at all. We cannot root for the widow or the judge, and we do not have enough information to speak about the opponent, but if he is tangled up with this widow, he may suffer guilt by association. Since we cannot find justice in the setting, we have to look elsewhere. We also have to cross-examine ourselves. What are our stereotypes of widows and judges, of the legal system and its relationship to religious confession? Of human nature and the drive for vengeance? Why do we want one person or group to succeed and another to fail? Does the end ever justify the means (as it does in this story)?

Jesus was invested in fairness, reconciliation, and compassion. The parable of the Widow and the Judge defies any sort of fairness. The "justice" the "unjust judge" (we should not forget that description) offers is not the justice of God or a program of fairness; it is granting a legal decision based not on merit, but on threat. There is no reconciliation in this parable; there is only revenge. There is no compassion, neither by the judge for the widow nor by the widow for the judge.

With his story, Jesus forces us to find a moral compass. At the same time, we learn that to do so, we need to interrogate our stereotypes and then ask the right questions, the ones we hesitate to ask.[68]

CHAPTER 9

The Rich Man and Lazarus

And some person was wealthy, and he dressed in purple and linen, feasting daily, splendidly. And some poor person, named Lazarus, was lying by his gates, being (covered with) sores. And he was wishing to be fed from the things falling from the table of the wealthy, but rather the dogs, coming, were licking his sores.

And it happened that when died the poor man and he was brought by the angels into the bosom of Abraham, and also died the wealthy, and he was buried. And in Hades, raising his eyes, being in torment, he sees Abraham from a distance and Lazarus in his bosom. And he himself calling out said, "Father Abraham, have mercy on me and send Lazarus so that he might dip the tip of his finger into water and cool my tongue, because I am suffering in this flame."

And said Abraham, "Child, do you remember that you received your good in your life, and Lazarus likewise the bad. And now here he is being comforted, but you are in pain. And in all these things between us and you a great chasm stands, so that the ones wishing to cross over from here to you are not able, nor from there to us can one cross over."

And he said, "I ask you, therefore, Father, so that you might send him to the house of my father. For I have five brothers, so that he might witness to them, in order that not will they come to this place of torment."

And says Abraham, "They have Moses and the prophets; let them listen to them."

And he said, "Not, Father Abraham, but if someone from the dead would come to them, they would repent.

And he said to him, "If to Moses and to the prophets not do they listen, neither if someone from the dead would rise would they be persuaded."

Luke 16.19–31

T his is not a story about the afterlife"—so goes one refrain among biblical scholars. It is not about final judgment, eternal damnation, or heavenly reward. The motifs of Lazarus resting comfortably in paradise and the rich man frying in hell are merely folklore or metaphor. "The parable proves absolutely nothing about a hereafter; it does not document either heaven or hell. . . . No, if Jesus told the story, he merely was playing around with a folktale tradition."[1] Some of us resist taking the parable in literal fashion, because we are uncomfortable with the idea of a real heaven and a real hell, of harps and halos, devils and pitchforks.[2]

Some of us resist this conclusion, because the judgments seem unfair. The rich man did ignore poor Lazarus, but he's hardly Hitler or Pol Pot. As for Lazarus, despite liberation theology's claim of God's "preferential option for the poor," we readers recognize that the poor are just as capable of sinning as the rich and that to romanticize poverty helps no one. Lazarus displays no pious action; he shows no action at all. Thus we want his fate to be explained by something other than his poverty; we do not want victimization to be rewarded.

Perhaps some of us resist the idea that the parable is about life after death because Lazarus appears to be "saved" apart from the cross. The storyteller, Jesus, has not yet died. If one can be saved apart from the sacrifice Jesus makes, then Jesus's sacrifice is not of universal import. The parable cannot be about life after death; it's too otherworldly, superstitious, or inconsistent. It is also a Christian message of limited salvation. As such, it is much more likely to come from Jesus himself, because its message is antithetical to the major claims of his followers.

"This is not (really) a story about economics"—so goes the other common refrain. Surely Jesus is not saying that wealth in and of itself is bad or that poverty is good. Religion professor Ronald Hock captures the consensus through at least the mid-1980s: "Scholars are quick to rule out the rich man's principal characteristic, his wealth (v. 19), as the reason for his judgment, or to impugn his life-style of wearing fine clothing and feasting daily (v. 19), or to assume that the rich man had gained his wealth, or maintained it, from usury, fraud, or exploitation of slaves."[3] Jesus does not tell everyone to "sell all you have and give the money to the poor." Moreover, according to 1 Timothy 6.10 (cf. Heb. 13.4), it is *the love of money* that is "the root of all kinds of evil," not money itself. Granted, Jesus says, "How hard it is for those who have riches to enter the kingdom of God" (Luke 18.24), but hard is not impossible, especially with God's help. The parable cannot be about changing the economic system, whether in the first century or the twenty-first: the idea is too earthly, too communistic.

Since we refuse to take the fates of the rich man and Lazarus literally, and since we resist reading the parable as about economics—that is, since we ignore what the parable does say—we are forced to interpret it in light of what it doesn't say. Thus we conclude that the rich man was condemned not simply because he ignored the man at his gate, but because he earned his wealth by exploiting the poor. Or we conclude that Lazarus was not only poor but also pious.[4]

Once we have the rich man as not simply rich, but also evil, and Lazarus as not simply poor, but also righteous, we then easily slide into vague social reversals. For some readers, the parable becomes another iteration of the beatitudes or Mary's Magnificat. It assures that the poor and the meek—with whom we readers identify—will be blessed; we can rest easy that God "has filled the hungry (us) with good things, and sent the rich (them) away empty" (Luke 1.53). The "good news to the poor" that Jesus proclaims (4.18) is that someday the poor (we readers) will live in the heavenly high-rent district, Abraham's bosom, where we can watch the rich (those not in our immediate group) suffer forever. That this reading offers pie in the sky rather than food for the hungry does not seem to bother most folks.

On both popular and scholarly levels, we find other, more pernicious readings. Over and over again we are told, "At the time of Christ, impoverished beggars were regarded as sinners being punished for their sins,"[5] and, "Judaism of that period would likely conclude that the miserable condition of Lazarus was the result of God's punishment for sin, and wealth, such as enjoyed by the rich man, indicated God's blessings."[6] "The prevailing understanding of prosperity and poverty [was] in terms of divine reward and retribution."[7] Lazarus "belongs among the outcasts of society. He is the type of person about whom it would have been socially acceptable for the rich man to be indifferent."[8] "It is strange in that the reversal of fortunes it depicts contradicts the widespread belief that wealth was a sign of God's favor and poverty a sign of sin."[9] "Jesus's audience, or at least a significant part of it, would have been steeped in the belief that riches were a blessing for obedience, with suffering a punishment for sin," and thus they were "outraged" to hear that Lazarus had been received by Abraham.[10]

For the last-quoted author, who goes on to note the contrary view expressed in Proverbs, Job, Ecclesiastes, and many psalms, the ancient "Jewish expectation" is found in today's "prosperity gospel."[11] Who knew Jews invented the prosperity gospel?

We also find in studies of this parable the anticipated condemnation of Temple and purity, despite the fact that the parable says nothing about either. For example, the rich man is understood to be one of the "urban elites who lived at the expense of the poor [and who] twisted Torah and Temple to serve their ends. They read the Prophets for their comfort and Moses to study the purities lest they should become unclean."[12]

In these popular readings, which do preach well, the shock of the parable is that the rich may not be God's darlings and the poor may not be sinful. The subtext for today's Christians is that Jews glorified wealth and worshipped Mammon, while Jesus invented social conscience and liberation theology. The message from the pulpit is, once again, thank God Jesus came to restructure the value system. That many folks in the pews don't actually take this restructuring to heart, as they step over the street people and make their way to brunch, does not matter: Jesus has given them the corrective. Surely we can do better.

What if the parable does say something about the afterlife, which is what the church fathers thought[13] and probably what the majority of the original auditors of the parable—who hadn't read the latest issue of *Biblical Theology Bulletin* or *Review and Expositor,* but who did believe in a just God, who resurrected the dead and proclaimed a final judgment—thought as well? What if we took seriously Jesus's own concern for how people related to each other, or how they might live if they already had one foot in the kingdom of heaven? What if the parable does say something about economic status, a major concern of both the scriptures of Israel and Jesus of Nazareth?

That's how people in Jesus's audience would have heard it; we do well to hear it as they would have.

And some person was wealthy, and he dressed in purple and linen, feasting daily, splendidly. **(Luke 16.19)**

Anytime a parable begins, "There was a rich man who . . . ," we know that the rich man is a poor role model. The scriptures of Israel, Jewish literature of the Second Temple period, rabbinic sources, and numerous quotes attributed to Jesus of Nazareth all agree that wealth is a snare, that the rich should but usually do not care for the poor, and that God has special concern for the disadvantaged. The rich man's lack of name—his traditional identification as *Dives*, Latin for "rich man," which morphed into a proper name in the Middle Ages—shows his conventional character.[14] He represents any rich man.

For Jesus's initial audience, the reference not simply to a "rich man," but to one who lives a hedonistic life would convey a negative impression. Despite the claim by numerous scholars that the parable has "no reference to the good deeds of Lazarus or the evil deeds of the rich man,"[15] the point is only half correct. The rich man has sinned by omission—he has failed to extend his hand to the poor.

For that initial audience, the rich man is not "one of us." He does not merely have extraordinary wealth; he ostentatiously displays it. His "purple cloth" (Gk. *porphyra*) was among the most expensive of textiles. His "fine linen" (Gk. *bussos*), elegant material, was the same as that used to create the clothing used in the wilderness sanctuary and by the high priests; the term occurs repeatedly in the book of Exodus (LXX) to describe their special garments. But the priests wear their linen to serve in the sanctuary; the rich man wears his to sit at his dinner table. He is not serving God or neighbor; he is the epitome of one who is self-serving. His purple outer garment and his linen undergarments are the height of fashion: nothing nattier in Nazareth. Not one to save his best garments for the Sabbath, our rich man treats every day as another opportunity to indulge. That the verb for "dressed" (Gk. *enedidysketo*) is in the imperfect tense reinforces this daily indulgence.

What goes on his body is matched by what goes into it. *Euphraino*, translated here as "feasting," has the connotation of "cheering" or "rejoicing"; it is what people should do at major festivals. For example, in Deuteronomy 16.11, Moses exhorts the people to observe the Festival of Weeks (Heb. *Shavuot*; Gk. *Pentecost*), "Rejoice [Gk. *euphraino*; the underlying Hebrew is *simcha*] before the LORD your God—you and your sons and your daughters, your male and female slaves, the Levites resident in your towns, as well as the strangers, the orphans, and the widows who are among you . . . ."

The rich man is not celebrating sacred time, and he is not, as far as we know, celebrating with strangers and widows and orphans. Worse, he is forcing his staff—his servants and his slaves—to provide him the food, the entertainment, whatever he needs to sate himself. Jesus had dismissed "those who put on fine clothing and live in luxury" (Luke 7.25), and such folk, like Herod Antipas or Caiaphas, would not have been seen by the Jewish majority as epitomizing righteousness.

We can speak of the rich man as engaging in conspicuous consumption—something present-day culture often condemns even as it relishes reality shows that display it. The parable could be heard as proclaiming an alternate view of what is to be appreciated. Rather than relish indulgence or cluck to ourselves how shameful such consumption is, why not name it to be what it is—obscene? That may get us somewhere.[16]

The rich man is, like the Pharisee of Luke 17, a caricature; he is too rich even to be recognized and outside any system of social responsibility. Roman readers would have expected the rich to aid the poor as part of their role in the patronage system. Jewish readers would have expected such patronage, given that they were also part of the Roman world, but they also would have condemned the man for failing to provide support. Such care is commanded in Torah: "Since there will never cease to be some in need on the earth, I therefore command you, 'Open your hand to the poor and needy neighbor in your land'" (Deut. 15.11). Those commentators who are convinced that Jews would have been surprised that our rich man wound up damned perhaps missed looking at such passages.

Jesus makes the same point: "When you give a luncheon or a dinner, do not invite your friends or your brothers or your relatives or rich neighbors, in case they may invite you in return, and you would be repaid. But when you give a banquet, invite the poor, the crippled, the lame, and the blind. And you will be blessed, because they cannot repay you, for you will be repaid at the resurrection of the righteous" (Luke 14.12–14). In Luke 18.22, he tells his would-be follower, "Sell all that you own and distribute the money to the poor, and you will have treasure in heaven." Earlier he told his disciples, "Sell your possessions, and give alms. Make purses for yourselves that do not wear out, an unfailing treasure in heaven, where no thief comes near and no moth destroys" (12.33). He is not being religiously innovative here; he is reflecting his Jewish culture.

Jesus's reference to salvation in relation to economics fits within a Second Temple Jewish context, for at this time support for the poor increasingly had taken on a soteriological dimension. Indeed, the Hebrew term for "giving alms" (*tzedakah*) comes from the same root as the term for "righteousness" (*tzedek*). The book of Tobit offers the advice:

> Give alms from your possessions, and do not let your eye begrudge the gift when you make it. Do not turn your face away from anyone who is poor, and the face of God will not be turned away from you. If you have many possessions, make your gift from them in proportion; if few, do not be afraid to give according to the little you have. So you will be laying up a good treasure for yourself against the day of necessity. For almsgiving delivers from death and keeps you from going into the Darkness. (4.7–10)

Biblical studies scholar Gary Anderson suggests that the rabbinic notion of "drawing down one's treasury in this world" might make a fruitful comparison to our parable: "If this rabbinic motif was relevant, one of the points of Luke would be that the rich man had enjoyed all the fruits of his labors in this world and as a result had nothing left in the world to come."[17] Had he supported the poor, he could have erased the debt to God created by sin.

The rich man refused to give alms, even when a poor man was at his gate. Of course he will suffer in the afterlife. He had laid up nothing for it. Jesus's Jewish audience knew this. They would not have been on the side of the rich man, they would not have regarded his wealth as a sign of righteousness, and they would not have been surprised at his fate.

And some poor person, named Lazarus, was lying by his
gates, being (covered with) sores. And he was wishing
to be fed from the things falling from the table of the
wealthy, but rather the dogs, coming, were licking his sores.
(Luke 16.20-21)

Standard English translations may be more mellifluous than the Greek, but what they gain in narrative flow they lose in pathos. The NRSV and the NIV both begin v. 20 with "At his gate"; the Greek, however, begins with "And some poor person" (*ptochos;* the same term used in the beatitude "Blessed are you who are poor" [Luke 6.20; cf. Matt. 5.3, which speaks of the "poor in spirit"]). The focus is not on the location; it is on the man's economic condition. "Some rich person" is in direct contrast to "some poor person." That Jesus proclaimed the poor blessed finds enactment in this parable.

In Jesus's sense of justice, those who suffer on earth find not just spiritual peace, but physical peace as well in another sphere. Those who would limit his interests to social policy do not do justice to his Jewish context or his Jewish sensibilities, which are replete with the sense that the doing of justice is part of God's involvement with humanity.

The NIV muddles the Greek even more by identifying the figure not as a poor man, but as a "beggar." Not all poor are beggars, and not all beggars are poor. *Ptochos* appears thirty-four times in the New Testament, where it describes people in states of poverty, most of whom do not beg. The "poor widow" who puts her two coins into the Temple treasury begs from no one (Mark 12.42–43; Luke 21.3). When Paul, in Romans 15.26, states, "Macedonia and Achaia have been pleased to share their resources with the poor among the saints at Jerusalem," he is not talking about messianicly inclined beggars. James 2.2 condemns the congregation that affirms a "person with gold rings and in fine clothes," but dishonors "a poor person in dirty clothes."

A beggar (Gk. *prosaites*) actively begs; that is his job. According to Mark 10.46, as Jesus was leaving Jericho, he encountered "Bartimaeus son of Timaeus, a blind beggar, . . . sitting by the roadside." In John 9.8, speaking of the blind man whom Jesus had healed, "The neighbors and those who had seen him before as a beggar began to ask, 'Is this not the man who used to sit and beg?' " Lazarus neither sits nor begs. He is in worse shape than a beggar. And thus he too is "not one of us." Like the rich man at the other extreme, he is a figure so poor that we cannot identify with him. We are neither the rich man nor Lazarus.

Lack of identification is not the same thing as lack of sympathy, however. To conclude that Lazarus has "broken society's unspoken code" and therefore the audience is not likely to sympathize overstates, just as to conclude that Job, who is in worse shape than Lazarus, does not garner sympathy would be to overstate.[18] To argue that Lazarus "is the type of person about whom it would have been socially acceptable for the rich man to be indifferent"[19] suggests an abhorrent society. That the rich man is indifferent condemns him. To ignore suffering—especially when it is at one's doorstep—is never "socially acceptable." To the contrary, perhaps the reason Lazarus is at the gate in the first place is because the people who placed him there expected the rich man to act.

Lazarus is supposed to have our sympathies. The scriptures of Israel repeatedly express God's concern for the poor, the widow, the orphan, and the stranger—if they deserved their states, then the divine concern makes no sense. Further, for the parable, what Lazarus did or did not do does not matter. One commentator, J. Mary Luti, gets it right: "Luke's parable . . . doesn't say, for example, if Lazarus was deserving or lazy, drug-addicted, mentally ill, or a good Joe down on his luck."[20] He deserves readers' pity, and, like Job, he receives it.

The storyteller's art also leads readers toward this empathy. Before we know of Lazarus's circumstances beyond the stark notice of his poverty, we learn his name. In parables, characters are rarely named. There are landowners and tenants, fathers and sons, widows and judges, kings and peasants, but there are no Reubens or Rachels, Moshes or Miriams. In the

Gospels, Lazarus and his "father" Abraham are the only named figures in a parable.

In Hebrew, "Lazarus" would be "Eliezer," which means "God helps" (see Exod. 18.4; Eliezer is the name of Moses and Zipporah's second son, and Moses glosses the name, "The God of my father was my help, and delivered me from the sword of Pharaoh"). The term *ezer* is familiar from names like Ebenezer (see 1 Sam. 7.12) and the identification of the human being's partner in Genesis 2.18 as an *ezer k'negdo*, a "helper who is like him." The irony is apparent: the only help Lazarus will get will come from God, since the rich man is not doing what God had commanded.

Less likely is the claim that Lazarus is meant to evoke Abraham's servant Eliezer, although it does show up in sermons on occasion. Here's how this connection is supposed to work. In Genesis 15.2, Abraham prays, "Lord God, what will you give me, for I continue childless, and the heir of my house is Eliezer of Damascus?" "Aha," suggests the biblical reader with a good concordance, "two matches!" Lazarus of the parable must be Eliezer, and the confirmation of the connection is that both Luke 16 and Genesis 15 mention Abraham. Then, once the connection is made, a few exegetes come to the conclusion that our Lazarus, related to Abraham's gentile servant, represents the (Christian) gentiles, who replace the money-loving Jews, represented by the rich man, in salvation history. The parable then becomes an allegory about the salvation of the gentiles and "the severity of the judgment of Israel if she persists in her unrepentant state."[21] This configuration equates Jews with the damned rich and Christian gentiles with the righteous poor.

There is no reason for first-century Jews to associate a figure named Lazarus with gentiles from Damascus, any more than readers of the Gospel of John would associate the Lazarus whom Jesus raised from the dead with them. Further, Eliezer does *not* inherit Abraham's estate; Abraham's son Isaac does. Further, Abraham's servant in Genesis enters the Greek language, through the Septuagint, not as "Lazarus," but as "Eliezer." The connection to Genesis and so of our Lazarus to gentiles works only when what the Bible actually says is ignored and an ugly supersessionism deforms the Gospel.

However, the association of our Lazarus with the Johannine story does have some merit. In John 11, Jesus raises Lazarus; in our parable, the rich

man pleads with Abraham to send Lazarus to his brothers, for "if someone from the dead would come to them, they would repent" (16.30). We
might conclude that Luke knew the story of the raising of Lazarus in John's
Gospel, or from a common source to which both evangelists had access, and
so named the figure in the parable Lazarus. Or we might conclude that John
knew Luke's parable and turned the parable into a narrative. Or we might
conclude that Jesus himself, anomalously, named a figure in a parable.

I am attracted to the idea that Jesus provided the name. Luke is not known
for any affinity for Hebrew or Aramaic terms (Mark's Aramaic drops out of
Luke's text), and there is no reason to think that Luke's Greek-speaking audience would have known these languages either. Jesus, good storyteller and
Aramaic-speaker that he was, would have known the nuances of the name,
of which for the parable there are at least three.

First, the rich man knows Lazarus by name, and that knowledge condemns him. The man at his gate was not a stranger; the rich man cannot
plead ignorance. Second, the name translated "God helps" raises the question of the presence of the divine. For our Lazarus, the only way that God
will help him is if those who claim to be followers of God follow the Torah,
doing their share. Third, the name shows that the storyteller attends to this
man—the storyteller also knows his name. The name forces us to notice the
man by the gate. He is not just "some guy"; he is Lazarus.

Placed by His Gates

The parable does not detail Lazarus's arrival at the rich man's gate. The Greek
verb in Luke 19.20 is *ballo,* which in the active voice means "to throw" or "to
cast," but in the passive voice it means something closer to "to be placed";
hence "was lying." A few commentators who stop at the lexicon, do not go
on to see how the term is used in context, and do not check the grammati-
cal form conclude that Lazarus was "tossed" outside, like garbage. The same
term, *ballo,* describes Peter's mother-in-law whom Jesus heals ("lying in
bed," Matt. 8.14), and I have no reason to believe that Peter or his wife was
engaging in elder abuse. It describes the paralytic, carried by several people
toward Jesus ("lying on a bed," Matt. 9.2). It describes the erstwhile demon-
possessed Canaanite daughter, whom the mother finds "lying" (*ballo*) on her

bed (Mark 7.30), and so on. Thus the term not only need not have, but also should not have, a negative connotation.

The anonymous people who placed the poor man at the gate may have put him there *because* they knew that the rich man had funds or because they knew that his friends and relatives would enter the gate and see him.

Wishing to Be Fed

Lazarus desired only the scraps from the rich man's table. The Greek echoes the wish of the prodigal (Luke 15.16), desperate to eat even the pods fed to the pigs. Numerous claims that diners would use pieces of bread as napkins that they would then toss to the hungry are as ahistorical as the claim that the folded "napkin" (KJV) described in John 20.7 as part of Jesus's burial indicates that Jesus would return for dinner.

The hungry prodigal rehearses the speech he will give to his father. The hungry Lazarus says nothing; throughout the parable, he remains silent. Thus we readers have to give him a voice. Whether Lazarus desired also that the rich man choke on his own food, or that the rich man have a conversion experience and turn into an ancient Jewish Francis of Assisi who divests of his possessions and lives humbly among the poor, we do not know.

Good Dogs, Sores, and More Mistaken Views of Jewish Culture

The reference to dogs increases the pathos. Lazarus cannot get a crumb, but the dogs, who lick his sores, turn his body into their meal. He provides for them what he himself lacks. At the same time, they aid him. That the saliva of dogs had healing properties was already known in antiquity. In his biography of Apollonius of Tyana (43), the second-century CE author Philostratus presents a healing narrative in which Apollonius

> bade the dog lick the wound all round where he had bitten the boy, so that the agent of the wound might in turn be its physician and healer. . . . Nor did the sage neglect the dog either, but after offering a prayer to the river he sent the dog across it; and when the dog

had crossed the river, he took his stand on the opposite bank, and began to bark, a thing which mad dogs rarely do, and he folded back his ears and wagged his tail, because he knew that he was all right again.[22]

As might now be expected, Lazarus's distress becomes the occasion for negative characterizations of Jewish practices and attitudes, especially in relation to sin and purity. We read, "It is Lazarus—who is ritually unclean because of his sores and the dogs licking those sores (16:20)—who was made clean by God";[23] "Both Lazarus's running sores and the dogs licking his sores would have rendered him ritually impure";[24] "He cannot even defend himself from [the dogs'] actions, which render him more degraded and unclean."[25] The logical conclusion from these stereotypes is that Lazarus was ignored by the (purity-obsessed) rich man in part because he was unclean.

The parable of course says nothing about "ritual impurity." The sores are not necessarily sources of impurity; nor are dogs. How then does this mischaracterization arise?

Some scholars suggest that Lazarus would have been seen as sinful because he suffers a fate comparable to that of King Ahab, about whom 1 Kings 21.19 states, "In the place where the dogs licked up the blood of Naboth, dogs will also lick up your blood." Licking the blood of a dead king is not the same thing as licking the sores of a poor, hungry, and still living man. The corpse and so the blood streaming from it are impure; the sores, although they have a strong "ick" factor, are not.

Although Lazarus gives his name in numerous languages to lazarettos (i.e., places where people suffering from leprosy are quarantined) and although St. Lazarus is the patron of those suffering from leprosy, nothing in the parable indicates that Lazarus's ulcers or sores are leprous and therefore sources of impurity. The Greek term *elkos* appears in the New Testament elsewhere only in Revelation (16.2, 11), where it refers to the "sores" or perhaps "wounds" of those who bear the mark of the beast. The Septuagint for Leviticus 13 indicates that such "sores" need to be diagnosed by a priest to determine if leprosy is present. The sore itself is not equivalent to the disease; rather, the disease breaks out in the sore. More often, *elkos* appears in terms of a physical ailment detached from concerns for purity or leprosy. In Exodus 9.9–11 it refers to the plague of "boils" inflicted on the Egyptians;

Deuteronomy 28.27 connects these boils to "ulcers, scurvy, and itch." These sores are also suffered by Job (2.7), but even here there is no mention of leprosy or impurity. Josephus uses the cognate *elkosis* to describe one of the many disgusting symptoms suffered by Herod the Great[26] and to condemn the anti-Jewish Egyptian priest Apion, who, as Josephus recounts, "was circumcised himself of necessity, on account of an ulcer (*elkosis*) in his penis."[27] Gross, yes, but not leprosy.

As for the dogs, missing from most of these studies is the notice that some Jews kept dogs as pets. The book of Tobit, a very Jewish book found in the Deuterocanonical literature, presents Tobias, the volume's hero, as accompanied by a pet dog. These readings also miss the numerous references in the Mishnah to dogs owned by Jewish householders (e.g., *Kilaim* 8.6; *Baba Qamma* 5.3; 7).

Dogs are not sources of uncleanness—that is not the image Jesus's audience would take from the description of Lazarus. Rather, they would realize that the dogs provided him his only comfort. The dogs realized what the rich man did not—that people in pain need help. In feeding the dogs, Lazarus provides them a service; in licking his wounds, the dogs reciprocate. Suggestions that the dogs are the rich man's "guard dogs"[28] or that they serve to clean the floors after the diners have left are at best speculation. Nothing suggests they are pit bulls or have a place in the rich man's home.

Lazarus is not a leprous poster child for the evils of Jewish purity laws. We might see him as a first-century Job—covered in sores and mistreated by those who should have befriended him, including not a few New Testament interpreters.

And it happened that when died the poor man and he was
brought by the angels into the bosom of Abraham, and also
died the wealthy, and he was buried. **(Luke 16.22)**

Lazarus, as far as we know, has no earthly familial support. We cannot be certain, however, that he was left unburied. Jewish tradition speaks extensively about the importance of treating a dead body with utmost respect and burying corpses (as we saw in our discussion of the Good Samaritan parable in chapter 2). In contrast, the rich man's burial suggests a family plot and therefore anticipates the reference to his brothers. It is with the rich man's burial and Lazarus's angelic travels that their fates are shown to be the reverse of their lives on earth.

Whereas the Greek speaks of the *kolpos,* the "breast," "chest," or "bosom" (so the KJV), of Abraham, the NRSV has the sanitized "to be with Abraham" and the NIV "Abraham's side." The Greek conveys connotations of both intimacy and feasting. For intimacy, *kolpos* in antiquity primarily suggested parental love and protection in the "bosom" of the family.[29] Father Abraham holds his child Lazarus and thus provides him the nurture he did not receive at the rich man's gate. For feasting, Lazarus is reclining on Abraham's chest, just as the beloved disciple reclined on Jesus's chest at the Last Supper (John 13.23). The posture suggests a banquet, a motif that might be expected given Jesus's focus on food and banqueting and the parable's detailing of food and drink. The poor man, who had no food, is now reclining at the heavenly banquet. Gospel readers may recall Jesus's comment, "Many will come from east and west and will eat (recline at table) with Abraham and Isaac and Jacob in the kingdom of heaven" (Matt. 8.11). *First Enoch* 62.14 similarly teaches that the righteous "shall eat and rest and rise with that Son of Man forever and ever." What the poor man lacked in life—human companionship, food, comfort—he now has.

Like the name Lazarus, the reference to Abraham—the other named figure in a parable—suggests several roles: father figure, protector, symbol of hospitality, eschatological judge, and more. That Lazarus is the "father" of the people Israel is a point reinforced by the rich man's address "Father Abraham." The image would have been a familiar one. The "Jews" in the Fourth Gospel claim, "Abraham is our father" (8.39), and John the Baptist warns, "Do not presume to say to yourselves, 'We have Abraham as our ancestor (father)'; for I tell you, God is able from these stones to raise up children to Abraham" (Matt. 3.8–9).

To be "father" meant more than to hold a position of authority or even to protect. It also signaled the provision of food and so of hospitality. Thus Jesus notes that the birds of the air neither sow nor reap, "yet your heavenly Father feeds them" (6.26), advises that people pray, "Our Father," when they ask for their "daily bread" (6.9, 11), and queries, "Is there anyone among you who, if his child asks for bread, will give a stone?" (7.9; the NRSV, in its gender-inclusive language, strips out the clear reference to a male parent in the Greek). Abraham, the archetypal "father," provides food. By the Second Temple period, Abraham's hospitality had become one of his dominant characteristics. Unlike the rich man, Abraham welcomed strangers to dine with him (Gen. 18.1–15). The rich man is not a true child of Abraham, in that he did not behave as Abraham would have.

In the Second Temple period as well, Abraham was also known as having access to heavenly knowledge and associated with the afterlife. According to 4 Maccabees 7.19 (also 16.25), "Our ancestors Abraham and Isaac and Jacob do not die to God, but live to God." That same text proclaims, "For if we so die, Abraham and Isaac and Jacob will welcome us, and all the fathers will praise us" (13.17). In John 8.56, Jesus tells his Jewish interlocutors, "Your ancestor (father) Abraham rejoiced that he would see my day; he saw it and was glad." In Luke 13.28, Jesus speaks of the division of the righteous and the sinners: "There will be weeping and gnashing of teeth when you see Abraham and Isaac and Jacob and all the prophets in the kingdom of God, and you yourselves thrown out." The parable is a visual enactment of this prediction.

Along with eschatological knowledge comes soteriological influence. The pseudepigraphon known as the *Testament of Abraham,* which also emphasizes Abraham's hospitality, describes the patriarch's tour of heaven. Abraham sees the small gate that leads to the salvation of the (few) righteous and the narrow gate that leads to the damnation of the (many) sinners. In the story's longer version, Abraham initially prays for the condemnation of sinners, but later intercedes with God for their salvation. That the rich man might ask for Abraham's intercession fits within these numerous roles.

Finally, as we noticed in the discussion of the parable of the Pharisee and the Tax Collector, Abraham's role as "father" may have also evoked the *zechut avot,* the idea that Jews, seeking forgiveness could appeal to the righteous behavior of their ancestors. God would remember that righteous behavior of the patriarchs and transfer its value to their repentant descendants. This notion may underlie the Baptist's comment about the people's reliance on father Abraham. The Rich Man and Lazarus then shows the limits of these merits. Some Jews may have thought that Abraham would plead for them all; Jesus thought otherwise.

～～～

And in Hades, raising his eyes, being in torment, he sees
Abraham from a distance and Lazarus in his bosom.
(Luke 16.23)

Cautionary tales of postmortem reversals of fortune are part of global storytelling. The Babylonian Talmud (*Sanhedrin* 23c; cf. *Hagigah* 77d) recounts the story of a fellow named Ma'jan, "a rich tax collector" known for evil deeds, who died the same day as did a poor Torah scholar. The tax collector received a magnificent funeral; the scholar was ignored. The story continues: "Now, one of the student's friends had a dream, in which he saw the fate of the two men after their death. The student was in paradise, the garden of the King, enjoying its beauty and the richness of its vegetation and streams. The man who had been rich in his life, Ma'jan, was also standing on the banks of the stream, trying to reach the water, but unable to do so."

For this rabbinic story, wealth is connected with evil deeds and tax collecting; wealth itself is not the problem. The Torah scholar, by virtue of his occupation, is deemed righteous. The rationales for the verdicts on the rich man and Lazarus are less clear, although the former's wealth and the latter's poverty are necessary components to the judgment.

Our rich man's fate is already anticipated by his introduction in the parable: "There was a rich man who . . ." It is confirmed by the details of his self-indulgence, and it is sealed with the notice of his failure to notice Lazarus. In good folkloric fashion, the rich man's damnation would be complemented by the poor man's salvation. The motif of reversal does not require any details for *why* Lazarus finds himself comforted in Abraham's bosom. The parable is, moreover, focused on the rich man, with whom the story begins and to whom the story gives voice.

Even when readers today seek an explanation for Lazarus's heavenly reward, the focus is nevertheless more on the evils of wealth than on the virtues of poverty in general or Lazarus in particular. We could claim, "Lazarus is judged innocent and so finds lasting comfort in the bosom of Abraham, not so much because of his assumed faith as because of his poverty, which excluded him from the damning life of the rich man."[30] Or we might take the next step and suggest that poverty is itself unjust and therefore those who suffer from it must receive recompense.

Given its focus on the rich man, the parable works well without any need for explaining what Lazarus *did* to *earn* a place in Abraham's bosom. The Mishnah affirms, "All Israel has a share in the world to come" (*Sanhedrin* 10.1), save for those who say there is no resurrection of the dead according to Torah, for apostates, and for Epicureans. By failing to extend his hand to the poor and instead by living an epicurean life—a life marked by luxury and not generosity—the rich man had placed himself outside the system.

Folkloric though the parable may be, it speaks to early Jewish views of the afterlife. Already Daniel 12.2 mentions postmortem rewards for the righteous: "Many of those who sleep in the dust of the earth shall awake, some to everlasting life, and some to shame and everlasting contempt." The Wisdom of Solomon proclaims, "The souls of the righteous are in the hand of God, and no torment will ever touch them," whereas "the ungodly will be punished as their reasoning deserves, those who disregarded the righteous and rebelled against the Lord" (3.1, 10). According to *1 Enoch* 22.8–11, the righteous will be rewarded and the sinners (whom Enoch equates with the rich) will face "scourges and torments" for eternity.

According to Josephus, the Pharisees taught, "Every soul is imperishable, but only the soul of the good passes into another body, while the souls of the wicked suffer eternal punishment."[31] The Essenes "declare that for the good souls there is reserved an abode beyond the ocean, a place which is oppressed neither by storms nor snowfalls nor burning heat but is refreshed by the ever gentle west wind blowing from the ocean; but they banish the wicked souls to a gloomy and stormy dungeon, full of never-ending punishments."[32]

The notion that in the afterlife, the saved and the damned could see each other also appears in various texts. *Fourth Ezra (2 Esdras) 7.36–37* predicts, "Then the pit of torment shall appear, and opposite shall be the place of rest; and the furnace of hell shall be disclosed, and opposite the paradise of delight. Then the Most High will say to the nations that have been raised from the dead, 'Look now, and understand what you have denied, whom you have not served, whose commandments you have despised.'" According to various Jewish pseudepigrapha, including *Jubilees* 23.30–31; *1 Enoch* 95.3; 96.1; and *2 Baruch* 51.5–6, the righteous witness the suffering of the sinners.

Such descriptions serve several practical purposes. First, they function as disincentives. "Don't ignore the poor, or in the afterlife they will get to watch you while you suffer" has a visceral quality to it. Second, they provide a sense of justice for those who see the uncaring rich prosper and the poor suffer. Third, they function as safeguards against violence: rather than attack the rich man, open his home for public housing, and distribute his treasures on earth to those in need—that is, rather than provoke a slave revolt or motivate social banditry—postmortem compensation suggests that whatever violence is to occur is not in human hands.

And yet . . . the parable raises much more difficult questions than "Is Lazarus saved because he is poor?" First, if we remain unfazed by the idea of endless pain, then we are no better than the rich man whose punishment we praise. If the body is in the image and likeness of the divine, is torturing it to be celebrated or condemned? What purpose does eternal punishment serve, other than certain revenge fantasies of those who are not being tortured? Schadenfreude may be a source of emotional pleasure, but it is not nice.

Second, do we wish ourselves in Lazarus's place in the afterlife—because if we do, we should be prompted to imagine ourselves in his place in the present life. Does heavenly reward take us off the hook for helping the poor who are always with us? For both men (to whom are we closer on the economic spectrum, the fabulously wealthy or the desperately poor?) perhaps their fates are already determined. What of ours?

Finally, what is our notion of justice, or of God? The Pharisees promulgated the concept of resurrection of the dead, and for the Mishnah the concept has what might be seen as doctrinal status. Justice has to be found somewhere. If not in this life, then where? Then when?

And he himself calling out said, "Father Abraham, have
mercy on me and send Lazarus so that he might dip the tip
of his finger into water and cool my tongue, because I am
suffering in this flame." **(Luke 16.24)**

"Father Abraham"—the familial language evokes the *zechut avot* even as it
suggests an intimacy with the patriarch. The wealthy man's cry is also not
dissimilar to the prodigal's evoking of his filial relationship, "Father, I have
sinned" (Luke 15.18, 21). Indeed, the rich man's repeated use of "Father"
coupled with his concern for his brothers, but not wife and children, suggests that he might be an indulged son, with no responsibilities of his own,
no wife and children. His wealthy dress and sumptuous feasting also remind
us of the prodigal, who gets the "first robe" and the "grain-fed calf." I doubt
the prodigal was all that repentant, and I see no acknowledgment of sin on
the rich man's part either. His appeal to Abraham will not yield its desired
results, because he has not fulfilled his role in Abraham's family; he has
failed to display hospitality on earth, and he has failed, even in the pain of
torture, to understand his sin.

The rich man knows Abraham's name and Abraham's role, as he knew the
name and the circumstances of the man in anguish by his gates. Knowledge
without action will count for nothing. He refused to recognize on earth
that Lazarus too was a child of Abraham and so should have been treated as
a welcome member of the family. He had the resources; he had the opportunity; he had the commandments of Torah. He did nothing, and he still
does nothing.

Instead, he continues to think of Lazarus as nothing more than a servant
or a dog, who is to fetch something for the master. He fails to recognize the
irony of his request. Lazarus would have been happy with a crumb; the rich
man wants even less—a drop of water. He will receive exactly what he gave
to Lazarus. But now the circumstances are different.

In Genesis 19, Abraham prays for the few righteous in Sodom. In the *Testament of Abraham,* he prays for the salvation of sinners. Perhaps one needs
to be an atheist to resist the idea that eternal damnation is a righteous idea.

Or do we just rejoice in our salvation and say, with all literalness, "The hell with them"?

As for Lazarus, in his *Last Temptation of Christ,* Nicholas Kazantzakis imagined that Lazarus prayed on behalf of the rich man.[33] Would Lazarus have provided the aid? Would we?

And said Abraham, "Child, do you remember that you
received your good in your life, and Lazarus likewise the bad.
And now here he is being comforted, but you are in pain.
And in all these things between us and you a great chasm
stands, so that the ones wishing to cross over from here to
you are not able, nor from there to us can one cross over."
(Luke 16.25–26)

Abraham responds to the rich man, but it is not the response he wants. The translation "child" (Gk. *teknon*) is the same term Luke uses to show the anguish Mary and Joseph felt when they thought they had lost Jesus in Jerusalem: "Child, why have you treated us like this? Look, your father and I have been searching for you in great anxiety" (2.48). In the parable of the Lost Son(s), it is the entreaty the desperate father makes to his older son, "Child, you are always with me, and all that is mine is yours" (15.31). It is the term used to describe how God is able to raise up children to Abraham (Matt. 3.9). Abraham acknowledges his relationship to the rich man, but he can do nothing for him except provide explanation of his present circumstances.

The patriarch's explanation is a restatement of Luke 6.20, 24: "Blessed are you who are poor, for yours is the kingdom of God. . . . But woe to you who are rich, for you have received your consolation." The Greek reinforces the connection: "consolation," *paraklesis* (the Gospel of John's reference to the "Paraclete," "Comforter," or "Advocate," who teaches in Jesus's absence) reappears in 16.25 to describe Lazarus's "comfort" (*parakaleo*).

The point is not the reversal of roles. Lazarus is not living a life of conspicuous consumption; the rich man is suffering from pain and deprivation, but his suffering is worse, for it is endless. Perhaps he is also experiencing the envy he hoped to cause in others who would have observed his conspicuous consumption. Lazarus had the dogs for comfort; the rich man has, instead, the vision of Lazarus and Abraham. He will spend eternity seeing what he cannot have.

The "chasm" (that is the Greek term) that separates the rich man from Abraham and Lazarus secures the separation. The gate that separated them in life has now become an impassable gorge.

And he said, "I ask you, therefore, Father, so that you might send him to the house of my father. For I have five brothers, so that he might witness to them, in order that not will they come to this place of torment." **(Luke 16.27–28)**

Biblical scholars are inclined to assign vv. 27–31 to Luke, based on the arguments that the dialogue is unnecessary to the plot and that the concern for an appearance by a dead man seems a bit "Christian." Moreover, some of the vocabulary reappears in Luke 24, the encounter of the two disciples with Jesus on the road to Emmaus. A few scholars even suggest Luke tacked on the ending to condemn Jews who refused to accept the proclamation of Jesus's resurrection.[34] The arguments are possible, but not necessary.

Jesus is just as capable of speaking of Moses and the Prophets and postmortem judgment as is any other Jew. The last verses increase the pathos of the parable, make clear that we already have the resources we need in order to lead righteous lives, accentuate the point that familial connections ultimately cannot help in marking righteousness, and place the responsibility for appropriate behavior not in the supernatural, but in the very real.

These concerns are more likely to stem from Jesus than from Luke. For Luke, the Torah and Prophets can only be understood through Jesus's interpretation; that is one of the points of the Road to Emmaus story. For the parable, Torah and Prophets are abundantly clear to anyone who reads them carefully. For Jesus, more important than familial connection is the family of faith. He states, "Whoever does the will of my Father in heaven is my brother and sister and mother" (Matt. 12.50); family is determined ultimately by appropriate action, not biological connection. Finally, Jesus does not call any of his "brothers" or "sisters" (the other children in the household of Mary and Joseph) to be in the inner circle of the Twelve. Could Jesus tell a story in which a man's "brothers" were not faithful to what he saw to be correct behavior? Absolutely. Even if the words are from Luke, the ideas fit what we know from multiple other sources about Jesus of Nazareth.

The rich man's paternal invocation and familial emphasis continue, but again he has not yet learned what landed him in torment in the first place. He wants to save his brothers from torment, not to ease the pain felt by the millions who lack food, shelter, or health care. Whether he even has a clue that saving his brothers by teaching them appropriate behavior would in fact result in the improvement in the lives of the poor remains unlikely. Further, the rich man wants the message just for them; he has yet to learn that Abraham's paternity is to more than his family, indeed to more than just the Jews, for Abraham is the father of "many nations" (Gen. 17.4).

Had he been more clever, the rich man might have asked Abraham for permission to take the message to his brothers himself. If he thinks Lazarus can move from Abraham's bosom to earth, he might have asked for the same opportunity. At least the short trip would have eased his torments. But the rich man cannot divest himself of his status or change his ways: Lazarus is still the slave whose job it is to serve the master, still the laborer who will do whatever is necessary to survive. Although the NRSV sees the rich man as "begging" Abraham, that translation overstates his self-perception. A person who "begs" realizes his subordinate position. The rich man does not beg; he merely "asks" (Gk. *erotao*).

His request is not without precedent; both Jews and pagans told stories of people who return from the dead, whether as ghosts or in dreams. The medium of Endor conjures the spirit of Samuel at Saul's request (1 Sam. 28). In Luke 24.39, Jesus has to reassure the disciples that he is not one even as he suggests that ghosts exist: "Look at my hands and my feet; see that it is I myself. Touch me and see; for a ghost does not have flesh and bones as you see that I have." In *On Divination,* Cicero recounts a tale of a ghost on a rescue mission in the story of Simonides, who found the dead body of a stranger lying on the road and buried it. He was about to embark on a ship, when the man he had buried appeared to him in a dream and warned him not to undertake the voyage, for he would perish. He returned home, but all the other people who sailed on that vessel were lost. In the *Iliad,* Homer depicts the appearance of the dead Patroclus to Achilles in a dream. Ovid recounts the apparition of Romulus to Julius Proculus. Pliny, Suetonius, and Plutarch, among others, all attest to a popular belief in ghosts.[35]

A first-century audience would not have seen the rich man's request as odd. Ghosts, or the spirits of the dead, can and do visit the living. Although Lazarus cannot get to the rich man because of the "chasm," there is nothing that suggests that he cannot visit the rich man's brothers. Abraham's refusal is not based on geographical barriers. It is based, rather, on his own decision. Abraham can advocate for the rich man; he chooses not to do so.[36]

And says Abraham, "They have Moses and the prophets; let them listen to them." **(Luke 16.29)**

The concern in Jewish scripture, broadly defined, is not what we *have,* but what we *do.* Deuteronomy 15.7 mandates, "If there is among you anyone in need, a member of your community in any of your towns . . . do not be hardhearted or tight-fisted toward your needy neighbor." Isaiah 58.7 had already taught: "Share your bread with the hungry, and bring the homeless poor into your house; when you see the naked, to cover them, and not to hide yourself from your own kin."

The parable's emphasis on the importance of Torah disturbs those readers who want to set up a law-versus-grace dichotomy, see the Law as impossible to follow (hence the need for the Christ), or are worried about works-righteousness. But this commendation of the Law and the Prophets would not have disturbed Jesus's initial audience, and it makes good sense on the lips of Jesus the rabbi.

And he said, "Not, Father Abraham, but if someone from the
dead would come to them, they would repent." And he said
to him, "If to Moses and to the prophets not do they listen,
neither if someone from the dead would rise would they be
persuaded." **(Luke 16.30–31)**

This final appeal to filial relationship, whether read as comic, or tragic, or pathetic, does not succeed. The rich man, dead himself, still thinks of Lazarus as an available servant. He has not repented from his failure to aid Lazarus; he has not recognized his sin. Nor does he find Torah self-evidently compelling.

Abraham refuses his request; the brothers, like the rich man, know what they should have done. Once they are dead, they will not get a second chance; there is no postmortem do-over.

The suspicion that a "Jewish audience would have felt that the rich man's punishment was unjust, since he was given no warning of the critical importance of passing through the gate"[37] is overstated; that warning occurs again and again in the Torah and Prophets. The fact is repeated, twice, by Abraham: he knows that the brothers can "listen"—the warning has already been given. The concern for almsgiving was part of the culture. So was love of neighbor. The problem is not the message; the problem is that people don't listen.

Some people, we learn, will never change. They condemn themselves to damnation even as their actions condemn others to poverty. If they think that they can survive on family connections—to Abraham, to their brothers—they are wrong. If they think their power will last past their death, they are wrong again.

The parable ends with a cautionary note. Heed the commands to aid the poor and the sick and hungry, or you will eventually suffer worse poverty, greater pains, deeper hunger. Do not just contribute to the food drive, but invite the hungry into your home. Do not just put money in the collection plate, but use your resources to provide jobs and support for those in need. Do not treat the sick as burdens, but as beloved family members who deserve love and care. Know the names of the destitute; each has a story to tell. Recognize, as Jesus puts it, that you cannot serve both God and mammon (Luke 16.13; Matt. 6.24).

Postmortem Assessment

According to John Dominic Crossan, "We are not told that the rich man did anything wrong or the poor man did anything right. Yet their roles in this world are reversed in the next world. . . . What if, in the next life, this life's nonsuffering *haves* will become suffering *have-nots* and this life's suffering *have-nots* will become nonsuffering *haves*? A simple reversal of fortune?"[38] Richard Bauckham asks whether "the rich man suffers in the next life just because he was rich in this life, while the poor man is blessed in the next life just because he was poor in this life."[39] Whatever answer we choose to give these queries, the very point that we can ask them should challenge our views of justice, economics, and soteriology.

Neither Torah nor Prophets condemns wealth qua wealth or commends poverty qua poverty. Yet voluntary poverty was a viable option in a first-century Jewish context, just as it is in Buddhist culture today, just as it is for Catholics who take vows of poverty along with those of chastity and obedience. The parable speaks to the dangers of wealth. Can a rich man enter the kingdom of heaven? The question remains open.

Given the enormous wealth of our rich man—a wealth so extreme that we cannot identify with him—the parable also asks about what the average person should do. Where is the artisan, the peasant, the elementary-school teacher, or the carpenter in this tale? Are we, we average people, separated from the wealthy man and Lazarus? Do we dream of the rich man's clothes and food? Do we fear becoming destitute? The parable interrogates our priorities as well.

For many readers, the judgment of the parable is emotionally satisfying. The salvation of the sick, suffering, and destitute and the damnation of the obscenely wealthy would likely have appealed to Jesus's audience, as it continues to have an appeal today. Yet once we judge the rich man as deserving of his fate—eternal torment—we condemn ourselves as barbaric. Once we envy Lazarus for his eternal reward and forget or, worse, romanticize his poverty, we again condemn ourselves.

The parable suggests that the gift of eternal life in paradise is possible. "Heaven," however understood, is ours, but it is also ours to lose. The point is not that we have to "earn" it. The point is that we uphold our part of the covenant by behaving as human beings should behave: we care for the poor; we are our brothers' and sisters' keepers. If we expend everything on ourselves, then there is nothing left in our heavenly treasury.

When asked why he became a doctor and went to what was then French Equatorial Africa (now Gabon), Albert Schweitzer cited this parable. He recognized that although the rich man, representing Europe, had access to medical care, Lazarus, representing Africa, did not.[40] In a 2006 article, Olubiyi Adeniyi Adewale, of Benson Idahosa University in Benin City, Nigeria, makes a similar argument: the parable "gives a veiled warning to the Western Church, which appears complacent and unruffled about the plight of their covenant brethren in Africa."[41]

The parable tells us that we do not need supernatural revelation to tell us that we have the poor with us. We do not even need the threats of eternal torture. If we cannot see the poor person at our gate—on the street, in the commercials that come into our homes, in the appeals made in sermons, in the newspapers—then we are lost.

Ironically, what the rich man asked Lazarus to do—to warn his brothers of the threat of hell—the parable does for readers.[42] Will the five brothers, who may hear Torah's insistence that they "love the neighbor" and "love the stranger," listen? We do not know. Will we?

The Power of Disturbing Stories

Jesus told parables because they serve, as *Song of Songs Rabbah* notes, as keys that can unlock the mysteries we face by helping us ask the right questions: how to live in community; how to determine what ultimately matters; how to live the life that God wants us to live. They are Jesus's way of teaching, and they are remembered to this day not simply because they are in the Christian canon, but because they continue to provoke, challenge, and inspire.

Jesus knew that the best teaching concerning how to live, and live abundantly, comes not from spoon-fed data or an answer sheet. Instead, it comes from narratives that remind us of what we already know, but are resistant to recall. It comes from stories that prompt us to draw our own conclusions and at the same time force us to realize that our answers may well be contingent, or leaps of faith, or traps. It comes from stories that community members can share with each other, with each of us assessing the conclusions others draw, and so reassessing our own.

The parables, if we take them seriously not as answers but as invitations, can continue to inform our lives, even as our lives continue to open up the parables to new readings.

Jesus knew that the best teaching comes from stories with memorable characters who are both familiar and strange, who play upon our stereotypes even as they confront them. The concept of a good Samaritan would have been an oxymoron for Jesus's audience. The idea that a tax collector could tap into the righteousness of both the Temple system and the Pharisee would have been recognized, but I suspect not particularly liked. The idea that an elder brother—Cain, Ishmael, Esau, the second lost son—is sympathetic again prompts a challenge to our expectations, and perhaps a recuperation of our history and our family. As for the kingdom of heaven being compared to a high-end wholesaler, or leaven, or mustard seed . . . If this can be the case, the kingdom can be compared to anyone or anything.

The parables, if we take them seriously not as historical portraits of real people but as challenges to our stereotypes, help us to locate both our eccentric traits and our excellent talents; they can inspire and humble, challenge and comfort.

Jesus knew that the best teachings come from stories that make us laugh even as they make us uncomfortable. The rabbi from Nazareth offers us images of a conniving young man, amid the pigs, salivating over the bread enough to spare available at his father's table; tenacious widows threatening judges with physical harm; a rich man unable to realize that death has changed his position of privilege; a baker surreptitiously hiding yeast in dough that will produce more bread than can possibly feed a single family; a mustard seed that can provide shelter; a lucky fellow who finds treasure in a field . . . We smile, and at the same time we wonder. Are we to be sympathetic to the young man or not? Do we want the widow to achieve her goal? Should the rich man suffer even more, until he learns his place? What would we do with all that bread? Do seeds really have such potential, and if seeds, why not us?

The parables, if we take them seriously not as "meaning" but as soliciting our meaning making, and if we allow ourselves to be open to various interpretations, become not tools for shaming or inculcating guilt, but for good, hard lessons learned with a sense of playfulness.

Jesus himself, as we know from the rest of the Gospel tradition, cared deeply about reconciliation, and so he told stories about people torn apart and how they might be brought together. He constantly taught about laying up treasure in heaven rather than on earth, and so he told stories about rich men whose wealth does them no good and poor people who find the real treasure they need. Jesus insisted we should not judge, and that the criterion by which we judge others will be used to judge us. Therefore he offered parables in which those who judge others are trapped into being in relationship with them; he told parables in which those who judge themselves righteous may be wrong or may not realize the full implications of their righteousness.

He sought to prepare his people for the inbreaking of the kingdom of heaven, the time when we would recline at table with Abraham, Isaac, and Jacob, and so he set about enacting the messianic banquet among a mixed group of saints and sinners, tax collectors and patrons, women and men, faithful and doubters. He also told stories about baking and banquets and feasts and so in his stories nourished his followers even as he left them hungry for more.

To prepare his followers for that inbreaking, he also asked them to prioritize. What really matters, and what does not? The parables ask us questions. What is our pearl of great price? What would we do were we to find treasure in the field? What would satisfy us, and what *should* satisfy us?

Resisting What Should Be Irresistible

It may be that no matter how good the teachings, we will still resist them. Such resistance begins with the Gospels themselves. Luke tames the parables. For Luke, the parable of the Widow and the Judge is about the need to pray always, certainly not about women asserting themselves in public, and even more certainly not about threatening people if they do not get their way, regardless of the justice of their case. For Luke, the Lost Sheep, Lost Coin, and Lost Sons are about repentance and forgiveness, and thus provocative, humorous, and celebratory stories become tamed into banal statements of the obvious. For Luke, the parable of the Pharisee and the Tax Collector reinforces the idea of bad Pharisees and good tax collectors rather than calling into question the meaning of prayer, good deeds, repentance, and justification.

Domestication of the parables' provocation then continues as we move from text to interpretation. In many settings the Pearl of Great Price is about the importance of the church, or faith, or Jesus; surely Christians already know this. The Laborers in the Vineyard can't be about economics, we say, because that would completely discombobulate labor relations; imagine, a CEO who is interested in providing employment for those who need it, and a group of workers who are so selfish that they demand more than their original contract even while begrudging others a living wage. The Rich Man and Lazarus can't really be about heaven and hell, because that would suggest people could be saved apart from the cross or, conversely, that poverty and suffering may warrant heavenly reward, apart from good deeds.

The parables we have looked at in this volume, as well as all the others, began their process of domestication as soon as the evangelists wrote them down, and probably before that. This process should not surprise us. As much as we might respect the idea of divine freedom and mystery, we are ultimately more comfortable with answers rather than questions, with the tried and true rather than new thoughts. Debate can be messy; it can lead to disagreement, or worse. Better that everyone remain on the same page.

Jesus understood that God does not play by our rules. His God is a generous God, who not only allows the sun to shine on both the just and the unjust, but also gives us the ability to live into what should be rather than what is. The parables help us with their lessons about generosity: sharing joy, providing for others, recognizing the potential of small investments.

His God wants us to be better than we are, because we have the potential to be. We are made but a little lower than the divine (Ps. 8.6; see Heb. 2.7); we should start acting in a more heavenly matter. Those who pray, "Your kingdom come," might want to take some responsibility in the process, and so work in partnership with God. We too are to seek the lost and make every effort to find them. Indeed, we are not only to seek; we are to take notice of who might be lost, even when immediately present. The rich man ignores Lazarus at his gate, and the father of the prodigal ignored the elder son in the field. For the former, it is too late; for the latter, whether it is too late or not we do not know. But we learn from their stories. Don't wait. Look now. Look hard. Count.

These are all hard lessons, despite the humor with which they are delivered. Therefore we resist them. Worse, our resistance, our efforts in refusing the challenges parables make to our presuppositions often take the form of anti-Jewish stereotypes. When I began working on this volume, years ago, I knew of certain problematic readings, but I was actually shocked to find out how pervasive and persuasive they are. Rather than accept the challenge, including those challenges that, were we honest, would convict ourselves, we turn the parables into screeds against Jewish practice, ethics, or theology.

Such approaches, as we've seen throughout the volume, misread Jesus, and misread Judaism. We can do better.

Foretastes of the Messianic Banquet

Parables will continue to be open to new understandings, but not all understandings have the same weight. If our approach is to learn more about ourselves, we can simply say, "What does the parable mean to me?" If we find a challenge, so much the better. If we want to learn more about Jesus, we have to do a bit more work.

If the interpretation requires an answer key or a decoder ring, then we are not hearing it as those who first heard it did. Jesus told parables, not allegories.

If the interpretation is a platitude or a banality—be generous, God loves you, the kingdom of God is important, pray a lot—we may have a surface reading, but we are not fully appreciating the genius of Jesus's storytelling or the respect he had for the people who listened to him.

If the interpretation of a story told by a Jew to other Jews is based on or yields a negative stereotype of Judaism, then the interpretation has gotten more lost than the sheep, coin, or sons, and it cannot and should not be recovered.

If the interpretation does not raise for us more questions, if it does not open us up to more conversation, if it creates a neat and tidy picture, we need to go back and read it again.

Once we are open to the challenge, we can turn to other parables. Jesus tells us of a dishonest manager who makes others complicit in his crimes, and does so in such a way that his former employer can only commend him for his shrewdness (Luke 16.1–8). Poor Luke goes through numerous machinations to turn this story into a lesson about evangelism: "Make friends for yourself by means of dishonest wealth (unrighteous mammon)" (16.9). That may be what the manager did, but that's not a great lesson for matters of reconciliation, justice, or compassion. Something else must be going on.

Jesus tells the story of the Five Wise and Five Foolish Virgins, also called the Ten Bridesmaids (Matt. 25.1–13). The parable might just as easily be called that of the "Woefully Delayed Groom," but that would be too

Christologically edgy for those who still anticipate a second coming. The reading "bridesmaids" is odd, given that the parable never mentions a bride (Matt. 25.1–13; I do worry about that missing bride, just as I worry about the absent mother of the prodigal and prudent).

All ten young women fall asleep, and thus they all fail to do what Jesus exhorts, "Keep awake" (e.g., Mark 13.37; Matt. 24.42). Five fail to share their oil, and they exhort their companions who have run out to go to the local 7-Eleven for more. If the only conclusion we draw from this is, "Be prepared" (turning the first five virgins into Boy Scouts—the type of gender-bending the organization is still not prepared to sanction), Jesus has wasted his time.

Domestication begins as soon as this bridegroom is seen as Jesus himself. With this move, conservative readers conclude that Jesus is being autobiographical. He is the bridegroom, we can be assured of the second coming, we will be prepared with our faith (and perhaps even our good deeds), and we, but not others, will enter the messianic banquet. There is no challenge here; there is at best either self-satisfaction or the development of neurosis as we try to stay awake. For liberals, the idea that Jesus is the bridegroom leads to the conclusion that the parable could not be by Jesus at all; rather, it must be a creation of the early church worried that people will lose heart at the delay of the Parousia, the Second Coming.

What if the parable is from Jesus, but is *not* autobiographical? What if the virgins are virgins, the bridegroom a delayed suitor, and the oil just oil and not "good deeds" or "sufficient faith"? With this nonallegorical reading, the right questions can be answered. When is selfishness appropriate and when not? Do we rejoice at the suitor's coming or condemn him from showing up late? Do we want to go into the banquet with a delayed suitor who slams the door in the face of our friends (after all, it is a good party), or do we stay outside with the women just returned from the 7-Eleven with more oil? Might there be a third way, so that all can rejoice?

In the parable of the Wicked Tenants (Matt. 21.33–46; Mark 12.1–12; Luke 20.9–19), Jesus tells a story about a vineyard, and most hearers would conclude that the vineyard is Israel. We saw the same association with the parable of the Laborers in the Vineyard: the connection to Isaiah 5.1–7 is unavoidable. But Jesus shifts the focus immediately, for the problem in this parable is not with the vineyard that does not yield grapes, but with the tenants. The vineyard according to Isaiah is not destroyed; in this parable it is.

Already we are challenged, because we do not know how far to push the association.

Once we move into allegory, we are challenged again. Is the landowner God or just a landowner? Is God an *absentee* landowner? If so, the parable can be taken as a critique of God, which would be much at home in a Jewish setting, where laments and complaints serve theological purposes. If we insist the tenants are the Jews, their leaders, or the Pharisees, what do we learn? What if they are instead the various nations who conquered Israel: Babylon, Persia, Greece, Rome? Matthew tells us that the heir is Jesus (21.42). Would first-century Jews get this point? Or would they first think, "This is a tragic story, and the horror does not end"?

What do we do with a landowner who finds his slaves abused, one after the other, and then decides to send his son, with the surety, "They will respect my son"? How foolish is this? Yes, we rush to allegory, but not so fast. We do the same thing today. We send battalion after battalion to the front, and we keep thinking, with "shock and awe," that "they" will respect us. They do not. Yet we keep expending our resources even when we know there is no chance of recuperation. We keep at the quest for honor and power, even when the cause is lost. We insist that we were always right, because we are unable to realize our policies were misguided.

And what do we do with the ending? The tenants say to themselves, "This is the heir. Come let us kill him and get his inheritance." Do we want them to succeed, as if they are representative of a peasant revolt? Do we want them to be punished, so that they suffer the same fate as they meted out to the messengers and then the heir? What is the resolution when violence escalates? The landowner will let the farm out to other tenants. Will the violence be repeated?

The parable of the Wedding Banquet or Great Dinner (Matt. 22.2–14; Luke 14.16–24) is similarly disturbing in its violence. It ends with dead slaves, a burned city, dinner guests who are compelled to attend the party, and an expelled guest doomed to torture because he lacked the right outfit. That any of this speaks to what the "kingdom of heaven" is like should come as a surprise. If the parable is about salvation, then it is about a type of salvation in which free will is obviated. If the parable is about the grace of the divine, then it is a grace that burns an entire city because of the sins of a few of its citizens. If the parable is about the messianic banquet, then it is a banquet that nobody eats. If the lord or king in the parable is God, then we should wonder if this is the type of God we want to worship.

The parable should disturb. If we hear it and are not disturbed, there is something seriously amiss with our moral compass. It would be better if we perhaps started by seeing the parable not as about heaven or hell or final judgment, but about kings, politics, violence, and the absence of justice. If we do, we might be getting closer to Jesus.

Jesus recounts the parable of the Sheep and the Goats (Matt. 25.31–46), in which people are judged not on whether they worshipped Jesus or not, but on whether they cared for the poor, fed the hungry, or visited people in prison. Otherwise put, Jesus asks, "Did you go the extra mile?" The parable still convicts, even while it is happily read in churches by people who have never set foot in a prison, never invited a homeless person to lunch, never held a shivering baby with AIDS, or sat by the bed of a childless widow with stage-four cancer. We might know, when that final judgment occurs, to get into the sheep line rather than the goat line, but then what? Do we rejoice at the condemnation of others, do we remain silent like Lazarus in the bosom of Abraham, or do we finally conclude that perhaps God's mercy is greater than what we think it to be?

One does not need to worship Jesus as Lord or Savior for the parables to have meaning. The people who first heard him did not, at first, worship him. Yet they paid attention, because for those with ears to hear and some patience to ponder, the parables spoke to their hearts. I do not worship Jesus as Lord and Savior, but I continue to return to these stories, because they are at the heart of my own Judaism. They challenge, they provoke, they convict, and at the same time they amuse. At each reading, when I think I've got all the details explained, something remains left over, and I have to start again. The parables have provided me countless hours of inspiration, and conversation. They are pearls of Jewish wisdom. If we hear them in their original contexts, and if we avoid the anti-Jewish interpretation that frequently deforms them, they gleam with a shine that cannot be hidden.

Acknowledgments

My gratitude to David Buttrick, with whom I had the privilege of co-teaching a course on parables at Vanderbilt Divinity School, cannot be overstated. Thanks are also due to Marianne Blickenstaff, for her editorial skills, good humor, and short story of her own; for their encouragement and advice, appreciation goes to Michael Peppard, Richard I. Pervo, Barbara Reid, Febbie Dickerson, and Myrick Shinall Jr. To Mickey Maudlin at Harper-One I extend my deep appreciation for his sage counsel, and his patience. Thanks also to copyeditor Ann Moru and production editor Lisa Zuniga.

Over the past decade, I have been reading parables with numerous clergy, church, synagogue, and civic groups. In particular, I express my appreciation to Dr. Rowan Strong and his colleagues at Murdoch University, Perth, for hosting me in 2013 as their "Theologian in Residence" and providing me the conversation partners with whom I could refine several of the essays in this volume. Gratitude is also owed the Loyola School of Theology and the Maryhill School of Theology, both in the Philippines; the University of Richmond (Weinstein-Rosenthal Lectureship); Auburn Theological Seminary (Jack and Lewis Rudin Lecture); Australian Catholic University, Melbourne; University of Sydney; the Christian Scholars Group on Jews and Judaism; University of Dallas (Landren Lecture); Allegheny College; Coe College; Sixth National Symposium on Religious Education and Ministry, Sydney; Oklahoma City University; University of North Alabama; New Orleans Baptist Theological Seminary; University College London; Chapman University; Manhattanville College; High Point University; Fordham University; Santa Clara University; Ignatian Center, Saint Mary's University College, Calgary; Carleton University (Edgar and Dorothy Davidson Lecture); Dickinson College and St. John's Episcopal Church on the Square, Carlisle, Pennsylvania; Nazareth College (Melbourne); Kilbreda College (Melbourne); Mt. Saint Mary's College, Claremont Graduate University, and Claremont School of Theology (11th Pat Reif Memorial Lecture); Averett College; and St. Norbert College.

In Nashville: Greater Nashville Unitarian Universalist Church; Westminster Presbyterian; West End United Methodist; Vine Street Christian Church; Calvary United Methodist; Christ Church Cathedral; Woodmont Christ Church; The Temple, Congregation Ohabai Shalom; Brentwood United Methodist; St. Paul's Episcopal (Franklin).

The Chatauqua Institute (New York), Kalamazoo Diocese (Roman Catholic); TriState Forum for Continuing Theological Education (ELCA); Christian Church/Disciples of Christ of MidAmerica; Fresno Interfaith Scholar Weekend and Department of Philosophy, California State University–Fresno; Stetson University Pastors' School; University Park United Methodist Church (Denver); All Saints Episcopal Church, Ann Evans Woodall Lecture (Atlanta); Bible Fest (Boston); The Fountains, a United Methodist Church/Beth Hagivot Congregation (Arizona); Sisters of Sion (Melbourne); Chapel by the Sea (New South Wales); Foundation for Contemporary Theology (Houston); Limmud–UK; Limmud–South Africa; First United Methodist Church (Perkins Lectures), Wichita Falls, Texas; Barbara Noojim Wathall Bible Studies Series, Independent Presbyterian Church (Birmingham, Alabama); Snowstar Institute (Ontario); Mayer's Prayer Breakfast (Lincoln, Nebraska); Catholic Diocese of Green Bay, Congregation Cnesses Israel, Ecumenical Center of the University of Wisconsin Green Bay, First United Church of Christ, First United Methodist Church, Grace Lutheran Church, Moses Montefiore Synagogue (Appleton), St. Anne's Episcopal Church, Union Congregational Church, West Side Moravian Church, Winnebago Presbytery (Green Bay); Mountaintop Lecture Series/Cherry Log Christian Church (Georgia); Saint Michael and All Angels Episcopal Church (Dallas); Stephen Wise Free Synagogue (New York); St. Luke's United Methodist Church (Indianapolis); Royal Poinciana Chapel Center for Spiritual Inquiry (Palm Beach); Calvary Church (Memphis); First Christian Church (Fullerton); Church of the Foothills (Santa Ana); the D. L. Dykes Foundation; Countryside Community United

Church of Christ/ADL/Tri-Faith Initiative (Omaha); St. James Episcopal (New York City); Catholic Education Office, Ballarat, Victoria; Progressive Christian Network, Victoria; First United Church of Bloomington (Indiana); Sanibel Congregational United Church of Christ/Congregation Bat Yam (Sanibel, Florida); and the Episcopal Diocese of Southern Ohio.

Notes

Introduction: How We Domesticate Jesus's Provocative Stories

1. Brian M. Howard, "I Just Wanna Be a Sheep," Mission Hills Music © 1974, 2002. One does not need to invent unfortunate songs that (unintentionally?) reinforce negative stereotypes; for the full lyrics to this popular ditty, see http://lyricstranslate.com/en/Worship-Songs-I-just-wanna-be-sheep-lyrics.html. The other groups disclaimed by the children are "Sadducees," "hypocrites," and in some versions "goats."

Chapter 1: Lost Sheep, Lost Coin, Lost Son

1. Jerome, *Lives of Illustrious Men,* chap. 135.

2. *Aristotle's Nichomachean Ethics,* trans. Robert C. Bartlett and Susan D. Collins (Chicago: Univ. of Chicago Press, 2012), 70 (4.1.1120b 31ff.).

3. http://www.prodigalmagazine.com.

4. http://www.prodigal.com.au.

5. See Carol Shersten LaHurd, "Recovering the Lost Women in Luke 15," *Biblical Theology Bulletin* 24 (1994): 66–76 (67).

6. Mikeal C. Parsons, in a fascinating study of the parable's reception history, offers numerous examples from art and literature in which the elder brother is not mentioned or depicted. See his "The Prodigal's Elder Brother: The History and Ethics of Reading Luke 15.25–32," *Perspectives in Religious Studies* 23 (1996): 147–74.

7. Tertullian, *On Repentance* 8; cited in Brad H. Young, *The Parables: Jewish Tradition and Christian Interpretation* (Peabody, MA: Hendrickson, 1998), 132. Young correctly adds, "No one crucified rabbis for telling parables."

8. Eduard Schweizer, *Jesus* (London: SCM, 1971), 29; cited in Young, *Parables,* 133.

9. Klyne R. Snodgrass, *Stories with Intent: A Comprehensive Guide to the Parables of Jesus* (Grand Rapids, MI: Eerdmans, 2008), 94.

10. The Letters of St. Jerome, vol. 1, ed. *Johannes Quasten and Walter J. Burghardt* (Mahwah, NJ: Paulist Press, 1963), 124 (*Letter* 21).

11. Parsons, "Prodigal's Elder Brother," 152.

12. Parsons, "Prodigal's Elder Brother," 154, citing John Calvin, *Commentary on a Harmony of the Evangelists, Matthew, Mark, and Luke,* 2 vols., trans. William Pringle (Edinburgh: Calvin Translation Society, 1845), 2:50.

13. Cited in Marsha Witten, *All Is Forgiven: The Secular Message in American Protestantism* (Princeton, NJ: Princeton Univ. Press, 1993), 94–95, and referenced in Parsons, "Prodigal's Elder Brother," 166, n. 64. See also Witten's earlier "Preaching About Sin in Contemporary Protestantism," *Theology Today* 50 (July 1993): 243–53.

14. As with all parables in the Gospels, questions of tradition versus redaction remain a scholarly staple. On Luke 15, see, e.g., Charles E. Carlston, "Reminiscence and Redaction in Luke 15:11–32," *Journal of Biblical Literature* 94 (1975): 368–90.

15. Arland J. Hultgren, *The Parables of Jesus: A Commentary* (Grand Rapids, MI: Eerdmans, 2000), 469.

16. Luke Timothy Johnson, *The Gospel of Luke,* Sacra Pagina (Collegeville, MN: Liturgical, 1991), 242. Reading the prodigal son as an "outcast" is an exegetical staple; see also Hultgren, *Parables of Jesus,* 85.

17. *The Shari Lewis Show* replaced *The Howdy Doody Show* in October 1960 on NBC; a ventriloquist, Shari Lewis (née Hurwitz) gave voice to, among other things, a sock puppet named Lamb Chop. In 1993, Lamb Chop offered testimony before Congress on the import of children's television.

18. Hultgren, *Parables of Jesus,* 54.

19. Robert J. Miller, *The Complete Gospels: Annotated Scholars Version* (Santa Rosa, CA: Polebridge Press, 1992), 321.

20. Hultgren, *Parables of Jesus,* 57–58, citing Kenneth E. Bailey, *Poet and Peasant and Through Peasant Eyes: A Literary-Cultural Approach to the Parables in Luke* (Grand Rapids, MI: Eerdmans, 1983), 147; *Finding the Lost Cultural Keys to Luke 15* (St. Louis: Concordia, 1992), 65; Joachim Jeremias, *"poime,"* in G. Kittel and G. Friedrich, eds., *Theological Dictionary of the New Testament* (Grand Rapids, MI: Eerdmans, 1964–76), 6:488–89; and Bernard Brandon Scott, *Hear Then the Parable* (Minneapolis: Fortress, 1989), 413–14. Following Joachim Jeremias (*Jerusalem in the Time of Jesus* [Philadelphia: Fortress, 1969], 303–5, 310), Barbara E. Reid says, "It is a shock for respected religious leaders to be asked to think of themselves as lowly shepherds" (*Parables for Preachers, Year C* [Collegeville, MN: Liturgical, 2000], 184).

21. Scott, *Hear Then the Parable,* 414.

22. Snodgrass, *Stories with Intent,* 102.

23. Ralph F. Wilson, "Shepherds in Bethlehem (Luke 2:8–20)," Jesus Walk Bible Study Series (© 1985–2014); http://www.jesuswalk.com/lessons/2_8-20.htm, and from there to countless sermons.

24. Philo, *On Agriculture* 60 in *The Works of Philo,* trans. C. D. Yonge (Peabody, MA: Hendrickson, 1993), 179.

25. *The Mishnah: Translated from the Hebrew with Introduction and Brief Explanatory Notes,* trans. Herbert Danby (Oxford: Oxford Univ. Press, 1933; Peabody, MA: Hendrickson, 2011), 329.

26. Geza Vermes, *The Dead Sea Scrolls in English,* 4th ed. (Sheffield: Academic, 1995), 111.

27. The comparison between early Judaism and the Taliban appears in former president Jimmy Carter's Bible studies on Ephesians in *Leading a Worthy Life: Sunday Mornings in Plains: Bible Study with Jimmy Carter* (New York: Simon & Schuster, 2007).

28. Hultgren, *Parables of Jesus,* 64, following Bailey, *Poet and Peasant,* 158; *Finding the Lost Cultural Keys,* 93.

29. David Buttrick, *Speaking Parables: A Homiletic Guide* (Louisville, KY: Westminster John Knox, 2000), 197.

30. Snodgrass, *Stories with Intent,* 114, citing Augustine, *Exposition of the Psalms* 121–50.

31. Luise Schottroff is among the few who do not see an insult in the son's request (*The Parables of Jesus,* trans. Linda M. Maloney [Minneapolis: Fortress, 2006], 139).

32. Witten writes: "For some pastors, the sin of the prodigal son is the ultimate transgression. They interpret the son's untimely demand for his inheritance as a symbolic act of patricide" ("Preaching About Sin," 244).

33. Bernard S. Jackson, *Essays on Halakhah in the New Testament,* Jewish and Christian Perspectives Series 16 (Leiden: Brill, 2007), 116, n. 11. See also in the same note Jackson's comments on the "methodologically questionable premise: that one should interpret both the parable and near contemporary Jewish sources against a construct of 'Middle Eastern' custom heavily informed by medieval Arab Christian interpretation and contemporary Arab custom." Jackson goes on to observe that the Mishnah (e.g., *Baba Batra* 8.7) regulates such advances of inheritance, and that the Elephantine papyri acknowledge gifts as opposed to bequests in one's testament.

34. The Mishnah, *Baba Batra* 8.4–5, suggests that fathers were assigning inheritance according to their own standards, not necessarily those of Deuteronomy. On inheritance issues, see the informative comments in Jackson, *Essays on Halakhah,* 140–41.

35. Young condemns the older brother for failing to fulfill his role as familial mediator (*Parables,* 141); however, the only source he has for this "traditional" role is Bailey's reflection on Arab Christian culture (Young cites *Poet and Peasant,* 194–203 and *Peasant Eyes*).

36. Philo, *On the Contemplative Life,* 47.

37. Suggested by Mark Allen Powell.

38. Suggested by Grace Imathiu.

39. Craig L. Blomberg, *Preaching the Parables: From Responsible Interpretation to Powerful Proclamation* (Grand Rapids, MI: Baker Academic, 2004), 36.

40. Bernard Brandon Scott, *Re-Imagine the World: An Introduction to the Parables of Jesus* (Santa Rosa, CA: Polebridge, 2001), 73, 76. Similarly, following N. T. Wright's reading of the parable as an allegory of Israel's exile and restoration (*Jesus and the Victory of God* [Minneapolis: Fortress, 1996], 126), Hultgren suggests that the prodigal's story corresponds "with the recurring story of Israel (apostasy, repentance, and return)" (*Parables of Jesus,* 84). He does not, however, follow Wright in identifying the older brother with the Samaritans.

41. J. Albert Harrill, "The Indentured Labor of the Prodigal Son (Luke 15.15)," *Journal of Biblical Literature* 115 (1996): 714–15.

42. Buttrick, *Speaking Parables,* 43. Donald Juel remarks: "In reading the story of the prodigal son, I chose to play the younger son as a classic manipulator" ("The Strange Silence of the Bible," *Interpretation* 51 [January 1997]: 5–19 [10]).

43. See Philip Sellew, "Interior Monologue as a Narrative Device in the Parables of Luke," *Journal of Biblical Literature* 111 (1992): 239–53.

44. Schottroff, *Parables of Jesus,* 142, citing Joachim Jeremias, *The Parables of Jesus,* rev. ed. (New York: Scribner, 1965), 130.

45. Scott, *Hear Then the Parable,* 70, 75; see also *Re-Imagine the World,* 70, 75, 82.

46. Hultgren, *Parables of Jesus,* 78, following Bailey, *Finding the Lost Cultural Keys,* 144–45; and Bruce C. Malina and Richard L. Rohrbaugh, *Social Science Commentary on the Synoptic Gospels* (Minneapolis: Fortress, 1992), 372. See also Snodgrass, *Stories with Intent,* 126.

47. Buttrick, *Speaking Parables,* 203; similarly, Blomberg, *Preaching the Parables,* 39; and many others.

48. Reid, *Parables for Preachers, Year C,* 61.

49. The original connection of parable to practice appears to have come from David Daube in Calum Carmichael, ed., *New Testament Judaism: Collected Works of David Daube,* vol. 2

(Berkeley, CA: Robbins Collection, 2000), 813. It is developed by H. K. Rengstorf in *Die Re-investitur des verlorenen Sohnes in der Gleichniserzählung Jesu (Luk. 15, 11–32)* (Cologne: Westdeutscher, 1967); followed by Bailey, *Finding the Lost Cultural Keys,* 121–22; and Blomberg, *Preaching the Parables,* 37: the Prodigal "recognizes that his father may well have performed the standard Jewish ceremony of 'cutting off' his wayward son and disowning him"; and others. See the helpful discussion in Jackson, *Essays on Halakhah,* 127–32.

50. Blomberg, *Preaching the Parables,* 39 (emphasis mine). Blomberg is apparently following Kenneth Bailey on this "standard" and "common" Jewish practice; see 43, where he makes this acknowledgment. The only "primary" source he offers is the comment, "Recall Tevye with his youngest daughter in *Fiddler on the Roof*" (43).

51. Blomberg, *Preaching the Parables,* 43 (emphasis mine).

52. Bailey, *Finding the Lost Cultural Keys,* 143; Malina and Rohrbaugh, *Social Science Commentary,* 372. See also Scott, *Re-Imagine the World,* 75.

53. Reid, *Parables for Preachers, Year C,* 62.

54. Scott, *Re-Imagine the World,* 82.

55. Philo, *On Providence* 2.4–6; cited in Jackson, *Essays on Halakhah,* 136.

56. Carol Shersten LaHurd, "Reviewing Luke 15 with Arab Christian Women," in Amy-Jill Levine with Marianne Blickenstaff, eds., *A Feminist Companion to Luke,* Feminist Companion to the New Testament and Early Christian Writing 3 (Sheffield: Sheffield Academic, 2002), 259. See also her earlier article, "Rediscovering the Lost Women in Luke 15," *Biblical Theology Bulletin* 24 (1994): 66–76; when she "asked whether any part of the father's behavior was unexpected in the light of their experience of the Middle Eastern family, all answered negatively and provided stories about how the family serves as location of unconditional care" (67).

57. There are numerous rabbinic statements on forgiveness, and for sins much more damaging than the prodigal committed. From *Bamidbar Rabbah, Naso* 14.1, for example: "There was never a man more wicked than (King) Manasseh, yet, in the hour of his repentance, God accepted him, as it is written (2 Chron. 33:13), 'He prayed unto God, and God accepted his prayers.'" Discussion and additional citations appear in Young, *Parables,* 148–50.

58. Cited by numerous commentators, including Scott, *Re-Imagine the World,* 76.

59. Frank Stern, in *A Rabbi Looks at Jesus' Parables* (Lanham, MD: Rowman and Littlefield, 2006), suggests this connection (189).

60. For more details on the intertextual connections, see Jackson, *Essays on Halakhah,* 141–42.

61. Buttrick, *Speaking Parables,* 203; Reid sees the father's behavior as "very feminine" (*Parables for Preachers, Year C,* 66).

62. Buttrick, *Speaking Parables,* 203, quoting Bernard Brandon Scott, *Hollywood Dreams and Biblical Stories* (Minneapolis: Ausburg/Fortress, 1994), 64.

63. Suggested by Scott, *Re-Imagine the World,* 70.

64. Henri Nouwen, *The Return of the Prodigal Son: A Story of Homecoming* (New York: Doubleday, 1992), 50.

65. David R. Henson, "God Is the Prodigal Son: Reinventing Christianity's Most Beloved Parable (Lectionary Reflection)," *Patheos* (March 7, 2013,) [http://www.patheos.com/blogs/davidhenson/2013/03/god-is-the-prodigal-son-reinventing-christianitys-most-beloved-parable/].

66. Bailey, *Poet and Peasant,* 206.

67. Mikeal C. Parsons provides numerous examples from art and literature in which the elder brother is not mentioned or depicted; see his "The Prodigal's Elder Brother."

68. Richard Q. Ford, *The Parables of Jesus: Recovering the Act of Listening* (Minneapolis: Fortress, 1997), 110.

69. Suggested by Richard I. Pervo.

70. Hultgren, *Parables of Jesus,* 80.

71. Witten, "Preaching About Sin," 245.

72. Bailey, *Finding the Lost Cultural Keys,* 171–72.

73. Greg Forbes, "Repentance and Conflict in the Parable of the Lost Son (Luke 15:11–32)," *Journal of the Evangelical Theological Society* 42.2 (1999): 211–29 (223).

74. Reid, *Parables for Preachers, Year C,* 65. See also Heikki Räisänen, "The Prodigal Gentile and His Jewish Christian Brother, Luke 15.11–32," in F. Van Segbroeck et al., eds., *The Four Gospels 1992:* Festschrift Frans Neirynck (Leuven: Leuven Univ. Press, 1992), 2:1617–36 (1624–27).

75. Nancy Duff, "Between Text and Sermon (Luke 15:11–32)," *Interpretation* 49.1 (January 1995): 66–69 (67).

76. LaHurd, "Rediscovering the Lost Women," 67.

77. Tertullian, *On Modesty* 8–9.

Chapter 2: The Good Samaritan

1. http://www.samaritans.org/about-us.

2. http://www.samaritanspurse.org.

3. http://www.donkeyrescue.org.au.

4. http://www.cnn.com/ALLPOLITICS/inauguration/2001/transcripts/template.html.

5. http://news.bbc.co.uk/2/hi/uk_news/4125229.stm.

6. http://www.tonyblairfaithfoundation.org/news/2012/06/14–4.

7. http://www.holocaust-history.org/himmler-poznan/.

8. Klyne R. Snodgrass, *Stories with Intent: A Comprehensive Guide to the Parables of Jesus* (Grand Rapids, MI: Eerdmans, 2008), 339.

9. Josephus, *Against Apion* 1.60.

10. *Sifra Kedoshim* (Perek 4); see also *Genesis Rabbah* 24.27.

11. See Naim Stifan Atreek, "Who Is My Neighbor?" *Interpretation* 62.2 (2008): 156–65.

12. Josephus, *Against Apion* 2.146, in Steve Mason, ed., Flavius Josephus. *Translation and Commentary,* vol. 10: Against Apion (Leiden: Brill, 2007), 249–50. For additional insights on the Jewish view of "neighbor," see Michael Fagenblat, "The Concept of Neighbor in Jewish and Christian Ethics," in Amy-Jill Levine and Marc Z. Brettler, eds., *The Jewish Annotated New Testament* (New York: Oxford Univ. Press, 2011), 540–43.

13. Suggested by Herbert Basser.

14. For several examples, see Riemer Roukema, "The Good Samaritan in Ancient Christianity," *Vigiliae Christianae* 58.1 (2004): 56–74.

15. Barbara E. Reid, *Parables for Preachers, Year C* (Collegeville, MN: Liturgical, 2000), 116.

16. Sharon H. Ringe, *Luke,* Westminster Bible Companion (Louisville, KY: Westminster John Knox, 1995), 158.

17. Ringe, *Luke,* 158.

18. Bernard Brandon Scott, *Hear Then the Parable* (Minneapolis: Fortress, 1989), 197.

19. Josephus, *Antiquities* 20.206–7.

20. W. Eugene March, *The Wide, Wide Circle of Divine Love: A Biblical Case for Religious Diversity* (Louisville, KY: Westminster John Knox, 2005), 69. See also Brad Young, *The Parables: Jewish Tradition and Christian Interpretation* (Peabody, MA: Hendrickson, 1998), 109:

"The priest and the Levite were more interested in ritual purity than saving the life of another human being."

21. Christopher R. Matthews, "Luke," in Harold W. Attridge, ed., *The HarperCollins Study Bible* (San Francisco: HarperSanFrancisco, 2006), 1423.

22. Walter Wink, "The Parable of the Compassionate Samaritan: A Communal Exegesis Approach," *Review and Expositor* 76 (1979): 199–217 (209).

23. Richard Bauckham, "The Scrupulous Priest and the Good Samaritan: Jesus's Parabolic Interpretation of the Law of Moses," in *New Testament Studies* 44 (1998): 475–89.

24. Philo, *Hypothetica* 7.7.

25. Josephus, *Against Apion* 2.211.

26. Michel Gourgues, "The Priest, the Levite, and the Samaritan Revisited: A Critical Note on Luke 10.31–35," *Journal of Biblical Literature* 117.4 (1998): 709–13.

27. http://mlk-kpp01.stanford.edu/index.php/encyclopedia/documentsentry/ive_been_ to_the_mountaintop/, accessed through http://www.biblegateway.com/blog/2012/04/ why-didnt-they-stop-martin-luther-king-jr-on-the-parable-of-the-good-samaritan/.

28. Josephus, *Antiquities* 13.254–56.

29. Josephus, *War* 1.562; *Antiquities* 17.20.

30. Josephus, *Antiquities* 9.291.

31. Josephus, *Antiquities* 20.118–36.

32. See the very helpful work of Alan D. Crown, including his "Redating the Schism Between the Judaeans and the Samaritans," *Jewish Quarterly Review* 82.1/2 (1991): 17–50; see also Michael Fagenblat, "The Concept of Neighbor in Jewish and Christian Ethics," in Amy-Jill Levine and Marc Z. Brettler, eds., *The Jewish Annotated New Testament* (New York: Oxford Univ. Press, 2011), 540–43.

33. E.g., Wink, "Parable of the Compassionate Samaritan," 210; he dates the Mishnah to ca. 65/66 CE.

34. See the discussion in Charlotte Elisheva Fonrobert, "When Women Walk in the Ways of Their Fathers: On Gendering Rabbinic Claims for Authority," *Journal of the History of Sexuality* 10 (2001): 398–415.

35. Charles Hedrick, "The Victim Beside the Road in the Story of the Samaritan," Good Samaritan Interactive Project Textbase, http://homepages.bw.edu/~rfowler/abs/textbase/ textbase.html . See also Charles Hedrick, *Parables as Poetic Fictions* (Peabody, MA: Hendrickson, 1994), 110.

36. Charles Hedrick, e-mail, July 23, 2007.

37. Snodgrass, *Stories with Intent*, 696.

38. Walter Grundmann, *Die Geschichte Jesu Christi* (Berlin: Evangelische Verlagsanstalt, 1957), 90.

39. My thanks to Herb Basser, who tracked down this connection (personal correspondence). On Grundmann, and his enormous influence in post-war Germany and subsequently into New Testament scholarship to this day, see Susannah Heschel, *The Aryan Jesus: Christian Theologians and the Bible in Nazi Germany* (Princeton and Oxford: Princeton Univ. Press, 2008).

40. M. Gnanavaram, " 'Dalit Theology' and the Parable of the Good Samaritan," *Journal for the Study of the New Testament* 50 (1993): 59–83.

41. The connection of 2 Chronicles 28.8–15 to the parable was already proposed by John Dominic Crossan in *In Parables: The Challenge of the Historical Jesus* (New York: Harper & Row, 1973), 65. For development of this connection, see F. Scott Spencer, "2 Chronicles 28.5–15 and the Parable of the Good Samaritan," *Westminster Journal of Theology* 46

(1984): 317–49; Isaac Kalimi, "Robbers on the Road to Jericho: Luke's Story of the Good Samaritan and Its Origins in Kings/Chronicles," *Ephemerides Theologicae Lovanienses* 85/1 (2009): 47–53.

42. http://www.bbc.co.uk/news/uk-politics-10377842.

43. For more on the function of the innkeeper, see Bruce W. Longenecker, "The Story of the Samaritan and the Innkeeper (Luke 10:30–35): A Study in Character Rehabilitation," *Biblical Interpretation* 17.4 (2009): 422–47.

Chapter 3: The Kingdom of Heaven Is like Yeast

1. http://www.westarinstitute.org/projects/the-jesus-seminar/.

2. http://www.earlychristianwritings.com/jsem.html.

3. Joachim Jeremias, *The Parables of Jesus*, rev. ed. (New York: Scribner, 1965), 149. This citation is the starting point for many analyses of the parable, e.g., Robert W. Funk, "Beyond Criticism in Quest of Literacy: The Parable of the Leaven," *Interpretation* 25 (1971): 149–70 (citation 152). See also Jacobus Liebenberg, *The Language of the Kingdom and Jesus: Parable, Aphorism, and Metaphor in the Sayings Material Common to the Synoptic Tradition and the Gospel of Thomas,* Beihefte zur Zeitschrift für die Neutestamentliche Wissenschaft 102 (Berlin: de Gruyter, 2001); Liebenberg finds the primary message concerns "the inherent ability of the Kingdom to permeate the whole world and to change it" (349).

4. C. H. Dodd, *The Parables of the Kingdom* (New York: Scribner, 1961), 155–56; the comment is cited by Funk, in "Beyond Criticism," 153, but is not criticized.

5. Ernst Lohmeyer, *Das Evangelium des Matthäus* (Göttingen: Vandenhoeck & Ruprecht, 1958), 220; as summarized by Funk, in "Beyond Criticism," 159.

6. Funk, "Beyond Criticism," 165–66.

7. Noted by Luise Schottroff in *The Parables of Jesus* ([Minneapolis: Fortress, 2006], 206), who eloquently speaks of Jewish "ritual expression" in appreciating the "gift of God."

8. Funk, "Beyond Criticism," 166.

9. Plutarch, *Roman Questions* 109 in *The Roman Questions of Plutarch: A New Translation, with Introductory Essays & a Running Commentary,* trans. H. J. Rose (Oxford: Clarendon, 1924), 166.

10. Ignatius, *Epistle to the Magnesians* 10.2–3 in *Apostolic Fathers*, vol. I, trans. Kirsopp Lake. Loeb Classical Series 24 (Boston: Harvard Univ. Press, 1985), 207, as cited in Funk, "Beyond Criticism," 167.

11. Funk, "Beyond Criticism," 163.

12. Susan Marie Praeder, *The Word in Women's Worlds: Four Parables* (Wilmington, DE: Michael Glazier, 1988).

13. http://www.womenpriests.org/scriptur/praeder1.asp.

14. Audrey West, "Preparing to Preach the Parables in Luke," *Currents in Theology and Mission* (2009): 405–13 (411).

15. Bernard Brandon Scott, *Re-Imagine the World: An Introduction to the Parables of Jesus* (Santa Rosa, CA: Polebridge, 2001), 27.

16. Scott, *Re-Imagine the World,* 31, 34.

17. Barbara E. Reid, *Parables for Preachers, Year C* (Collegeville, MN: Liturgical, 2000), 300; cf. 304 on the inclusion of "corrupt gentiles" and extending the point to suggest preaching the parable to embrace all who might be excluded on the basis of race, ethnicity, class, gender, age, sexual orientation, and so forth.

18. David Buttrick, *Speaking Parables: A Homiletic Guide* (Louisville, KY: Westminster John Knox, 2000), 147. Buttrick follows Funk, "Beyond Criticism." Reid similarly states, "In every other instance in Scripture in which leaven occurs, it represents evil or corruption" (*Parables for Preachers*, 298).

19. Buttrick, *Speaking Parables*, 149.

20. For an exhaustive discussion of the source-critical question regarding the two parables, see Zeba Antonin Crook, "The Synoptic Parables of the Mustard Seed and the Leaven: A Test-Case for the Two-Document, Two-Gospel, and Farrer-Goulder Hypotheses," *Journal for the Study of the New Testament* 78 (2000): 23–48.

21. See the examples in Ryan S. Schellenberg's excellent article, "Kingdom as Contaminant? The Role of Repertoire in the Parables of the Mustard Seed and the Leaven," *Catholic Biblical Quarterly* 71 (2009): 527–43 (539–40). Helpful as always in providing ancient references is Klyne R. Snodgrass, *Stories with Intent: A Comprehensive Guide to the Parables of Jesus* (Grand Rapids, MI: Eerdmans, 2008), 229–30.

22. Philo, *Special Laws* 2.184–85; cited in Snodgrass, *Stories with Intent*, 229.

23. Scott, *Re-Imagine the World*, 27.

24. Scott, *Re-Imagine the World*, 25.

25. Scott, *Re-Imagine the World*, 34.

26. See Elizabeth Waller, "The Parable of the Leaven: A Sectarian Teaching and the Inclusion of Women," *Union Seminary Quarterly Review* 35 (1979–80): 99–109; Reid, *Parables for Preachers, Year C*, 302–3.

27. Robert J. Miller, *The Complete Gospels: Annotated Scholars Version* (Santa Rosa, CA: Polebridge Press, 1992), 320.

28. Conversely, Liebenberg insists that from *Thomas* "one can at least gather that the woman is not depicted in a positive light" (*Language of the Kingdom*, 345).

29. Waller, "Parable of the Leaven," 104.

30. For details of bread making in antiquity, see Praeder, *Word in Women's Worlds*, 11–16.

31. Waller moves in this direction with her observation, "It is Sarah who emerges from the epiphany 'full of God,' pregnant with a son" ("Parable of the Leaven," 103).

32. Cited in Snodgrass, *Stories with Intent*, 230, with reference also to *b. Niddah* 64b.

Chapter 4: The Pearl of Great Price

1. An earlier version of this chapter appears as "The World Was My Oyster, but I Used the Wrong Fork" (Oscar Wilde): The Parable of the Pearl Reopened," in Jason A. Whitlark et al., eds., *Interpretation and the Claims of the Text Resourcing New Testament Theology* (Waco: Baylor Univ. Press, 2014).

2. Arland J. Hultgren, *The Parables of Jesus: A Commentary* (Grand Rapids, MI: Eerdmans, 2000), 420. R. T. France speaks of "true discipleship" and the "single-minded commitment which discipleship must involve" (*The Gospel of Matthew*, New International Commentary on the New Testament [Grand Rapids, MI: Eerdmans, 2007], 540); Donald R. Hagner speaks of the "cost of absolute discipleship" ("Matthew's Parables of the Kingdom," in Richard N. Longenecker, ed., *The Challenge of Jesus's Parables* [Grand Rapids, MI: Eerdmans, 2000], 116). Jeffrey A. Gibbs, in "Parables of Atonement and Assurance: Matthew 13.44–46," summarizes: "Interpreters have treated this pericope as parables of sanctification which portray the 'cost of discipleship'" (*Concordia Theological Quarterly* 51.1 [1987]:19–43 [19]).

3. Hagner is emphatic: "The pearl in the story clearly represents the kingdom" ("Matthew's Parables of the Kingdom," 117).

4. E.g., Jan Lambrecht, *Out of the Treasure: The Parables in the Gospel of Matthew* (Louvain: Peters; Grand Rapids, MI: Eerdmans, 1992), 171.

5. Most recently, Ray C. Stedman, "The Case of the Valuable Pearl," accessed March 24, 2013, http://www.raystedman.org/new-testament/matthew/the-case-of-the-valuable-pearl. See also Otto Glombitza, "Der Perlenkaufmann," *New Testament Studies* 7 (1960–61), 153–61; Christoph Burchard, "Senfkorn, Sauerteig, Schatz und Perle in Matthäus 13," in *Studien zum Neuen Testament und seiner Umwelt* 13 (1988): 5–35; cited in Lambrecht, *Out of the Treasure,* 171. See Klyne R. Snodgrass, *Stories with Intent: A Comprehensive Guide to the Parables of Jesus* (Grand Rapids, MI: Eerdmans, 2008), 251, for discussion. Biblical scholars do not generally read homiletic works or troll the Internet for popular readings, despite our knowledge that we are not the only ones interpreting texts.

6. Juan Carlos Ortiz, quoted in Ross Cochrane, "You Are So Worth It All," accessed March 24, 2013, http://pastorross1.wordpress.com/2011/04/15/matthew-1345-46–you-are-so-worth-it-part-17/.

7. Cochrane, "You Are So Worth It All." Less floridly, Gibbs proposes, "*Margarites* ["pearl"] and *thesauros* ["treasure"] refer to the disciples of Jesus at Matthew 13:44–46. . . . In the eyes of the God of grace, these sinful, imperfect disciples appear as treasure; nay, as pearls!" ("Parables of Atonement and Assurance").

8. Carl H. Stevens, "The Great Pearl: Matthew 13:45–46," Greater Grace World Outreach, accessed March 23, 2013, http://www.ggwo.org/index.php?module=ministries&action=faiththoughtsdev&year=2007&month=11&day=29.

9. Attested in various ancient manuscripts such as Codex Ephraemi Syri Rescriptus (C) and Codex Bezae Cantabrigiensis (D) as well as by Origen and Cyprian.

10. Arland J. Hultgren, *The Parables of Jesus. A Commentary* (Grand Rapids, MI: Eerdmans, 2000), 491, following Joachim Jeremias, *Jerusalem in the Time of Jesus* (Philadelphia: Fortress, 1969), 31, and the rabbinic sources cited there. Jeremias writes: "T. Ter. x.9, 43; j. Peah i.6, 16c53 mention a priest's shop. T. Betz. Iii.8, 205 tells of two scholars . . . who were merchants 'all their life.' . . . The high priestly family too carried on a flourishing trade." How these references indicate "high respect" as opposed to data is not clear. There is no rabbinic citation that I could find that advises encouraging one's son to become a merchant.

11. Jeremias, *Jerusalem in the Time of Jesus,* 31.

12. On charges of Jeremias's anti-Judaism or anti-Semitism with particular attention to the parables, see Tania Oldenhage, *Parables for Our Time: Rereading New Testament Scholarship After the Holocaust,* American Academy of Religion Cultural Criticism Series (New York: Oxford Univ. Press, 2002), especially chap. 4, "Joachim Jeremias and the Historical-Critical Approach" (39–50). Biblical scholars, who often quote Jeremias as if he is gospel, are too often unaware of his presuppositions.

13. Josephus, *Antiquities* 20.34.

14. Pliny, *Natural History* 9.106. See Hultgren, *Parables of Jesus,* 419. Snodgrass adds Pliny's reference to Cleopatra's two pearls worth ten million sesterces and Caesar's gift to the mother of Brutus of a pearl worth six million sesterces (Suetonius, *Caesar* 50); see his *Stories with Intent,* 248.

15. Pliny, *Natural History* 9.119–21; Horace, *Sermons* 2.3.239–42. These details and discussions appear in B. Ullman's delightful (not a term loosely used for an academic article) "Cleopatra's Pearls," *Classical Journal* 52.5 (1957): 193–201, http://penelope.uchicago.edu/Thayer/E/journals/CJ/52/5/ Cleopatras_Pearls*.html.

16. Pliny, *Natural History* 9.107.

17. Thomas G. Long, *Matthew*, Westminster Bible Companion (Louisville, KY: Westminster John Knox, 1997), 157.

18. Hultgren, *Parables of Jesus*, 422. "Quest" language is also common in discussion of this parable. See, e.g., Long, *Matthew*, 157.

19. France, *Gospel of Matthew*, 541.

20. Hultgren, *Parables of Jesus*, 421.

21. Craig S. Keener, *A Commentary on the Gospel of Matthew* (Grand Rapids, MI: Eerdmans, 1999), 392.

22. M. Eugene Boring, "Matthew," in *The New Interpreter's Bible* 8 (Nashville, Abingdon: 1995), 313.

23. Pheme Perkins, *Hearing the Parables of Jesus* (New York: Paulist, 1981), 28. See also Paul W. Meyer, "Context as a Bearer of Meaning in Matthew," *Union Seminary Quarterly Review* 42 (1988): 69–72; according to Meyer, "From the world's point of view, [the ploughman and the merchant] act in curious ways, even queerly" (70). C. H. Dodd interprets the merchant's action as analogous to following Jesus as well as to "unpardonable rashness" and "throwing caution to the winds" (*Parables of the Kingdom* [1936; New York: Scribner, 1961], 86, 87).

24. The miraculous catch of fish is conventional; see also *b. Baba Batra* 133b and *Pesikta Rabbati* 23.6.

25. Robert J. Miller, *The Complete Gospels: Annotated Scholars Version* (Santa Rosa, CA: Polebridge Press, 1992), 317.

26. Craig L. Blomberg, *Preaching the Parables: From Responsible Interpretation to Powerful Proclamation* (Grand Rapids, MI: Baker Academic, 2004), 133, emphasis his.

27. Blomberg, *Preaching the Parables*, 133. For other examples of "sacrificial" readings, see David Buttrick, *Speaking Parables: A Homiletic Guide* (Louisville, KY: Westminster John Knox, 2000), 103; Bernard Brandon Scott, *Hear Then the Parable* (Minneapolis: Fortress, 1989), 317, following Jack Dean Kingsbury, *The Parables of Jesus* (London: SPCK, 1969), 115; Keener, *Commentary on the Gospel of Matthew*, 391, 392; Grant R. Osborne, *Matthew*, Exegetical Commentary on the New Testament (Grand Rapids, MI: Zondervan, 2010), 542; Michael J. Wilkins, "Matthew," *NIV Application Commentary* (Grand Rapids, MI: Zondervan, 2004), 488; Hagner, "Matthew's Parables of the Kingdom," 118; Robert H. Stein, *An Introduction to the Parables of Jesus* (Philadelphia: Westminster, 1981), 104–6. Long uses the language of the "auction block" (*Matthew*, 156).

28. W. D. Davies and Dale C. Allison Jr., *The Gospel According to St. Matthew*, vol. 2, International Critical Commentary n.s. (Edinburgh: Clark, 1991), 437.

29. Blomberg, *Preaching the Parables*, 133.

30. Luise Schottroff, *The Parables of Jesus* (Minneapolis: Fortress, 2006), 207.

31. Schottroff, *Parables of Jesus*, 208.

32. Warren Carter's claim that both parables "highlight for the audience the searching for, intense commitment to, and rejoicing which God's reign requires" ("The Parables in Matthew 13.1–52 as Embedded Narratives," in Warren Carter and John Paul Heil, *Matthew's Parables: Audience-Oriented Perspectives*, Catholic Biblical Quarterly Monograph Series 30 [Washington, DC: Catholic Biblical Association of American, 1998], 36–63 [55]) overstates the searching for the first parable and understates the shift in the second: the merchant was not initially searching for one pearl of great price, but for multiple pearls of value.

33. See John Paul Heil, "Narrative Progression in Matthew 13.1–52," in Carter and Heil, *Matthew's Parables*, 64–95 (88–89); Glombitza, "Der Perlenkaufmann," 153–61.

34. Blomberg, *Preaching the Parables*, 133.

35. Ivor H. Jones notes the space Matthew accords to "ascetic tradition" in *The Matthean Parables: A Literary and Historical Commentary* (Leiden: Brill, 1995), 355.

36. Brendan Byrne, *Lifting the Burden: Reading Matthew's Gospel in the Church Today* (Collegeville, MN: Liturgical, 2004), 115.

37. Byrne, *Lifting the Burden,* 115.

38. Hultgren, *Parables of Jesus,* 422.

39. Hultgren, *Parables of Jesus,* 420.

40. Buttrick, *Speaking Parables,* 103.

41. Snodgrass, *Stories with Intent,* 244. Osborne goes further: "Nothing is said about reselling it for profit. It could be this is simply assumed and omitted, but it is more likely that the omission has theological relevance" (*Matthew,* 531). The relevance is not, however, spelled out.

42. Scott, *Hear Then the Parable,* 319.

43. See Snodgrass, *Stories with Intent,* 671, n. 340.

44. Hinted at by Buttrick, *Speaking Parables,* 103.

45. Hultgren, *Parables of Jesus,* 422.

Chapter 5: The Mustard Seed

1. Arland J. Hultgren, *The Parables of Jesus: A Commentary* (Grand Rapids, MI: Eerdmans, 2000), 401.

2. For examples, see Hultgren, *Parables of Jesus,* 396; Barbara E. Reid, *Parables for Preachers, Year A* (Collegeville, MN: Liturgical, 2001), 103.

3. Frederick Dale Bruner, *Matthew: A Commentary,* vol. 2, *The Churchbook: Matthew 13–28* (Grand Rapids, MI: Eerdmans, 1990), 34. My thanks to former student Rev. Dr. Noel Schoonmaker, whose paper on this parable for a course on parables at Vanderbilt in spring 2006 pointed out numerous interpretive possibilities.

4. Barbara E. Reid, *Parables for Preachers, Year C* (Collegeville, MN: Liturgical, 2000), 295.

5. Reid, *Parables for Preachers, Year A,* 106.

6. David Buttrick, *Speaking Parables: A Homiletic Guide* (Louisville, KY: Westminster John Knox, 2000), 77; "despised and rejected" is an allusion to Isa. 53.3, the "suffering servant," understood in Christian interpretation as Jesus.

7. William E. Arnal, "Gendered Couplets in Q and Legal Formulations: From Rhetoric to Social History," *Journal of Biblical Literature* 116 (1997): 75–94 (84); cited in Ryan S. Schellenberg, "Kingdom as Contaminant? The Role of Repertoire in the Parables of the Mustard Seed and the Leaven," *Catholic Biblical Quarterly* 71 (2009): 527–43 (531).

8. Reid, *Parables for Preachers, Year A,* 106, following John Dominic Crossan, *The Historical Jesus* (San Francisco: HarperSanFrancisco, 1991), 276–80.

9. Reid, *Parables for Preachers, Year C,* 296–97, 304, following Douglas E. Oakman, *Jesus and the Economic Questions of His Day* (Lewiston/Queenston: Edwin Mellen, 1986), 125.

10. Bernard Brandon Scott, *Re-Imagine the World: An Introduction to the Parables of Jesus* (Santa Rosa, CA: Polebridge, 2001), 37–38; *Hear Then the Parable* (Minneapolis: Fortress, 1989), 381–82.

11. Reid, *Parables for Preachers, Year A,* 106.

12. Buttrick, *Speaking Parables,* 78.

13. Klyne R. Snodgrass, *Stories with Intent: A Comprehensive Guide to the Parables of Jesus* (Grand Rapids, MI: Eerdmans, 2008), 225.

14. Scott, *Re-Imagine the World,* 38–39.

15. Luise Schottroff, *Parables of Jesus,* trans. Linda M. Maloney (Minneapolis: Fortress, 2006), 118; she discusses the parable in a chapter entitled "Political Prophecy."

16. Joshua Garroway, "The Invasion of the Mustard Seed: A Reading of Mark 5.1–20," *Journal for the Study of the New Testament* 32.1 (2009): 57–76 (60).

17. Snodgrass, *Stories with Intent,* 220; see also nn. 202, 662.

18. For one early attempt at this exercise, see John Dominic Crossan, "The Seed Parables of Jesus," *Journal of Biblical Literature* 92 (1973): 244–66. Crossan suggests that the biblical allusions suggested by the birds nesting in the branches represent an addition to the original parable (255, 259), and whereas the (hypothetical) pre-Markan and Q texts agree on the sowing, growth, size, and shade for birds, the " 'large branches' of the former are more original than the 'tree' of the latter" (259).

19. "Q," from the German *Quelle,* meaning "source," is a hypothetical text New Testament scholars use to explain the materials common to the gospels of Matthew and Luke but missing from Mark.

20. Jacobus Liebenberg, *The Language of the Kingdom and Jesus: Parable, Aphorism, and Metaphor in the Sayings Material Common to the Synoptic Tradition and the Gospel of Thomas,* Beihefte zur Zeitschrift für die Neutestamentlich Wissenschaft 102 (Berlin: de Gruyter, 2001), 318–20; cited in Schellenberg, "Kingdom as Contaminant," 535.

21. Scott, *Hear Then the Parable,* 376.

22. Scott, *Re-Imagine the World,* 123; see also *Hear Then the Parable,* 375, 381–83, following Joachim Jeremias, *Parables of Jesus,* rev. ed. (New York: Scribner, 1965), 27, who is following Hermann Strack and Paul Billerbeck, *Commentary on the New Testament from the Talmud and the Midrash* (1926), 1:699; Buttrick, *Speaking Parables,* 77 (following Scott); and others.

23. Pliny, *Natural History* 29.54.170 in *Pliny: Natural History,* vol. 5, trans. H. Rackham. Loeb Classical Library 371 (Boston: Harvard Univ. Press, 1961), 529.

24. Schellenberg, "Kingdom as Contaminant," 536.

25. Buttrick, *Speaking Parables,* 77.

26. Schellenberg, "Kingdom as Contaminant," 537.

27. Details in Schellenberg, "Kingdom as Contaminant," 532. Schellenberg confirms these positive assessments by citing numerous other classical sources in agreement.

28. Pliny, *Natural History* 17.70.

29. Robert W. Funk, "The Looking Glass Tree Is for the Birds," *Interpretation* 27.01 (1973): 4, and following numerous commentators, including Scott, *Re-Imagine the World,* 38–40. On subverting the imperial dream of triumph, see also Reid, *Parables for Preachers, Year A,* 104–5; Buttrick, *Speaking Parables,* 77.

30. Snodgrass dryly notes, "One can see how people jump to the conclusion that the birds represent the Gentiles, but that is going too far" (*Stories with Intent,* 224).

31. Snodgrass, *Stories with Intent,* 223.

32. Buttrick, *Speaking Parables,* 77.

Chapter 6: The Pharisee and the Tax Collector

1. Citations in Klyne R. Snodgrass, *Stories with Intent: A Comprehensive Guide to the Parables of Jesus* (Grand Rapids, MI: Eerdmans, 2008), 741, n. 149.

2. William R. Herzog II, *Parables as Subversive Speech: Jesus as Pedagogue of the Oppressed* (Louisville, KY: Westminster John Knox, 1994), 173.

3. Bernard Brandon Scott, *Hear Then the Parable* (Minneapolis: Fortress, 1989), 97; cited in Herzog, *Parables as Subversive Speech,* 177.

4. See Luise Schottroff, *The Parables of Jesus,* trans. Linda M. Maloney (Minneapolis: Fortress, 2006), 8.

5. Robert Doran, "The Pharisee and the Tax Collector: An Agonistic Story," *Catholic Biblical Quarterly* 69 (2007): 259–70.

6. Craig L. Blomberg, *Preaching the Parables: From Responsible Interpretation to Powerful Proclamation* (Grand Rapids, MI: Baker Academic, 2004), 159.

7. Stephanie Harrison, "The Case of the Pharisee and the Tax Collector: Justification and Social Location in Luke's Gospel," *Currents in Mission and Theology* 32.2 (2005): 99–111 (citations 99, 105).

8. Josephus, *Antiquities* 18.60–62; see also *War* 2.175–77.

9. E.g., Timothy A. Friedrichsen, "The Temple, a Pharisee, a Tax Collector, and the Kingdom of God: Rereading a Jesus Parable (Luke 18.10–14a)," *Journal of Biblical Literature* 124/1 (2005): 89–119 (108), paraphrasing Michael Farris, "A Tale of Two Taxations (Luke 18:10–14b): The Parable of the Pharisee and the Toll Collector," in V. George Shillington, ed., *Jesus and His Parables: Interpreting the Parables of Jesus Today* (Edinburgh: T+T Clark, 1997): 23–33 (30).

10. F. Gerald Downing, "The Ambiguity of 'The Pharisee and the Toll-Collector' (Luke 18:9–14) in the Greco-Roman World of Late Antiquity," *Catholic Biblical Quarterly* 54 (1992): 80–99 (84).

11. Details in Downing, "Ambiguity of 'The Pharisee and the Toll-Collector,'" 88–89, 93.

12. Josephus, *Antiquities* 18.15.

13. Josephus, *Antiquities* 13.297–98.

14. See Josephus, *Life* 191, who states of the Pharisees, they "are supposed to excel others in the accurate knowledge of the laws of their country."

15. Herzog, *Parables as Subversive Speech,* 182.

16. Blomberg, *Preaching the Parables,* 159; Blomberg cites no sources.

17. Downing, "Ambiguity of 'The Pharisee and the Toll-Collector,'" 82.

18. Contra Harrison, "Case of the Pharisee," 106, citing several others.

19. Herzog, *Parables as Subversive Speech,* 179.

20. *Pace* Farris, "Tale of Two Taxations," 31.

21. Josephus, *War* 5.415.

22. Philo, *Special Laws* 2:196.

23. Herzog, *Parables as Subversive Speech,* 181, 191; following him, see Farris, "Tale of Two Taxations," 31. Missing are citations to such texts as *m. Demai* 3.1, "The House of Shammai say, 'They give that which is tithed to him who does not tithe.'"

24. David A. Neale, *None But the Sinners. Religious Categories in the Gospel of Luke* (Journal for the Study of the New Testament Supplement Series 58; Sheffield: JSOT Press, 1991), 67.

25. This is the reading on the website of the US Conference of Catholic Bishops (http://www.usccb.org/bible/luke/18).

26. Some translations are discussed in Hultgren, *Parables of Jesus,* 119, 122.

27. John R. Donahue, *The Gospel in Parable: Metaphor, Narrative and Theology in the Synoptic Gospels* (Philadelphia: Fortress, 1988), 188; cited in Herzog, *Parables as Subversive Speech,* 186.

28. Buttrick, *Speaking Parables,* 226.

29. Blomberg, *Preaching the Parables,* 160; Friedrichsen, "The Temple, a Pharisee," 97; following Kenneth E. Bailey, *Poet and Peasant and Through Peasant Eyes: A Literary-Cultural Approach to the Parables in Luke* (Grand Rapids, MI: Eerdmans, 1983), 148; Scott, *Hear Then the Parable,* 94.

30. Hultgren, *Parables of Jesus,* 122.

31. Observed, among others, in Friedrichsen, "The Temple, a Pharisee," 94.

32. Buttrick, *Speaking Parables,* 226, cites a prayer "from the Talmud" (he does not give the citation). See also Farris, "Tale of Two Taxations, 26.

33. Fredrick C. Holmgren, "The Pharisee and the Tax Collector: Luke 18:9–14 and Deuteronomy 26:1–15," *Interpretation* 48 (1994): 252–61 (257).

34. See, e.g., Blomberg, *Preaching the Parables,* 160; Snodgrass, *Stories with Intent,* 463, 465; Friedrichsen, "The Temple, a Pharisee," 93–94; Doran, "Pharisee and the Tax Collector," 266–67.

35. Suggested by Herzog (*Parables as Subversive Speech,* 176), who cites Pheme Perkins (*Hearing the Parables of Jesus* [New York: Paulist, 1981]), who follows R. B. Y. Scott (*The Way of Wisdom in the Old Testament* [New York: Macmillan, 1971]) as the source of the proverb. Perkins does cite Scott, but advances no primary source reference (172). She states only that Scott suggested that the parable could be converted into a proverb. Scott himself observes "how easily a parable like that of the Pharisee and the tax collector can be turned into a gnomic couplet" (77).

36. Doran, "Pharisee and Tax Collector," 267.

37. Eta Linnemann, *Jesus of the Parables: Introduction and Exposition,* 3d ed., trans. John Sturdy (New York: Harper & Row, 1966), 59; cited in Herzog, *Parables as Subversive Speech,* 185 (in seeking the original, I found instead the title *Parables of Jesus: Introduction and Exposition.*) See also, among others, Hultgren, *Parables of Jesus,* 123; Snodgrass, *Stories with Intent,* 467; Friedrichsen, "The Temple, a Pharisee," 111; Farris, "Tale of Two Taxations," 28.

38. Herzog, *Parables as Subversive Speech,* 183.

39. Hyam Maccoby, "How Unclean Were Tax Collectors," *Biblical Theology Bulletin* 31 (2002): 60–63, answers his titular question with the claim of no more and no less than others. See citation in Snodgrass, *Stories with Intent,* 741, n. 144.

40. Herzog, *Parables as Subversive Speech,* 185, citing Donahue, *Gospel in Parable,* 189.

41. Harrison, "Case of the Pharisee," 102.

42. Kenneth E. Bailey, *Through Peasant Eyes: More Lucan Parables, Their Culture and Style* (Grand Rapids, MI: Eerdmans, 1980), 149; cited in Herzog, *Parables as Subversive Speech,* 185. Snodgrass also adduces this connection, despite no reference to it in the parable (*Stories with Intent,* 468).

43. Bailey, *Through Peasant Eyes,* 153–54, followed by Herzog, *Parables as Subversive Speech,* 188; both are cited in Friedrichsen, "The Temple, a Pharisee," 112. Nahum 2.7 might be the only source for this claim.

44. Dennis Hamm, "The Tamid Service in Luke-Acts: The Cultic Background behind Luke's Theology of Worship (Luke 1:5–25; 18:9–14; 24:50–53; Acts 3:1; 10:3, 30)," *Catholic Biblical Quarterly* 25 (2003): 215–31.

45. Farris, "Tale of Two Taxations," 30.

46. Hultgren, *Parables of Jesus,* 124; cited approvingly in Friedrichsen, "The Temple, a Pharisee," 114.

47. Friedrichsen, "The Temple, a Pharisee," 114, following Scott, *Hear Then the Parable,* 97.

48. Herzog, *Parables as Subversive Speech,* 189.

49. Friedrichsen, "The Temple, a Pharisee," 103.

50. Friedrichsen, "The Temple, a Pharisee," 116.

51. See Lenn E. Goodman, *Judaism, Human Rights, and Human Values* (New York: Oxford Univ. Press, 1998), 40–42.

Chapter 7: The Laborers in the Vineyard

1. An earlier version of this chapter appears in Amy-Jill Levine and Myrick C. Shinall Jr., "Standard and Poor: The Economic Index of the Parables," in Robert Stewart, ed., *The Message of Jesus: John Dominic Crossan and Ben Witherington III in Dialogue* (Minneapolis: Fortress, 2013), 95–116.

2. See V. George Shillington, "Saving Life and Keeping Sabbath (Matthew 20.1b–15): The Parable of the Labourers in the Vineyard," in V. George Shillington, ed., *Jesus and His Parables: Interpreting the Parables of Jesus Today* (Edinburgh: Clark, 1997), 87–101, for a listing of commentators who take this theological reading and/or who approve of the owner.

3. Robert T. Fortna, "Exegesis and Proclamation," *Journal of Theology for Southern Africa* 72 (1990): 66–72 (72).

4. So Klyne R. Snodgrass's summary of Arland Hultgren's reading (*The Parables of Jesus: A Commentary* [Grand Rapids, MI: Eerdmans, 2000]), and many others. See Snodgrass's *Stories with Intent: A Comprehensive Guide to the Parables of Jesus* (Grand Rapids, MI: Eerdmans, 2008), 362.

5. Details in J. M. Tevel, "The Labourers in the Vineyard: The Exegesis of Matthew 20,1–7 in the Early Church," *Vigiliae Christianae* 46.4 (1992): 356–80 (362).

6. José David Rodríguez, "The Parable of the Affirmative Action Employer," *Currents in Theology and Mission* 15.5 (1988): 418–24 (420).

7. Rodríguez, "Parable of the Affirmative Action Employer," 420.

8. Joachim Jeremias, *The Parables of Jesus*, rev. ed. (New York: Scribner, 1963), 139.

9. See Dan O. Via, *The Parables: Their Literary and Existential Dimension* (Philadelphia: Fortress, 1967), 154–55.

10. Matthew Henry (1662–1714), in his *Concise Commentary on the Bible,* taught: "The direct object of this parable seems to be, to show that though the Jews were first called into the vineyard, at length the gospel should be preached to the Gentiles, and they should be admitted to equal privileges and advantages with the Jews" (http://www.ccel.org/ccel/henry/mhcc.xxxii.xx.html). Bernard Brandon Scott proposes that, in the Matthean context, "the latecomers are the disciples, and those first hired are the Pharisees. Furthermore, the lord of the parable is Jesus as judge" (*Hear Then the Parable: A Commentary on the Parables of Jesus* [Minneapolis: Fortress, 1989], 285). Matthew, however, does not depict Jesus as calling the Pharisees at all, let alone first.

11. Rodríguez, "Parable of the Affirmative Action Employer," 423.

12. Brendan Byrne, *Lifting the Burden: Reading Matthew's Gospel in the Church Today* (Collegeville, MN: Liturgical, 2004), 152–53. The view of those hired after the first group as "marginals," "outcasts," "sinners," or other generally undefined, but certainly negative types is common. See also Daniel Harrington, *Matthew* (Sacra Pagina [Collegeville, MN: Liturgical Press, 1991]), on the parable's defending "Jesus's special concern" for the "tax collectors and sinners" who were "marginal in Jewish society" (284); Craig L. Blomberg, *Matthew* (The New American Commentary: An Exegetical and Theological Exposition of Holy Scripture, vol. 22 [Nashville: Broadman, 1992]): "In its original historical setting, the latecomers to the kingdom were the 'tax collectors and sinners'" (305).

13. Craig S. Keener, *A Commentary on the Gospel of Matthew* (Grand Rapids, MI: Eerdmans, 1999), 481.

14. Hultgren, *Parables of Jesus,* 35. See also W. D. Davies and D. C. Allison Jr., *Matthew,* International Critical Commentary, vol. 3 (Edinburgh: Clark, 1996), 69, n. 20.

15. Thomas G. Long, *Matthew,* Westminster Bible Companion (Louisville, KY: Westminster John Knox, 1997). According to Blomberg, "The story scarcely models good management-labor practices" (*Matthew,* 303).

16. William R. Herzog II, *Parables as Subversive Speech: Jesus as Pedagogue of the Oppressed* (Louisville, KY: Westminster John Knox, 1994), 86; Luise Schottroff, "Human Solidarity and the Goodness of God: The Parable of the Workers in the Vineyard," in Willy Schottroff and Wolfgang Stegemann, eds., *God of the Lowly* (Maryknoll, NY: Orbis Books, 1984), 129–47 (133).

17. Herzog, *Parables as Subversive Speech,* 96–97.

18. Suggestions in Jonathan Reed's "Reappraising the Galilean Economy: The Limits of Models, Archaeology, and Analogy," presented at the Westar (Jesus Seminar) spring meeting, March 2008. For more on the economic situation and its apologetic interpreters, see my "De-Judaizing Jesus: Theological Need and Exegetical Execution," in Steven Ramey, ed., volume commemorating the Aaron Aronov Lecture Series in the Department of Religious Studies at the University of Alabama (forthcoming) as well as the earlier version of the article, "Theory, Apologetic, History: Reviewing Jesus's Jewish Context," *Australian Bible Review* 55 (2007): 57–78.

19. Matthew speaks of householders in 10.25; 13.27, 52; 20.1, 11; 21.33, and 24.43, and may think of the church in household-terms. See Michael H. Crosby, *House of Disciples: Church, Economics, and Justice in Matthew* (Maryknoll, NY: Orbis Books, 1988). While the church/household analogy is more a Matthean than "historical" Jesus issue, Matthew's view is a logical continuation of Jesus's teaching.

20. Hultgren states that the owner is "surely a metaphor for God" (*Parables of Jesus,* 36).

21. Other uses of *despotes* to refer to the divine include 2 Peter 2.1 ("Master"); Jude 4 ("Master and Lord, Jesus Christ"); and Revelation 6.10 ("Sovereign Lord").

22. Herzog, *Parables as Subversive Speech,* 84.

23. Levinas follows in a long line of Jewish philosophers who have found more recognition in Christian seminaries than in the synagogue; predecessors include Franz Rosenzweig, Martin Buber, and even Abraham Joshua Heschel.

24. Emmanuel Levinas, "Judaism and Revolution," in *Nine Talmudic Readings,* trans. Annette Aronowicz (Bloomington: Indiana Univ. Press, 1994), 97.

25. Douglas Oakman, "The Buying Power of Two Denarii," *Forum* 3 (1987): 33–38.

26. Herzog, *Parables as Subversive Speech,* 85.

27. Herzog, *Parables as Subversive Speech,* 86; see Hultgren, *Parables of Jesus,* 40, who says that this reading is "to ruin a good story."

28. Suggested in Long, *Matthew,* 225.

29. Fortna, "Exegesis and Proclamation," 67.

30. Fortna, "Exegesis and Proclamation," 67.

31. According to Hultgren, "The landowner who goes out to hire laborers is surely a metaphor for God. . . . To make him God is 'not to allegorize'; to fail to do so or to refuse to do so, is to tear the parables from their symbolic universe" (*Parables of Jesus,* 36).

32. Byrne, *Lifting the Burden,* 153.

33. David Buttrick, *Speaking Parables: A Homiletic Guide* (Louisville, KY: Westminster John Knox, 2000), 114.

34. William Loader, "First Thoughts on Passages from Matthew in the Lectionary," http://wwwstaff.murdoch.edu.au/~loader/MtPentecost14.htm.

35. Diedrik Nelson, "Exposition of Matthew 20:1–16," *Interpretation* 29.3 (1975): 288–92 (290).

36. A suggestion from Dr. Myrick C. Shinall.

37. Brosend, *Conversing with Scripture,* 64.

38. Less charitable and more on target is Snodgrass: "The view that the parable confronts exploitation of workers and that the owner is a negative figure has no basis" (*Stories with Intent,* 372).

39. Snodgrass, *Stories with Intent,* 365.

40. For a detailed study of rabbinic parables concerning labor and wages and a critique of those scholars, such as Joachim Jeremias, who set up unfortunate scenarios of law versus grace or pristine, truthful Jesus versus nit-picking rabbinism, see Catherine Hezser, *Lohnmetaphorik und Arbeitswelt in Mt 20:1–16: Das Gleichnis von den Arbeitern im Weinbery im Rahmen rabbinischer Lohngleichnisse,* Novum Testamentum et Orbis Antiquus 15 (Fribourg: Academic, 1990).

41. Whether original or not, the term precludes the parable from serving as an indication of the gap between elite and marginal, rich and expendable.

42. Fortna, "Exegesis and Proclamation," 69.

43. Fortna, "Exegesis and Proclamation," 70.

44. Fortna, "Exegesis and Proclamation," 66.

45. He is perhaps romantic in his claim that "In my opinion, often the poor are genuinely happy for an unexpected blessing that someone else in their station in life receives." See Brad H. Young, *The Parables: Jewish Tradition and Christian Interpretation* (Peabody, MA: Hendrickson, 1998), 78.

46. Hultgren, *Parables of Jesus,* 35. See also Davies and Allison, *Matthew,* 69, n. 20.

47. Josephus, *Antiquities* 20.220. Keener cites *Testament of Job* 12.3–4 as well as later rabbinic sources to indicate that "Jewish hearers would consider it pious to give wages even to those not expecting it" (*Commentary on the Gospel of Matthew,* 483).

48. Philo, *Life of Moses* 1.313. See the brief discussion in Davies and Allison, *Matthew,* 71.

49. Or again, Antigonus of Socho: "Do not be like workers who serve their master for the sake of receiving a reward" (*m. Avot* 1.3, reading *avadim,* "slaves," as "workers"). For other rabbinic parables with comparable images and themes, see also Hultgren, *Parables of Jesus,* 34–35.

50. Brian J. Capper, "Jesus, Virtuoso Religion, and the Community of Goods," in Bruce W. Longenecker and Kelly D. Liebengood, eds., *Engaging Economics: New Testament Scenarios and Early Christian Reception* (Grand Rapids, MI: Eerdmans, 2009), 60–80 (66).

51. Loader, "First Thoughts"; he also observes that "the rawness of being at other people's whim is humiliating, being an expendable resource to be exploited."

Chapter 8: The Widow and the Judge

1. An earlier version of this chapter appears as " 'This Widow Keeps Bothering Me' (Luke 18.5)," in David Balch and Jason T. Lamoreaux, eds., *Finding a Woman's Place: Essays in Honor of Carolyn Osiek, R.S.C.J.,* Princeton Theological Monograph Series (Eugene, OR: Pickwick, 2010).

2. Barbara E. Reid, *Taking Up the Cross: New Testament Interpretations Through Latina and Feminist Eyes* (Minneapolis: Fortress, 2007), 115–16. See also her "Beyond Petty Pursuits and Wearisome Widows: Three Lukan Parables" (*Interpretation* 56 [2002]: 284–94), where she finds in this parable "a bold portrait of the female face of God" (284). For another homiletic reading based on social location, see Mary Zimmer, "A Fierce Mother and a Widow: Models of Persistence," *Review and Expositor* 92 (1995): 89–93.

3. See Bernard Brandon Scott, *Hear Then the Parable* (Minneapolis: Fortress, 1989), 183; followed by Charles W. Hedrick, *Parables as Poetic Fictions: The Creative Voice of Jesus* (Pea-

body, MA: Hendrickson, 1994), 199; and especially Wendy Cotter, "The Parable of the Feisty Widow and the Threatened Judge (Luke 18:1–8)," *New Testament Studies* 51 (2005): 328–42, in which Cotter compares the widow's lack of a polite, formal approach to legal papyri (335).

4. François Bovon, "Apocalyptic Traditions in the Lukan Special Material: Reading Luke 18.1–8," *Harvard Theological Review* 90 (1997): 383–91 (387).

5. Arland J. Hultgren, *Parables of Jesus: A Commentary* (Grand Rapids, MI: Eerdmans, 2000), 259.

6. Luke Timothy Johnson, *The Gospel of Luke,* Sacra Pagina (Collegeville, MN: Liturgical, 1991), 269; Cotter notes that *ekdikeo* and *antidikos* ("opponent") are standard forensic terms ("Parable of the Feisty Widow," 336–37).

7. Ben Witherington III, "Jesus, the Savior of the Least, the Last, and the Lost," *Quarterly Review* (1995): 197–211 (203); cited in Cotter, "Parable of the Feisty Widow," 336.

8. Hedrick, *Parables as Poetic Fictions,* 199 (n. 48 offers papyrus details).

9. For similar nuances, see the sources collected in Edwin D. Freed, "Parable of the Judge and the Widow," *New Testament Studies* 33 (1987): 38–60 (46).

10. For other problems with the translation, especially concerning the verses I am suggesting are Lukan additions, see Bovon, "Apocalyptic Traditions."

11. John Dominic Crossan, "Discussion," in Daniel Patte, ed., *Semiology and Parables: Exploration of the Possibilities Offered by Structuralism for Exegesis* (Pittsburgh: Pickwick, 1976), 58–59; cited in Stephen Curkpatrick, "Dissonance in Luke 18:1–8," *Journal of Biblical Literature* 121 (2002): 107–21 (115, n. 24).

12. Freed goes too far in his claim that "the unjust judge serves only as a foil to emphasize the persistence of the widow" ("Parable of the Judge and the Widow," 51).

13. Bovon states, "In verses 2–5 resounds the ironic and original voice of the historical Jesus" ("Apocalyptic Traditions," 389).

14. For helpful summaries, among many, see Cotter, "Parable of the Feisty Widow," 328–31; Curkpatrick, "Dissonance in Luke 18:1–8." For the best case for unity for 18.2–8, see John M. Hicks, "The Parable of the Persistent Widow," *Restoration Quarterly* 33/4 (1991): 209–23. For a critical assessment of what may be additions both by Luke and by the tradition Luke inherited, see Bovon, "Apocalyptic Traditions."

15. Pheme Perkins, *Hearing the Parables of Jesus* (New York: Paulist, 1981), 195.

16. Reid, *Taking Up the Cross,* 116.

17. Hultgren, *Parables of Jesus,* 254.

18. Joel B. Green, *The Gospel of Luke,* New International Commentary on the New Testament (Grand Rapids, MI: Eerdmans, 1997), 640.

19. Richard Q. Ford, *The Parables of Jesus: Recovering the Art of Listening* (Minneapolis: Fortress, 1997), 65, 67.

20. Johnson, *Gospel of Luke,* 273.

21. Luise Schottroff, *Lydia's Impatient Sisters: A Feminist Social History of Early Christianity* (Louisville, KY: Westminster John Knox, 1995), 101.

22. Schottroff, *Lydia's Impatient Sisters,* 277, n. 197.

23. Brad H. Young, *The Parables: Jewish Tradition and Christian Interpretation* (Peabody, MA: Hendrickson, 1998), 58.

24. Dorothy Jean Weaver, "Between Text and Sermon, Luke 18:1–8," *Interpretation* 56 (2002): 317–19 (317).

25. Mary W. Matthews, Carter Shelley, and Barbara Scheele, "Proclaiming the Parable of the Persistent Widow (Lk. 18.2–5)," in Mary Ann Beavis, ed., *The Lost Coin: Parables of Women, Work and Wisdom* (London: Sheffield Academic, 2002), 46–70 (50).

26. David Buttrick, *Speaking Parables. A Homiletic Guide* (Louisville, KY: Westminster John Knox, 2000), 224.

27. Klyne R. Snodgrass, *Stories with Intent: A Comprehensive Guide to the Parables of Jesus* (Grand Rapids, MI: Eerdmans, 2008), 250–53 (n. 735). The account of Philip of Macedon is recorded by Plutarch, *Moralia* 179C–D.

28. For helpful comments on the relationship of rabbinic law to practices found in the Babatha archives, see Ranon Katzoff, "*P. Yadin* 21 and Rabbinic Law on Widows' Rights," *Jewish Quarterly Review* 97.4 (2007): 545–75.

29. See Hannah M. Cotton and Jonas C. Greenfield, "Babatha's Property and the Law of Succession in the Babatha Archive," *Zeitschrift für Papyrologie und Epigraphik* 104 (1994): 211–24.

30. Katzoff, "*P. Yadin* 21," 557.

31. Martin Goodman's comment that Babatha's willingness to enter into a bigamous relationship following the death of her first husband "may provide some indication of the helplessness of widows left with children" and that her "apparent lack of success in August A.D. 131 in compelling her son's guardians to pay more than two denarii a month for his upkeep . . . is testimony to her powerlessness after her second husband had died" ("Babatha's Story," *Journal of Roman Studies* 81 [1991]: 169–75 [174]) overstates the evidence. Babatha already owned property; her second marriage may have been as easily contracted for status, for her own desire to climb the economic ladder, or even for love. The date of 132 could indicate an increasingly difficult political situation rather than powerlessness on Babatha's part.

32. On widows' independence, see also Matthews's contribution to Matthews, Shelley, and Scheele, "Persistent Widow," 49. Contrast her coauthor Scheele, who defines widows at the time as having "the legal status of property, and when their owners died, they had to be transferred to other proprietors" (64).

33. Carolyn Osiek, "The Widow as Altar: The Rise and Fall of a Symbol," *Second Century* 3 (1983): 159–69.

34. Reid, *Taking Up the Cross,* 116.

35. Examples in Cotter, "Parable of the Feisty Widow," 333–35.

36. The commentaries frequently cite *m. Sanhedrin* 1.1, which mandates that property cases be heard by three judges; or follow Joachim Jeremias, who suggests that behind the text is the ruling in *b. Sanhedrin* 4b that "an authorized scholar may decide money cases sitting alone" and thus concludes that the case is about finances (*Parables,* 153); and/or follow J. D. M. Derrett's discussion of "customary" and "administrative" courts ("Law in the New Testament: The Parable of the Unjust Judge," *New Testament Studies* 18 [1972]: 178–91).

37. Cotter, "Parable of the Feisty Widow," 332, following Jill Harries, *Law and Empire in Late Antiquity* (Cambridge: Cambridge Univ. Press, 1999).

38. Hedrick suggests that the phrase conveys a sense of physical debilitation (*Parables as Poetic Fictions,* 187), but this seems an overread, given the parallel in Luke 11.

39. Ford, *Parables of Jesus,* 81; cited with approval in Donald Capps, "Pastoral Images: The Good Samaritan and the Unjust Judge," *Journal of Pastoral Care and Counseling* 63.1/2 (2009): 1–11 (11).

40. Hultgren, *Parables of Jesus,* 253. Hultgren, Scott (*Hear Then the Parable,* 180), and Young (*Parables,* 57) compare the judge's description to Josephus's negative description of King Jehoiakim (*Antiquities* 10.83).

41. See T. W. Manson, *The Sayings of Jesus* (London: SCM, 1957), 305. Green suggests that "she lacks the economic resources to offer the appropriate bribe necessary for a swift settlement" (*Gospel of Luke,* 640). Amos 5.12 speaks of judges who afflict the righteous and take bribes, but the widow may not be righteous, and the judge need not be corrupt.

42. Hedrick, *Parables as Poetic Fictions,* 196. See also Derrett, "Law in the New Testament," 190–91.

43. Hultgren, *Parables of Jesus,* 254; for a fuller reading of the judge in light of honor/shame motifs, see Scott, *Hear Then the Parable,* 178–87. Bruce J. Malina and Jerome Neyrey propose that the narrative demands "special sympathy for the precarious state of the 'shame' of the widow, the value worth more than gold" ("Honor and Shame in Luke-Acts: Pivotal Values of the Mediterranean World," in Jerome H. Neyrey, ed., *The Social World of Luke-Acts: Models for Interpretation* [Peabody, MA: Hendrickson, 1991], 25–65 [64]). Then again, economics can trump both honor/shame and gender systems. The judge's interest is not honor; the widow displays no honor for the court. Neither displays a concern for shame. According to Johnson, the middle voice of *entrepomenos* (18.2) "suggests someone incapable of shame" (*Gospel of Luke,* 269).

44. Bovon draws this connection ("Apocalyptic Traditions," 386).

45. Primary sources collected by, among others, Freed ("Parable of the Judge," 42) and Cotter ("Parable of the Feisty Widow," 331–32); see also Hedrick, *Parables as Poetic Fictions,* 195, nn. 29, 30.

46. Hedrick (*Parables as Poetic Fictions,* 200), Hultgren (*Parables of Jesus,* 253), and Young (*Parables,* 41–65) develop the connections between 11.5–8 and 18.1–8.

47. Green, *Gospel of Luke,* 636.

48. See the general discussion by Konrad Weiss, "*hypopiadzo* ...," in G. Kittel and G. Friedrich, eds., *Theological Dictionary of the New Testament* (Grand Rapids, MI: Eerdmans, 1964–76), 8:590.

49. Philip Sellew, "Interior Monologue as a Narrative Device in the Parables of Luke," *Journal of Biblical Literature* 111.2 (1992): 239–53.

50. Sharon H. Ringe, *Luke,* Westminster Bible Companion (Louisville, KY: Westminster John Knox, 1995), 224.

51. Hultgren, *Parables of Jesus,* 255.

52. William R. Herzog II, *Parables as Subversive Speech: Jesus as Pedagogue of the Oppressed* (Louisville, KY: Westminster John Knox, 1994), 230.

53. Buttrick, *Speaking Parables,* 186.

54. Joseph B. Tyson, *Marcion and Luke-Acts: A Defining Struggle* (Columbia: Univ. of South Carolina Press, 2006).

55. For a more positive reading of the women in Luke 8.1–3, see Esther A. DeBoer, "The Lukan Mary Magdalene and the Other Women Following Jesus," in Amy-Jill Levine with Marianne Blickenstaff, eds., *A Feminist Companion to Luke,* Feminist Companion to the New Testament and Early Christian Writings 3 (London: Sheffield Academic, 2002), 140–60.

56. Warren Carter, "Getting Martha Out of the Kitchen: Luke 10.38–42 Again," in Levine with Blickenstaff, eds., *Feminist Companion to Luke,* 197–213.

57. Acts includes the widows overlooked in the service (6.1–6) and the widows who mourn Dorcas (9.39–41). There may be other widows who are not designated as such, e.g., Mary the mother of John Mark, Lydia.

58. Richard Bauckham, *Gospel Women: Studies of the Named Women in the Gospels* (Grand Rapids, MI: Eerdmans, 2002), 98–99; Bauckham also argues for her historicity.

59. Bauckham, *Gospel Women,* 99–100.

60. Bauckham, *Gospel Women,* 98–99, n. 83.

61. Snodgrass, *Stories with Intent,* 449.

62. On the ambivalence and contradictions of parabolic details and Luke's framing of them to provide resolution, see Stephen Curkpatrick, "Parable Metonymy and Luke's Kerygmatic Framing," *Journal for the Study of the New Testament* 25 (March 2003): 289–307.

63. Barbara E. Reid, *Parables for Preachers, Year C* (Collegeville, MN: Liturgical, 2000), 234. See also her "Beyond Petty Pursuits"; there she says, "When one doggedly resists injustice, faces it, names it, and denounces it until justice is achieved, then one is acting as God does. Moreover, the parable displays godly power revealed in seeming weakness" (294). For others who read the widow as a divine image, see Matthews, Shelley, and Scheele, "Persistent Widow," 69, and sources there.

64. Reid, *Parables for Preachers, Year C,* 234.

65. Capps, "Pastoral Images," 11.

66. Schottroff, *Lydia's Impatient Sisters,* 114.

67. Herzog, *Parables as Subversive Speech,* 231.

68. With gratitude to Richard Pervo and to the Greater Nashville Unitarian Universalist Congregation (GNUUC) for discussions of the earlier draft of this chapter.

Chapter 9: The Rich Man and Lazarus

1. David Buttrick, *Speaking Parables: A Homiletic Guide* (Louisville, KY: Westminster John Knox, 2000), 218.

2. Outi Lehtipuu, *The Afterlife Imagery in Luke's Story of the Rich Man and Lazarus, Novum Testamentum* Supplement 123 (Leiden: Brill, 2007): 5.

3. Ronald F. Hock, "Lazarus and Micyllus: Greco-Roman Backgrounds to Luke 16:19–31," *Journal of Biblical Literature* 106 (1987): 447–63 (453).

4. See the very helpful summary of the history of interpretation in Lehtipuu, *Afterlife Imagery in Luke's Story,* chap 2, "Previous Research and Its Evaluation," 11–38; see also 163–64.

5. Buttrick, *Speaking Parables,* 217; the reference to "the time of Christ" separates Israel's scriptures from Second Temple Judaism.

6. George W. Knight, "Luke 16:19–31: The Rich Man and Lazarus," *Review and Expositor* 94 (Spring 1997): 277–83 (279). At least one evangelical Internet site repeats Knight's view; see Adrian Warnock, "The Shocking Parable of the Rich Man and Lazarus—Luke 16," August 23, 2009, http://www.patheos.com/blogs/adrianwarnock/2009/08/shocking-parable-of-rich-man-and/, "The Text This Week" (http://www.textweek.com/mtlk/lk16b.htm). Klyne Snodgrass summarizes the dominant view: "Many Jews would assume that the rich man was blessed by God and that the poor man was cursed (cf. John 9.2 and Job)" (*Stories with Intent: A Comprehensive Guide to the Parables of Jesus* [Grand Rapids, MI: Eerdmans, 2008], 425). John 9.2, a text in the New Testament, need not express what "many Jews" think; moreover, it has nothing to do with economic status: the text is about congenital blindness. Job, a book in the Jewish canon, demonstrates the *disconnect* between suffering and sin.

7. Karen E. Hatcher, "In Gold We Trust: The Parable of the Rich Man and Lazarus (Luke 16.19–31)," *Review and Expositor* 109.2 (2012): 277–83 (277–78).

8. Arland J. Hultgren, *The Parables of Jesus: A Commentary* (Grand Rapids, MI: Eerdmans, 2000), 116.

9. Alyce McKenzie, "Lectionary Reflection on the Rich Man and Lazarus, Luke 16:19–26," September 19, 2010, http://www.patheos.com/blogs/faithforward/2010/09/to-see-or-not-to-see-stepping-over
-lazarus-reflections-on-luke-1519–26/, (a website for sermon preparation).

10. Craig L. Blomberg, *Preaching the Parables: From Responsible Interpretation to Powerful Proclamation* (Grand Rapids, MI: Baker Academic, 2004), 48.

11. Blomberg, *Preaching the Parables,* 48.

12. William R. Herzog II, *Parables as Subversive Speech: Jesus as Pedagogue of the Oppressed* (Louisville, KY: Westminster John Knox, 1994), 128.

13. See L. J. van der Lof, "Abraham's Bosom in the Writings of Irenaeus, Tertullian, and Augustine," *Augustinian Studies* 26 (1995): 109–23.

14. Henry J. Cadbury, "A Proper Name for Dives," *Journal of Biblical Literature* 89 (1962): 399–402. Cadbury points out that in the Bodmer papyrus the rich man is named Neues, the origins of which remain unknown.

15. Richard Bauckham, "The Rich Man and Lazarus: The Parable and Parallels," in *The Fate of the Dead: Studies on the Jewish and Christian Apocalypses,* Novum Testamentum Supplement 93 (Leiden: Brill, 1998), 97–118 (100).

16. Greg Carey, "Commentary on Luke 16:19–31," *Working Preacher,* http://www.workingpreacher.org/preaching.aspx?commentary_id=679.

17. Gary A. Anderson, *Sin: A History* (New Haven, CT: Yale Univ. Press, 2010), 230, n. 37.

18. Bernard Brandon Scott, *Hear Then the Parable* (Minneapolis: Fortress, 1989), 151.

19. Hultgren, *Parables of Jesus,* 116.

20. J. Mary Luti, "Send Lazarus," *Christian Century* (September, 1998): 819.

21. C. H. Cave, "Lazarus and the Lukan Deuteronomy," *New Testament Studies* 15 (1969): 319–25 (323); cited in Lehtipuu, *Afterlife Imagery in Luke's Story* 30, n. 94; Lehtipuu correctly denies this connection.

22. Philostratus, *Life of Apollonius* 24.

23. E.g., David B. Gowler, " 'At His Gate Lay a Poor Man': A Dialogic Reading of Luke 16:19–31," *Perspectives in Religious Studies* (2005): 249–65 (263); following Bruce J. Malina, *Christian Origins and Cultural Anthropology* (Atlanta: John Knox, 1986), 163–70.

24. Snodgrass, *Stories with Intent,* 425.

25. Herzog, *Parables as Subversive Speech,* 119.

26. Josephus, *Antiquities* 17.169.

27. Josephus, *Against Apion* 2.143.

28. Herzog, *Parables as Subversive Speech,* 119.

29. Hock, "Lazarus and Micyllus," 456. For a superb study of the artistic appropriation of the scene, see Martin O'Kane, " 'The Bosom of Abraham' (Luke 16:22): Father Abraham in the Visual Imagination," *Biblical Interpretation* 4–5 (2007): 485–518.

30. Hock, "Lazarus and Micyllus," 462.

31. Josephus, *War* 2.8.14.

32. Josephus, *War* 2.8.11.

33. Cited in Lehtipuu, *Afterlife Imagery in Luke's Story,* 5, n. 10.

34. John Dominic Crossan, *In Parables: The Challenge of the Historical Jesus* (New York: Harper & Row, 1973), 67; developed by Scott, *Hear Then the Parable,* 142–46.

35. Cicero, *On Divination* 27; Homer, *Iliad* 23.65; Ovid, *Fasti* 2.503. For handy summaries, see Bauckham, "Rich Man and Lazarus," 108–14; Snodgrass, *Stories with Intent,* 422–23.

36. Bauckham, "Rich Man and Lazarus," 115.

37. Scott, *Hear Then the Parable,* 155.

38. John Dominic Crossan, *The Power of Parable: How Fiction by Jesus Became Fiction About Jesus* (San Francisco: HarperOne, 2012), 94.

39. Bauckham, "Rich Man and Lazarus," 104.

40. James Brabazon, *Albert Schweitzer: A Biography,* 2nd ed. (Syracuse: Syracuse Univ. Press, 2000), 347.

41. Olubiyi Adeniyi Adewale, "An Afro-Sociological Application of the Parable of the Rich Man and Lazarus (Luke 16.19–31)," *Black Theology* 4.1 (2006): 27–43 (27).

42. Darrell L. Bock, "The Parable of the Rich Man and Lazarus and the Ethics of Jesus," *Southwestern Journal of Theology* 40.1 (1997): 63–72 (69).

Index